ALCOHOL
IN
AMERICA

SUNY Series in New Social Studies
  on Alcohol and Drugs
Harry G. Levine and Craig Reinarman, Editors

Walter B. Clark
Michael E. Hilton
Editors

ALCOHOL

IN

AMERICA

Drinking Practices
and Problems

STATE UNIVERSITY OF NEW YORK PRESS

Published by
State University of New York Press, Albany

For information, address State University of New York
Press, State University Plaza, Albany, N.Y., 12246

Production by E. Moore
Marketing by Dana E. Yanulavich

Library of Congress Cataloging-in-Publication Data

Alcohol in America : drinking practices and problems / Walter B. Clark
    and Michael E. Hilton, editors ; with contributions by Raul Caetano
    . . . [et al.].
        p.   cm. — (SUNY series in new social studies on alcohol and
    drugs)
    Includes bibliographical references and index.
    ISBN 0-7914-0695-4 (alk. paper) ISBN 0-7914-0696-2 (pbk.)
    1. Alcoholism—United States.   2. Drinking of alcoholic beverages—
United States.   I. Hilton, Michael E., 1951–   . II. Clark,
Walter B., 1931–   . III. Caetano, Raul. IV. Series.
HV5289.A75   1991
362.29′2′0973—dc20   90-45048
                                                                 CIP

10 9 8 7 6 5 4 3 2 1

Contents

PART V: PROBLEMS

PART VI: CONTEXTS

PART VII: BLACKS AND HISPANICS

APPENDIX

Acknowledgments

An enormous debt of gratitude is owed to those who helped us to produce this book. Kim Bloomfield undertook a great deal of the editorial work for the preparation of the original manuscript. We recognize her able job of keeping track of manuscripts that came from several different sources and in several different formats. Clerical assistance was provided by Reuben Kuszel, David Casselman, and Yvonne Nouri. Patrick Mitchell and David Smith assisted in optically scanning documents submitted and translating documents from one word processing system to another. Judith Lubina took charge of preparing the manuscript in its final form. Her direction of the final phases of the manuscript preparation was superb.

Analyses of the data that were conducted at the Alcohol Research Group depended on the programming assistance of Gary Collins, Diane Davis, Gloria Bocian, Alex Millar, and Patrick Mitchell.

Robin Room was a guiding force behind this project from its earliest phases. His influence on the whole has been far greater than would be indicated by his authorship of three of the chapters.

All of the contributing authors are to be thanked as well, both for allowing us to include their work in this volume and for their patience with the process.

We would also like to acknowledge our appreciation for permission to edit and reprint copyrighted material previously published in various journals and monographs. Copyrights for the various chapters are as follows:

Chapter 3, "Measuring Alcohol Consumption in the U.S.: Methods and Rationales" is abridged with permission from Lynn Kozlowski et al., eds. *Research Advances in Alcohol and Drug Problems*, vol. 10, pp. 39–80, 1990. Copyright by Plenum Publishing Corporation, New York, N.Y. 10013.

Chapter 5, "The Demographic Distribution of Drinking Patterns in 1984" is reprinted with permission from *Drug and Alcohol Dependence*, vol. 22, pp. 37–47, 1988. Copyright by Elsevier Science Publishing Company, Inc., Limerick, Ireland.

Chapter 7, "Changes in American Drinking Patterns and Problems, 1967–1984" is reprinted with permission from the *Journal of Studies on Alcohol*, vol. 48, pp. 515–22, 1987. Copyright by Alcohol Research Documentation, Inc., Rutgers Center of Alcohol Studies, New Brunswick, N.J. 08903.

Chapter 8, "Trends in U. S. Drinking Patterns: Further Evidence from the Past Twenty Years" is reprinted with permission from the *British Journal of Addiction*, vol. 83, pp. 269–278, 1988. Copyright by the Society for the Study of Addiction to Alcohol and Other Drugs, London, United Kingdom.

Chapter 9, "Trends in Drinking Problems and Attitudes in the U. S.: 1979–1984" is reprinted with permission from the *British Journal of Addiction*, vol. 83, pp. 1421–1427, 1988. Copyright by the Society for the Study of Addiction to Alcohol and Other Drugs, London, United Kingdom.

Chapter 10, "Cultural Changes in Drinking and Trends in Alcohol Problems Indicators: Recent U.S. Experience" is reprinted with permission from Ragnar Waahlberg, ed. *Prevention and Control/Realities and Aspirations*, vol. 3, Proceedings of the 35th International Congress on Alcoholism and Drug Dependence, Oslo, Norway, pp. 820–831, 1989. Copyright by the National Directorate for the Prevention of Alcohol and Drug Problems, Oslo, Norway.

Chapter 12, "The U. S. General Population's Experiences of Responses to Alcohol Problems" is reprinted with permission from the *British Journal of Addiction*, vol. 84, pp. 1291–1304, 1989. Copyright by the Society for the Study of Addiction to Alcohol and Other Drugs, London, United Kingdom.

Chapter 13, "Demographic Characteristics and the Frequency of Heavy Drinking as Predictors of Self-Reported Drinking Problems" is reprinted with permission from the *British Journal of Addiction*, vol. 82, pp. 913–925, 1987. Copyright by the Society for the Study of Addiction to Alcohol and Other Drugs, London, United Kingdom.

Chapter 14, "The Effect of Average Daily Consumption and Frequency of Intoxication on the Occurrence of Dependence Symptoms and Alcohol-Related Problems" is an earlier version of an article whose published title is "The Relationship Between Ethanol Intake and DSM-III Alcohol Use Disorders: A Cross-Perspective Analysis" and is reprinted with permission from the *Journal of Substance Abuse*, vol. 1, pp. 231–252, 1989. Copyright by Ablex Publishing Corporation, Norwood, New Jersey 07648.

Chapter 17, "Regional Diversity in United States Drinking Practices" is reprinted with permission from the *British Journal of Addiction*, vol. 83, pp. 519–532, 1988. Copyright by the Society for the Study of Addiction to Alcohol and Other Drugs, London, United Kingdom.

Chapter 18, "The Presence of Alcohol in Four Social Situations: Survey Results from 1964 and 1984" is reprinted with permission from the *International Journal of the Addictions*, vol. 22, pp. 487–495, 1987. Copyright by Marcel Dekker, Inc., New York, N.Y. 10016.

Chapter 20, "Drinking Patterns in the Black Population" is adapted from Danielle Spiegler et al., eds. *Alcohol Use Among U. S. Ethnic Minorities*, NIAAA Research Monograph, no. 18, pp. 3–50, Washington, D. C.: USGPO, DHHS Publication No. (ADM) 89-1435, 1989. This material is in the public domain.

Support for this research, and for the preparation of this monograph, came from a National Institute on Alcohol Abuse and Alcoholism Research Center Grant (AA05595) to the Alcohol Research Group, Institute of Epidemiology and Behavioral Medicine, Medical Research Institute of San Francisco.

PART I. INTRODUCTION

WALTER B. CLARK

1

Introduction

This book contains the results of several survey studies of alcohol use and related matters among members of the adult general population of the United States. Interviewers, equipped with carefully designed questionnaires, went to the respondents, asked the survey's questions in face-to-face settings, and recorded the answers given. This is the strength and the weakness of survey research; it is the only way to learn what individual respondents do and think, and the sum of the individuals' responses provides a view of alcohol use among all U.S. adults. However, survey data obviously are just peoples' answers to the questions asked; that is, we learn what people are willing and able to tell us, which is not very different from our circumstances in everyday life. Survey data are not objective truths, they are accounts of what people do and think. Without such accounts, imperfect as they may be, we would know much less about drinking and its correlates—a point which will be made below in discussing survey data as compared to tax records of total amounts of beverages sold in a given year.

The 1984 national alcohol survey, the central focus of this book, took pains to replicate some of the questions and procedures used in past national alcohol surveys, especially those of 1964, 1967, and 1979.

This enables us to examine some of the changes in drinking practices over this span of time. As it turns out, this is an especially interesting period because alcohol use was increasing during the first fifteen years of this time, and may have peaked and begun to decline after 1980. The materials on trends in alcohol consumption below will provide much detail on this possibility.

In other sections below, the authors are concerned with describing the correlates of various drinking patterns, including the problems which some respondents attributed to their alcohol use. This makes an interesting tale, for while the rates of drinking patterns are higher among heavier drinkers, substantial numbers of heavier drinkers report no problems due to drinking, while some who drink less do report having had problems which they attribute to alcohol use.

Perhaps the most striking finding from surveys of alcohol use is the variability in drinking patterns among U.S. adults. The United States has substantial numbers of nondrinkers and even has quite a few prohibitionists. Variations in beverage preferences, in amounts drunk, in the places and situations where alcohol is used, and in rates of various kinds of problems related to drinking are shown in following chapters to be related to the social and demographic characteristics of drinkers. Since the 1984 survey, unlike previous ones, included large supplementary samples of Black and Hispanic respondents, the drinking patterns of these Americans are described below in greater detail than was done in prior works.

The first surveys of alcohol use in general populations were undertaken only about forty years ago, and the 1984 survey owes much to earlier studies. Forty years is not such a long time, yet in that time we have learned a great deal about alcohol use and its effects; we have also learned that many earlier ideas concerning drinking and drinking problems were seriously in error. This point, like those mentioned above, will be elaborated in pages below.

PAST SURVEYS OF ALCOHOL USE

The earliest public opinion polls concerning alcohol use among members of the general population were carried out by the Gallup organization in the late 1930s. These surveys asked respondents "whether they had occasion to use alcoholic beverages, or whether they were complete abstainers." The wording seems quaint, but the information produced is interesting. It tells us that then, as now, about a third of U.S. adults did not use alcoholic beverages (Gallup, 1939–1966). The Gallup surveys were not focused on alcohol use, and their analyses were limited to a few tabulations of responses to this question within categories of gender, age, location and the like. It was not until after World War II that surveys that did pay more attention to alcohol use were carried out. The earliest of these were by Riley and Marden (1947) and by Riley, Marden, and Lifshitz (1948) which were based on a national survey. These included questions about the frequency of drinking, and about the reasons people gave to explain their use of alcohol. There were few questions about drinking in these early surveys; for instance, there were none that asked about the quantities of alcoholic beverages used on an occasion of drinking. Another early study was that of Maxwell (1952) who described drinking in the state of Washington. Straus and Bacon's (1953) survey of a sample of college students was remarkable for that time in that it included questions about frequency of drinking, quantities typically taken per occasion and even about the occurrence of some kinds of problems resulting from drinking. The kinds of questions asked about alcohol use in this study were adopted by a good many studies that followed. Mulford and his associates carried out a number of surveys in the state of Iowa; then in 1964 there followed a study of alcohol use for the United States as a whole. Mulford's (1964) survey was one which, following Straus and Bacon's approach, asked not only about the frequency of drinking, but also about the typical quantities per drinking occasion and even about common problems resulting from drinking such as complaints about drinking by spouses, employers or others.

The early studies noted above were among those which, in the span of a few years, enlarged upon the questions asked in the Gallup studies. Room's discussion of measuring alcohol consumption (chapter 3) in the Methods section of this volume contains the details on these early studies as well as on those which followed in ever increasing numbers as the years went by. As his discussion makes clear, a reasonably complete description of the drinking practices of a general population requires that a good many questions be asked about kinds of beverages drunk, frequency of use of each and, most complicated of all, the amounts of alcohol taken per drinking occasion. If one's concern is with describing the correlates of alcohol use, the description of drinking patterns defined by these dimensions is a minimum requirement. In addition, since one central reason for doing such surveys is to determine the relationship of various drinking patterns to the occurrence of various kinds of alcohol-related problems, a long list of questions about such potential problems is also needed. These requirements seem obvious, and one might wonder why early surveys most often omitted these obviously essential elements. One reason was that many of the earlier surveys were not independent studies at all;

rather, a researcher was only able to tack a few questions onto a survey which covered many topics. Such "piggyback" or "omnibus" surveys yielded some information, though often less than the researcher wanted, but did so at very low cost when compared to the expense of conducting an entire survey dedicated to a single research question. Obtaining government funding for studies of drinking practices was rare in those decades. Other researchers who shared questionnaire space with those interested in alcohol use sometimes felt that including questions on drinking might jeopardize the success of the survey as a whole. Respondents, it was felt, would not want to answer such personal questions and would refuse to answer not only the alcohol researcher's questions, but everybody else's questions as well. Interestingly, many alcohol researchers shared these worries about asking questions on such a sensitive topic as drinking was assumed to be at that time. Several dodges were used by those who were worried about offending potential respondents. A first was to ask only a very few questions about drinking, and to couch these questions in soft words (Gallup's quoted above is an example). A second was to imbed questions about drinking in a list of other questions about recreational activities, nutrition, or what have you.

These dodges were poor things indeed; if one asked only a few innocuous questions or if one loaded the questionnaire with questions about which one cared but little, one ended up with small amounts of poor data. Attempts to disguise the real interests of the survey while obtaining enough information on drinking behavior often seemed silly in retrospect. Given a questionnaire of reasonable length, one could include only a few innocuous questions about food preferences or recreational activities before one had to get down to the real work of asking, say, two dozen detailed questions on how much and how often the respondent drank and whether his drinking was a source of some of his problems.

There were a few methodological studies at the time which suggested that researchers' fears, rather than respondents' sensitivities, were the real problem. However, the most convincing evidence came from survey experience itself; relatively few respondents broke off an interview once it had begun even though they did not know at the outset what the interview would cover. Even fewer refused to answer particular questions on drinking or its effects. Almost none voiced objections to having been asked about these supposedly sensitive topics. Bit by bit researchers began to ask their questions more directly and to ask for greater detail. This is not to say that there were no more worries about the validity of answers given to questions about drinking—there are still real concerns about this—but perhaps it is fair to say that researchers began to regard their own timidity as at least as great a problem as the respondents' sensitivities.

DRINKING PATTERNS

Given greater courage and greater funding, in the late 1960s researchers began to ask more detailed questions about alcohol consumption. For instance, early surveys sometimes asked respondents how often they drank as many as five drinks per occasion, which is a substantial amount of alcohol to drink in an hour or two. However, later surveys were to find that it was worthwhile to ask about much larger quantities drunk per drinking occasion because there are drinkers who often exceed five drinks per occasion, and these drinkers report somewhat higher rates of drinking problems than those who drink less. Later surveys asked about much larger amounts per occasion— the 1984 survey asked how often twelve drinks were taken, and the 1979 survey asked about eighteen drinks per occasion (see Room's discussion in the Methods section for details).

Later surveys also asked respondents how often they drank enough to get high, or tight, or drunk. A small but significant proportion of respondents in the general population readily answered that they sometimes did drink very large amounts and that they did get drunk. Males, younger people, the unmarried, urban residents, and those whose religion does not forbid drinking include more than average numbers of heavier drinkers. Not surprisingly, those who drink relatively heavily go more often to taverns, parties, and other wet settings than lighter drinkers do, and they report more drinking on each occasion and in all settings. Heavier drinkers commonly report that their friends include other heavier drinkers, while lighter drinkers and total abstainers are more likely to describe their friends as much like themselves as far as drinking is concerned. Such commonsensical findings and other less obvious ones are discussed in the Drinking Contexts section below.

DRINKING PROBLEMS

An important point from these descriptions of who drinks how much is this: The same demographic characteristics that are associated with heavier drinking are also associated with higher rates of almost all kinds of alcohol problems in general populations. For instance, heavier drinking is relatively common among young men, and it is in this group that the highest rates of nearly all kinds of alcohol problems were found. Clinical studies, and especially the works of E. M. Jellinek (1946, 1960), had led researchers to expect to find the highest rates of alcohol dependence, indications of lost control over drinking, and so forth, among middle aged men with long histories of very heavy drinking. That was not what was found. Instead, surveys found that reports of such alcohol problems were extremely common among all heavier drinkers, most of whom were not and would not become clinical alcoholics. This was astonishing at the time because of the widespread belief that such things as blackouts, tremors, and unplanned and unwanted drunkenness were indications that progressive alcoholism was either present or coming. Ultimately, the survey data showing that such problems were more common than had been believed, and that having one problem was not a strong predictor of having others, led to a drastic revision of ideas concerning the nature and course of alcoholism (more commonly called "alcohol dependence" in recent times).

Some details on these matters will be found below in the section on drinking problems. Here it is worth noting that the almost universally used survey questions about drinking problems, unlike questions about drinking patterns, were not developed by survey researchers. Instead, they were taken wholesale from clinical studies of alcoholics, and most particularly from E. M. Jellinek's studies of members of Alcoholics Anonymous. The very earliest surveys did not ask about alcohol problems at all, but soon surveys began to include at least a few. As in many other respects, Straus and Bacon's (1953) survey of college students was a leader in this; they inquired about drinking problems such as injured friendships, poor academic work and the like. Mulford's (1964) national survey did much the same for the United States as a whole. By the mid-1960s community studies were asking the entire range of drinking problems questions including questions on apparent dependence on alcohol, loss of control and, of course, interpersonal problems due to drinking (Knupfer, 1967; Clark, 1966. See Room, 1977, for a thorough discussion of the history of these measures). While the interpretation of the meaning of data from these questions and the analyses of the data have changed greatly in the years since then, the content has remained much the same to the present day.

It is interesting to note that questions about drinking problems are easily asked and easily answered because the "bad signs" such as blackouts, tremors after drinking, and all the rest are well known to drinkers everywhere either from personal experience or from common observation of others. That means, of course, that the drinker who affirms a question about, say, having shaky hands the morning after drinking has not only noted the tremors, but has also concluded that they were due to drinking. Similarly, questions about harmed friendships or marriages are dependent upon the respondent's judgment that such problems exist and that they are due to alcohol. To a great extent the respondents in epidemiological surveys of drinking and drinking problems are thus participants in the work, and not naive research subjects.

WHAT SURVEYS TELL US

The surveys discussed in this volume cover only the years from 1964 through 1984. However, as will be discussed, this is an interesting span of time for it includes a time when alcohol consumption was increasing, and it may also include the beginning of a downturn in consumption. As noted, all the papers in this volume make use of 1984 national alcohol survey data, but some also make comparisons with data from earlier national alcohol surveys, especially those carried out by the Alcohol Research Group in 1964, 1967, and 1979. The most recent survey was designed to facilitate such comparisons by including identical questions on amount of drinking and other key variables, and by using comparable high quality sampling and fieldwork procedures in all surveys.

Survey data, with all their faults, provide the only means of describing variations in alcohol use in general populations. In doing this, surveys have had important consequences; in the past twenty-five years they have added to our knowledge of the correlates of various drinking patterns, and have forced us to revise our ideas concerning alcohol problems, including dependence and alcoholism. By showing variations in alcohol use and its correlates, surveys put flesh on the bones of aggregate statistics such as those concerning the production or sales of alcoholic beverages. And aggregate data alone are bare bones indeed. For instance, aggregate data on alcohol production and sales are available for a much earlier period of time, including the early years of this century when total alcohol consumption was falling rapidly in the United States, as it was in most other western European nations. As Cahalan (1988) notes, apparent alcohol consumption, estimated from tax records, has fluctuated over the years of this century. Yearly per capita consumption of absolute alcohol per person aged fifteen years or older was in excess of 2.5 gallons in the early 1900s, but it was falling rapidly in the years leading to the prohibition period. In 1933 when prohibition ended, apparent consumption was a little less than one gallon of absolute alcohol per person per year. This drop in consumption suggests an enormous shift in public sentiments concerning drinking, but aggregate data tell us nothing about the behavior or feelings of the people involved. Historical and sociological studies such as Gusfield's (1963) work on the temperance movement provide rich descriptions of the views of leaders for and against prohibition, and they provide useful descriptions of organizational activities, but they tell us relatively little about the man in the street.

From 1933 on, the consumption of alcoholic beverages increased. With the exception of the World War II years when consumption fell off briefly, the increase in per capita consumption continued until, in 1981, it reached over 2.75 gallons per capita per year (Cahalan, 1988, p. 2). Again, these great changes in alcohol use speak of great shifts in public sentiments, but it is only for the last two decades that we have national survey data to tell us who was doing what with alcoholic drinks. However, this recent two decades may turn out to be an interesting period, for around 1981 alcohol consumption in the United States began to decline. The total apparent per capita consumption decreased in 1982, and again in 1983, and again in 1984. In 1985, the per capita consumption was 2.58 gallons, a decrease of over six percent from 1981. That isn't much of a decline compared to the early decades of this century, but it is worth watching. As noted, there have been periods before in this century when consumption fell only to rise and exceed its former level. However, there is some reason to believe that the recent decline is no mere dip in the upward curve; Room's discussion of cultural changes in drinking (chapter 10 of this volume) suggests that the recent decline in consumption is matched by changes in public sentiment toward drinking and drinking problems. Further declines in apparent consumption may follow.

The usefulness of survey data lies chiefly in the description of variations in alcohol consumption and its correlates, variations concealed in the aggregate consumption statistics. For instance, the relatively high per capita consumption figure of 2.8 gallons of alcohol per year is only about one ounce of alcohol each per day. It has often been noted that if each person did in fact drink his daily share, there would be no drinking problems. However, the United States is remarkable among modern industrial nations in the variety of drinking patterns within its population, and knowledge of this variation is central to the epidemiology of alcohol problems, as the several papers in the Alcohol Problems Section demonstrate. However, while heavy drinking is an obvious concern of researchers, those who do not drink are also of interest—only partly because their numbers qualify what the per capita consumption figures mean. Further, "heavy drinking" is an ambiguous term which sometimes refers to total consumption over, say, a year and sometimes refers to the amount of alcohol consumed on a single occasion. Those who drink large amounts on occasion may experience drunkenness and may experience alcohol problems and yet their total consumption of alcoholic beverages may be relatively low. The earlier surveys in this series have provided descriptions of abstainers and of those who often drink to the point of drunkenness. Some details about these two groups may be of interest.

ABSTAINERS

Genevieve Knupfer (1961) was among the first to use survey data to describe those who abstain from alcohol. This survey was based on a probability sample of the adult population of Berkeley, California— not an area in which one would expect to find many nondrinkers. She pointed out, quite rightly, that abstainers in that population were in the minority. Since the norm for the population was to drink, abstinence was "deviant" from that norm, a term she used in that scholarly paper. The wire services transmitted a synopsis of her article to newspapers, and that synopsis also contained the word "deviant" as applied to nondrinkers. Quite a few newspapers printed a paragraph or two about her article. Dozens of angry letters from news editors, clergymen, and offended abstainers arrived in Knupfer's mail. The gist of these was that the term 'deviant' should not be used to describe people whose behavior was morally correct. Had the writers of these angry letters read the article, perhaps they would have found little to object to. Knupfer's description of abstainers and drinkers was objective. The two groups differ on many dimensions, but most of these differences are of degree. It is difficult to find attributes held by a large majority of one group which are held by only a small minority of the other. For instance, while a large proportion of abstainers agree that "drinking does more harm than good," a substantial, if smaller, proportion of drinkers also agree with that statement. Among abstainers, however, there are some who are militantly so, and some of these took the trouble to write to Knupfer upon reading the news report of her research. Interestingly, what Knupfer found in Berkeley does not differ radically from what was later found for the nation as a whole. Abstainers, including those who abstain on principle, are not rare in the United States, and their numbers have remained reasonably constant over many years.

The United States is not the highest in per capita consumption among those nations providing such figures, but it is above the median (Cahalan, 1988, p. 4). This measure of apparent consumption would be higher still were it not that about a third of U.S. adults abstain from drinking alcoholic beverages, a proportion of the population that has not changed greatly since the mid-1930s (Room, chapter 10 in this volume; Hilton, 1986; Knupfer and Room, 1970). Thus, the noted increases in U.S. per capita consumption since then cannot be attributed to changes in the proportion of drinkers. Further, the relatively high and stable proportion of abstainers makes the United States unusual among industrial nations. Armyr, Elmer, and Herz (1982) report some estimates for many nations. Norway and Sweden may each have 20% of abstainers among adults, Canada has perhaps 15% to 20%, and Finland may have 15% reporting they never drink. The figures for other nations are much lower: Austria, 6%; Belgium 5% to 10%; France perhaps 13%; Great Britain 8%; and West Germany 5% to 10%.

Thus the one-third of U.S. adults who abstain is significantly higher than the proportions found in these other countries. Further, in the United States another 15% of adults report they use alcohol less often than once a month. This 15% of infrequent drinkers plus the one third who do not drink at all means that nearly half of adults make little or no use of alcoholic beverages (Cahalan, Cisin, and Crossley, 1969; Clark and Midanik, 1982).

Thus it is that per capita consumption figures, while useful, obscure much variation in alcohol use in the United States. There is further variation among abstainers as well. In the opinion of some, no drinking differs even from drinking a little, and in the 1979 national alcohol survey, 63% of current abstainers (those who had used no alcohol in the preceding year) reported that they were lifelong abstainers. Interestingly, only 6% of these current abstainers reported having been heavy drinkers at some time in the past (Hilton, 1986).

Comparing results from 1979 and 1964, using data from the national surveys in this series, Hilton (1986) found no significant decline in the proportion of abstainers among U.S. adults. The descriptive characteristics of abstainers also were quite similar in both surveys. Relatively more women than men abstain from alcohol, relatively more older than younger people, and relatively more of those with little education than those with more. Also, as is now well known, the East South Central census region of the United States—sometimes called the Bible Belt—contains a greater proportion of abstainers than other regions do. Affiliation with a fundamentalist Protestant group underlies some of the latter; Hilton's (1986) analysis indicates that this was so in 1979 as in 1964. A few studies have suggested that the rates of abstention may be declining in traditionally dry areas of the country (Smith and Hanham, 1982), or that differences in rates of abstention between the sexes may be decreasing (Wechsler and McFadden, 1976), or that the influence of religion on abstention is declining (Nusbaumer, 1981). However, the 1979 national survey data do not support these findings; nor did the earlier findings of Johnson et al. (1977) include signs of such changes in their analysis of several other sets of national survey data. In fact, another look at such matters may well be worthwhile, for the 1984 national survey data reported in the papers in the Trends Section of this volume suggest there may be signs of increasing rates of abstinence in at least some demographic categories. In any event, as was the case twenty years ago, a substantial proportion of U.S. adults are abstainers today, and many have abstained all their lives.

There are many reasons why one might choose not to drink, and the 1979 national survey asked lifelong abstainers about their reasons for not drinking. Sixty percent or more reported that they came from families that didn't drink, that drinking would damage their reputations with family and friends, that their religion forbids use of alcoholic beverages, and that drinking is morally wrong (among other reasons). Such reasons for not drinking as these suggest the social forces which have sustained the abstaining fraction of U.S. adults all through a period of generally increasing use of alcohol. Clark (1977) and Knupfer and Room (1970), analyzing different sets of survey data, found that many abstainers reported they socialized with others who did not drink, and few abstainers went to taverns or to parties where alcohol was served. This speaks of a separation of people according to a lifestyle, and in fact the same survey data found that heavier drinkers also reported associating with others like themselves as far as drinking was concerned.

As several past surveys have found, some people do not drink because they don't like the taste or smell or the effects of alcoholic beverages (Knupfer, 1961; Knupfer and Room, 1970). But Hilton (1986) notes that it is one thing to choose not to drink and quite another to feel that no one should drink. Yet a substantial fraction of U.S. adults feel that no one should drink, and some feel that no one should be permitted to drink. Hilton's data show that 9% of all U.S. adults interviewed in 1979 disapprove of any drinking by anyone, and Room's paper (chapter 10) in the Trends Section reports Gallup data from the same year indicating that nearly one in five of those interviewed would have favored a law forbidding all alcohol sales in the country.

Thus in the United States today, despite the apparent ubiquity of alcoholic beverages, almost half of adults either drink less often than once a month, or else do not drink at all, and a substantial minority would prefer that no one used alcohol.

DRUNKENNESS

In contrast to those who abstain are those who sometimes use alcoholic beverages to get drunk. These people also comprise a significant proportion of U.S. adults. Several of the surveys in this series have asked respondents how often they have gotten drunk in the past year. Predictably, the majority of U.S. adults report no instances of drunkenness, and even among current drinkers the majority say they've not been drunk in the past year. However, among men aged eighteen through twenty-five, about three-quarters of those who drank at all during the preceding year also reported having been drunk at least once. Among women drinkers in the same age range, just under half said they had been drunk at least once in the last year (Clark, 1982a, 1977). By and large, the demographic and social characteristics associated with higher rates of drunkenness are the reverse of those associated with abstinence. Details on the correlates of drunkenness can be found in the references cited; here we will focus on the relationships among drunkenness, total amount of drinking, and rates of some common drinking problems. But first, some background information will be useful.

As Knupfer (1984) has shown, drunkenness is risky, and drunkenness is not identical to heavy drinking—at least as that latter term is commonly used. In a year, the frequent drinker of small amounts may drink as much as the infrequent drinker of large amounts, but it is the latter who runs the greater risk of almost all the kinds of drinking problems found in general populations. Knupfer's point is that it is intoxication, not amount of drinking, that often is associated with violations of the norms governing acceptable behavior, and it is intoxication that leads the drinker himself to worry about his drinking. Her analysis makes it clear that the frequency of drinking very large amounts on an occasion of drinking is associated with high rates of drinking-related interpersonal problems, and with such problems as blackouts, shaking hands, and so forth—things commonly taken as indications of alcohol dependence. Knupfer's approach was to infer drunkenness from respondents' reports of having drunk five drinks in a day as often as three times a week over the past year, or of having drunk eight drinks in a day at least that often. She also included respondents' reports of having been drunk or high—whatever those terms meant to them—with similar frequencies. Using all these criteria, she found that among all those who reported frequent intoxication, there were still variations in rates of some kinds of alcohol problems. Women who drank at the highest levels encountered more problems than men, and among men, younger men and married men reported more problems than older men or single men.

Hilton's "Higher and Lower Rates of Reported Problems Among Heavy Drinkers" (chapter 15 in this volume) follows Knupfer's lead in trying to puzzle out why some heavy drinkers have problems while others do not. He defined intoxication in terms of reports of drinking large amounts per occasion, but unlike Knupfer he did not include respondents' reports that they had been drunk as one measure of intoxication. Knupfer's central focus was elsewhere, but she did show that self reported drunkenness was strongly but not perfectly correlated with reports of drinking large amounts per occasion. There is therefore still another question that can be explored in this area: namely, the interrelationships among amount of drinking, frequency of self reported drunkenness, and rates of various alcohol problems.

Surveys concerned with measuring alcohol consumption typically ask respondents how often they drink, how much per occasion, and so on, which is quite different from asking how often they get drunk. First, a given amount of alcohol will produce different blood alcohol levels depending upon such things as beverage type, stomach contents, and the amount of time given over to drinking. Drinkers also vary in body size, proportion of fatty tissue, tolerance for alcohol, and so forth, which also affect degree of intoxication. Beyond these substantial sources of variation lies another, that of the drinker's perceptions of his degree of intoxication and his willingness to categorize some degree of intoxication as being drunk. In the 1979 national alcohol survey, respondents were asked to describe their drinking patterns and they were asked how often they had gotten drunk in the past year (Clark, 1982a). These data indicate that, among drinkers, amount of drinking expressed in alcoholic drinks per month is correlated with frequency of drunkenness, but only to a moderate degree (the product-moment correlation coefficient is 0.422). Quite small proportions of lighter drinkers report that they have gotten drunk in the past year; larger proportions of moderate drinkers, and substantial proportions of the heavier drinkers report drunkenness, and relatively frequent drunkenness. However, even among the heaviest drinkers fully 40% of women and 23% of men report never having been drunk in the past year. Lest it be thought that these people were simply denying having been drunk, we should recall that they had already described how much and how often they drank, and substantial proportions of heavier drinkers went on to describe current personal problems which they blamed on their drinking.

"Drunk" was not defined for respondents in this survey; if they asked what was meant by it they were told, "whatever it means to you." Thus in the survey, as in the language itself, the term was left ambiguous. However, it is clear that "drunk" means severe intoxication to most U.S. adults, for respondents were also asked, "How many drinks do you think you would have to have before you would feel drunk?" Men drinkers reported a mean of 9.8 drinks (SD 5.58) and women drinkers said 5.7 drinks (SD 3.0) in order to feel drunk. That is a lot, and the word "drunk" must mean extreme intoxication to many of these respondents. Interestingly, the frequency of reported drunkenness in the past year was not correlated with the reports of the numbers of drinks it would take to feel drunk. However, the total amount of drinking in the past year was correlated with the amount to feel drunk (r = 0.45). It is that last which is important, for it indicates that lighter drinkers (overall) reported that it took less alcohol to make them drunk than heavier drinkers required.

The demographic correlates of frequency of drunkenness are not surprising: among drinkers, more men than women reported frequent drunkenness, and many more young people than older people reported having been drunk at any given frequency in the past year. Overall, 9% of men drinkers reported having been drunk at least once a month in the past year, another 9% said four to eleven times, 22% said one through three times, and 61% said they had never been drunk in the past year. Among women drinkers only 4% reported at least monthly drunkenness, another 3% said four through eleven times, 18% said one through three times, while 74% said they had not been drunk in the past year (Clark, 1982a).

As noted above, total amount of drinking was found to be correlated with frequency of drunkenness, but that relationship was only of moderate strength, and some heavy drinkers reported no drunkenness while some light and moderate drinkers did report having been drunk in the past year, and even reported having been drunk at least as often as once a month. A regression analysis indicated that— independently of frequency of drunkenness—total amount of drinking was related to reports of drinking problems including indicators of loss of control, dependence symptoms and interpersonal problems due to drinking. The regression also indicated that frequency of drunken-ness—regardless of whether the respondent was a light, moderate or heavy drinker—also was related to these same kinds of drinking problems. Thus it seems fairly clear that a pattern of drinking which includes drunkenness carries an increased risk of drinking problems; and relatively heavy drinking without subjective feelings of drunkenness also carries an increased risk of drinking problems. Those who are heavy drinkers and who get drunk fairly often are at substantially greater risk of drinking problems than are the other two groups, and those other two groups are about equal in terms of rates of problems which they attribute to their use of alcoholic beverages.

Thus survey data provide insight into the degree to which variations in drinking patterns among U.S. adults are related to alcohol problems. Drunkenness, as abstainers frequently report, can interfere with a drinker's ability to carry out his responsibilities, and spouse, friends, and even the drinker himself may properly object. Heavy drinking, involving lesser degrees of intoxication than outright drunkenness still carries some risk of such problems. However, it should also be noted that not all heavy drinkers, and not even all heavy drinkers who report frequent intoxication, have reported drinking problems. In that same data set, 84% of the heaviest drinkers who also reported at least monthly or more frequent drunkenness reported no dependence symptoms such as shaking hands after drinking, blackouts or the like. Nearly 40% of these same heavy drinking, frequently drunk respondents reported no indications of loss of control over drinking such as unintended drunkenness, fears of losing control over alcohol, and so forth, in the past year (Clark and Midanik, 1982). Thus, if these things are taken at face value, there are risks associated with drinking and drunkenness, but the risks of severe alcohol problems are far from certain. No doubt such observations have been made by many drinkers. One may go on to ask why some drinkers experience problems while others whose drinking patterns are similar remain problem free. This question is addressed in several places in the section on Drinking Problems, and several characteristics of drinkers beyond their reported habits of alcohol consumption seem important. Material in the section on the Contexts of Drinking also bears the matter. Intoxication is normatively acceptable for some social statuses, less so for others. Even more striking is the apparent agreement among U.S. adults concerning the kinds of situations or settings in which intoxication is permissible, even encouraged. Some of the variation in drinking problem rates can be attributed to descriptions of who is drinking how much in which settings, and further information on this can be found in the Contexts section. However, these materials are far from conclusive; why some heavy drinkers experience problems while others do not is still an unanswered question.

The reports from thousands of respondents concerning alcohol are summarized and analyzed in the chapters below. The diversity of drinking patterns and their correlates is striking. Above it was noted that abstinence is not rare in U.S. society, and neither is drunkenness. But in the chapters following it will be shown that most adults do drink and yet avoid drunkenness. Intoxication, of course, has much to do with the problems that arise from alcohol use, but the intoxicating properties of beverage alcohol also have much to do with the popularity of such beverages. As everyone knows, alcohol can cause problems for the drinker and for others, but most drinkers do not report experiencing problems related to their drinking. In the chapters below, a detailed description of who drinks how much and with what effects and consequences is given for the United States in the mid-1980s.

PART II.   METHODS

WALTER B. CLARK

2

Some Comments on Methods

SURVEY STUDIES

The use of survey techniques to study alcohol use and its correlates is now about forty years old. In that time there have been some major improvements, perhaps the most important of which was the introduction of area-probability sampling methods. Allowing, as such methods do, each person in the study population to have nearly an equal chance of being selected for interviewing means that the sample can provide unbiased estimates of the true, unknown proportions in the population from which it was drawn. These expensive statistical tools have, for academic research projects, largely replaced the quota sampling and the "convenience samples" of earlier days. On the other hand, gaining cooperation from potential respondents has become increasingly difficult over this same span of time; where once it was considered just acceptable to complete interviews with 90% of respondents chosen by probability methods, 75% is often a difficult goal to reach today. There are weighting schemes which are designed to compensate for losses to the sample due to nonresponse (those used in the 1984 survey are described below) but these are not as satisfactory as a near perfect completion rate.

Information has accumulated over the last forty years on the kinds of questions about drinking and related problems that can be used in surveys. In general, the questions asked of respondents in recent times are more numerous, more detailed, more probing and more focused than those of earlier works. Having a base of previous surveys to build upon has helped in this, and the collective experience of survey researchers around the world has grown greatly in recent years. The international associations of researchers who share data, experience and critical reviews of work have reduced the need to invent measures anew, and replications of past work are becoming more common. There is a need for replication of past studies, but asking the same questions in the same format also means that any defects in the old are also in the new. Since questionnaire length is always limited, new questions cannot simply be added on to the old. In the 1984 survey, questions on frequency and quantity of drinking were taken from the earlier surveys of 1964 and 1967, as were some questions on alcohol-related problems (along with a few new ones). By this decision the trend studies in this volume were made possible, but it also ruled out using newer measures of alcohol use and alcohol problems, and some of these newer measures would have been better for other tasks.

RESEARCH METHODS

The 1984 national alcohol survey is based on a representative sample of people aged eighteen years or more who were living in households within the contiguous states at the time of the survey. Each respondent contributed about an hour in answering a long series of standardized questions which were asked by an interviewer. Questions about alcohol use and possible problems related to drinking were a central part of these interviews, but many other questions were asked to provide a means of describing the demographic characteristics of the respondents and their opinions and attitudes on many matters.

Since all the papers in this volume make some use of the data from the 1984 national survey, and since all are concerned in some way with alcohol use or alcohol problems in the general population, a general description of research methods will be given here. Similar descriptions have been deleted from the individual papers, which now contain only methodological points that are specific to the particular paper.

SAMPLING AND INTERVIEWING

The survey was designed to yield a representative sample of adults aged eighteen years or older who were living in households within the forty-eight contiguous states during 1984, the year the survey was conducted. Temple University's Institute for Survey Research was responsible for sampling and fieldwork. The multistage, area-probability sampling procedure used one hundred primary sampling units for the primary sample. In addition to this, ten additional sampling units were selected from geographical areas containing relatively high proportions of Black or Hispanic residents. This, combined with systematic oversampling of Black and Hispanic residents, provided large, nearly representative samples of Blacks and Hispanics in addition to the sample of all adults. These supplementary samples permitted detailed analyses of Black and Hispanic drinking patterns in the United States, which are separately reported in the section below concerned with drinking patterns in these segments of the population. In other sections Blacks and Hispanics are included, but the focus is on the total adult population. The total number of respondents interviewed in the three samples was 5,221, of which 1,947 came from the sample of Blacks and 1433 from the Hispanic sample. Completion rates for interviewing were reasonably high: 73.2% for the non-Black, non-Hispanic sample, 75.9% for the Black, and 72.2% for the Hispanic sample.

Given the oversampling of Blacks and Hispanics, it was necessary to weight these cases down to their true proportions in the total population for some purposes. In addition, additional case weights were applied to all samples to take into account the number of eligible adults living in a household which fell into the sample, and the completion rates of interviewing among men and women, among those over and under thirty-five years of age, and within four census regions of the United States. The weighting scheme produced an N of 2,167 cases which is the actual number of non-Black, non-Hispanic respondents plus a proportionally down-weighted case weight attached to each Hispanic and each Black respondent. The combined weights have been used in calculating population estimates of percents, and so forth, but the numbers of cases shown are unweighted in most analyses reported on here, and even those which are weighted do not make use of greatly inflated totals. (The few variations in these procedures are described in the papers to which they apply.)

The questionnaires designed by the Alcohol Research Group to elicit information on drinking and related matters include newly developed materials but there are also questions identical or similar to those used in past national alcohol surveys. Of course, it would have been desirable to replicate exactly that past research, but since there have been over a half-dozen past surveys which differ from each other, it was not possible to include questions identical to all used in past work on the present survey. What was done was to exactly replicate questions on frequency and quantity of drinking used in the 1964 national survey, and to replicate exactly some of the drinking problem questions from the 1967 survey. This permits exact comparisons to be made with the current data, and such twenty year comparisons are included in the section on trends in these pages. In other cases, the current survey included questions similar to, but not identical with, those asked in past surveys. This permits comparisons between current data and several past surveys; it sacrifices exact comparability for multiple comparisons. Again, the individual papers contain details on these matters. The questionnaires used in 1984 were highly structured and almost all responses to the questions were recorded by means of checking an appropriate answer category. The asking of the questions and recording of answers was done by interviewers of the Institute for Survey Research of Temple University, which organization also verified the quality of interviews and produced the final data tape used for the analyses reported in these pages. The face-to-face interviews were almost always done in the respondents' homes, and those Hispanic respondents who preferred to be interviewed in Spanish were furnished with a bilingual interviewer and a Spanish language version of the questionnaire. On the average, each interview required a little over an hour.

VALIDITY QUESTIONS

The 1984 survey interviews consist of carefully written questions which were tested before use to make sure they contained no unplanned ambiguities. During interviews, interviewers read the questions aloud to respondents and recorded answers by means of checking categories, and any further probing questions needed to make a respondent's meaning clear were given to all interviewers during the training period, as were explanations they might provide to respondents about what the questions meant. Thus care was taken to provide each respondent with the same interview, and to record his answers in the same way. However necessary uniformity in interviewing may be, self-reported information is always what respondents are willing and able to say to interviewers. The usefulness of survey data, the only source of individual-level data, must be assessed not in comparison to unknown objective reality, but in comparison to what could be learned by other methods.

A large part of the 1984 survey consisted of asking people's opinions and attitudes concerning alcohol use, and there is no other way to learn about these matters. Other questions ask about earnings, education and the like—things which could in principle be verified, but which in practice would be an impossibly large task. However, the substantial literature on the validity of self-reported drinking patterns makes it clear that this is one area in which researchers are not all willing to accept respondents' answers as useful data.

One good reason for their doubts is that data on alcohol production and sales indicate that more alcohol is sold than the respondents in surveys say they drink. Pernanen (1974) reviewed the literature on this and concluded that surveys "account for" one-half to two-thirds of alcohol known to have been sold in a given area. This discrepancy would not be a great problem if the size and direction of these response errors were known. They are not, and some researchers have shown that, in at least some study populations, heavier drinkers and drinkers with problems tended to minimize their drinking to a greater extent than lighter drinkers (see Midanik, 1982; 1988 for a recent review of this literature). Other researchers have reported better success with self-reported information on drinking patterns both among patients in alcoholism treatment centers and among members of general population groups (Midanik, 1982). One study of men in the U.S. Air Force (Polich and Orvis, 1979) found that these young men's self-reports of drinking accounted for over 80% of the alcohol known to have been purchased.

Thus, among researchers opinions are mixed on the degree of accuracy of self-reports of amounts of drinking—and even more mixed on the nature of the reporting errors that must exist. Some are concerned with denial of excessive drinking, some think forgetfulness is more important, some stress that seasonal variation in drinking, and especially heavy drinking around the holidays, is not well covered in surveys done at other times in the year. Others have compared various methods of eliciting and recording amounts of drinking, and research supportive of various procedures can be found (including drinking diaries, respondent's summaries of their usual patterns, interviewer-assisted recollection of all drinking in past days, weeks or months, reports of the last drinking occasion, or of the last week's drinking, randomized response questions which conceal from the interviewer the nature of the question being answered by the respondent, phony saliva tests thought to encourage truthful responses, and real breath, blood, urine, and sweat tests to check on respondents' reports of amount of drinking in a relatively brief period before testing. Midanik, 1988, contains a discussion of these).

Self-reports of problems related to alcohol use have also been scrutinized by researchers, and questions about validity have been raised. Some drinking problems cannot be verified: respondents' reports of being worried about their drinking, or reports of craving for alcohol or inability to control the amount they drink on an occasion are examples. Other kinds of drinking problems such as arrest records, admission to alcoholic treatment programs and the like are subject, at least in theory, to external verification. The few such studies concerned with these kinds of self-reports in general populations have found that some respondents' reports do not match what the records show, but they also show that some respondents report more than the records contain (see Polich, 1982, Polich and Orvis, 1979; O'Farrell and Connors, 1982; Knupfer, 1967; Robins, 1966).

From such studies it seems that for the foreseeable future respondents' self-reports are the best source of information of amount of drinking and on related problems. Official records, biochemical tests, additional interviews with spouses, relatives, and so on, are less useful for general population studies and often cannot be obtained.

Surveys make use of less than precise data, and unexpected research findings are tentatively accepted only because much of the same data is expected by those who know the study population from being members of it. Thus repeatedly finding that men report more drinking, intoxication, and alcohol problems than women do fits with our experience, and lends some credence to less obvious findings, such as moderate drinkers who report they sometimes get drunk have somewhat higher rates of some drinking problems than heavier drinkers who report they never get drunk (Clark and Midanik, 1982).

A FINAL NOTE

Below are two methodological studies that pertain to the 1984 national survey. A third is contained in the Appendix. That one, by Robert Santos, describes the sampling methods he and his colleagues at Temple University's Institute for Survey Research used. His technical description is important and useful, but beyond this, one is impressed by the enormous amount of work that was done before a data tape could be produced.

The next paper is Room's discussion of the history and practice of obtaining from respondents useful descriptions of their patterns of alcohol use. Room makes well the point that capturing useful descriptions of human behavior by means of a relatively few survey questions is not simple; he also makes clear that researchers must choose one or another approach in this task, and that their choices will affect what the research will find upon analysis.

Hilton's discussion of the questions asking about potential problems resulting from drinking shows that describing these problems is no less complicated than describing drinking patterns. The complexity becomes more marked when various single items relating to particular kinds of drinking problems must be combined into indexes of alcohol dependence and the like. Hilton's discussion makes these points well, and he also notes some of the controversies that exist concerning the measurement of alcohol problems in general populations.

Here again we should note that these papers on research methods are not just celebrating technical niceties. The interpretation of the data depends upon the decision to use one measure rather than another, one index rather than others. The methods provide a lens—good or poor—through which we examine what the respondents have told us.

3

Measuring Alcohol Consumption in the U.S.: Methods and Rationales

INTRODUCTION

This paper aims to lay out the methods of measuring alcohol consumption that have been used in survey studies of the general population of the United States, and to discuss their development and rationales. As was already clear by 1970 (Room, 1970b), there are two major strategies for asking respondents about their current pattern of drinking: (1) to ask them to list all recent drinking occasions; and (2) to ask them to summarize their current patterns. In general terms, British and Scandinavian researchers have followed the first strategy, while North American researchers have followed the second (see Room, 1977, and Auth and Warheit, 1982–1983 on U.S. traditions). Recently, some European researchers have challenged U.S. traditions of measuring drinking patterns, arguing in favor of the "recent occasions" approach (Duffy, 1982, 1984; Alanko, 1984). On the other hand, a recent empirical analysis of Finnish data concluded that "for most descriptive purposes" on a population level, "the choice of measurement procedure is irrelevant," and furthermore, that an approach in the U.S. tradition may least underestimate consumption among the heaviest drinkers (Simpura, 1987). These discussions and analyses, along with recent discussions by U.S. researchers (e.g., Greenfield, 1986; Knupfer, 1987, forthcoming), do serve to remind us of "the extremely complicated structure of the concept of alcohol consumption" (Alanko, 1984, p. 209) and of the need for new developmental work taking account of the different national traditions. As Alanko concludes, our "awareness of the problems" in existing approaches "should stimulate further research leading to improved methodology" (p. 224).

In sketching the history and development of measurements of amount of drinking in North American surveys, this paper focuses on surveys of the general adult population, although, as noted below, two other quantitative research traditions—studies of teenage drinking, and studies of amount of drinking among clinical alcoholics—have intersected with the tradition of adult drinking practices surveys. Our attention is on the logic and procedures of measurement and of aggregation for reporting; readers are referred elsewhere for general reviews on the validity of measures of alcohol consumption (Pernanen, 1974; Midanik, 1982).

NORTH AMERICAN APPROACHES TO MEASURING AMOUNT OF DRINKING

Methodological discussions of the best way to measure drinking patterns and problems date back at least to Pearl's discussion (1926; pp. 69–92) of the importance of separating steady daily drinkers from occasional heavy drinkers. Until the 1950s, however, surveys of the general population confined themselves to simple distinctions between drinking and abstaining (e.g., Gallup, 1972; Billings, 1903) or by frequency of drinking (Riley and Marden, 1947). The crucial step in moving to a fuller measurement of alcohol consumption was to start asking also about amount of drinking on an occasion or in a given period.

In this sense, the modern North American tradition of questions on amount of drinking starts with Straus and Bacon's pathbreaking study (1953) of *Drinking in College*. Straus and Bacon's approach to measuring patterns of drinking was to ask for each type of beverage (wine, beer, and spirits), the frequency of drinking, and the average amount ordinarily consumed at a sitting. A similar method was adopted in the Iowa general population studies of Mulford and associates, starting in the late 1950s (Fitzgerald and Mulford, 1982; their 1979 survey specified the time period covered to the last thirty days.) Variations on this method have been widely used.

Meanwhile, a separate tradition, starting with the San Francisco Bay Area studies of the California Drinking Practices Study in the early 1960s (Knupfer et al. 1963; Knupfer and Room, 1964), asked for each beverage type, the frequency of drinking, and then the proportion of drinking occasions on which one or two drinks, three or four drinks, and five or more drinks were consumed. This series of questions was carried over to the national drinking surveys of Cahalan and associates (1969) and to studies by Jessor and associates (1968; pp. 483–486). They have also been used in a number of other surveys. To maintain comparability with the 1964 and 1966 national alcohol survey data-sets, the questions have also been repeated, along with others, in some more recent surveys of the Alcohol Research Group, including the 1984 national alcohol survey.

Those using this approach were critical of the "usual quantity" approach, pointing out that someone who drinks small amounts frequently and larger amounts infrequently would quite truthfully respond that their usual quantity was one beer: "a person who drinks seven days a week and is drunk on only two of those days could not be regarded as one who 'usually' gets drunk when he drinks. Yet by using his usual drinking behavior this person becomes classified with others who drink daily and never have more than two drinks" (Fink, 1962; see also Knupfer, 1966). The method of asking proportions of drinking occasions on which particular quantities were used lent itself naturally to defining two dimensions of quantity of drinking for each beverage type: the "modal quantity", that is, the amount consumed "more than half the time", and the "range", that is, the amount consumed at least "once in a while." The summary measures derived from these measures (discussed below) were based on combinations of these two dimensions and the dimension of frequency of drinking.

By the mid-1960s, however, as attention shifted from partitioning the general population by drinking patterns to measuring drinking-related problems and their correlates, Knupfer and her associates were growing increasingly uncomfortable with an upper range category that started as low as five drinks. The 1964 reinterview of the San Francisco sample extended the range substantially by asking about "the times when you had the most to drink" in the last year, with an upper coding category of "twelve or more" drinks, and found that substantial proportions of current drinkers—23% of men and 3% of women—reported having drunk this much (Room, 1968). The researchers in the Berkeley group also moved away from the "proportion of occasions" questions in favor of straightforwardly asking respondents how often they drank at different levels of consumption. The result, first used in a 1967 survey of San Francisco males, was a series of questions about how often the respondent drank at least twelve, eight to eleven, and four to seven drinks, as well as an overall frequency of drinking question. The different beverage types were combined in asking these questions, with respondents being given equivalents in terms of different bottle sizes for the number of drinks in question. The 1967 National reinterview study, in addition to using the beverage-specific "proportion of occasions" question series, also asked about the timing and amounts of drinking on the last two drinking occasions (Room, 1970a).

The 1969 national alcohol survey of males combined two methods by using the beverage-specific "proportion of occasions" questions for five or more, three to four, and one to two drinks, and then adding cross-beverage questions for eight to eleven and twelve or more drinks. Whereas earlier surveys had simply asked the questions in the present tense, and the 1967 San Francisco and most later surveys in this tradition used a time period of one year, the 1969 survey used a three year reporting period. To maintain comparability with earlier surveys, the 1984 national alcohol adult survey also adopted this combination of two methods, but with a one year reporting period.

The first national alcohol survey financed under contract by the National Institute of Alcohol Abuse and Alcoholism (NIAAA)—carried out by Louis Harris and associates in 1970—used the beverage-specific "proportions of occasions" questions derived from the studies by Knupfer, Cahalan and their associates (see Room and Beck, 1974). However, the five succeeding federally contracted surveys, carried out in 1972–1975 by Harris and by Opinion Research Corporation as evaluations of NIAAA's public service advertisement campaigns, shifted back to a version of the Straus and Bacon series on usual quantity of each beverage type (reanalyzed in Johnson et al. 1977; see Noble, 1979; pp. 7–13; Rappeport et al. 1975). By 1972 NIAAA was deeply committed to an alcoholism treatment monitoring and evaluation system (see references in Room, 1980), which had adopted a usual-quantity formulation in asking clients at intake about their drinking in the previous month (Armor et al. 1978; p. 303), and the reversion to usual-quantity questions in the general-population surveys probably reflected the influence of this monitoring and evaluation effort, and the desire to collect general-population data in comparable form (see chapter 3 in Armor et al. 1978).

Meanwhile, the four national surveys of drug use carried out under contract between 1974 and 1979 for the National Institute on Drug Abuse combined some elements of two traditions in their summary questions on amount of drinking, using both Straus and Bacon-type questions and questions about frequency of drinking five or more drinks (Abelson and Atkinson, 1975; Abelson and Fishburne, 1976; Abelson et al., 1977, 1980).

In the last few years, there has been some convergence between the Berkeley Alcohol Research Group (ARG) tradition and that represented by RAND Corp. researchers and NIAAA contractors. Starting with the 1975 San Francisco and Marin studies, some ARG surveys have included questions about days of drinking at particular levels in the last thirty days, with higher quantities measured over the past year. Polich and Orvis (1979) adopted a similar method, asking for each beverage type and the amount drunk in a typical day during the last thirty days, while also asking the frequency of drinking eight or more drinks in the last year. The Sobells and associates (1980) have proposed and used on clinical samples a "Time-Line" method of eliciting data on drinking behavior, using a detailed reconstruction of the respondent's drinking in the context of life events over the last 30 days. Such a method amounts to being a variant "recent occasions" method. Most recently, Armor and Polich (1982) have recommended an approach in terms of frequency and usual quantity in the last thirty days, plus a series of questions asking how often the respondent had drunk five to ten and eleven or more drinks in the preceding twelve months.

The picture has been further muddied by two recent studies performed under NIAAA contract, which each used a hitherto unused time period and a new formulation for the alcohol consumption questions. The 1983 Health Interview Survey special questionnaire on drinking used a two week base period, asking for the usual number of drinks in a day on a drinking day in the period, and for the total number of drinks in the period for each beverage, while the special Hispanic Health and Nutrition Examination Survey (Hispanic HANES) of 1982 used the same questions for a four week base period (Alcohol Epidemiology Data System, 1984).

So far, this discussion has focused on three traditions of asking about quantity of drinking, each of which asks the respondent to summarize his or her drinking patterns: the "usual quantity" approach, the approach in terms of the "proportion of occasions" at a given level, and the "frequency of specific levels of drinking" approach. Each of these methods has been used in a number of adult general population surveys in North America. (See figures 2, 4, and 6 in Room, 1990). A few North American studies have also used the alternative method of the "listing of drinking occasions" in the last week. The list of such studies is primarily composed of methodological studies and community surveys designed to maintain comparability in cross-national comparisons.

AGGREGATE MEASURES OF ALCOHOL CONSUMPTION

Whatever method of asking about amount of drinking is used, most studies move to aggregate the data from the different questions into summary measures or scores. It has been at this level of aggregate measures that most of the published North American discussions of measuring amount and patterns of drinking have been pitched. It has also been the level at which there has been the maximum of confusion—both because of failure to distinguish between methods of questioning and methods of aggregation, and because of confused terminology and designations.

From the beginning there have been two main types of aggregate measures of amounts of drinking: single-dimensional orderings, and multidimensional (mostly bidimensional) typologies. The choice of type and form of measure reflected a combination of influences on the investigator: substantive interests, presumptions about relations with correlates, and available or preferred analytical methods. Investigators whose main object was describing drinking patterns in the population tended to report amount of drinking in discrete categories (particularly in the days of analysis by counter-sorter), often using a typology. Frequently, such investigators have offered a "profile analysis" of the correlates of the different "types" of drinking pattern. On the other hand, investigators interested in using amount of drinking as a predictor in multiple regression or similar analyses tended to prefer at least an ordered and if possible an interval unidimensional measure of consumption.

Straus and Bacon's "Q-F" (Quantity-Frequency) Index, later adapted by Mulford and others, set the style of multidimensional typologies of amount of drinking, cross-classifying the dimensions of frequency and usual quantity of drinking. Other measures in this style, each with their own categories and construction rules, included the "F-Q" (Frequency-Quantity) measures of Knupfer and associates (1963) and the "Q-F" (Quantity-Frequency) categorization of Edwards and associates (1972). Knupfer et al.'s F-Q was composed from three dimensions: frequency of drinking, modal quantity of drinking, and range of drinking, in terms of drinks per occasion.

Cahalan et al. (1969) used the same three component dimensions to compose the measure in the main text of *American Drinking Practices*, "Q-F-V" (Quantity-Frequency-Variability), but this measure is in the end an essentially unidimensional measure of the "heaviness" of drinking. As Bowman, Stein, and Newton (1975) point out, Cahalan et al.'s Q-F-V tends to give greater weight to quantity than to frequency, pushing infrequent heavy drinkers into the "heavy" category, particularly as compared with Straus and Bacon's Q-F.

Perhaps the most straightforward way of treating amount of drinking unidimensionally is to compute the total volume of drinking, that is, how many litres of absolute alcohol (or some other measure) are consumed per given time period. The computation is simple for Straus and Bacon-style questions: for each beverage-type, the number of occasions per time period is multiplied by the average quantity per occasion, and the results for the three beverage types are summed. For the Knupfer et al. style of questions, numeric proportions must be assigned also to the responses "once in a while," "less than half the time," "more than half the time," and "nearly every time." In the late 1960s, Jessor and associates (1968; pp. 483–486) and Cahalan and associates (Cahalan and Cisin, 1968; Cahalan et al. 1969; pp. 213–215) devised independent and different ways of computing a volume measure from the Knupfer et al. questions.

Confusingly, Jessor et al. named their volume measure a "Q-F" (Quantity-Frequency) Index, and this name was adopted by NIAAA contract researchers from the RAND Corp. and elsewhere as a generic term for volume-of-drinking measures, although their Q-F volume measure (sometimes called "A-A") was usually based on Straus and Bacon-style questions, and the designation Q-F had previously been used for typologies rather than a unidimensional score (see, for example, Armor et al., 1978; p. 86; Polich and Orvis, 1979; p. 144.)

The primary initial use made by Cahalan and associates of their volume measure was as one dimension of a two-dimensional typology, "V-V" (Volume-Variability), of which the other dimension was the range of drinking (specifically, whether the respondent at any time drinks as many as five drinks at a sitting) (see Cahalan et al. 1969; pp. 211–224). Recently, Greenfield (1986) has proposed a new two-dimensional "Volume-Maximum Index" where the maximum quantity criterion slides upward with increasing volume of drinking.

In other work, the Berkeley group has made use of yet another dimension originally derived from the Knupfer et al. question series: how often the respondent drinks five or more drinks, usually trichotomized between not at all, less than once a week, and at least once a week, with the last category denominated "Frequent Heavy Drinker" (Room, 1972.) The measure was a major component of the "Index of Frequent Intoxication" used in Cahalan's *Problem Drinkers* (1970; p. 28). A "Quantity/Frequency typology" crossing the "frequency of heavy drinking" dimension with frequency of drinking has been used in a number of reports (see, for example, Cahalan et al. 1976; Cahalan and Treiman, 1976 (using four or more drinks); Wallack, 1978; Caetano and Herd, 1984; Herd, 1985d; Hilton, 1987).

DIFFERENCES IN RESULTS WITH DIFFERENT
QUESTION APPROACHES

There are surprisingly few empirical studies comparing results in general populations with different methods of questioning. Most such studies are based on asking a respondent to report drinking patterns by alternative methods in the same interview. Given that the study has other purposes as well, this approach has the advantage of being inexpensive. But it is an approach which tries the respondent's patience and which probably underestimates discrepancies between different methods, since respondents may attempt to maintain consistency in their responses.

Comparing Summary and Recent-Occasions Methods

A number of studies have compared results between "recent occasions" questions and summary-pattern questions. The comparisons have usually focused on frequency of drinking or on volume of drinking. Such comparisons raise the complication of how to treat the relationship between the time since recent occasions—particularly since the last drinking occasion—and the average time between occasions (this issue is of course also intrinsic to the computation of a volume measure from recent-occasions measures). Let us consider two examples to pose the issue, assuming in both cases that interviews are randomly distributed in time—for example, by day of the week. (1) For respondents who drank at regular intervals, say every fourth day, the average time since the last drinking occasion would be one-half the average time between occasions. (2) But for respondents who drink only on Friday and Saturday nights every week, the average time since the last occasion would be almost the same interval as the average time between occasions. In cultures where patterns like the latter example are frequent, assuming the time since the last occasion is equal to the average time between occasions may be a better choice in estimating frequency. Notice also that the problem is not solved by taking the time between the last two occasions as equivalent to the average time between occasions: with the "only on Friday and Saturday" pattern, using this interval would result in a substantial overestimate of frequency of drinking. Of course, the problem of the relationship between average frequency and the time since drinking occasions is considerably muted when many occasions are measured.

There have been several statistical discussions of this problem as it applies to measuring frequency and volume of alcohol consumption or purchases.[1] From statistical reasoning, Skog (1981) shows that an estimation based on the time between the last two occasions "will generally lead to overestimation of the individual consumption level" even for drinkers with a fairly regular pattern. A number of empirical studies have compared results from the two methods, with varying results (see Room, 1990). Representative is Simpura's analysis (1987) of the 1984 Finnish national survey. Simpura found that a volume of drinking computed on Straus and Bacon-like "usual quantity" questions yielded a somewhat higher coverage of national sales (34%) than volumes based on the last week's drinking occasions (29%) or on a variable period including at least the last four drinking occasions (26%). However, the usual quantity computation, unlike the other two, did not exclude home-made beverage consumption.

Comparing Different Summary Methods

Surprisingly few studies have compared results with the different methods of summary estimation of drinking patterns. Using a U.S. nationwide sample of males aged twenty-one to fifty-nine, Room (1971b) showed that adding questions on the frequency of drinking eight to eleven and twelve or more drinks to the Knupfer et al. series which stopped at five and more drinks raised the overall average volume of drinking by 16%. In the study of drinking among U.S. Air Force personnel conducted by Polich and Orvis (1979), adding questions on the frequency of drinking eight plus drinks for each beverage type in the last year to the Straus and Bacon-type "usual quantity" questions concerning the last thirty days raised the overall average volume of drinking by 36% (Armor and Polich, 1982). On the other hand, a computation based only on "frequency of particular quantities" questions was reported to result in an average overall volume of only 91% of the Straus and Bacon series (computed from Armor and Polich, 1982; the sample and questions used in these comparisons are not specified). Using a student sample at the University of Oregon (N = 484), Gwartney-Gibbs (1982) compared an average daily volume computed by asking respondents the total number of beers, glasses of wine, and shots of liquor they had drunk in the past week with a volume computed from asking on how many days the respondent had drunk one or more, four or more, eight or more and twelve or more drinks in the last four weeks. While the aggregate mean volume reports by the two methods were almost exactly the same—0.87 and 0.88 drinks per day, respectively—the distribution of responses by volume showed some differences: 31% had not had a drink in the last week (vs. 16% in the last four weeks), and 22% reported a daily volume of one and one-half or more drinks in the last week (vs. 19% in the last four weeks).

Drawing on data from annual nationwide surveys of the number of occasions of drug use among high-school seniors, Bachman and O'Malley (1981) found that for alcohol consumption, across the whole range of answers they could test (between one and thirty-nine occasions in a year), respondents reported on the average 3.2 times as many drinking occasions in the last week as would be expected from their report of drinking occasions in the last year. The ratio seemed consistent from one class to the next, and held also for marijuana use; for illicit drugs, the ratio was consistently lower, in the range 2.4–2.9. The authors relate these findings to the general finding from studies of the reporting of health events that underreporting increases relatively rapidly with the time since the event (Cannell et al. 1977).

The 1979 U.S. national alcohol survey used two alternative methods of asking about amount of drinking. For each beverage type, respondents were asked their frequency in the last year of drinking eighteen or more drinks on an occasion, and then of fifteen to seventeen, twelve to fourteen, eight to eleven, five to seven, three to four and one to two drinks. Respondents were also asked about their drinking of each beverage type in the last month, in terms of frequency and how much they usually had "at one time, on the average." From these two separate sets of questions, an overall volume in drinks per month was computed. Table 3.1 compares the results on these two measures. It will be seen that for each beverage type and overall, the "frequency of specific levels" approach yields a higher volume estimate more often than the "usual quantity" approach—38% higher in the case of the overall volume of drinking (data not shown). The higher estimates by the "frequency of specific levels" approach arise in two ways: (1) a substantial proportion of the sample has had a few drinks in the last year, but reports no drinking in the last month; and (2) a high proportion of relatively heavy drinking respondents—presumably particularly those who often drink more than their "usual" quantities— give a higher volume estimate by the "frequency of specific levels" approach.

Simpura (1987) also investigated the intercorrelations and correlates of volume scores computed from his three different questioning methods. The "usual quantity" estimate correlated 0.81 with the "period" estimate from four or so occasions; both measures had a lower correlation with an estimate from the last week's drinking occasions, due to the substantial number of respondents who had no drinking in the last week (0.67 with "period" estimate, 0.61 with "usual quantity" estimate; all correlations on logarithmically transformed measures).

TABLE 3.1
Comparison of Volumes Computed from "Usual Quantity" and from
"Frequency of Specific Levels" Questions, 1979 U.S. National
Drinking Survey, $N = 1,772$, in percent
(based on weighted data)

	Wine	Beer	Liquor	Overall
0 drinks on both measures	54%	51%	50%	33%
Higher by "usual quantity" questions:				
3+ drinks/month higher	7	10	10	17
0.1–2.9 drinks/month higher	9	10	10	10
Lower by "usual quantity" questions:				
0.1–2.9 drinks/month lower	21	12	17	14
3+ drinks/month lower	9	17	13	26

DIFFERENCES IN RESULTS WITH DIFFERENT SCORES AND MEASURES

There is a somewhat more developed literature in this area, although it has been curiously noncumulative. Survey reports in the 1960s often presented different aggregations based on the same data; Cahalan et al.'s discussion on Volume-Variability in an appendix to *American Drinking Practices* (1969), for instance, includes a comparison with the Quantity-Frequency-Variability variable used in the main text.[2]

A few reports in the course of the 1970s focused on the differences between the heavy drinking category of the various aggregate measures. A 1971 report (Room, 1971a) showed that the prevalence of heavy drinking varied between 7% and 20% according to five different measures of heavy drinking built on the same questions in the same sample; altogether 34% of the sample was defined as a heavy drinker by one or another of the measures. The paper also showed that the relationship between heavy drinking and social class could be completely reversed, depending on the heavy drinking measure which was chosen. Streissguth et al. (1977) studied the interrelations of Q-F-V, Volume Variability (V-V), and "Jessor's A-A" (a volume measure) in a sample of pregnant women—a sample mostly composed of relatively light drinkers—and found that, although the three measures identified much the same proportions as heavy drinkers, there was considerable divergence in which members of the sample were thus identified— only 70% of those with over 1 oz. absolute alcohol on the A-A measure were "High Volume-High Maximum" (HVHM) drinkers, while only 70% of HVHM drinkers met the 1 oz. criterion on the AA, for instance. Noting that the "poor interrelationship" of the scores might be partly "due to the attempt to oversimplify relatively complex drinking activity by reducing it to a single scale or a small number of categories," the authors concluded that "it is probably advisable to use multiple alcohol assessments in a study of this type" (p. 418). Another report on a study of pregnant women (Little et al., 1977) proposed a new "A-A—Q-P" measure, conceptually related to the "Frequent Heavy Drinking" measure. Cross-tabulating the Q-P categorization with Q-F-V, V-V, and A-A categories, the authors concluded that Q-P "expresses the average frequency of massed drinking with greater precision than either" Q-F-V or V-V; for instance, "these indicators...fail to differentiate between weekly and monthly massed drinking, although weekly binging is a much more dangerous pattern than monthly intoxication on payday, for instance" (p. 560). A study based on an alcohol treatment sample (Bowman et al., 1975) proposed a two-dimensional "Volume-Pattern Index" where the "pattern" dimension was conceptualized in terms analogous to the standard deviation of the respondent's daily consumption. The relations between the "Volume-Pattern" grid and the categories of the Q-F, Q-F-V, and V-V measures were shown graphically. To the authors' surprise, the Pattern dimension was not related to five measures of social adjustment, although the Volume measure was. It was concluded that "pattern of intake may have a very different meaning for severe problem drinkers requiring hospitalization and for the social drinkers who were most numerous" in general-population studies.

The 1984 national alcohol survey of drinking conducted for the Alcohol Research Group by Temple University's Institute for Survey Research included questions on drinking from which several measures of the volume of drinking could be created:

1. A volume measure (Cahalan method) computed as in Cahalan et al.'s Volume-Variability (but including a volume for all drinking at least once a year), based on the Knupfer et al. questions on the proportion of consumption occasions for each beverage type on which five or more, three to four and one to two drinks were consumed.
2. A volume measure computed from the same questions, but according to the method specified in Jessor et al. (1968). (The metric in this computation is ounces of absolute alcohol/day, and in the other volume measures is drinks per month. Assuming 0.5 oz. absolute alcohol per drink, all measures are converted to "drinks per month" by multiplying the Jessor-method result by sixty.)
3. A volume measure (Optimum method) adding the extra volume attributable to questions on the frequency of drinking eight to eleven and twelve or more drinks to the volume computed in one above. Assuming that the eight to eleven and twelve or more drinks

occasions would also have been reported as five or more occasions—and thus already counted with a value of six—the frequency of drinking eight to eleven drinks was multiplied by 3.5, and the frequency of drinking twelve or more by 7.0, to reflect the "extra" drinks, and these products were added to the volume computed in one above.

4. A volume measure ("last two occasions" method) computed on the basis of the time since the last two drinking occasions and amount consumed on these occasions. The computation of volume in drinks per month added together the amounts for the last two occasions, divided by the number of days since the second-to-last drinking occasion, and multiplied by thirty. This computation assumes that the time since the last occasion is the same as the time between occasions, which gives a volume estimate which usually will err on the side of overestimation (Skog, 1981).

Table 3.2 shows the means and standard deviations of these four volume measures. The aggregate volume estimate for the last two occasions method is only 76% of the estimate by the method used by Cahalan et al. (despite the inflationary estimation procedure used). On the other hand, adding two questions on the frequency of drinking eight to eleven and twelve or more drinks adds 13% extra volume to the estimate (Optimum method).

TABLE 3.2
Means, Standard Deviations, and Median for Four Volume Measures,
1984 National Drinking Survey
(drinkers only, N = 3,647, weighted data)

Volume Measures (Drinks Per Month)	Mean	Standard Deviation	Median
Cahalan method	39.93	78.93	12.80
Jessor method*	47.82	92.94	16.80
Optimum method	45.18	94.67	14.05
Last two occasions method	30.31	62.40	8.57

*Multiplied by 60 to convert to drinks/month.

It will be seen that the Jessor method also results in a higher estimate, by 19%, than the Cahalan method, although they are based on exactly the same questions. The differences between the Cahalan method and the Jessor method derive from two sources. (1) The Cahalan method assumes that all drinks have equivalent alcohol content (set at 0.5 oz. absolute alcohol in table 2), whereas the Jessor method assigns

0.6 oz. to a glass of wine, 0.48 oz. to a beer, and 0.675 oz. to a liquor drink. While the Jessor method overestimates the proof strength of wine and liquor drinks today, it has been argued that wine and liquor drinks consumed at home frequently contain a greater volume of alcoholic beverage than assumed in the Cahalan method (Gross, 1983; pp. 126–132). (2) The Cahalan method distinguishes between all available response categories in assigning proportions of occasions to the five or more, three to four, and one to two levels, while the Jessor method lumps "once in a while" with "less than half the time," and "more than half the time" with "nearly every time." The methods also differ in how the pattern of responses to the three levels is taken into account. The net result of the Jessor method is to give more weight to low-proportion responses such as once in a while. In the Jessor method, for instance, a quantity consumed "nearly every time" has only twice the weight of a quantity consumed once in a while, while by the Cahalan method the ratio varies between 4:1 and 10.6:1 according to the pattern of other responses. The main result of elevating the estimates of "once in a while" occasions is to push a substantial number of low-volume drinkers into the middle volume range (table 3.3). Although there is a good deal of assumption involved in either method, it seems to me that the relative weights assigned to the response categories in the Cahalan method are closer to their probable meanings to the respondents. This, then, is a case in which in my view a higher volume estimate is not necessarily a better estimate.

TABLE 3.3
Comparison of Volume Computation Methods,
1984 National Drinking Survey
($N = 5,221$, weighted data) (Corner Percentages)

	Cahalan et al. Method (drinks per month)				
	0	0.01–17.4	17.5–44.9	45+	Total
Jessor et al. Method (oz. absolute alcohol per day)					
0	31.1%	0	0	0	31.1%
0.01–0.21	—	29.9	0	0	29.9
0.22–0.99	—	8.1	12.0	2.6	22.7
1.0+	0	0	1.0	15.3	16.3
Total	31.1%	38.0	13.0	17.9	100.0

Table 3.4 shows the intercorrelations of the four methods of estimating volume, and their correlations with overall frequency of drinking, with frequency of drinking eight or more drinks, and with

selected demographic variables. It will be seen that there is a very high intercorrelation between the Jessor method, Cahalan method, and Optimum method indices. A good part of this relation must be attributed, of course, to the fact that they are aggregated in large part or in whole from the same questions and responses. The correlation of each of these three measures with the volume estimate based on the last two occasions is considerably lower, as might be expected on substantive as well as procedural grounds. The correlations with this volume estimate are, in fact, lower than those with the overall frequency question, which is not a component of any of the volume measures.

It will be noted in table 3.4 that there is very little relation of any of the volume measures with age, education, or family income, while the relation with gender is moderate. Both overall frequency of drinking and frequency of drinking eight or more drinks show a stronger relationship with being male, while the frequency of drinking eight or more drinks is fairly strongly related to youth. We shall return to the issue of the strength of correlates of different drinking measures below.

DISCUSSION

Questions about amount of drinking are asked of many populations and with many purposes in mind. In picking our way through the implications of the material laid out above, it is perhaps best to work backwards through the aggregate measures to the questions.

Aggregate Measures

Volume of drinking continues to exercise a strong attraction as a single overall measure of amount of drinking. It is easy to conceptualize, it captures all the drinking, and it has strong technical attractions: it is unidimensional and is in principle a continuous variable. It is the appropriate measure for the main check on the aggregate validity of survey data—alcohol sales data for the population surveyed. Work in the tradition of Ledermann has helped focus attention on the volume dimension. It is a comfortable measure for epidemiologists concerned with a variety of behavioral risk factors in morbidity and mortality; and indeed the dimension may well be the most closely related to risk of long-term health consequences of drinking such as cirrhosis.

Yet for many purposes volume is an inappropriate or awkward measure; and, for that matter, for many purposes the individual's drinking cannot adequately be summarized by any single dimension. The argument can be seen laid out in 1926 in Pearl's *Alcohol and Longevity*.

TABLE 3.4

Correlations of Volumes Computed by Different Methods, and with Demographic and Other Measures, 1984 National Sample, Drinkers Only
(N = 3,272, weighted data)

	Volume Jessor Method	Volume Optimum Method	Volume Last Two Occasions	Overall Frequency	Frequency Drinks	Age	Education	Family Income	Gender
Volume Cahalan Method	0.98	0.97	0.52	0.68	0.52	-0.02	-0.03	0.02	-0.21
Volume Jessor Method		0.95	0.50	0.68	0.50	-0.02	-0.01	0.04	-0.19
Volume Optimum Method			0.55	0.64	0.60	-0.03	-0.04	0.01	-0.21
Volume Last Two Occasions				0.45	0.51	-0.07	-0.02	0.03	-0.19
Overall Frequency					0.42	0.01	0.04	0.10	-0.27
Frequency 8+ Drinks*						-0.24	-0.10	-0.03	-0.27
Age							-0.15	-0.07	0.02
Education								0.42	0.02
Family Income									0.07

*Frequency 8+ drinks: this measure takes as the "frequency of drinking 8+ drinks" whichever response to the 8-11 and 12+ drinks levels is more frequent, except that if the two levels are drunk with equal frequency they are raised one category—e.g., if both are drunk "once or twice a week," the "8+ frequency" is set at "three or four times a week."

In an earlier study he had grouped the cases studied essentially on a dimension of volume of drinking, remarking that "I realize fully that in placing the moderate and temperate but *steady* daily drinker in the 'Heavy' category that I am going contrary to common opinion and the common usage of descriptive language," but defending the choice as "sound from a purely biological point of view." An English committee remonstrated that Pearl's classification did not reveal "whether moderate drinking, using the word moderate in its colloquial sense, is prejudicial to longevity. Are a daily pint or two of beer, or a daily bottle of claret, or a few glasses of whiskey and soda per diem harmful?" In his new study, Pearl therefore adopted a distinction between those who were "moderate in amount, steady in frequency" and those who were "heavy in amount, occasional as to frequency," noting that "surely it is in accord with common usage to call a person who gets drunk a heavy drinker. Also it is common usage to call a person who drinks a little but never gets drunk a moderate drinker" (p. 73). Pearl further remarked that "the basis of the present classification is the same as that which we use regarding drinking in everyday life. It is that of the immediate *effect* of the drinking on the drinker. If a person drinks enough to get drunk it is *prima facie* evidence that he is a heavy drinker" (p. 75).

The problem with a volume measure, then, is that it is relatively insensitive to differences in the patterning of drinking that are of social importance in terms both of correlates and of consequences. As can be seen in table 3.4, volume of drinking is relatively insensitive to variations in the U.S. population by such significant social differentiations as age or social class: the less frequent and heavier drinking of the younger and the poorer is balanced by the relatively more frequent and lighter drinking of the middle-aged and middle-class. More crucially, many of the adverse consequences of drinking—notably casualties and social problems—are fairly specific to heavy drinking occasions. Knupfer (1984) has recently reemphasized this point: "the average amount a person drinks seems to us of little importance, from the point of view of social norm violation or driving accidents: what matters, we contend, is frequency of intoxication. Indeed, it is difficult to see what interest there is, unless one is doing some sort of market research, in average amounts or total amounts." It is for this reason that, as attention turned in U.S. studies in the mid-1960s to measuring drinking-related problems as well as drinking patterns, researchers began to seek typologies or measures with a dimension reflecting the drinking of significant amounts on an occasion.

It might be noted that the adequacy of a volume measure (number of cigarettes consumed in a given interval) is now questioned even in the current literature on tobacco smoking—where, given the nature of smoking habits and the emphasis on long-term health consequences, one might have expected it to have been seen as an adequate measure. "In times past," one of the participants (Fredericksen, 1983) at a recent conference on measurement in the field noted, "smoking rate (number of cigarettes per unit time) was considered to be an adequate descriptor of smoking behavior. . . . In recent years, it has become increasingly clear that this is a far too simplistic picture. . . . Overall it becomes apparent that while our concern is 'risk', an adequate description of smoking must involve the assessment of what is smoked, the rate or temporal pattern of that consumption, and smoking topography (puff rate, puff size, interpuff interval, puff volume, etc.)." Similarly, contributors discussing the measurement of smoking among youth proposed that "less weight should be given to the quantity (i.e., absolute number) of cigarettes young people smoke. Instead, more attention ought to be put on the timing and situational patterns of youth's tobacco consumption" (Schinke and Gilchrist, 1983).

However patterns of drinking are measured and aggregated, U.S. survey reports on drinking have commonly cut the drinking population up into discrete categories of drinking. Such categorizations, often with relatively few cells, have been criticized by European researchers as often hiding the character of the overall distribution of consumption. It is clear, also, that comparisons of such categorized variables can be quite misleading when the focus is on changes in drinking (Caetano et al. 1982). Such categorizations were a necessity in the era, through the late 1960s, when most analysis was done on the counter-sorter, but categorizations are still commonly used for presentation in tabular and other analyses comparing statistics across parts of the sample. Behind the categorizations adopted are at least two implicit criteria: that the categories be describable and appear meaningful, and that each category include a decent sized "chunk" of the sample. The latter criterion means that shifting patterns of drinking may render a particular categorization less useful because of shrinking chunks: in the 1984 U.S. national alcohol sample, most high- and medium-volume drinkers at least occasionally drink five or more drinks, so that the Volume-Variability measure defined on the 1964 U.S. national alcohol sample (Cahalan et al. 1969, Appendix I) no longer yields usable chunks. Sometimes a third and more controversial criterion, of maximizing differences on or the linearity of relations with important correlates, also enters into consideration. One difficulty with categorizations is that different choices by researchers on where to set the boundaries of categories can make comparisons difficult or impossible, even when the underlying items or scores are comparable.

Despite their problems, categorizations remain useful in describing patterns of drinking in a population. The alternative—to work only with summary statistics—gives a far less detailed picture of patterns, and frequently leaves interesting patternings hidden.

Along with categorizations of volume and other single-dimensional variables, U.S. researchers have often used *drinking typologies* composed of two or more dimensions. Many of the early typologies, such as Q-F-V, while composed from several dimensions, added them together into a partly or wholly unidimensional measure, so that they amounted to weighted and categorized volume measures, in which some patterns of drinking (often those drinking relatively large amounts on an occasion) were given a special weight. The advantage of such a weighted measure over a simple volume of drinking measure has not been systematically argued in the survey literature; it presumably parallels the tendency of some clinically-based measures to assess a special "penalty" for binge drinking (Milton and Lee, 1967; Ewing, 1970). It might be noted that since the computation of volume itself frequently rests on a substratum of plausible but arbitrary assumptions, the analyst's choices of assumptions often in fact amount to differential weights within what is conceptually a volume measure.

More recently, typologies have usually been constructed from the intersections of two distinct dimensions. The Volume-Variability index, for instance, is composed of a volume dimension and a dichotomous dimension of whether the respondent reports drinking five or more drinks on an occasion at least once in a while. Many typologies include overall frequency of drinking as one dimension, often cut into categories according to the periods of everyday life—daily, weekly and monthly. A typology which has often been used at the Alcohol Research Group (e.g., Cahalan et al., 1976; Wallack, 1978; Caetano and Herd, 1984) cross-cuts this with a trichotomous division on drinking five or more drinks on an occasion—that the respondent does this at least once a week, that the respondent does it once in a while, or that the respondent does not do it at all. Such a typology makes a serviceable classification of current U.S. drinking patterns, and complements without duplicating a drinking volume measure (table 3.5; the "infrequent-high maximum" category—one to eleven times a year, sometimes five or more—would often be combined with another category).

Whether or not typologies are used, the general tendency of the literature has been towards a *dimensional approach* to summarizing drinking patterns. There is an almost endless choice of dimensions for summarizing a behavior as complex as drinking. Frequency of drinking is perhaps the most commonly reported dimension. The logical complement to this would be *average drinks per occasion*, that is,

TABLE 3.5
Typology of Frequency of Drinking by Frequency of Drinking 5+ Drinks
1984 U.S. National Drinking Survey
(*N* = 5,221, weighted data)
(Percentaged on total sample)

	Frequency of Drinking 5+ Drinks		
	Drinks 5+ Once a Week	*Drinks 5+ Less Often*	*Doesn't Drink 5+*
Overall Frequency			
At least once a week	11.2%	12.5%	12.0%
1–3 times a month		6.3%	12.3%
1–11 times a year		1.7%	13.6%
Abstainer			30.2%
			100%

volume/frequency. This dimension has been little used, although it has an interestingly small relation with frequency of drinking in current U.S. data (table 3.6). Various measures of variability have been proposed, but the most frequently used have been some form of "maximum quantity on an occasion," which is easily interpretable but taps only one element of variability. There has been some convergence of different approaches on the "frequency of drinking specified amounts" as a useful operational representation of heavy drinking; Finnish researchers, for instance, taking body-weight into account, have used the frequency of drinking enough to reach a given blood alcohol level (Bruun, 1969), while U.S. researchers have tended to use the frequency of drinking five or more or 8 or more drinks.

At least since the mid-1960s, U.S. survey research on drinking patterns in the general population has been primarily conducted in the context of studies of drinking-related problems. This tradition, which differs for instance from the Scandinavian tradition of studies of drinking patterns without much attention to drinking problems, has meant that primary attention has been paid to drinking dimensions and levels which might be regarded as "problematic." Although studies of clinical populations have sometimes been interested in the occurrence and proportion of small-quantity occasions, for instance, since this bears on discussions of addiction models, this dimension has not been prominent in general-population studies. Rather little attention has been paid in U.S. analyses, since the 1969 study by Cahalan and associates, to differential patterning by type of beverage, although even from a

TABLE 3.6

Average Number of Drinks per Occasion (Cahalan Method)
by Overall Frequency of Drinking, 1984 National Drinking Survey
Current Drinkers Only (total N = 5,221, weighted data)

	Overall Frequency of Drinking		
	Nearly daily or more often	1–4 times a week	Less than once a week
Average drinks* per occasion			
4.4+	29.0%	30.7%	22.5%
2.4–4.39	32.6	35.6	37.1
0–2.39	38.4	33.6	40.4
(N)	(477)	(1,084)	(1,631)
Pearson's r = 0.07			

*Average number of drinks is computed from the Volume-Cahalan method divided by the overall frequency (in occasions per month). Percentages are based on weighted data, Ns are unweighted.

drinking-problems perspective there are some interesting differences in patterning between beer, wine and spirits consumption (Room, 1976).

Asking Questions about Drinking

It will be clear from the discussion and data above that much of what we think we know about asking questions about drinking is based on presumption and lore rather than on detailed quantitative studies. Given the substantial underestimation of aggregate alcohol consumption in survey data, the criterion usually offered for choosing between methods is whether the method yields a higher average volume of drinking (Midanik, 1982). Yet a higher volume estimate for a population as a whole is not necessarily the best criterion. A set of questions and method of aggregation that yields a high estimate may nevertheless be indefensible on logical or statistical grounds (Skog, 1981). Also, a volume criterion assigns a primary role to frequent and heavier drinkers, giving little weight to the handling of the lighter and more infrequent drinkers who form the bulk of the population.

The choice of method should in fact depend on the main analytical purposes for which the data is being collected. As outlined above, there are only a few main choices of approach in asking questions about amount of drinking. But besides these main choices, there are many detailed decisions to be made by the researcher, some of which are discussed in what follows.

Recent Occasions Questions: Quite a number of studies have asked about the last two drinking occasions (or about drinking occasions on the last two drinking days, which is not the same thing). As will be apparent from the discussion and references above, there are severe statistical problems in using the last two occasions to estimate volume of drinking, mostly because of the difficulty of estimating the frequency of drinking. More generally, summarizing respondents' drinking on the basis of one or two occasions will be unreliable to the extent the respondents are not absolutely regular in their rhythm and amounts of drinking. Nevertheless, asking about recent occasions has several potential uses: it is a way of securing information on contexts of drinking; it can give a good sampling (though weighted towards infrequent drinkers) of drinking person-occasions; and it may yield reliable population estimates despite the unreliability at the individual level.

Several studies—notably the World Health Organization (WHO) Community Response Study in Mexico, Zambia, and Scotland (Roizen, 1981)—have asked about the occasion on which the respondent drank the most in the last month and the occasion on which the respondent drank the most in the last year. Such questions are potentially useful descriptively, and along with a frequency question can form the minimum data needed for a frequency-maximum quantity typology.

Substantial studies using the recent-occasions approach usually enquire about the drinking days and/or occasions for at least the last week. This is the basic approach used for governmental surveys in Britain (Dight, 1976), and in the WHO Community Response Study. Such an approach excludes many drinkers in cultural situations, such as Zambia and Mexico, where many drinkers drank quite infrequently. Accordingly, respondents in the WHO study were asked about their last two drinking days, at a minimum. The Finnish approach to this problem has been to vary the time period asked about according to the reported overall frequency of drinking. As Mäkelä (1971) showed, the drawback of asking about longer periods is the greater forgetting of occasions in earlier weeks.

At a minimum, such approaches ask about the amount and type of beverages consumed, and usually also the length of the drinking occasion, the setting and the number and type of companions. The questioning involved in this method is often quite lengthy—on the average perhaps twenty minutes of interview time in the 1979 Contra Costa County survey. A less obvious cost of this method is the substantial programming job involved in collating and aggregating the "occasions" data into summary scores.

In my view, the extended recent-occasions or "survey period" approach yields a rich data-set for contextual analyses of drinking, but is not clearly superior to other approaches in characterizing the respondent's overall drinking patterns. This view is not shared by many European researchers, however: in Alanko's view, "the survey period approach gives unbiased estimates for most existing drinking styles and is thus the one to be preferred in actual survey work" (Alanko, 1984; p. 220.)

Recent Period Summary Methods: A number of U.S. studies in recent years, particularly NIAAA contract studies, have moved to asking about drinking in a fixed period of time—usually thirty days. Unlike the recent-occasions methods, these studies ask the respondent to summarize his or her drinking in the period. A questionnaire used in 1975 Alcohol Research Group studies—and since used in college drinking studies (Greenfield and Haymond, 1980; Greenfield et al. 1980; Greenfield, 1986)—asks respondents to report on how many days in the last month they had any drinks, four or more drinks, eight or more drinks, and twelve or more drinks. A method originally used in clinical follow-up studies has been adopted by Armor and Polich and others (e.g., Polich and Orvis, 1979) for use in the general population. The method asks about drinking of each beverage type in the thirty days before the last drinking occasion: on how many days did the respondent drink that beverage, and what was the usual quantity? Adaptations for NIAAA contract studies use a two week period (1983 Health Interview Survey Supplement) and a four week period (Hispanic HANES study), and add a question about the total number of drinks of the beverage consumed during the period (Alcohol Epidemiology Data System, 1984).

These methods represent something of a hybrid between the recent-occasions and other summary methods. Specifying responses to a particular time period perhaps puts the respondent in mind of specific drinking occasions, and does put all responses on an equal time-footing; many overall summary methods specify no time period beyond the use of the present tense. But the method runs the risk that the time period is not typical of the respondent's consumption over a longer period. The 1975 ARG questions and the Armor and Polich (1982) recommendations partly remedy this by asking also about frequency of consumption of larger amounts over a one year period.

Recent questionnaires also often ask for the amount of beverage in the respondent's usual "drink"; the differing sizes of drinks, particularly for wine and spirits, is increasingly seen as a major contributor to survey underestimation of drinking in the United States (see Gross, 1983; p.126–132). The questions about the total number of drinks in the time period in the new NIAAA formulations are presumably intended to recapture infrequent large amounts for the volume accounting, but it is difficult to believe that frequent drinkers really find it possible to add drinks across all occasions in a thirty day period.

Overall Summary (Customary Drinking) Methods: For the many nondrinking studies which want a summarization of the respondent's drinking, but which do not have the questionnaire time to spare for exhaustive questioning, a few overall summary questions are probably the best compromise. The Alcohol Research Group has had good results with just two questions added to "caravan surveys" in monitoring drinking practices in California:

> Now, please think of all the times during *the last* twelve months when you had something to drink. How often have you had some kind of beverage containing alcohol, whether it was wine, beer, whiskey, or any other drink? Just give me the letter A, B, C, or whatever fits your answer...About how often during the last twelve months would you say you had five or more drinks?[3]

Beyond this bare minimum, the refinements lie in many directions. A majority of U.S. drinking surveys ask about beverage types separately, although there is no published study of how much difference this makes. Some studies provide tables of equivalence between drinks and common beverage container sizes; as noted above, some also ask about the average size of drinks. A fundamental difference remains between approaches soliciting the respondent's estimate of "usual quantity" and those requesting information about the drinking of specific amounts, although as mentioned some current studies compromise between the approaches. In my view, usual quantity is a flawed approach to asking about amount of drinking in the general adult population (in teenage populations and in treatment samples, where drinking may be more of an all-or-nothing proposition, usual quantity questions may work adequately—although see Harford, 1979). The Knupfer et al. "proportion of occasions" series represent an improvement, but except where comparability is needed it seems preferable to ask about actual frequencies of different drinking levels. It should be noted that respondents may be daunted by an overelaboration of levels of drinking: the 1979 national alcohol survey asked for each beverage type about the frequency of drinking at the levels of eighteen or more, fifteen to seventeen, twelve to fourteen, eight to eleven, five to seven, three to four and one to two drinks; anecdotally, it seemed that such elaboration became self-defeating.

It is also an improvement to specify a time period to be covered— whether a year or a week. But in the choice of a time period, researchers seem to be faced with a paradox. So long as the respondent's frame of reference is remembering specific drinking occasions, the shorter the time period the better the recall. Yet the shorter the time period, the more potential for misclassification of respondents because the period is "unusual." On the other hand, there is little evidence that the time period specified makes much difference in the aggregate when the respondent is being asked about his or her customary behavior.

Future consideration of and work on improving questions on amount of drinking must also take into account the results of Blair et al.'s experimental study manipulating the form of questions about amount of drinking of beer, wine and liquor in the last year. The study (Blair et al. 1977), carried out on a nationwide "probability sample with quotas" (N = 1,172), systematically varied the form of questions on three dimensions: open-ended versus closed-ended questions; long questions (with at least thirty words) versus short questions; and questions using words of the respondent's choice rather than standard wordings (the last variation was applied only to liquor). Higher annual volumes were reported in answer to open-ended, to long, and to familiarly-worded questions. The cumulative effect was striking: drinkers reported two hundred eight drinks of liquor in the last year with a long, open, familiar question, as against eighty drinks with a short, closed, standard question.

In presenting in some detail the diversity of U.S. approaches to measuring and aggregating responses on amount of drinking, this paper aims to contribute to bringing some coherence to a field where too often researchers have paid little attention to others' methods, and in particular to contribute to a dialogue between North American and European researchers. There is by now an enormous investment in the different national traditions; for comparability over time it is inevitable that at least part of previous methods will be maintained. But perhaps in the future we may be able to move towards a cross-fertilization of methods that would allow more detailed cross-national analyses.

4

A Note on Measuring Drinking
Problems in the 1984 National Alcohol Survey

THE MEASUREMENT OF DRINKING PROBLEMS
IN GENERAL POPULATION SURVEYS

The measurement of drinking problems in general population surveys is by no means a generally agreed upon process. In the 1984 National Alcohol Survey, we used a series of forty-five items that are the products of some twenty years of cumulative experience. The intellectual history of these items perhaps best begins with Clark's (1966) paper reporting on the operationalization of drinking problems in a 1964 San Francisco survey, although earlier influences on that work must also be recognized (Jellinek, 1946, 1952; Keller, 1962; Mulford and Miller, 1960b; Bailey et al. 1965). Measurement issues in the same survey were also discussed by Knupfer (1967a). These local studies influenced a series of national surveys, including those done in 1967 (Cahalan 1970), 1969 (Cahalan and Room, 1974), and 1979 (Clark and Midanik, 1982). The items used in the 1984 survey were substantially similar to those used in the 1969 and 1979 surveys. The course of these developments has also been influenced both by survey projects conducted at other institutions (Polich et al. 1981; Fitzgerald and Mulford, 1984a; Wilsnack et al. 1984; Vaillant, 1983) and by various theoretical contributions (especially Edwards and Gross, 1976; but also Keller, 1972, 1976, 1977; and Plaut, 1967). These studies have posed a number of issues, many of them unresolved, about how drinking problems should be measured in a general population survey.

One of the developments in this series of studies has been the growing recognition of a tripartite distinction between (1) the respondent's quantity and frequency of alcohol consumption, (2) a set of drinking behaviors and immediate sequelae of drinking which, though perhaps not problematic in and of themselves, are thought to be indicative of either dependence or a drinking problem, and (3) a set of problematic consequences that can arise because of drinking. Herein, these conceptually distinct domains will be referred to as Intake, Dependence, and Consequences. We must be especially cautious about the second of these labels. Dependence includes certain behaviors, attitudes, and immediate consequences of the drinking event such as, not feeling able to stop until the onset of intoxication, skipping meals, and morning drinking. Though the term would seem to imply that these behaviors indicate some underlying and unidimensional entity called alcoholism or problem drinking, we are not committed to such an interpretation. We only intend to refer to a set of behaviors and experiences which accompany the drinking event itself without adopting such an interpretation.

Intake measures were combined with Dependence measures in most of the surveys cited above. However, Room (1977) and Clark and Midanik, (1982) recognized that such items as the frequency of drunkenness and heavy intake should properly be considered as separate from other problem indicators and that the goal of analysis should be to demonstrate the relationship between the two rather than to assume it at the outset. How intake should best be measured is itself the subject of much debate (Room, 1977, chapter 3 in this volume), although it does seem that the frequency of drunkenness is a critical element (Knupfer, 1984).

Dependence is the most controversial of the three domains. As conceptualized by Cahalan and Room (1974), "Problematic Drinking," as they called it, can be subdivided into the categories of (1) Psychological Dependence (drinking for escape or relief), (2) Symptomatic Behaviors (morning drinking, shakes, sweats, blackouts, and the like), (3) Loss of Control (inability to control amount per occasion or to abstain entirely), and (4) Binge Drinking (drinking for twenty-four hours or more). One controversy is whether these are indeed separate phenomena or whether they represent a single underlying phenomenon. Cahalan and Room listed these as separate categories, but also summed their composite items together into a summary score. On the basis of a factor analysis, Polich et al. (1981) included measures of symptoms, loss of control, and bingeing in a six item index. This procedure was vigorously rejected by Clark and Midanik (1982), who argued that Loss of Control and Symptomatic Behavior were separate from each other as well as from Consequences; they advised that these phenomena be kept analytically distinct precisely so that such relationships could be assessed. Seeing no clear resolution to this debate at present, we have chosen a middle course which should offer something to advocates of either side. In this paper, the categories of Loss of Control, Symptomatic Behavior, and Binge Drinking are considered separately so that the interrelations between the three can be investigated. Yet, we also provide a summary index of Dependence in which all three are combined.

A crucial part of the above controversy rests on the issue of whether there is some set of problem indicators that taps an underlying unitary phenomenon. In other words, the debate is about whether one subset of the problem items has a conceptual pre-eminence over the rest. As the label Symptomatic Behavior suggests, the behaviors in this category (morning drinking, shakes, sweats, blackouts, and the like) have been thought to be symptomatic indications that a dependence on or an addiction to alcohol exists (Polich et al. 1981, followed this line of reasoning, drawing heavily on the dependence conceptualization of Edwards and Gross, 1976.) Others, notably Room (1980a), Clark and Midanik (1982), and Roizen et al. (1978) have sharply disagreed. A major element of their position has been that the items included in this category better represent short term physical consequences of the ingestion of large amounts of alcohol than signs of long term physiological dependence. Hence, they should be given no primacy over other problem indicators.

An older issue regarding Dependence is the conceptual status of psychological dependence. Psychological dependence is often viewed as an early stage in the development of alcoholism, and an assessment of one's reasons for drinking could serve as an early warning of possible problems under this perspective. Hence, items that ask the respondent whether he or she drinks for relief of anxiety or escape were included in many of the surveys on the above list. However, the utility of these questions has been significantly challenged over the years, leading to Clark and Midanik's conclusion that: "the notion of 'escape drinking' as an indicator of severe alcohol problems should be scrapped" (Clark and Midanik, 1982, p. 24).

The drinking consequences domain has been much less controversial over the years. It is widely agreed that these are separate from Dependence and that they are more loosely interrelated than are the Dependence indicators. Also, over the years there has been a quiet but steady growth in the number of different kinds of Consequences that have been included in surveys (a tradition which we continue here by creating a new category for accidents caused by drinking). Within the domain, it has been recognized that those consequences that depend on the reactions of other people in the drinker's environment are different from the ones that do not (Room, 1977). The rates of the former can be heavily influenced by the general level of social disapproval of drinking in the drinker's environment. Here, we have continued the practice of Cahalan and Room (1974) of creating a Social Consequences score out of a subset of the total of Consequences items.

Given the above issues and developments in survey experience, the 1984 survey included a set of forty-five drinking problems items, grouped into twelve problem areas. (figure 4.1).

FIGURE 4.1
Drinking Problem Items in the 1984 Survey

I. DEPENDENCE

A. *Loss of Control*

1. Once I started drinking it was difficult for me to stop before I became completely intoxicated.
2. I sometimes kept on drinking after I had promised myself not to.
3. I deliberately tried to cut down or quit drinking, but I was unable to do so.
4. I was afraid I might be an alcoholic.
5. Sometimes I have needed a drink so badly that I couldn't think of anything else.

B. *Symptomatic Behavior*

6. I have skipped a number of regular meals while drinking.
7. I have often taken a drink the first thing when I got up in the morning.
8. I have taken a strong drink in the morning to get over the effects of last night's drinking.
9. I have awakened the next day not being able to remember some of the things I had done while drinking.
10. My hands shook a lot the morning after drinking.
11. I need more alcohol than I used to, to get the same effect as before.
12. Sometimes I have awakened during the night or early morning sweating all over because of drinking.

C. *Binge Drinking*

13. I stayed intoxicated for several days at a time.

(continued)

FIGURE 4.1 (continued)

SOCIAL CONSEQUENCES SUBSET

II. CONSEQUENCES

D. *Belligerence*

14. I have gotten in a fight while drinking. (2)
15. I have gotten in a heated argument while drinking. (1)

E. *Spouse Problems*

16. Did your spouse's feelings about your drinking break up your relationship with him/her or threaten to break it up? (3)
17. A spouse or someone I lived with threatened to leave me because of my drinking. (3)
18. A spouse or someone I lived with got angry about my drinking or the way I behaved while drinking. (2)
19. Was there ever a time when you felt that your drinking had a harmful effect on your home life or marriage? (2)
20. Did your spouse or someone you lived with feel that you should drink less or act differently when you drank? (1)

F. *Problems with Relatives*

21. Did your mother's feelings about your drinking threaten to break up your relationship with her? (3)
22. Did your father's feelings about your drinking threaten to break up your relationship with him? (3)
23. Did any other relative's feelings about your drinking threaten to break up your relationship with him or her? (3)
24. Did your mother feel that you should drink less or act differently when you drank? (1)
25. Did your father feel that you should drink less or act differently when you drank? (1)
26. Did any other relative feel that you should drink less or act differently when you drank? (1)

G. *Problems with Friends*

27. Did a girlfriend's or boyfriend's feelings about your drinking threaten to break up your relationship with him or her? (3)
28. Did any other friend's feelings about your drinking threaten to break up your relationship with him or her? (3)
29. Was there ever a time when you felt that your drinking had a harmful effect on your friendships and social life? (2)
30. Did your boyfriend or girlfriend feel that you should drink less or act differently when you drank? (1)
31. Did any other friend feel that you should drink less or act differently when you drank? (1)

H. *Job Problems*

32. I have lost a job, or nearly lost one, because of drinking. (3)
33. Drinking may have hurt my chances for promotion, or raises, or better jobs. (2)

(continued)

FIGURE 4.1 (continued)

H. Job Problems (continued)
  34. Was there ever a time when you felt that your drinking had a harmful effect on your work and employment opportunities? (2)
  35. People at work indicated that I should cut down on drinking. (1)
I. Problems with Police
  36. I had trouble with the law about drinking when driving was not involved. (2)
  37. I have been arrested for driving after drinking. (2)
  38. A policeman questioned or warned me because of my drinking. (1)

END OF SOCIAL CONSEQUENCES SUBSET

J. Health Problems
  39. I had an illness connected with drinking which kept me from working on my regular activities for a week or more. (3)
  40. A physician suggested I cut down on drinking. (2)
  41. I felt that my drinking was becoming a serious threat to my physical health. (1)
  42. Was there ever a time when you felt that your drinking had a harmful effect on your health? (1)
K. Accidents
  43. My drinking contributed to getting hurt in an accident in a car or elsewhere. (2)
  44. My drinking contributed to getting involved in an accident in which someone else was hurt or property, such as an auto, was damaged. (2)
L. Financial Problems
  45. Was there ever a time when you felt that your drinking had a harmful effect on your financial position? (2)

In figure 4.1 above, numbers in parentheses follow each of the items that refer to Consequences of drinking. These numbers reflect our judgment about the severity of each consequence. The values are the same as those used by Cahalan and Room (1974) wherever the questions are the same, except that we use a score of three rather than four as the highest value. Where the questions are new, we have assigned values that are consistent with the severity levels present in Cahalan and Room's system. Respondents who answered affirmatively to any of the questions were then asked if they had experienced that problem within the past year. If so, the problem was counted as a current problem. Otherwise, it was counted as a past problem. The term "lifetime problems" will be used to refer to problems experienced either currently or in the past. Most of the present analysis deals with current problems.

SCORING PROCEDURES

From these forty-five items, two levels or tiers of scores were constructed. First, scores were constructed for each of the twelve problem areas appearing in the above list. These will sometimes be called problem groups in the analysis below. These first tier scores were fairly simple ones, distinguishing between those with no problems, those with minimal problems, and those with moderate problems within each problem group. The second set of scores was calculated for three broader, combined categories: Dependence, Consequences, and its subset of Social Consequences. The score for Dependence was formed by combining the items in the Loss of Control, Symptomatic Behavior, and Binge Drinking areas. The score for Consequences was formed by combining the items from the remaining nine problem groups, Belligerence through Financial Problems. Social Consequences, a subset of Consequences, was formed by combining items from six of these nine groups, Belligerence through Police Problems (i.e., Social Consequences includes all of the Consequences except those under the headings Health Problem, Accidents, and Financial Problems.) (See figure 4.1).

At both levels, the scoring procedure for the Dependence items is different from that used for the Consequences items. This difference reflects our adherence to the position taken earlier by Cahalan and Room (1974) and Cahalan (1970) that a priori determinations of the severity of Dependence items cannot be legitimately made. We do accept such judgments about the Consequences items, although we recognize them as subjective and crude. Hence, the procedures for scoring the Consequences items makes use of these severity values (which appear in parentheses in the above list) while the procedures for scoring Dependence do not.

To begin with the first tier, scores for Loss of Control were created by simply summing the number of items affirmed by the respondent. Those with two or more items affirmed were counted as having a moderate level problem. Those with only one item affirmed were counted as having a minimal level problem. Those with no items affirmed were counted as having no problem. Symptomatic Behavior was scored similarly except that three or more items affirmed was the standard for a moderate level problem. Again, one or more items affirmed was the minimal level standard. Since Binge Drinking was only a single item problem, a slightly different procedure was required. Any indication of binge drinking was automatically counted as a moderate level problem. This is consistent with the scoring system used earlier by Cahalan and Room (1974). Hence, all respondents who affirmed the sole binge item were counted as having a moderate problem in the Binge Drinking area.

For the nine remaining problem groups, Belligerence through Financial Problems, severity levels were assigned based on the highest-valued item that the respondent affirmed within each category. If the respondent affirmed an item valued at two or three, he or she was counted as having a moderate level problem in that area. If only items of value one were affirmed, the respondent was counted as having a minimal level problem. If no items were affirmed, the respondent was classified as having no problems in that area.

The second tier of scores, those for Dependence, Consequences, and Social Consequences, were constructed in a similar way. For Dependence, we simply summed the number of items affirmed out of the 13 in the category. Four levels of problems were assigned. Those with no items affirmed were counted as having no problem. Those with only one or two items affirmed were counted as having a minimal problem. Those with three or more items affirmed were counted as having at least a moderate problem. Those with four or more items were counted as having a problem at a high level. Note that these are hierarchical rather than mutually exclusive categories. All those counted in the high problem group are also included in the moderate problem group. For indices of both Consequences and Social Consequences, we summed together the severity values of the items affirmed. Those with scores of zero were counted as having no problem. Those with scores of one through three were counted as having a minimal problem. Those with scores of greater than four were counted as having at least moderate problems. Such a score would correspond to the affirmation of at least four minimal level (value of one) problem items or the affirmation of two or more items of at least moderate (value of two or more) severity or some other combination of similar severity. Those with scores of eight or more were counted as having a high level of problems. Most of the analyses to follow deal with the moderate and minimal problem levels. While attention will also be paid to the high level, it should be noted that analyses of high problems are hindered by the smaller Ns involved.

In the Consequences area and its subset, the Social Consequences area, the moderate problem level corresponds to the affirmation of at least four minimal level (value of one) problem items or the affirmation of two or more items of at least moderate (value of two or more) severity or some other combination of similar severity. We feel that this criterion represents a problem level that should be of concern to the drinker and that can justifiably be referred to as problematic. The high level is more extreme and can scarcely be achieved without scoring more than minimal problems in several areas. We feel that this level represents the existence of substantial alcohol problems.

THE PREVALENCE OF DRINKING PROBLEMS

Tables 4.1 and 4.2 show the frequency distributions for the Dependence, Consequences, and Social Consequences indices. (Note that here and throughout this chapter, weighted data are used for all prevalence estimates and statistical calculations but reported Ns are unweighted.) The indices were computed for current problems and percentages were calculated on the basis of current drinkers. At the minimal level, respondents who had scores of one or more on any of the three indices would be counted as having experienced problems during the past year. The figures indicate that 20% of the current drinkers experienced at least one of the Dependence items, 21% experienced at least one Consequence, and 19% experienced at least one Social Consequence. For men, the figures were higher; 26% experienced one of the Dependence items, 26% experienced at least one Consequence, and 24% experienced at least one Social Consequence. For women, 14% experienced at least one of the Dependence items, 16% experienced at least one Consequence, and 14% experienced at least one Social Consequence. These rates are very high and far in excess of conventional impressions of the prevalence of drinking problems. But they indicate that when occasional or mild problems are included, the experience of drinking problems is reported by a fairly large proportion of the population.

TABLE 4.1
Frequency Distribution of Dependence Items among Current Drinkers

		Percent of Respondents	
Index Score	*Total*	*Men*	*Women*
1 or more	20	26	14
2 or more	11	14	7
3 or more*	7	9	4
4 or more**	4	6	3
5 or more	3	4	1
6 or more	2	3	1
N	(3,185)	(1,513)	(1,672)

* criterion for moderate level problems
** criterion for high level problems

At the moderate level, 7% of all drinkers can be counted as experiencing Dependence, 10% experienced Consequences, and 8% experienced Social Consequences. Calculated on the base of all adults rather than of all drinkers the figures would be 5% Dependence, 7%

TABLE 4.2

Frequency Distributions of Consequences and Social Consequences
among Current Drinkers

	Percent of Respondents					
	Consequences			*Social Consequences*		
Index Score	*Total*	*Men*	*Women*	*Total*	*Men*	*Women*
1 or more	21	26	16	19	24	14
2 or more	15	20	11	14	19	9
4 or more*	10	14	6	8	12	4
6 or more	7	10	4	6	9	2
8 or more**	5	7	2	4	7	2
12 or more	3	5	1	2	4	1
16 or more	2	2	1	1	2	1
N	(3,194)	(1,572)	(1,673)	(3,194)	(1,521)	(1,673)

* criterion for moderate level problems
** criterion for high level problems

Consequences, and 6% Social Consequences. Men, of course, had higher problem rates than women.

All three of the problem distributions in tables 4.1 and 4.2 are quite gradual. The data themselves do not suggest any clear divisions or gaps along a gradient of increasing problem levels. While this finding has been contained in a number of previous studies, its implications bear repeating. The gradient between drinkers with few problems and those with many is such that the data themselves never suggest a convenient, empirically derived dividing line that can be used to separate problematic from non-problematic drinkers. Instead, analysts must rely on arbitrary cutpoints. Criteria can be established at greater or lesser levels of severity and prevalence estimates will vary accordingly. Given this state of affairs, it must be recognized that it is not possible to give a simple answer to the question "How many alcoholics (or problem drinkers) are there in the United States?" The answer depends heavily on the cutpoints that are chosen.

Table 4.3 shows the rates of each of the twelve problem groups. Again, the calculations refer to current problems only and the percentages are based on current drinkers. The figures show the percentages of drinkers who had a problem in each area according to both the minimal and the moderate criteria. A variety of observations can be made about these results. To begin with, the rates of minimal problems in the Symptomatic Behavior area were quite high (18% overall, 23% among men, 12% among women). This essentially reflects the high frequency of affirming the "skipped meals while drinking" and "forgot what I did while drinking" items. On the other hand, Binge Drinking and Accidents were both quite rare. The most often mentioned of the various Consequences groups were Problems with Spouse and Problems with Friends. Belligerence was quite a common problem at the lower level. This reflected the frequent occurrence of having heated arguments while drinking. But the gap between the minimal and moderate problem levels for Belligerence was large, indicating that actual fights were much more rare than arguments. A wide gap also appeared between the minimal and moderate levels of Health Problems. Many respondents felt that drinking was deleterious to their health, but relatively few had had this feeling confirmed by either the advice of a physician or the experience of a drinking-related illness.

ANALYSIS OF INDIVIDUAL PROBLEM ITEMS

The percentage of respondents who experienced each of the forty-five individual problems during the past year is given in table 4.4. Overall, these problem rates are quite low. Only 10% of the respondents checked the most frequently mentioned items—having had a heated argument while drinking and lapse of memory after drinking—but for the great majority of the items, the percentages were far lower. The minimum rate occurred on the item that asked whether the respondent's father had threatened to break off his relationship with the respondent. Only ten respondents mentioned this item. Averaging across all forty-five items, the mean percentage of respondents experiencing each individual problem was 2.8% (standard deviation 2.5%). Of those respondents who reported a problem, most reported only one or two. While 72% of all drinkers reported no problems, 10% reported only one problem, 14% reported three or more problems, and only 9% reported five or more of the forty-five problems on the list (not shown on table).

The five most frequently mentioned individual problems were: had a heated argument while drinking (10%, item no. 15), loss of memory !10%, item no. 9), skipped meals (9%, item no. 6), spouse or equivalent got angry about respondent's drinking (8%, item no. 18), and respondent kept on drinking after promising to stop (7%, item no. 2).

The question about memory loss was included as an indicator of blackouts, complete short term memory losses that can be experienced as a physiological consequence of a session of heavy drinking and that are thought to be one indicator of alcohol dependence. Skipping meals on a regular basis has been considered an indicator of the salience of drink-seeking behavior, and therefore of alcohol dependence. The frequency with which these items were mentioned by our respondents

TABLE 4.3
Percentage of Drinkers with Current Problems

	Total		Men		Women	
	At least minimal problem	At least moderate problem	At least minimal problem	At least moderate problem	At least minimal problem	At least moderate problem
Loss of control	10	4	12	5	7	3
Symptomatic behavior	18	3	23	5	12	2
Binge drinking	1	1	2	2	1	1
Dependence	20	7	26	9	14	4
Belligerence	11	4	13	5	8	2
Problems with spouse	10	9	14	13	6	5
Problems with relatives	5	#	7	1	4	#
Problems with friends	8	6	10	8	6	5
Job problems	3	2	4	3	2	1
Problems with police	3	2	4	3	1	#
Health problems	7	2	7	2	7	1
Accidents	1	1	2	2	1	1
Financial problems	3	3	4	4	2	2
Consequences	21	10	26	14	16	6
Social Consequences	19	8	24	12	14	4
	N = 3,185		N = 1,513		N = 1,672	

Less than 0.5%

TABLE 4.4
Percentage of Drinkers Affirming Individual Problem Items

Item #		Total	Men	Women
Loss of Control				
#1	Could not stop	3	5	1
#2	Broke promise	7	8	5
#3	Tried to stop	3	4	2
#4	Afraid, alcoholic	2	2	2
#5	Preoccupation	1	1	1
Symptomatic Behavior				
#6	Skipped meals	9	12	6
#7	Morning drinking	2	4	1
#8	Hangover remedy	2	3	1
#9	Memory loss	10	13	6
#10	Tremors	4	4	3
#11	Tolerance	4	5	3
#12	Night sweats	2	2	2
Binge Drinking				
#13	Binge drinking	1	2	1
Belligerence				
#14	Fight	4	5	2
#15	Argument	10	12	8
Problems with Spouse				
#16	Spouse, relationship	1	2	1
#17	Spouse threatened to leave	2	4	1
#18	Spouse angry	8	11	4
#19	Harmed marriage	5	7	2
#20	Spouse objected	4	6	3
Problems with Relatives				
#21	Mother, relationship	#	1	#
#22	Father, relationship	#	#	#
#23	Relative, relationship	#	#	#
#24	Mother objected	4	6	3
#25	Father objected	2	3	1
#26	Relative objected	2	2	2
Problems with Friends				
#27	Girl/boyfriend, relationship	1	1	#
#28	Friend, relationship	#	#	#
#29	Harmed friendships	5	7	4
#30	Girl/boyfriend objected	3	4	1
#31	Friend objected	1	1	1
Job Problems				
#32	Lost job	1	1	#
#33	Hurt promotion	1	1	#
#34	Hurt job	2	3	1
#35	Workmates advised	1	1	#

(continued)

TABLE 4.4 (continued)

Item #	Total	Men	Women
Problems with Police			
#36 Legal trouble	1	2	#
#37 DUI arrest	1	1	#
#38 Policeman	2	4	1
Health Problems			
#39 Illness	#	#	#
#40 Physician advised	1	2	1
#41 Health threat	2	3	2
#42 Harmed health	6	6	7
Accidents			
#43 Accident, self hurt	1	1	#
#44 Accident, others hurt	1	2	#
Financial Problems			
#45 Harmed financial position	3	4	2
Minimum N for any one item	(3,144)	(1,484)	(1,649)

Less than 0.5%

seems to indicate that they interpreted both questions more loosely. In the former case, affirmative responses may have referred only to inconsequential lapses of memory which would not qualify as alcoholic blackouts. In the latter case, the occasional skipping of meals in order to prolong a drinking occasion may not necessarily imply dependence and seems to be a more common occurrence than is envisaged in the clinical literature. The items referring to heated arguments and to anger on the part of spouses may be related to the extent that they refer to instances of heated arguments between the drinkers and their spouses. The least often experienced problems were: drinking threatened to break up the relationship between the respondent and the respondent's father (0.1%), drinking threatened to break up the relationship between the respondent and some other relative (0.2%), drinking threatened to break up the relationship between the respondent and the respondent's mother (0.3%), drinking threatened to break up the relationship between the respondent and a friend (0.3%), and the respondent had an illness related to drinking (0.3%). These four problems occurred primarily among young respondents, who are less able than older drinkers to distance their drinking from the eyes of disapproving parents and family members. Of the respondents who reported that drinking threatened to break up relations with fathers, mothers, other relatives, or friends, 64% were under the age of twenty-five.

The types of problems most frequently experienced were similar for both sexes (table 4.4). For men, the most frequently experienced problems were: loss of memory (13%), had a heated argument (12%), skipped meals (12%), spouse got angry (11%), and continued to drink after promising to stop (8%). Among women, the order was only slightly different: had a heated argument (8%), felt that drinking had harmed health (7%), skipped meals (6%), memory loss (6%), and continued to drink after promising to stop (5%). Spouse got angry was sixth in popularity (4%). Thus, there was a fairly strong agreement between the genders as to what the most commonly experienced problems were.

Among the remaining items, there were occasional cases where the percentage of women experiencing the problem was roughly the same as to the percentage of men experiencing it. These included: had an illness related to drinking, was afraid that I might be an alcoholic, sweats in the night, a friend's criticism of the respondent's drinking, and a relative's criticism of the respondent's drinking. These were the only areas where women's problem rates drew even with men's. For the item about feeling that drinking had been harmful to health, the women's rate actually surpassed the men's (6.5% vs. 6.1%).

RELATIONSHIPS BETWEEN DRINKING PROBLEMS

Table 4.5 contains an intercorrelation matrix of the relationships between the individual drinking problems. The coefficients are phi coefficients between the dichotomous (presence or absence) problem indicators. The figures above the diagonal were computed for problems at the moderate level of severity; those below the diagonal were computed for problems at the minimal level of severity. In making these calculations, we included only those respondents who indicated the presence of at least one problem of any severity. As discussed by Cahalan and Room (1974), this procedure reduces the artificial inflation of the coefficients that is brought about because the great majority of the respondents have neither of any given pair of problems. The calculations were also made on the basis of current problems only.

On the whole, the relationships between problems were not strong. Coefficients of 0.30 and above are achieved for several relationships, but coefficients of above 0.35 are quite rare. It must be recognized that the skewed marginal distributions of problem indicators constrain the maximum size that these phi coefficients can take, but the relationships were modest nonetheless. While there appear to be more high coefficients among the moderate level problems (above the diagonal) than among the minimal level problems (below the diagonal), there are also more low coefficients in the upper half of the table. Thus the average relationship is not much greater above the diagonal than

TABLE 4.5
Phi Coefficients of Interrelationships between Problem Groups

Above diagonal—moderate level of problems
Below diagonal—minimal level of problems

	(1)	(2)	(3)	(4)	(5)	(6)	(7)	(8)	(9)	(10)	(11)	(12)
1. Loss of Control	—	0.42	0.30	0.23	0.27	0.15	0.38	0.23	0.20	0.21	0.07	0.30
2. Symptomatic Behavior	0.18	—	0.42	0.31	0.32	0.13	0.31	0.22	0.34	0.17	0.13	0.34
3. Binge Drinking	×	×	—	0.30	0.20	0.09	0.21	0.18	0.30	0.12	0.06	0.27
4. Belligerence	0.26	0.16	×	—	0.31	0.13	0.24	0.15	0.20	0.08	0.27	0.25
5. Problems with Spouse	0.26	0.10	×	0.31	—	0.10	0.32	0.21	0.18	0.17	0.04	0.22
6. Problems with Relatives	0.30	0.15	×	0.23	0.26	—	0.12	0.03	0.21	0.02	0.05	-0.02
7. Problems with Friends	0.22	0.02	×	0.22	0.25	0.43	—	0.27	0.19	0.14	0.11	0.34
8. Job Problems	0.16	0.05	×	0.18	0.19	0.16	0.22	—	0.24	0.05	0.14	0.41
9. Problems with Police	0.24	0.15	×	0.23	0.26	0.33	0.20	0.26	—	0.08	0.27	0.13
10. Health Problems	0.20	-0.02	×	0.06	0.14	0.19	0.23	0.23	0.05	—	-0.01	0.11
11. Accidents	×	×	×	×	×	×	×	×	×	×	—	0.05
12. Financial Problems	×	×	×	×	×	×	×	×	×	×	×	—

× Not appropriate, Binge Drinking, Accidents, and Financial Problems have no minimal level score.

it is below. For moderate problems, the average coefficient was 0.19 (standard deviation 0.10) while for minimal problems, the average coefficient was 0.20 (standard deviation 0.09).

At the moderate level, there did seem to be a consistent indication of interrelationship between the problems in the Dependence area. Loss of Control and Symptomatic Behavior were quite firmly related (phi = 0.42). Binge Drinking was also related to these two (phi = 0.30 and 0.42 respectively). Unfortunately, the strong relationship between Loss of Control and Symptomatic Behavior was not reproduced at the minimal problem level (phi = 0.18). Other individual relationships of note among the moderate level problems were as follows: Loss of Control was related to Problems with Friends (phi = 0.38) and with Financial Problems (phi = 0.30). Symptomatic Behavior was related to Belligerence (phi = 0.31), Problems with Spouse (phi = 0.32), Problems with Friends (phi = 0.31), and Financial Problems (phi = 0.34). Binge drinking was related to Belligerence (phi = 0.30), and Problems with Police (phi = 0.30). The latter of these relationships seems reasonable insofar as intoxication for prolonged periods is likely to be accompanied by behaviors that would attract the notice of the police. Oddly enough, Belligerence was not strongly related to Problems with the Police (phi = 0.20). It was, however, related to Problems with Spouse (phi = 0.31). Problems with Spouse was related to Problems with Friends (phi = 0.32), indicating some degree of mutual occurrence between these most frequent of the Consequences. Problems with Friends was also related with Financial Problems (phi = 0.34). Job Problems was firmly related to Financial Problems (phi = 0.41); this was expected given that financial position is generally dependent on employment.

At the minimal problem level, there were fewer relationships of note. Belligerence and Spouse Problems were related (phi = 0.31), repeating a relationship found at the moderate level. Problems with Relatives was strongly related to Problems with Friends (phi = 0.43) and more weakly related to Loss of Control (phi = 0.30). Also, Problems with the Police was related to Problems with Relatives (phi = 0.33).

Another way to study these interrelationships is to examine the percentage of drinkers with problems in any one group who had problems in another group. Table 4.6 presents such figures. The table is organized so as to indicate the percentage of drinkers who had the problem listed in the row heading who also had the problem listed in the column heading. Thus, of the one hundred fifty six drinkers who reported Loss of Control at the moderate level, 47% also reported experiencing Symptomatic Behavior at the moderate level. Eighty six percent of these same fifty-five drinkers reported at least one other moderate level problem besides Loss of Control.

TABLE 4.6

Joint Occurrence of Current Drinking Problems at the Moderate Level*

	(1)	(2)	(3)	(4)	(5)	(6)	(7)	(8)	(9)	(10)	(11)	(12)	Any Other Problem	N
1. Loss of Control	—	47%	20%	33%	66%	6%	64%	25%	17%	18%	8%	35%	86%	156
2. Symptomatic Behavior	52	—	28	41	73	6	59	25	26	16	12	40	92	135
3. Binge Drinking	59	73	—	59	76	7	63	32	36	18	10	50	99	60
4. Belligerence	33	37	21	—	70	6	48	20	17	10	19	31	86	109
5. Problems with Spouse	24	24	10	26	—	3	38	16	10	10	6	19	93	319
6. Problems with Relatives	54	44	20	48	71	—	62	15	42	8	12	7	92	33
7. Problems with Friends	36	30	13	28	60	4	—	23	13	11	8	30	75	197
8. Job Problems	38	34	17	29	64	3	59	—	23	8	14	52	91	87
9. Problems with Police	42	58	31	42	68	12	57	38	—	13	27	27	90	63
10. Health Problems	43	35	16	24	71	2	48	14	13	—	3	25	75	73
11. Accidents	24	32	11	55	48	4	44	28	33	4	—	18	86	38
12. Financial Problems	42	43	21	37	62	1	63	42	13	12	7	—	88	107

* Read table horizontally. For example, of the 156 respondents reporting Loss of Control, 47% also reported Symptomatic Behavior.

The following percentages were relatively large and therefore indicate findings of note. Fifty-two percent of those who reported Symptomatic Behavior also reported Loss of Control. Fifty-nine percent of the few individuals who reported Binge Drinking also reported Loss of Control, 73% of them reported Symptomatic Behavior, and 59% of them reported Belligerence. Of the very few who reported Problems with Relatives, 54% also reported Loss of Control. Of those who had Job Problems, 52% also had Financial Problems, which is a consequence of job problems that we would expect. Of those who reported Problems with the Police, 58% also reported Symptomatic Behavior. Finally, of those few who reported accidents, 55% also reported Belligerence— giving some support to the notion that belligerence and impairment may combine in many accident situations. In general, these are the same relationships that emerged from the analysis of the phi coefficients.

Overall, a very high proportion of drinkers with any one problem also had another problem in at least one other area. Percentages expressing this relationship (rightmost column of table 4.6) range from 99% for Binge Drinking to 75% for Problems with Friends and Health Problems. Thus, although the presence of any one problem at the moderate level was not generally a good predictor of any other particular problem, we can conclude that most respondents who experienced one problem did have another problem of some kind.

SUMMARY

This paper establishes the definitions of alcohol-related problems that are used in several other sections of this book. This description has included both a thumbnail history of the development of the measurement approach used here and a specification of the scoring procedures involved.

Basic prevalence estimates are also given here. It does bear noting, however, that any estimate of the prevalence of drinking problems in the general population depends heavily on the criteria used in measuring those problems. At what we feel to be a moderate level of severity, 9% of men who drank and 4% of women who drank experienced Dependence in the past year while 14% of men who drank and 6% of women who drank experienced Consequences of drinking. Estimates based on a higher standard of severity were much lower.

Relationships between individual problem items as well as between problem subcategories were shown to be fairly weak. This lack of a strong clustering among drinking problems is typical of survey results of this kind. However, such an outcome pulls against the notion that experiencing drinking problems is largely confined to a small number of alcoholics or problem drinkers.

PART III. OVERVIEW

MICHAEL E. HILTON

5

The Demographic Distribution of Drinking Patterns in 1984

INTRODUCTION

Using data from the 1984 National Alcohol Survey, this paper reports ths distribution of alcohol consumption across a variety of demographic variables. Its purpose is to update sections of Cahalan, et al.'s (1969) *American Drinking Patterns*, the first detailed national survey of drinking patterns in the United States. One tribute to the quality of that work is that it is frequently cited as a source of prevalence estimates for drinking and heavy drinking. However, those results are now more than two decades old, and there is unease regarding the accuracy of such dated prevalence estimates. This paper notes any substantial differences between the 1984 results and those of the Cahalan et al. study. However, this is not a trend study per se; readers should see Hilton and Clark (chapter 7 in this volume), and Hilton (chapter 8) for trend studies using these data.

METHODS

A number of alcohol consumption variables were constructed from items on the 1984 National Alcohol Survey questionnaire. Abstainers were defined as persons who drank alcoholic beverages less often than once a year or who never drank them. All persons not defined as abstainers were defined as current drinkers. The frequency of drinking was taken from the following question: "How often do you usually have any kind of beverage containing alcohol, whether it is wine, beer, or whiskey, or any other drink?" An estimate of the monthly volume of consumption was constructed according to the technique developed by Cahalan et al. (1969). Measures of the frequency of consuming five or more drinks per occasion and of consuming eight or more drinks per day are discussed in Hilton (chapter 13)[1]. The frequency of self-reported drunkenness was derived from the question "How often in the past year did you drink enough to feel drunk?" The use of several consumption measures, as opposed to a single measure or typology, reflects the view that drinking patterns can be measured across a variety of relevant dimensions and that no single axis of measurement is superior to any other in its descriptive or analytical utility.

RESULTS

Six indicators of alcohol consumption are presented in table 5.1. The results show that 76% of men and 64% of women are current drinkers. American abstention rates were relatively unchanged between 1964 and 1979 (Hilton, 1986), and these data show that abstention rates continue to be fairly stable. In addition to the abstainers, 10% of men and 19% of women drink less often than once a month. Thus, the proportion of the population that never or rarely drinks is substantial. On the other hand, 49% of men and 25% of women drink at least once a week. For 12% of men and 4% of women, drinking is a daily experience.

The most often reported measure of alcohol use is the volume consumed during a specified time period, and the present results include volume so that comparisons to other studies may be drawn. By the commonly used standard of sixty or more drinks per month, 21% of men and 5% of women can be counted as high-volume drinkers. A higher cut point of one hundred twenty or more drinks per month produces estimates of 8.9% for men and 1.8% for women (data not shown in table). It is noteworthy that many people are very light drinkers: 30% of men and 42% of women drink fifteen or fewer drinks

TABLE 5.1

Distributions of Selected Alcohol Consumption Measures; by Sex (Percents)

	Men	Women	Total
1. *Percent Drinkers*	76	64	69
2. *Frequency of Drinking*			
Daily[a]	12	4	7
Weekly[b]	37	21	28
Monthly[c]	16	20	19
Yearly[d]	10	19	15
Abstainer	24	36	31
3. *Monthly Volume Consumed*			
60 or more drinks	21	5	13
30–59.9 drinks	14	9	11
15–29.9 drinks	10	8	9
0–14.9 drinks	30	42	36
Abstainer	24	36	31
4. *Frequency of Drinking Five or More Drinks on an Occasion*			
Weekly	24	6	14
Monthly	12	6	9
Yearly	7	7	7
Never	33	44	39
Abstainer	24	36	31
5. *Frequency of Drinking Eight or More Drinks in a Day*			
Weekly	8	2	4
Monthly	6	1	3
Yearly	18	9	13
Never	45	52	49
Abstainer	24	36	31
6. *Frequency of Getting Drunk*			
Weekly	5	1	3
Monthly	6	2	4
Yearly	30	22	26
Never	34	39	37
Abstainer	24	36	31
N	2,093	3,128	5,221

[a] Once per day or more often.
[b] At least once per week but less often than once per day.
[c] At least once per month but less often than once per week.
[d] At least once per year but less than once per month.

per month in addition to the 24% of men and 36% of women who are abstainers.

Despite its ubiquity, volume has been justly criticized as masking important differences between those who drink daily in small amounts and those who drink to intoxication infrequently. Following Knupfer's (1984) advice that the critical datum is the frequency of intoxication, the frequencies of drinking five or more drinks on an occasion and of drinking eight or more drinks per day are presented. Twenty-four percent of men and 6% of women consume five or more drinks as often as once a week, but a large proportion of both sexes (57% of men and 80% of women) never drink as many as five drinks at a time. Similarly, 8% of men and 2% of women drink eight or more drinks per day as often as once a week, but 69% of men and 88% of women never drink that much per day. Knupfer (1984) also suggested that drinking eight or more drinks per sitting as often as three times a week should be the criterion of heavy drinking. By this standard, only 3.5% of men and 0.6% of women would be counted as heavy drinkers (data not shown in table).

A given number of drinks can have differing effects because of such factors as weight and metabolism. It is therefore useful to look at self reported intoxication, even though this is heavily influenced by subjectivity. Five percent of men and 1% of women reported weekly or more frequent intoxication. Note that these proportions are considerably lower than the proportions consuming eight or more drinks per day as often as once a week, indicating, it would seem, a reluctance to admit to intoxication.

The Demographic Distribution of Consumption

Table 5.2 presents the proportion of respondents who are drinkers and the proportion who fall in the highest category on each consumption measure across several demographic categories. It is well established that drinking and heavy drinking are more prevalent among the young than the old (Cahalan et al., 1969; Clark and Midanik, 1982; Johnson et al. 1977). The current data confirm this. Several other points can be noted. By most measures, prevalence estimates are progressively lower in older age categories (Readers should not draw longitudinal conclusions from these cross-sectional data). It is surprising that this does not hold for daily drinking, which continues to have a high prevalence among older respondents. The proportion of those aged sixty and over who drink every day is unexpectedly large.

Additional findings merit a brief note. The finding that a greater proportion of men in their thirties than men aged eighteen to twenty-nine are drinkers is probably anomalous to this data set, most surveys

TABLE 5.2

Demographic Distributions of Selected Alcohol Consumption Measures
(Percents)

	Drinkers	Daily Drinkers	60+ Drinks per Month	5+ per Occasion Weekly	8+ per Day Weekly	Drunk Weekly	N
1. Age							
Men							
18–29	82	9	24	33	13	10	621
30–39	87	11	22	26	8	4	511
40–49	78	12	25	26	6	4	305
50–59	71	16	22	20	4	1	235
60 and over	58	14	14	8	2	1	413
Women							
18–29	74	2	5	7	2	2	894
30–39	69	5	7	10	3	2	766
40–49	62	5	6	8	2	*	406
50–59	62	3	6	2	*	*	358
60 and over	49	5	1	1	*	*	679
2. Race							
Men							
White	76	12	22	24	8	5	1,297
Black	72	11	17	18	6	5	768
Other	75	4	15	15	7	13	28
Women							
White	65	4	5	6	1	1	1,825
Black	54	3	4	5	1	1	1,267
Other	54	*	11	11	11	*	36

(continued)

TABLE 5.2 (continued)

	Drinkers	Daily Drinkers	60+ Drinks per Month	5+ per Occasion Weekly	8+ per Day Weekly	Drunk Weekly	N
3. Hispanic Background							
Men							
Hispanic	78	8	17	20	6	4	605
Non-Hispanic	76	12	22	24	8	5	1,488
Women							
Hispanic	54	1	4	3	1	*	848
Non-Hispanic	64	4	5	6	2	1	2,280
4. Marital Status							
Men							
Married	73	12	20	21	5	3	1,220
Never married	84	8	24	31	15	10	481
Divorced and separated	78	16	27	29	11	4	290
Widowed	61	21	13	10	3	8	100
Women							
Married	63	4	5	5	1	1	1,399
Never married	72	3	9	12	4	3	620
Divorced and separated	69	3	4	8	2	1	631
Widowed	49	4	1	2	*	*	478
5. Religion							
Men							
Catholic	89	15	29	32	8	6	701
Liberal Protestant[a]	83	12	23	25	8	3	349

5. Religion (continued)

Men

Conservative Protestant[b]	56	8	13	15	5	4	788
Jewish	89	*	7	15	6	*	26
Other	83	14	27	29	12	11	225

Women

Catholic	77	6	7	8	2	1	1,029
Liberal Protestant	71	4	6	5	1	*	520
Conservative Protestant	42	1	2	3	1	1	1,383
Jewish	88	*	*	*	*	*	32
Other	80	8	9	15	4	3	159

6. Income

Men

$10,000 and under	67	13	18	20	8	8	702
$10,001 to $20,000	69	11	19	19	7	4	563
$20,001 to $30,000	77	7	17	20	8	3	321
$30,001 to $40,000	82	9	27	29	7	4	210
$40,001 and over	91	16	32	35	8	5	173

Women

$10,000 and under	49	3	3	3	1	2	1,438
$10,001 to $20,000	65	4	6	8	3	1	702
$20,001 to $30,000	72	3	5	6	2	1	383
$30,001 to $40,000	68	5	8	7	2	1	211
$40,001 and over	81	5	5	6	*	*	165

(continued)

TABLE 5.2 (continued)

	Drinkers	Daily Drinkers	60+ Drinks per Month	5+ per Occasion Weekly	8+ per Day Weekly	Drunk Weekly	N
7. Education							
Men							
Less than high school	63	14	19	20	7	4	802
High school graduate	78	10	24	26	11	7	625
Some college	77	8	19	24	5	5	374
College graduate or more	88	16	22	23	4	3	28
Women							
Less than high school	45	3	2	3	1	1	1,261
High school graduate	67	4	6	7	3	1	1,003
Some college	70	4	5	8	1	*	561
College graduate or more	79	4	5	4	*	*	295
8. Urbanicity							
Men							
Metropolitan cities 50,000 and over	79	13	26	28	8	6	1,121
Metropolitan towns under 50,000	80	12	24	25	9	5	579
Nonmetropolitan areas	66	10	14	17	5	3	393
Women							
Metropolitan cities 50,000 and over	66	3	7	8	3	1	1,675
Metropolitan towns under 50,000	70	4	4	4	1	*	840
Nonmetropolitan areas	53	4	4	6	1	1	612
9. Region							
Men							
Northeast[c]	84	13	20	22	8	3	400

9. Region (continued)

Men							
Midwest[d]	83	13	27	29	5	3	348
Pacific[e]	78	12	22	27	10	5	339
South[f]	65	9	17	19	7	6	900
Mountain[g]	69	17	26	23	14	12	106
Women							
Northeast	75	6	5	5	1	1	590
Midwest	67	4	6	7	2	1	535
Pacific	71	4	7	9	3	3	476
South	52	2	3	3	1	1	1,422
Mountain	55	3	9	10	5	*	105

* Less than 0.5 percent.

a All Protestant denominations not counted as Conservative Protestant (see b).

b Includes: Baptist, Pentecostal, Assembly of God, Church of God, Nazarene, Holiness, Apostolic, Evangelical, Sanctified, Disciples of Christ, Christian Reformed, Jehovah's Witness, Seventh Day Adventist, Mormon, Brethren, Spiritual and Salvation Army.

c Includes New England and Mid-Atlantic states.

d Includes East North Central and West North Central states.

e Includes only Pacific states.

f Includes South Atlantic, East South Central, and West South Central states.

g Includes only Mountain states.

Percentages based on weighted data.
Ns based on unweighted data.

having found a greater prevalence in the younger category. By virtually any measure, the prevalence of heavy drinking among those aged sixty and older is extremely low. Finally, very heavy drinking, as measured by the eight or more drinks per day weekly and the drunkenness weekly indicators, is far more prevalent among men aged eighteen to twenty-nine than among any other age/sex group.

An especially useful feature of this data set is its focus on the drinking patterns of Blacks and Hispanics. The prevalence of drinking is higher among Whites than among Blacks for either sex. Among women, this difference is quite strong (65% vs. 54%), but among men it is much smaller and some might say unimportant (76% vs. 72%). Among women there is very little difference in the prevalence of heavy drinking between Whites and Blacks. For men, two measures seem to indicate a higher prevalence of heavy drinking among Whites: drinking sixty or more drinks per month (22% vs. 17%) and drinking five or more per occasion once a week or more often (24% vs. 18%). But the pattern is not consistent insofar as the other indicators do not suggest that heavy drinking is more prevalent among Whites than among Blacks. Similar findings have been discussed by Herd (1985d).

These are different conclusions than Cahalan et al., reached. There, on the basis of a much smaller number of Black respondents (82 men and 118 women) it was concluded that "White and Negro men varied little in their rates of drinking. However, Negro women differed from White women both in their much higher proportion of abstainers and in their higher rate of heavy drinkers." (Cahalan et al. 1969; p. 48). Since no particular effort to represent minority populations was made by Cahalan et al., whereas the current survey was explicitly designed to obtain a large and nationally representative sample of Black as well as Hispanic respondents, the present results must be preferred to those of the earlier survey.

With regard to Hispanics, the results show that Hispanic women are less likely to be drinkers than are non-Hispanic women, although Hispanic men are about equally likely to be drinkers as non-Hispanic men. Daily drinking was much more prevalent among non-Hispanics than among Hispanics (for either sex). Finally, the remaining indices of heavy drinking (sixty or more drinks per month, weekly drinking of five or more at a sitting, weekly drinking of eight or more per day, and weekly drunkenness) all show slightly lower prevalences among Hispanics than among non-Hispanics (for either sex). Additional details on Hispanic drinking patterns can be found in Caetano (1986; 1987c; 1988a; see also chapter 19). Cahalan et al. paid little attention to Hispanic ethnicity, except by way of including "Latin American-Caribbean" as one of several "National Identity" categories. Since only fifty-eight of its respondents fell into this category and since it was administered only in English, the Cahalan et al. survey did not adequately portray Hispanic drinking patterns.

These data confirm that marital status is related to drinking patterns. The highest prevalence of heavy drinking is found among those who have never been married or those who are divorced or separated. The next highest rate is found among those who are married (which, in these data, includes those who are living with someone in a marriage-like relationship). The lowest prevalence rate is among those who have been widowed. This pattern is much the same as that appearing in Cahalan et al. An interesting exception is that among women marital status does not seem to make much difference in the prevalence of daily drinking. Also note that among *men*, the divorced and separated have prevalence patterns similar to those who have never been married, while divorced and separated *women* have prevalence patterns more similar to married women than to never married women. This might reflect the impact of child-care responsibility on drinking patterns. Presumably divorced or separated women who have children would find relatively little time for heavy drinking, sharing this with married women who have children, while divorced and separated men, usually with far fewer responsibilities toward children, might have more opportunity to drink heavily. Neither of these results was apparent in Cahalan et al.'s data. The former was absent because daily drinking was not included as a variable in the analysis. That the latter did not appear gives caution that the previous statements on the drinking styles of divorced men vis a vis divorced women may be an overinterpretation of the present results. Finally, the rather low proportion of never married men who report daily drinking and the relatively high proportion of widowed men who report weekly drunkenness were unexpected findings.

Religion has long been recognized as a factor in the prevalence of heavy drinking. Table 5.2 separates Jews, Catholics, Liberal Protestants, and Conservative Protestants, with the latter including the following denominations: Baptist, Pentecostal, Assembly of God, Church of God, Nazarene, Holiness, Apostolic, Evangelical, Sanctified, Disciples of Christ, Christian Reformed, Jehovah's Witness, Seventh Day Adventist, Mormon, Brethren, Spiritual, and Salvation Army. Although their numbers in the sample are small, Jews reported a very high prevalence of drinking and a very low prevalence of heavy drinking, a pattern which has often been observed (Cahalan, et al. 1969; Glassner and Berg, 1985). Among Christians, a familiar three way split emerged. The prevalence of both drinking and heavy drinking was highest among Catholics, less high among Liberal Protestants, and lowest among Conservative Protestants. This was consistent for all measures and for both sexes. Findings for Catholics and Liberal Protestants were very similar, the gap being between these two and Conservative Protestants. This is a different result from that reported by Cahalan et al., in whose data the Liberal Protestants occupied a halfway position between Catholics and Conservative Protestants. This difference may reflect a blurring of the importance of religious background over the last twenty years.

The results show a strong and familiar relationship between income and the prevalence of abstention, but there are curiosities here as well. For men, there were surprising positive relationships between income and consuming sixty or more drinks per month and consuming five or more drinks at a sitting as often as once per week. However, this pattern was not matched by the results for eight or more at a sitting or weekly drunkenness. One wonders whether higher income respondents are more likely to under report drunkenness or occasions of especially heavy drinking. Another curiosity among men is the U-shaped distribution of daily drinking. For women, on the other hand, there was little evidence of any variation in the prevalence of heavy drinking across income categories.

The analysis of a second indicator of socioeconomic status, education, confuses the picture further. Again, there seems to be a consistent relationship between education and the prevalence of drinking, but among men, the distributions of the heavy drinking variables suggest that higher education is not necessarily associated with heavier drinking. Instead, the heaviest drinking group of men seems to be the "high school graduate" category. This finding is faintly suggested for women as well. In sum, these results confirm the existence of a rather strong relationship between socioeconomic status and the prevalence of drinking but, do not lead to a clear understanding of the relationship between socioeconomic status and the prevalence of heavy drinking.

Cahalan et al.'s analysis (1969) showed the same result with regard to the prevalence of drinking. With regard to heavy drinking, however, their results were inconsistent with the present findings. For example, Cahalan et al. found a lower prevalence of heavy drinking at the lower end of the income spectrum, but not any suggestion of a higher prevalence of heavy drinking at the higher end of the spectrum. This lack of corroboration between studies leads one to conclude that the relationship between socioeconomic status and the prevalence of heavy drinking is not well understood.

Since the turn of the century, drinking has been thought of as a sin of the big city, but this has not always been the case. As Rorabaugh

(1979) reminds us, whiskey was one of the principal rural commodities during the early nineteenth century, when underdeveloped transportation systems made it difficult to store and ship surplus corn in any other form. Today, we see that drinking and heavy drinking tend to be more prevalent among men in both the larger metropolitan cities (those with populations of 50,000 and more) and the smaller metropolitan cities (those with populations under 50,000) than in the nonmetropolitan areas (those outside of Standard Metropolitan Statistical Areas). Among women, the findings are not as strong; only a few percentage points separate the three categories, one might think of the frequency of daily drinking as an index of the normative penetration of alcohol into everyday life. It should therefore be more prevalent in the sophisticated larger cities than in the countryside. The results belie this, showing only small differences in the prevalence of daily drinking by urbanicity. However, the measures of heavy drinking generally do fall in the expected direction, being highest in the metropolitan cities and lowest in nonmetropolitan areas. The results of Cahalan et al. were similar in showing heavy drinking to be least prevalent in the rural areas but are different insofar as they found that the prevalence of heavy drinking was higher in the suburban localities (corresponding roughly to the smaller metropolitan cities category used here) than in the central cities.

The regional distribution of drinking patterns in this data set has been discussed elsewhere (Hilton, chapter 17 in this volume). Here it is sufficient to note the following. Rates for the prevalence of drinking follow their traditional pattern, being higher in the Wetter regions of the country (Northeast, Midwest and Pacific states) than in the Drier regions (South and Mountain states) for both men and women. Differences in the prevalence of daily drinking are not as great as would be expected under the interpretation that these data signify the normative acceptance of drinking. Heavy drinking is relatively more prevalent in the Wetter regions, but these results also show a high prevalence of heavy drinking, among respondents in the Mountain states for both men and women. Had this latter result not also been reported by other surveys (Clark and Midanik, 1982), one would be tempted to regard it as anomalous.

DISCUSSION

A comparison of the present findings to those of Cahalan et al. (1969) produces conclusions of three sorts. First there are findings that confirm those reported twenty years ago. Among these are the following examples: that men are more often heavier drinkers than women, that the prevalence of drinking and heavy drinking is greater among the young than the old, and that the prevalence of drinking among Jews is high while the prevalence of drinking problems among Jews is low. In these instances, the principal utility of the present data is to provide more up-to-date prevalence estimates than are available elsewhere.

A second category includes findings that were not investigated or were inadequately investigated in earlier studies. These include the findings about minority drinking patterns. Also falling into this category are findings with regard to drinking indicators that were not reported in previous studies were used here. Examples of this type include the finding that there is not much difference in the prevalence of daily drinking across categories of urbanicity, that daily drinking continues to be quite prevalent among older respondents, and that weekly drunkenness is not notably more prevalent among higher income men.

In the third category are findings that contradict earlier results. These include the findings on socioeconomic status (income and education) and heavy drinking, where the inconsistencies between variables (i.e., income and education), between different measures of heavy drinking, and between the 1964 survey and the 1984 survey create a confusing picture indeed. Continued study in this area would seem desirable. The finding that the drinking patterns of divorced women resemble those of married women while the drinking patterns of divorced men resemble those of never married men was not reported in earlier studies. Two kinds of further research seem needed here: longitudinal studies of respondents who become divorced and cross sectional studies in which variables indicating the presence of children in the home are included. (Unfortunately, the present data do not contain such a variable.)

For the most part, the drinking patterns of the general population have been well studied over the years and consequently they are known in broad outline although specific details may vary from survey to survey. Continuing study can broaden and refine existing knowledge, although it rarely leads to startlingly new conclusions. The results here add to this accretion of basic descriptive information on drinking patterns.

MICHAEL E. HILTON

6

The Demographic Distribution
Of Drinking Problems in 1984

INTRODUCTION

The previous chapter (chapter 5) presented data on the distribution of drinking patterns across various demographic categories. The purpose was to update data reported by Cahalan et al. (1969) some twenty years ago. The present paper serves as a followup to that chapter by presenting data on drinking problems. There are several purposes that this followup paper hopes to fulfill. First, it complements the previous chapter, extending the findings from drinking patterns to drinking problems. Second, like the previous chapter it provides an update of existing studies, in this case national alcohol surveys by Cahalan (1970), Cahalan and Room (1974), Clark and Midanik (1982), Johnson (1982), and Wilsnack et al. (1986). Third, this report provides a point of comparison for other studies. Future national alcohol surveys, local surveys, and surveys undertaken in other countries could all benefit from the availability of prevalence rates from the 1984 national survey.

The analysis to follow invites two comparisons, each involving an expectation of how the results will turn out. First, we compare the present results to the distributions of drinking patterns shown in the previous chapter. We expect to find that problem rates will be high wherever the prevalence of heavy drinking is high. That is because heavy drinking is the principal risk factor for drinking problems (Hilton, chapter 13 in this volume; Harford and Grant and Hasin, chapter 14). The relationship may not be straightforward to the extent that certain demographic factors may condition the relationship between consumption and problems. To the extent that these factors operate, drinking problems will not be distributed across demographic categories in precisely the same way that alcohol consumption is. Recent investigations of this relationship (Hilton, chapter 13 in this volume; Harford and Grant and Hasin, chapter 14), while not agreeing among themselves as to whether demographic variables influence the risk function, have agreed that alcohol intake is the dominant factor. To the extent that consumption predominates over other risk factors, problem distributions should resemble consumption distributions.

Second, we compare the present results with those of earlier national alcohol surveys (Cahalan, 1970; Cahalan and Room, 1974; Clark and Midanik, 1982; Johnson, 1982; Wilsnack et al. 1986). We expect problem rates to be distributed across demographic categories in much the same way that they were in other studies. Variations in item wording between surveys and secular trends in problem prevalences (Hilton and Clark, chapter 7 in this volume; Hilton, chapter 8; Hasin et al., in press) will produce variations in prevalence estimates from study to study, but the gross relationships between problem rates and demographic variables should remain roughly the same.

METHODS

Drinking problems were measured using the same system discussed in other papers in this volume (see chapter 4). Two scores were computed, one for dependence and the other for drinking-related consequences. Alcohol dependence items included questions about attempts to cut down on drinking, memory loss, tremors, morning drinking and binge drinking. Alcohol-related consequences included items about arguments with spouse, loss of employment, encounters with the police, accidents, alcohol-related health problems, and the like. Respondents were asked whether they experienced these problems during the past year or at any time during their lives. Only problems experienced during the past year, or current problems, are discussed in this report.

Items in the two problem areas were scaled differently. For the dependence scale, the number of problem items endorsed by each respondent was simply totaled, and a score of three or more items was defined as a moderate level problem. A score of four or more was defined as a high level problem. For drinking-related consequences, the items were given values between one and three before they were summed. These values, indicated in parenthesis in figure 4.1, which reflect the presumed relative severity each consequence, were originally developed by Cahalan and Room (1974). In this system, the loss of a job because of drinking added three points to the total while a warning about drinking from a police officer added one point to the total. After summing these values across the set of thirty-two consequences items, total respondent scores of four or more were defined as a moderate level of drinking-related consequences; scores of eight or more were defined as a high level of drinking-related consequences.

In the analysis to follow, the figures reported and the statistics calculated from them are based on the weighted data, but the Ns reported are unweighted. Note that the base for the rates of alcohol problems in the first table is the number of respondents and not just the number of drinkers. This is useful because it shows the rate of problems among the members of important population segments. However, current problems occur only among current drinkers, and the proportion of users of alcohol also varies within the population. Thus, a table giving problem rates among those who report at least some use of alcohol in the last year is also presented (table 6.2).

RESULTS

Gender is one of the most important covariates of drinking behavior (Cahalan et al. 1969; Wilsnack et al. 1986), and the present results reaffirm this (table 6.1). The prevalence of current drinking problems, however measured, was notably higher among men than among women. This finding is consistent with the introductory paper's report that heavy drinking was much more prevalent among men.

Problem prevalences decrease with age, as has been shown many times (Cahalan, 1970; Cahalan and Room, 1974; Clark and Midanik, 1982; Wilsnack et al. 1986). Heavy drinking also decreases with age (Cahalan et al. 1969; Clark and Midanik, 1982; Wilsnack et al. 1986), as was reaffirmed in chapter 5. In the present data, younger respondents scored higher on both dependence and consequences than older respondents. Generally, the pattern was for progressively lower prevalences to be found in progressively older age categories. There

TABLE 6.1
Percentage of All Respondents Reporting Drinking Problems (in percents)

	Dependence			Consequences		
	Moderate Level	High Level	N	Moderate Level	High Level	N
1. Sex						
Men	6.7	4.3	2,075	10.5	5.6	2,083
Women	2.8	1.6	3,119	3.9	1.4	3,120
2. Age						
Men						
18–29	11.0	6.8	615	16.4	10.3	618
30–39	7.0	4.2	504	9.6	3.7	508
40–49	5.9	4.1	304	13.0	7.8	304
50–59	3.6	1.7	233	5.8	3.0	233
60 and over	2.7	2.3	411	4.2	1.0	412
Women						
18–29	4.8	1.6	893	8.5	2.3	893
30–39	3.8	3.2	763	3.9	2.5	764
40–49	3.4	2.7	403	3.4	1.4	403
50–59	0.3	0.2	356	1.1	0.2	356
60 and over	0.3	0.2	679	0.1	0.0	679
3. Race						
Men						
White	6.4	3.9	1,287	9.9	5.0	1,291
Black	9.9	7.3	760	14.0	9.5	764
Other	6.6	6.6	28	17.9	11.1	28
Women						
White	3.0	1.7	1,818	3.8	1.5	1,818
Black	1.7	1.2	1,265	3.4	1.1	1,266
Other	0.0	0.0	36	11.0	0.0	36
4. Hispanic Background						
Men						
Hispanic	5.3	4.0	600	8.3	4.3	602
Non-Hispanic	6.8	4.3	1,475	10.7	5.7	1,481
Women						
Hispanic	1.9	0.5	842	2.0	0.5	842
Non-Hispanic	2.8	1.7	2,277	4.0	1.5	2,278
5. Marital Status						
Men						
Married or living together	4.4	2.6	1,210	7.9	3.7	1,214
Never married	11.4	6.7	477	15.8	9.1	481
Divorced and separated	11.9	10.7	288	17.7	11.0	288
Widowed	9.5	7.7	98	9.4	7.5	98

(continued)

TABLE 6.1 (continued)

	Dependence			Consequences		
	Moderate Level	High Level	N	Moderate Level	High Level	N
5. *Marital Status (continued)*						
Women						
Married or living together	2.6	1.5	1,394	4.0	1.7	1,394
Never married	5.6	3.3	619	6.7	0.9	620
Divorced and separated	2.6	1.7	629	2.7	1.7	629
Widowed	0.3	0.3	477	0.4	0.2	477
6. *Religion*						
Men						
Catholic	6.5	3.8	697	9.2	3.8	700
Liberal Protestant[a]	5.3	3.8	345	10.5	5.6	345
Conservative Protestant[b]	5.4	3.0	781	8.2	3.8	784
Jewish	3.5	0.8	25	0.7	0.7	26
Other	14.8	10.7	223	21.9	15.3	224
Women						
Catholic	2.3	1.2	1,022	3.9	1.6	1,022
Liberal Protestant	2.5	1.6	520	2.9	1.2	520
Conservative Protestant	2.6	1.6	1,381	3.6	1.2	1,382
Jewish	0.0	0.0	32	0.0	0.0	32
Other	7.8	4.2	159	10.8	3.1	159
7. Income						
Men						
$10,000 and under	9.7	6.8	695	16.3	10.0	699
$10,001 to $20,000	7.4	4.7	558	7.8	5.2	562
$20,001 to $30,000	2.1	0.8	319	8.2	2.9	319
$30,001 to $40,000	6.9	3.4	207	8.6	3.0	207
$40,001 and over	7.9	5.5	173	13.8	7.2	173
Women						
$10,000 and under	3.4	2.0	1,435	3.9	2.2	1,435
$10,001 to $20,000	2.7	1.5	698	3.6	1.1	699
$20,001 to $30,000	3.8	2.5	382	5.1	1.9	382
$30,001 to $40,000	3.0	2.1	211	3.3	1.8	211
$40,001 and over	0.0	0.0	165	1.6	0.0	165
8. *Education*						
Men						
Less than high school	6.7	4.0	797	10.7	5.5	801
High school graduate	10.6	7.3	618	13.0	8.3	619
Some college	3.6	2.2	370	9.6	2.5	373
College graduate or more	3.3	1.4	286	7.0	4.4	286
Women						
Less than high school	3.8	1.4	1,259	5.1	2.2	1,259
High school graduate	3.2	2.4	997	4.6	1.5	998

(continued)

TABLE 6.1 *(continued)*

	Dependence			Consequences		
	Moderate Level	*High Level*	*N*	*Moderate Level*	*High Level*	*N*
8. *Education (continued)*						
Women						
Some college	2.0	1.0	560	2.8	1.4	560
College graduate or more	1.2	1.2	295	1.7	0.0	295
9. *Urbanicity*						
Men						
Metropolitan cities 50,000 and over	8.0	4.5	1,113	13.1	7.9	1,118
Metropolitan cities under 50,000	6.7	4.9	575	11.0	5.6	576
Nonmetropolitan areas	5.2	3.1	387	6.9	3.0	389
Women						
Metropolitan cities 50,000 and over	3.7	2.7	1,667	5.6	2.3	1,668
Metropolitan cities under 50,000	1.8	0.4	839	1.9	0.7	839
Nonmetropolitan areas	3.0	2.0	612	4.5	1.3	612
10. *Region*						
Men						
Northeast[c]	6.3	4.7	398	10.2	4.3	399
Midwest[d]	7.2	3.0	342	5.6	2.4	345
Pacific[e]	6.5	5.8	335	10.9	6.7	337
South[f]	6.3	3.7	898	12.4	7.9	898
Mountain[g]	10.1	8.1	102	20.9	8.7	104
Women						
Northeast	2.8	0.5	589	4.0	0.4	589
Midwest	2.1	1.4	533	3.5	0.8	534
Pacific	7.2	5.2	474	7.1	4.6	474
South	1.3	0.8	1,419	2.7	1.3	1,419
Mountain	3.8	3.8	104	5.1	1.9	104

[a] All Protestant denominations not counted as Conservative Protestant (see b).
[b] Includes: Baptist, Pentecostal, Assembly of God, Church of God, Nazarene, Holiness, Apostolic, Evangelical, Sanctified, Disciples of Christ, Christian Reformed, Jehovah's Witness, Seventh Day Adventist, Mormon, Brethren, Spiritual and Salvation Army.
[c] Includes New England and Mid-Atlantic states.
[d] Includes East North Central and West North Central states.
[e] Includes only Pacific states.
[f] Includes South Atlantic, East South Central, and West South Central states.
[g] Includes only Mountain States.

Percents based on weighted data.
Ns based on unweighted data.

were a few noteworthy exceptions. First, women aged thirty to thirty-nine had a higher prevalence of dependence measured at the high level than did women aged eighteen to twenty-nine. Second, the reported prevalence of dependence, and to a lesser extent consequences, dropped sharply for women after the age of forty-nine. Third, men in their forties reported a rather high prevalence of alcohol-related consequences when compared to adjacent groups. This latter finding may indicate that heavy drinking finally "catches up" with men during their forties and precipitates adverse reactions. However, this finding may be a peculiarity of the present data set. It is not supported by other drinking practices surveys (Cahalan and Room, 1974; Clark and Midanik, 1982; Johnson, 1982) though Cahalan (1970) noted a similar effect among lower socioeconomic status men.

The relationship between race and drinking problems was conditioned by gender. Black men reported higher prevalences of dependence and consequences than White men. However, the same was not true for Black women. Since the introductory chapter did not report that heavy drinking was more prevalent among Blacks, one is tempted to offer the explanation that racism causes Black men get into more trouble than White men for the same amount of drinking. Yet, two other analyses of these same data failed to support this supposition (Hilton, chapter 13 in this volume; Harford, Grant and Hasin, chapter 14). Previous surveys have not always been careful to report the relationship between race and drinking problems. Cahalan and Room (1974) reported that race was correlated both with "problematic intake" and "tangible consequences" among men, which seems to have been reaffirmed here.

Problem rates among Hispanic respondents were slightly, but not much, lower than those of non-Hispanics. This was true for both men and women, for both dependence and consequences, and at both the moderate and the high levels. This is consistent with the findings of the introductory chapter, which found the prevalence of heavy drinking to be lower among Hispanics than non-Hispanics. This gives additional evidence that alcohol use is not a more severe problem among this minority community than it is among the general population. This conclusion contradicts Cahalan and Room's (1974) finding of a high problem prevalence among "Latin American-Caribbean" respondents; however, that study included only a small number of such persons. Elsewhere, the literature has rarely commented on problem prevalences among Hispanics, an exception being the work of Caetano (1984a, 1987c).

The relationship between marital status and drinking problems was a complex one. Among men, the highest problem rate was reported by those who were divorced and separated, followed by those who had never been married. Problem rates were much lower among men who were either married or living with someone in a marriage-like relationship. Among women, problem rates were also relatively high among the never married, but they were much lower among the divorced and separated, where they were at levels comparable to those who were either married or living in a marriage-like relationship.

This echoes the findings of chapter 5, where it was suggested that divorced and separated women, many of whom assume the responsibilities of raising children, tend to share the lighter drinking habits of married women, while divorced and separated men, most of whom are free from such responsibilities, tend to take on the heavier drinking style of single men. Other surveys have been divided on this point. Clark and Midanik (1982) found much the same pattern as here but Wilsnack et al. (1986) and Johnson (1982) both reported high problem rates among divorced and separated women.

Problem rates were unusually high among widowed men. This was unexpected both because chapter 5 did not find an unusually high prevalence of heavy drinking among widowers and because other surveys have typically found low problem rates among this group (Johnson, 1982; Wilsnack et al. 1986). However, Clark and Midanik (1982) also found a high problem rate among widowers.

Catholics, Liberal Protestants, and Conservative Protestants had similar problem rates. Problem rates were very low among Jews, as expected (Cahalan and Room, 1974; Glassner and Berg, 1985), although this finding is based on a small number of cases (twenty-six Jewish men and thirty-two Jewish women). Among those classified as "Other" religious preference, problem rates were quite high. This category consisted predominantly of people who specified "no religious preference." These findings are consistent with chapter 5, as well as other surveys reporting on drinking patterns by religion (Cahalan et al. 1969). It is noteworthy, however, that drinking problems, as distinct from drinking patterns, have not been widely reported. Of existing national alcohol surveys, only Cahalan and Room (1974) have reported of problem rates by religious preference, and those results only include men.

Distributions across income categories were complex. Among men, consequences rates were high in both the top and the bottom categories. Men's rates of dependence contained a weaker suggestion of this U-shaped pattern and a surprisingly low prevalence in the middle category ($20,001 to $30,000). Among women, rates varied much less across income categories, except that rates were quite low in the highest income group. Note also that among high income respondents, problem rates were high for men but low for women. This suggests a gender-income interaction that has not been explored in previous literature. The introductory chapter showed that high income men but not women had a higher prevalence of heavy drinking, so these findings are consistent with those achieved earlier.

Education presented a somewhat clearer picture of the relationship between drinking problems and socioeconomic status. For both men and women and for both dependence and consequences, prevalences were higher for the two lower educational categories than for the two higher ones. Also, it was often the case that the second lowest educational category (high school graduate) had the highest problem rates. Consistent with this, the analysis in the introductory chapter found that this same category contained the highest prevalence of heavy drinking.

Previous surveys have not reported distributions of drinking problems separately by income and education. Instead, they have reported a combined index of socioeconomic status, usually only dichotomized into an upper and a lower status group (Cahalan, 1970; Johnson, 1982) although Cahalan and Room (1974) presented a four-fold classification. The consensus of these studies has been that lower status respondents have higher problem rates. The present findings suggest a more complex, non-linear relationship. They also suggest a relationship that is sensitive to the way that socioeconomic status is operationalized.

Problem prevalences were usually highest in large cities for both men and women. Among men, the next highest prevalences were found in metropolitan towns,[1] followed by the lowest prevalences in nonmetropolitan areas. However, among women, the problem rates were much lower in metropolitan towns than they were in the nonmetropolitan areas. One might speculate that it is the conformist lives of suburban women that are reflected in these low rates. This conformity, however, only seems to affect the reporting of problems. These same suburban women did not report remarkably low rates of heavy drinking in the preceding chapter. Previous studies have also shown problem prevalences to be highest in large cities (Cahalan and Room, 1974). The introductory chapter showed that the highest prevalence of heavy drinking occurred in large cities, followed by the metropolitan towns, followed in turn by the non-metropolitan areas.

The regional distributions showed that the rates of both dependence and consequences were very high among men in the Mountain states. In contrast, men in the Midwest reported low rates of dependence at the high level and of consequences at either level. Among women in the Pacific region, rates for both dependence and consequences were very high. Among women in the South, rates for both types of problems were generally lower than in other regions. For the most part, these regional variations reflected the distributions of heavy drinking that were shown in the introductory chapter. However, that analysis did not find that men in the Midwest had a low prevalence of heavy drinking, in fact there were some indications of the opposite. Clark and Midanik (1982) also reported unusually high problem rates for Mountain states respondents, but they found that it was Pacific men rather than Pacific women who reported high problem rates.

Since only those who drink are at risk to report drinking problems, it is also useful to examine problem prevalences computed on a base of current drinkers (those who reported drinking at least as often as once a year). These figures are given on table 6.2. For the most part, they show patterns similar to those in table 6.1. However, there are a few important differences that warrant some discussion.

TABLE 6.2
Percentage of Current Drinkers Reporting Drinking Problems (in percents)

	Dependence			Consequences		
	Moderate Level	High Level	N	Moderate Level	High Level	N
1. *Sex*						
Men	8.9	5.7	1,513	13.9	7.4	1,521
Women	4.4	2.6	1,672	6.1	2.3	1,673
2. *Age*						
Men						
18–29	13.5	8.3	489	20.2	12.6	492
30–39	8.1	4.9	421	11.0	4.2	425
40–49	7.6	5.3	228	16.8	10.1	228
50–59	5.2	2.4	159	8.2	4.2	159
60 and over	4.7	4.0	210	7.3	1.7	211
Women						
18–29	6.5	2.2	571	11.5	3.2	571
30–39	5.5	4.7	467	5.6	3.6	468
40–49	5.4	4.3	215	5.5	2.2	215
50–59	0.5	0.4	171	1.8	0.3	171
60 and over	0.5	0.5	244	0.2	0.1	244
3. *Race*						
Men						
White	8.4	5.1	968	13.0	6.6	972
Black	13.9	10.2	525	19.5	13.2	529
Other	8.9	8.9	20	23.9	14.9	20

(continued)

TABLE 6.2 *(continued)*

	Dependence			Consequences		
	Moderate Level	High Level	N	Moderate Level	High Level	N
3. *Race (continued)*						
Women						
White	4.6	2.7	1,001	5.8	2.3	1,001
Black	3.2	2.3	651	6.2	2.1	652
Other	0.0	0.0	20	20.6	0.0	20
4. *Hispanic Background*						
Men						
Hispanic	6.8	5.2	443	10.6	5.6	445
Non-Hispanic	9.0	5.7	1,070	14.1	7.5	1,076
Women						
Hispanic	3.5	0.9	364	3.8	0.9	364
Non-Hispanic	4.4	2.7	1,308	6.2	2.3	1,309
5. *Marital Status*						
Men						
Married or living together	6.1	3.5	869	10.8	5.1	873
Never married	13.7	8.0	377	18.9	10.9	381
Divorced and separated	15.2	13.6	216	22.5	14.0	216
Widowed	15.7	12.7	49	15.5	12.5	49
Women						
Married or living together	4.0	2.4	764	6.4	2.7	764
Never married	7.8	4.5	380	9.3	1.2	381
Divorced and separated	3.8	2.5	362	4.0	2.5	362
Widowed	0.5	0.5	166	0.8	0.4	166
6. *Religion*						
Men						
Catholic	7.4	4.3	563	10.4	4.3	566
Liberal Protestant[a]	6.4	4.5	271	12.7	6.8	271
Conservative Protestant[b]	9.6	5.3	474	14.5	6.8	477
Jewish	4.0	0.9	179	0.8	0.8	180
Other	17.9	12.9	22	26.5	18.5	23
Women						
Catholic	3.0	1.6	566	5.1	2.1	566
Liberal Protestant	3.5	2.3	339	4.1	1.8	339
Conservative Protestant	6.1	3.7	618	8.5	2.9	619
Jewish	0.0	0.0	124	0.0	0.0	124
Other	9.8	5.3	24	13.5	3.9	24
7. *Income*						
Men						
$10,000 and under	14.5	10.3	464	24.4	14.9	468
$10,001 to $20,000	10.8	6.9	399	11.3	7.5	403

(continued)

TABLE 6.2 (continued)

	Dependence			Consequences		
	Moderate Level	High Level	N	Moderate Level	High Level	N
7. Income (continued)						
Men						
$20,001 to $30,000	2.7	1.0	254	10.6	3.7	254
$30,001 to $40,000	8.4	4.2	164	10.6	3.7	164
$40,001 and over	8.7	6.0	153	15.2	7.9	153
Women						
$10,000 and under	7.0	4.0	639	7.9	4.5	639
$10,001 to $20,000	4.1	2.4	407	5.5	1.7	408
$20,001 to $30,000	5.2	3.5	264	7.1	2.6	264
$30,001 to $40,000	4.4	3.1	148	4.8	2.7	148
$40,001 and over	0.0	0.0	128	2.0	0.0	128
8. Education						
Men						
Less than high school	10.6	6.4	512	17.0	8.6	516
High school graduate	13.6	9.4	472	16.7	10.6	473
Some college	4.7	2.8	285	12.5	3.3	288
College graduate or more	3.7	1.6	242	7.9	5.0	242
Women						
Less than high school	8.5	3.2	488	11.5	4.8	488
High school graduate	4.7	3.5	591	6.9	2.3	592
Some college	2.9	1.4	369	4.0	2.0	369
College graduate or more	1.5	1.5	224	2.2	0.0	224
9. Urbanicity						
Men						
Metropolitan cities 50,000 and over	10.1	5.7	814	16.5	10.0	819
Metropolitan cities under 50,000	8.4	6.2	438	13.7	7.0	439
Nonmetropolitan areas	8.1	4.8	261	10.5	4.6	263
Women						
Metropolitan cities 50,000 and over	5.6	4.1	890	8.5	3.6	891
Metropolitan cities under 50,000	2.5	0.6	492	2.7	1.0	492
Nonmetropolitan areas	5.7	3.8	290	8.4	2.4	290
10. Region						
Men						
Northeast[c]	7.5	5.6	298	12.1	5.1	299
Midwest[d]	8.6	3.6	277	6.8	2.8	280
Pacific[e]	8.3	7.4	262	14.0	8.6	264

(continued)

TABLE 6.2 (*continued*)

	Dependence			Consequences		
	Moderate Level	High Level	N	Moderate Level	High Level	N
10. *Region (continued)*						
Men						
South[f]	9.7	5.8	605	19.2	12.3	605
Mountain[g]	15.1	12.2	71	30.6	12.7	73
Women						
Northeast	3.7	0.7	356	5.3	0.5	356
Midwest	3.2	2.1	334	5.2	1.1	335
Pacific	10.1	7.4	274	10.0	6.4	274
South	2.5	1.5	646	5.1	2.5	646
Mountain	6.9	6.9	62	9.3	3.5	62

[a] All Protestant denominations not counted as Conservative Protestant (see b).
[b] Includes: Baptist, Pentecostal, Assembly of God, Church of God, Nazarene, Holiness, Apostolic, Evangelical, Sanctified, Disciples of Christ, Christian Reformed, Jehovah's Witness, Seventh Day Adventist, Mormon, Brethren, Spiritual and Salvation Army.
[c] Includes New England and Mid-Atlantic states.
[d] Includes East North Central and West North Central states.
[e] Includes only Pacific states.
[f] Includes South Atlantic, East South Central, and West South Central states.
[g] Includes only Mountain States

Percents based on weighted data.
Ns based on unweighted data.

First, among current drinkers (table 6.2), the differences in problem rates between Black men and White men were even greater than they had been when all respondents were examined (table 6.1). However, there were not corresponding differences among women. Second, in the current drinker data, divorced and separated men had even higher problem rates (for both dependence and consequences) than single men. Yet again, there were not corresponding differences among women; divorced and separated women had rates similar to those of married and cohabitating women. Third, religious differences became sharpened by the exclusion of abstainers from the analysis. In the table 6.2 data, problem rates were higher among Conservative Protestants than among either Liberal Protestants or Catholics. This was true for both men and women and for both dependence and consequences, though the effect was not strong for consequences at the high level.

Regarding income, basing the figures on current drinkers raised the prevalence rates among the poorest respondents. For men, this accentuated the already high problem rates among the poorest group. For women, this raised the problem rates so that those in the lowest income group had the highest rates. A similar effect occurred with regard to the lowest educational category. Again, the relatively high prevalence of abstainers in this group meant that problem prevalences were notably raised when abstainers are excluded from the analysis.

DISCUSSION

The findings here have been a mixture of new and old. While many reconfirm the findings of earlier surveys, some have not been reported before. Among the old findings are that men have higher problem rates than women, that problem rates are higher among the young, that married respondents have low problem rates and single respondents have high ones, that Jews have low problem rates, and that problem rates are high in large cities. In most instances, we found that the relationships between problem prevalences and demographic variables were consistent with the results of previous surveys. This confirmed the second of the two general expectations that were raised in the introduction.

Some of the new findings concerned subjects inadequately covered in previous surveys. Among these are the findings on Blacks and Hispanics, which the 1984 survey was especially designed to collect. Problem rates were relatively high among Black men but not among Hispanics of either gender. Another topic covered inadequately in previous studies is socioeconomic status. Here, a separate reporting by both income and education has replaced the previous practice of reporting a combined index of socioeconomic status (usually crudely dichotomized). The result raised more questions than were answered, however, with the findings showing complex picture that remains to be sorted out by future research.

The results generally confirmed the second major expectation given in the introduction, that the distributions of drinking problems would match the distributions of heavy drinking described in the introductory chapter. This was true in a general way for all 10 of the demographic variables that were studied. However, there were some details where the findings of this paper departed from those in the introduction, and these are exceptions to the overall finding. Black men had much higher rates of drinking-related consequences than would have been expected on the basis of their prevalence of heavy drinking. Widowed men had a high rate of problems but not of heavy drinking. Women in metropolitan towns of under 50,000 population had lower problem rates than would have been expected on the basis of their drinking patterns. And finally, men in the Midwest had problem rates that were unexpectedly low, given their rates of heavy drinking.

Finally, these results showed that on some issues, existing surveys are not in agreement. In these areas, the 1984 results are supported by some previous surveys but contradicted by others. One such area is that being separated or divorced seems to have a much different effect on the drinking patterns of men than it does on women. Another is the high rate of problems among respondents from the Mountain states. A third is the finding that men in their 40s reported an unusually high rate of drinking-related consequences. Most of these are matters of detail, and therefore this does not mitigate the more general finding that the relationships established by previous surveys were, by and large, confirmed here. However, they do point to areas where future research would seem warranted.

PART IV.   TRENDS

MICHAEL E. HILTON
WALTER B. CLARK

7

Changes in American Drinking Patterns and Problems, 1967–1984

INTRODUCTION

The single-distribution theory of alcohol consumption is one of the best known theses in the alcohol studies literature. Based on the contributions of Ledermann (1956), Skog (1982a, 1983), and others, the theory asserts that there is a relationship between the average per capita alcohol consumption of a population and the proportion of heavy drinkers in that same population. Expressed dynamically, the theory predicts that an increase in the average per capita volume of consumption will be accompanied by an increase in the proportion of heavy drinkers. Furthermore, it predicts that the increase in the proportion of heavy drinkers will be greater in magnitude than the increase in mean consumption volume. Presumably, there would also be an increase in the proportion of people reporting drinking problems. Collecting data for the consumption side of this argument is relatively easy since government statistics on alcohol consumption are readily available. For example, the rise in per capita alcohol consumption between 1967 and 1984 was 11.8% (Doernberg and Stinson, 1985; Doernberg et al. 1986). According to the theory, this increase should have been accompanied by an even larger increase in the proportion of drinkers who can be classified as heavy drinkers. However, it is much more difficult to observe changes in the relative proportion of heavy drinkers or in the proportion of drinkers who report problems due to drinking. Making such an observation would require that two general population surveys using precisely the same items for measuring intake and problems be administered, separated by a span of several years. Given the cost and time involved, such observations are understandably rare. However, the 1984 national alcohol survey undertaken by the Alcohol Research Group did collect data, about both intake and problems, which are precisely comparable to those collected in a 1967 national alcohol survey (Cahalan, 1970).

Here, we present some data from these two surveys on whether there have been any changes in either the prevalence of heavy drinking or the prevalence of self reported drinking problems. Our purpose is not so much the analytic one of testing the single distribution hypothesis as the descriptive one of providing evidence about possible increases in the rates of heavy drinking and drinking problems at a time when per capita consumption is known to have increased. Since these consumption increases have created the expectation that prevalence rates for heavy drinking and drinking problems have been rising, it might be argued that greater resources should be directed at prevention and treatment efforts. Such policy discussions should be informed by any available evidence regarding changes in prevalence rates, and here we intend to provide just such information.

Similar studies of trends in drinking patterns have generally tended to report that there have been few changes over time. Fitzgerald and Mulford (1981) found few changes in the prevalence of heavy drinking in Iowa between 1961 and 1979, although changes in light and moderate drinking were noted. Most national studies of trends stem from Johnson et al. (1977), a compilation of eight nationwide polls (mostly Harris polls) taken between 1971 and 1976. Clark and Midanik (1982) added data from the 1979 National Alcohol Survey to this sequence of studies, and more recently Wilsnack et al. (1984 and 1986) have added their 1981 results, which focus on drinking patterns among women. Taken together, the series of data accumulated in all three studies shows little change in drinking patterns between 1971 and 1981. Additional literature containing trend comparisons, including those by Room (1983), Room and Beck (1974), and Hilton (1986), seem to confirm this general conclusion.

The present study differs from these previous studies in three important respects. First, it covers a much longer time span than most of the others, assessing changes that have taken place over a seventeen year interval. Second, this study does not measure consumption on the basis of responses about typical or usual amounts of alcohol consumed (as did Wilsnack et al. 1984, 1986 and Johnson et al. 1977). As Room (1977) has noted, high-intake occasions can be masked by responses about typical drinking occasions, and this will yield inaccurate volume estimates. Also, estimates based on volume alone fail to make use of the amount per occasion as a second dimension of the respondent's drinking pattern. Third, the present study examines trends in drinking problems as well as in drinking patterns. Drinking problem items tend to be much less standardized than drinking pattern items, and therefore drinking problem trend studies that use strictly comparable items are especially rare. Finally, we give a caveat to the reader: our purpose is simply to describe changes that have taken place without supplying explanations for why these changes have occurred.

METHODS

Both the 1984 and the 1967 national alcohol surveys used strict area-probability sampling methods, and both asked a set of identical questions about drinking patterns and drinking problems. In both cases, face-to-face interviews of about an hour's length were conducted with adults living in households within the forty-eight contiguous states. By comparing the data from both surveys, we will be able to describe the changes that have occurred between 1967 and 1984.

The 1967 survey was the second wave of a longitudinal study, the first wave having been conducted in 1964 and the results published as *American Drinking Practices* (Cahalan et al. 1969). The second wave was conducted in 1967 and the results published as *Problem Drinkers* (Cahalan, 1970). The 1964 survey did not ask any questions about drinking problems and hence is not discussed here. Only persons aged twenty-one years or older were interviewed in 1964, which means that all respondents in the 1967 survey were at least twenty-three years old. In analyzing the 1984 data, we will similarly limit the analysis to those who were at least twenty-three years old. This exclusion of younger respondents is unfortunate because it is well known that the youngest age categories include relatively large numbers of both drinkers and problem drinkers

The interview completion rate in the 1967 sample was 72% (allowing for losses in both 1964 and in 1967). Those selected for reinterview in 1967 were disproportionally sampled from among heavy drinkers. However, the selection of these heavy drinkers was made according to probability methods, thus permitting reweighting to represent the adult population. In this paper we have weighted the 1967 data set for this differential selection and for the number of adults living within each selected household. These weights were constructed in such a way that the resultant N equals the actual number of people interviewed. Thus all 1967 figures in the analysis to follow are weighted figures, but the N's are not inflated beyond the overall number of people interviewed.

For each of three beverage types—wine, beer, and liquor—respondents were asked who often they drank one or two glasses, three or four glasses, and five or more glasses. From the responses, we computed the number of drinks consumed per month of each individual beverage, and of all beverages combined. To replicate the work done by Cahalan et al. (1969, Appendix I), we used a typology of drinking that takes into account not only the number of drinks consumed per month but also the amounts per occasion. We call this measure "Volmax," and can be briefly described as follows:

1. Abstainers are those who drink less often than once a year or who never drink.
2. Low Volume-Low Maximum drinkers are those who drink less than 17.5 drinks per month and who never have more than two drinks per occasion.
3. Low Volume-Medium Maximum drinkers are those who drink less than 17.5 drinks per month and who drink three or four drinks per occasion at least "once in a while" but who never drink five or more drinks per occasion.
4. Low Volume-High Maximum drinkers are those who drink less than 17.5 drinks per month and who drink five or more drinks per occasion at least "once in a while."
5. Medium Volume-Low Maximum drinkers are those who drink between 17.5 and 44.9 drinks per month and who never have more than two drinks per occasion.
6. Medium Volume-Medium Maximum drinkers are those who drink between 17.5 and 44.9 drinks per month and who drink three or four drinks per occasion at least "once in a while" but who never drink five or more drinks per occasion.
7. Medium Volume-High Maximum drinkers are those who drink between 17.5 and 44.9 drinks per month and who drink five or more drinks per occasion at least "once in a while."

8. High Volume-Low Maximum drinkers are those who drink forty-five or more drinks per month and who never have more than two drinks per occasion.
9. High Volume-Medium Maximum drinkers are those who drink forty-five or more drinks per month and who drink three or four drinks per occasion at least "once in a while" but who never drink five or more drinks per occasion.
10. High Volume-High Maximum drinkers are those who drink forty-five or more drinks per month and who drink five or more drinks per occasion at least "once in a while."

RESULTS

Drinking Patterns

Table 7.1 serves two purposes. It compares the sample distributions of selected demographic characteristics to census figures for 1970 and 1980 and it points out demographic trends in the population that could affect our analysis insofar as they are related to drinking patterns and drinking problems. The two samples were representative of census distributions on most characteristics including sex, region, race and education. One concern, however, is that the 1967 sample underrepresented younger people by 3.2%. This might have the effect of lowering the intake and problem estimates for that year inasmuch as younger people are known to be heavier drinkers and to have higher problem prevalences. Also, the 1967 survey underrepresented men (and overrepresented women) by 4.9%. Since the results presented here are controlled for sex, this underrepresentation should not alter the conclusions reached.

Several demographic trends in the underlying population will have to be kept in mind during the analysis. For instance, levels of educational attainment have increased, with substantially more people having completed high school in 1984 than had in 1967. The age distributions have also changed. Compared with the earlier sample, the 1984 sample had a larger percentage of respondents in their thirties, which accurately reflects population changes due to the maturation of those born during the "baby boom." The 1984 sample also had a smaller percentage of respondents in their forties, who would have been born during the late depression and war years. Since these characteristics are associated with drinking patterns, discovered changes in per capita consumption may reflect only a shift in the age or education distribution of the population. However, by looking at changes that have occurred within various categories of education and age, we should be able to

TABLE 7.1
Comparisons of the Survey Sample with Census Data
on Selected Demographic Characteristics (percents)[a]

	1967 Survey (N=1359)	1970 Census	1984 Survey (N=1904)	1980 Census
Sex				
Male	43.8%	48.7%	46.9%	48.8%
Female	56.2	51.3	53.1	51.4
Age				
23–29	14.0%	17.2%[b]	19.0%	19.8%[b]
30–39	21.0	19.5	24.0	23.5
40–49	24.0	20.8	17.0	16.1
50–59	19.0	18.2	14.0	15.1
60+	22.0	24.7	26.0	25.4
Region				
Northeast	24.0%	24.1%	22.0%	21.1%
North Central	31.0	27.8	26.0	25.2
South	32.0	30.1	33.0	34.0
West	13.0	17.1	19.0	19.7
Race [c]				
White	92.0%	89.3%	88.0%	86.6%
Black	7.0	9.8	10.0	10.9
Other	1.0	1.2	2.0	2.5
Education[d]				
Less than four years of high school	46.0%	47.7%	26.0%	27.9%
High school graduate	27.0	31.1	35.0	37.7
Some college or more	27.0	21.3	39.0	34.4

[a] Source of Census figures: Statistical Abstract of the United States 1982-83. 103rd Edition, U.S. Department of Commerce, 1982. The survey data are weighted figures as described in the text.
[b] Census figures for ages 20–24.9 adjusted to survey age categories of 23–24.9 by multiplying census figure by 0.6 (Stat. Abst., p. 28).
[c] Census figures for Race are ages 18 and older, survey data include those 23 years or those 23 years or older. (Stat. Abst., p. 28).
[d] Census figures for education are based on those 25 years and older. Survey data include those 23 years and older (Stat. Abst., p. 134).

distinguish between trends that have occurred within these categories and trends that have occurred because of changes in the distribution of respondents among categories. Both kinds of changes are real, of course, but they call for different interpretations.

The data indicate that beverage preferences have changed. For wine use, the mean increased from 3.95 drinks per month (SD 14.34) to 6.76 (SD 22.81) (significant at the 0.05 level). For beer use, the mean number of drinks per month increased from 19.36 (SD 55.07) to 24.89 (SD 64.05) (significant at the 0.05 level). A substantial decline in the volume of distilled drinks per month was reported; in 1967 the mean was 14.93 (SD 44.38) while in 1984 the mean was 9.33 (SD 30.19) (significant at the 0.05 level). (All figures were calculated on the basis of current drinkers.) Combining the three beverages into a measure of total drinks per month revealed an overall increase from 38.25 in 1967 (SD 77.36) to 40.92 (SD 81.52) in 1984, a difference that was not significant.

Although these findings correctly indicate that beverage preferences have changed between 1967 and 1984, they do not reflect all of the increase in per capita consumption that took place. The per capita consumption of absolute alcohol from all beverages combined was approximately 2.37 gallons in 1967 and approximately 2.65 gallons in 1985 (Doernberg and Stinson, 1985; Doernberg et al. 1986). This was an 11.8% increase, whereas our survey figures show only a 7.0% increase. We suspect that the questions on quantity of drinks per occasion are to blame for this undercoverage. In the 1967 survey the "five or six" drinks per occasion was the highest quantity asked about. No doubt many drinkers exceeded this amount per occasion, and for these drinkers, the volume measurements obtained must have been inaccurate, which in turn resulted in inaccurate aggregate estimates.

The distribution of the Volmax measure among various age categories and for each sex is shown in table 7.2. The "total" columns on the right of the table compare the two samples, and there we note that there were no significant differences between the drinking patterns of 1967 and 1984. In the second to last column we note that among women the drinking patterns of 1967 and 1984 also did not differ significantly. Among men however (third column from the right) there was one significant difference at the 0.05 level: the proportion of men who reported no current alcohol use was 25% in 1984 as compared to 20% in the 1967 survey.

Within the body of the table there were a few other differences between the findings of the two surveys, but these did not seem to form a pattern. For instance, in the twenty-three to twenty-nine age groups for each sex, the proportion of abstainers was greater in 1984 than it was in 1967. Also, among men aged sixty years or more, the proportion who reported themselves as abstainers was greater in 1984 than it was in 1967. Among women aged forty through forty-nine the proportion of abstainers was significantly greater in the later survey. Because these findings do not seem to form a meaningful pattern and because they are at variance with those of Hilton (1986), we are not inclined to place

TABLE 7.2

Quantity-Frequency of Drinking (Volume-Variability) by Sex and Age for 1967 and 1984 (Percent)[a]

	Men										Women									
Age	23–29		30–39		40–49		50–59		60+		23–29		30–39		40–49		50–59		60+	
Years	'67	'84	'67	'84	'67	'84	'67	'84	'67	'84	'67	'84	'67	'84	'67	'84	'67	'84	'67	'84
Volume-Variability																				
Abstainers	8%	17%*	13%	13%	18%	23%	25%	29%	32%	42%*	17%	27%*	34%	31%	26%	38%*	41%	38%	56%	51%
Low Volume																				
Low Max	12	9	15	12	13	24*	14	11	23	21	25	18	22	24	30	26	30	29	29	32
Medium Max	8	8	15	9	13	10	8	10	5	5	21	15	20	10*	11	7	8	10	3	4
High Max	14	13	12	13	10	6	8	11	3	2	15	12	7	11	8	7	5	4	1	1
Medium Volume																				
Low Max	4	1	1	2	2	2	5	2	6	2	0	1	2	1	6	1*	1	3	4	3
Medium Max	3	3	5	6	3	2	2	4	3	4	10	8	2	5	2	4	2	5	0	2
High Max	19	17	8	14	15	6*	7	5	3	2	7	11	4	7	7	5	2	2	2	1
High Volume																				
Low Max	0	1	1	–b	1	–	7	1*	11	8	1	1	–	1	3	1	2	2	3	3
Medium Max	3	–	1	1	4	–	7	5	5	4	1	–	2	–	2	3	4	3	1	2
High Max	28	30	29	29	23	27	19	22	10	10	4	8	7	10	5	7	5	4	2	1
	99%	99%	100%	99%	102%	100%	102%	100%	101%	100%	101%	101%	100%	100%	100%	99%	100%	100%	101%	100%
Ns	104	193	156	220	180	136	143	123	168	221	92	193	129	243	157	175	106	141	124	258

TABLE 7.2 *(continued)*

Years	Total Men '67	Total Men '84	Total Women '67	Total Women '84	Total '67	Total '84
Volume-Variability						
Abstainers	20%	25%*	36%	38%	29%	32%
Low Volume						
Low Max	16	15	27	26	22	21
Medium Max	10	8	12	9	11	9
High Max	9	9	7	7	8	8
Medium Volume						
Low Max	3	2	3	2	3	2
Medium Max	3	4	3	4	3	4
High Max	10	9	4	5	7	7
High Volume						
Low Max	4	2	2	2	3	2
Medium Max	4	2	2	2	3	2
High Max	21	23	5	6	12	14
	100%	99%	101%	101%	101%	101%
Ns	751	892	608	1010	1359	1902

[a] Percents and Ns are weighted figures.
* Percent difference significant at 0.05 level by difference of proportion test.
[b] Less than 0.5%

much emphasis on these differences. We think it more important to note the commonplace finding in both surveys that relatively more women than men in each age category were abstainers, and that the proportion of abstainers tended to increase with age among both sexes.

We crosstabulated drinking patterns as measured by Volmax against various other demographic categories (not shown). As above, the few statistically significant differences found did not seem to be patterned. Among men in the Northeast, the proportion of abstainers was greater in 1984 (16%) than in 1967 (9%), but not among women (25% in 1984 vs. 26% in 1967). In the northcentral region, relatively more women reported abstinence in 1984 (35%) than in 1967 (25%), but men did not (17% in 1984 vs. 19% in 1967). In the South, more men reported High Volume-High Maximum drinking in 1984 (19%) than was true in 1967 (11%). No such difference was found for women (3% in 1984 vs. 4% in 1967). There were regional differences in drinking patterns in both surveys, notably a greater proportion of abstainers in the South compared to other regions. Within categories of education, relatively more of both sexes who had less than a high school education were abstainers in 1984 than in 1967 (men in 1984: 38%; women in 1984: 56%; men in 1967: 27%; women in 1967: 43%). Men who had completed high school included relatively more abstainers in 1984 (24%) than in 1967 (15%), but that was not true for women (35% in 1984 vs. 33% in 1967). The relation of marital status to drinking patterns was much the same in 1984 as in 1967. One significant difference noted was that 26% of the married men reported themselves to be abstainers in 1984 as compared with 19% in 1967. Among women the only significant difference was that relatively fewer of those who never married were abstainers in 1984 (29%) than in 1967 (48%). There were few differences in religious affiliation between the surveys. Relatively more male Conservative Protestants reported being abstainers in 1984 (40%) compared with 1967 (30%), yet a greater proportion of male Conservative Protestants were High Volume-High Maximum drinkers in 1984 (17%) than were in 1967 (11%). We dichotomized total family income at the median in both surveys in order to provide a comparable measure for both years. The only significant income difference between the two surveys was found among women—among those of higher than median income the proportion of abstainers was higher in 1984 (28%) than in 1967 (19%).

We have focused only on differences between the two surveys and not on the relationships between various sociodemographic variables and drinking patterns. What we found regarding the latter (relatively few systematic differences between 1967 and 1984) suggests that the relationships between these demographic characteristics and patterns of alcohol use have not changed very much over the years.

Drinking Problems

The 1984 survey precisely duplicated fourteen questions on drinking problems that originally appeared in the 1967 survey. The fourteen items can be grouped into two categories; the first can be called "dependence items" and includes: "I have skipped a number of regular meals while drinking," "I have awakened the next day not being able to remember some of the things I had done while drinking," "I stayed intoxicated for several days at a time," and "Once I started drinking it was difficult for me to stop before I became completely intoxicated." The other ten items can be called "problem consequences" and include such things as trouble with spouse, employer, friends, police, and so forth, that were due to drinking in the respondent's judgment. Table 7.3 indicates the problem areas that these items covered. In Cahalan's work (1970) these items were categorized as "tangible consequences" of drinking. The analysis to follow will concentrate on two problem measures constructed from the fourteen items: any of four dependence problems reported in the past year and any of nine problem consequences reported in the past year (one item was dropped from the second measure for reasons discussed below.) Problems must have occurred within the past twelve months to have been counted.

The overall rates of both individual and aggregated problems in 1967 and in 1984 are shown in table 7.3 Between 1967 and 1984 there were statistically significant increases (for either one sex or the other) in the rates of almost half of the individual problem items. The rate for any individual problem was small, however, usually under 5%. Increases in the rates of problems were therefore sometimes quite small in absolute terms. In relative terms, however, a doubling or a tripling

TABLE 7.3

Changes in Rates of Various Drinking-Related Problems, 1967–1984

Percentages of Drinkers Reporting the Occurrence of
Each Problem in the Past Twelve Months

	Men		Women	
	1967	*1984*	*1967*	*1984*
Skipped meals[a]	4.1	10.9*	2.1	6.1*
Loss of memory[a]	4.9	11.8*	3.5	4.8
Couldn't stop until intoxicated[a]	2.4	4.3	0.4	1.1
Binge drinking[a]	1.6	1.1	0.3	0.9
Harmed friendships or social life[b]	2.3	6.4*	2.3	2.7
Harmed marriage or home life[b]	2.8	6.1*	0.6	2.6*
Harmed health[b]	5.8	6.3	6.3	6.1
Harmed work or employment opportunities[b]	0.9	2.9*	0.1	1.2*
Harmed finances[b]	2.2	3.2	0.8	1.5
Had an accident[b]	0.3	0.8	0.0	0.1
Legal trouble other than DUI[b]	0.6	1.1	0.0	0.0
Lost or nearly lost a job[b]	0.0	0.8*	0.3	0.4
People at work told me to cut down[b]	1.0	1.0	0.0	0.0
Physician told me to cut down	3.4	2.0	2.9	0.9*
Any of 4 dependence problems	8.2	18.8*	5.2	8.2*
Any of 9 problem consequences	10.8	13.3	8.0	7.1
Base N *(drinkers only)*	*476*	*666*	*492*	*630*

* Significant at 0.05 level; difference of proportions test.
   All figures based on weighted data.
[a] Indicates items counted as one of four dependence problems.
[b] Indicates items counted as one of nine problem consequences.

of problem rates can be found in the table. As in other surveys "skipping meals" and "blackouts" (loss of memory) were the most frequently reported experiences, and the greatest relative increases also occurred on these items. For "skipped meals" the differences were significant for both sexes; for "blackouts" the difference was significant only for men.

Other differences between the 1967 problem rates and the 1984 problem rates were that "harmed marriage" and "harmed work" were significantly higher among both sexes in 1984, and that "harmed friendships" and "loss of a job" (the latter very rare) were significantly greater in 1984 for men only. Increases in rates were found among most other items as well, but these were not statistically significant. In both survey years, the problem rates were lower for women than for men. This is consistent with the data on drinking patterns, in which relatively more men than women were heavier drinkers in both surveys.

An exception to the general pattern of increasing rates occurred in response to the item, "A physician suggested I cut down on drinking." Here, a lower proportion reported the problem in 1984 compared to 1967 for both men and women, significant for women only. This was the only item for which a significant decrease was noted. Because of the unusual behavior of this item relative to the other problem items, we excluded it from the problem consequences index, not wanting the interpretation of the index as a whole to be confounded by a strongly deviant item. Though conclusions based on a single item are necessarily weak, the findings here raise the question of whether physicians were less likely to advise their patients to reduce alcohol intake in 1984 than in 1967 even though per capita consumption had increased.

A greater proportion of both men and women reported experiencing one or more of the four dependence problems during the past year (p $\square$ 0.05). However, there were no statistically significant differences in the proportion of either men or women who reported experiencing one or more of the nine problem consequences. Thus, the overall picture appears to be one of higher rates of dependence problems in 1984 but of stable rates of problem consequences.

Since the proportion of respondents reporting any of four dependence items increased between 1967 and 1984, it would seem useful to examine the distribution of this change among various demographic categories. Table 7.4 presents data for such an analysis. A higher proportion of women reported one or more of the dependence items in 1984 than had in 1967. However, when this difference was examined within various demographic categories, with consequent reduction in N, no significant differences were seen. The only exception to this was in the western region, where the rate of dependence problems changed from 1.2% in 1967 to 17.0% in 1984.

TABLE 7.4
Percentage of Drinkers in Selected Demographic Categories
Reporting the Occurrence of any of Four Dependence Problems
in the Past Twelve Months

	Men		Women	
	1967	1984	1967	1984
Total	8.2%	18.8%*	5.2%	8.2%*
	(474)[a]	(665)	(492)	(630)
1. Age				
23–29	13.5	31.0*	9.5	18.1
	(73)	(158)	(96)	(142)
30–39	7.5	18.0*	6.0	9.3
	(108)	(188)	(108)	(168)
40–49	7.6	21.9*	5.2	8.4
	(120)	(105)	(131)	(108)
50–59	9.1	8.8	1.2	0.5
	(86)	(87)	(85)	(88)
60+	3.1	9.2	3.3	0.6
	(88)	(127)	(72)	(125)
2. Education				
Less than high school	8.4	21.0*	6.6	12.1
	(192)	(145)	(204)	(115)
High school graduate	7.8	22.2*	2.2	5.7
	(122)	(222)	(152)	(235)
Some college	9.9	16.3	7.2	8.3
	(75)	(125)	(75)	(155)
College graduate or more	6.9	14.4	5.5	9.0
	(84)	(174)	(61)	(125)
3. Marital status				
Married	7.7	14.9*	4.6	5.7
	(418)	(486)	(389)	(426)
Divorced, separated, never been married	13.7	29.0*	15.8	18.5
	(49)	(161)	(49)	(143)
4. Region				
Northeast	9.5	14.1	7.1	5.3
	(135)	(163)	(133)	(169)
North Central	6.5	20.5*	3.5	7.1
	(145)	(196)	(182)	(168)
South	9.8	18.6*	7.6	5.4
	(121)	(179)	(119)	(165)
West	6.5	22.4*	1.2	17.0*
	(73)	(128)	(57)	(127)

(continued)

TABLE 7.4 *(continued)*

	Men		Women	
	1967	*1984*	*1967*	*1984*
5. *Religion*				
Catholic	12.2%	17.5%	7.0%	7.9%
	(144)	(197)	(188)	(209)
Liberal Protestant	4.1	14.9*	4.9	6.6
	(92)	(132)	(90)	(128)
Conservative Protestant[b]	6.7	21.1*	4.3	8.0
	(197)	(240)	(180)	(215)
6. *Income*				
Above median	8.6	20.4*	5.9	9.0
	(208)	(247)	(222)	(263)
Below median	8.1	17.7*	4.8	7.6
	(259)	(381)	(261)	(334)
7. *Urbanization*				
Large metropolitan	12.7	22.3*	6.5	11.1
	(170)	(229)	(188)	(217)
Small metropolitan	6.3	15.2*	2.6	5.7
	(140)	(273)	(145)	(261)
Nonmetropolitan	5.1	19.9*	6.2	8.2
	(164)	(163)	(158)	(152)

* Significant at 0.05 level; difference of proportions test.
[a] Numbers in parentheses are base *N*s.
[b] Conservative Protestant includes the following denominations: Baptist, Methodist, United Brethren, Pentecostal, Assembly of God, Church of God, Nazarene, Holiness, Apostolic, Evangelical, Sanctified, Disciples of Christ, United Church of Christ, Christian Reformed, Jehovah's Witness, Congregational, Seventh Day Adventist, Latter-Day-Saint (Mormon), Brethren, Spiritual, Mennonite, Moravian, and Salvation Army.

Among men, significant differences were found in the younger age categories and the lower educational categories. Of men with either high school or less than high school education, a greater proportion reported a dependence problem in 1984 than had in 1967. A greater proportion of both married and single men reported a dependence problem in 1984 than had in 1967. Regionally, differences in the proportions were significant in the northcentral, southern, and western states. In 1984, higher rates were found among both categories of Protestant men, but differences were especially large among men from Conservative Protestant backgrounds. Differences were larger for those with higher incomes, which is inconsistent with the finding that greater differences can be found at lower educational levels. Differences were significant for men in all three categories of urbanization. However, whereas rural areas formerly had substantially lower rates than large metropolitan ones, they later came to have similar rates of these problems. Thus, these data suggest a general pattern of increase in the proportion of men reporting one or more of the dependence indicators but not in the proportion of women reporting one or more of them.

A parallel analysis of problem consequences yielded few findings of interest (data not shown). Significant decreases in the proportions reporting these problems were found among women in the South and women who were divorced, separated, or who had never been married. Significant increases were found among men from small metropolitan areas and among men who were Conservative Protestants.

DISCUSSION

We have searched for evidence of changes in alcohol consumption and drinking problems between the years 1967 and 1984 by analyzing data from two general population surveys. Since only items that were identically worded in both surveys were included in the analysis, our focus was restricted to a small set of problem items, and these may not be indicative of the full range of drinking problems that are typically experienced. Another limitation is that the survey items did not ask the respondents how often they drank more than five or six drinks per occasion, and we suspect that this is an important limitation on our ability to account for the total volume of alcohol consumed as this is estimated from published consumption statistics. The findings should be viewed with these limitations in mind.

Beverage preferences did change between 1967 and 1984. According to survey responses, Americans consumed more wine and beer but less distilled spirits in 1984 than they did in 1967. For total alcohol from all beverage types, however, the volume of drinks consumed did not change significantly. There were few significant differences in drinking patterns between 1967 and 1984, as these were measured by the Volmax index. An exception to this finding was a small increase in the percentage of men who were abstainers. Other scattered differences were observed when the data were analyzed according to various demographic breakdowns, but these did not fit into a recognizable pattern of change.

With regard to drinking problems, mixed findings were obtained. Little difference was found over time in the proportion of respondents experiencing any of nine problem consequences, but there was an increase between 1967 and 1984 in the proportion who reported experiencing one or more of four dependence problems. More specifically, increases were found for skipping meals because of drinking and experiencing memory losses after drinking. Among men, increases in dependence problem rates were unevenly distributed across demographic categories, especially across: age (with greater increases reported among younger respondents), educational attainment (with greater increases reported among the less educated respondents), and religious affiliation (with greater increases reported among Protestants, especially Conservative Protestants).

Finally, we must comment on the status of these findings as evidence for or against the single distribution theory. On the basis of that theory, increases of greater than 11.8% would have been expected in the prevalence of heavy drinking. Our finding was that there was not a significant increase in the prevalence of heavy drinking between 1967 and 1984. At first glance this might seem evidence that the relationship between increases in per capita consumption and increases in heavy drinking is not necessarily what it has been specified to be under the single distribution hypothesis. But on closer inspection, we realize that the observed increase—from a prevalence of 12% to one of 14% among the total population—was of the expected magnitude. This increase may have failed to be significant only because the sample sizes employed were insufficiently large. Thus, the present findings do not necessarily count as counterevidence against the single distribution theory. Nevertheless, this analysis has been of value since a known increase in consumption has created the expectation that heavy drinking and drinking problems are rising substantially. Though some increases do seem to be afoot, the present findings suggest that they have not been very large.

8

Trends in U.S. Drinking Patterns:
Further Evidence from the Past Twenty Years

INTRODUCTION

Hilton and Clark (chapter 7 in this volume) explored trends in drinking patterns and drinking problems between 1967 and 1984. One conclusion of their analysis was that there had been few significant changes in the prevalence of heavy drinking over that time period. This lack of change was contrary to the expectation that known increases in the per capita consumption of alcohol over that period would be accompanied by increases in the prevalence of both heavy drinking and drinking problems. The purpose of this paper is to broaden the search for trends in drinking patterns by making additional comparisons between the 1984 data and other data sets. Two sets of comparisons will be offered. First, a three-way comparison between 1964, 1979, and 1984 national alcohol survey data sets will be presented. (All three data sets were collected by the Alcohol Research Group and its predecessor organization, the Social Research Group). Second, the 1984 results will be compared against a collected series of data sets, first conflated by

Johnson et al. (1977) and later supplemented by Clark and Midanik (1982) and Wilsnack et al. (1986). (Here, this combined set of data will be called the Johnson series.) This paper also broadens the original findings by including a wider variety of measures of drinking patterns than were used in the Hilton and Clark paper. Whereas the earlier paper rested exclusively on an analysis of a quantity-frequency typology, a variety of intake variables are used here.

The Hilton and Clark study adopted a standard of strict comparability. Only items that were identical in both surveys were included in the analysis. In order to widen the net of comparison, this standard of comparability will have to be considerably relaxed. Existing surveys differ substantially among themselves in both the items used to assess alcohol intake and the procedures by which the responses to these items are translated into consumption measures. Fortunately, the drinking patterns questions used in the 1984 survey were identical to those used in 1964, so that a precise replication of measures is possible over this twenty year period. However, the 1984 items were not at all the same as those used in the 1979 survey nor in the Johnson series (which, furthermore, differ among themselves). Comparing these surveys is only possible through the use of monthly volume estimates that have been computed from fundamentally different sets of items. While the comparability flaws of this procedure are obvious, the question of trends in drinking patterns has been of sufficient public and scholarly interest that such compromises have been offered in previous work, along with appropriate caveats (Clark and Midanik, 1982; Johnson et al. 1977; Wilsnack et al. 1986). The results given here are presented in the same spirit of caution.

One weakness of the Hilton and Clark study was that it compared data from only two points in time. Thus, it was not able to rule out the possibility that prevalences could have risen and fallen during the interval but ended at the same level that they had begun, thus showing no change when beginning-point and end-point are compared. Adding both the 1984 and the 1964 data to the existing Johnson series will provide eleven data points, a much firmer basis for detecting such outcomes. From the point of view of those interested in the growth of the Johnson series, this study has the advantage of being able to place a new data point at both the beginning and the end of the existing series.

The addition of a middle comparison point (1979) to the 1964–1984 comparison will help capture the dynamics of changes in per capita alcohol consumption. As figure 8.1 shows, per capita alcohol consumption rose steadily from 1964 through the mid 1970s and then levelled off. By 1984 it had fallen slightly from its peak level. Given these figures (and assuming a constant rate of abstention), the single distribution theory would lead one to expect to find an increase in the prevalence of heavy drinking between 1964 and 1979 and stability (or a slight decline) in that prevalence between 1979 and 1984 (Skog, 1982a; 1983).

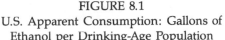

FIGURE 8.1
U.S. Apparent Consumption: Gallons of
Ethanol per Drinking-Age Population

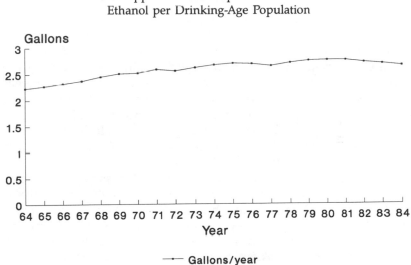

—•— Gallons/year

Source: Doernberg & Stinson (1985) and Doernberg et al. (1986).

Because it examines three points in time, this study parallels Simpura's (1986) analysis of Finnish survey data from the years 1968, 1976, and 1984. As in the American case, Finnish consumption figures rose between 1968 and 1979 followed by a stabilization between 1976 and 1984. The Finnish data generally supported the expectation that these trends in consumption would be accompanied by corresponding changes in the prevalence of heavy drinking.

Existing American research on trends in drinking patterns does not encourage us to expect similar support from the present analysis. The comparison of 1984 and 1967 data in the preceding paper (chapter 7) did not show increases in heavy drinking over that period. A trend toward increased prevalence of heavy drinking among men was discerned between 1971 and 1976 in the original Johnson et al. analysis (Johnson et al. 1977); however, later additions to that series seem to show rather stable rates between 1973 and 1981 (Wilsnack et al. 1986). In Iowa data, Fitzgerald and Mulford (1981) did not find much change in the prevalence of heavy drinking between 1961 and 1979. On the basis of these studies, it was not clear whether the current analysis will show that known changes in apparent consumption have been matched by changes in the prevalence of heavy drinking.

METHODS

Details of the 1964 national alcohol survey appear in Cahalan et al. (1969), while details of the 1979 national alcohol survey appear in Clark and Midanik (1982). Both of these surveys were also national area-probability surveys with face-to-face interviews. In the 1964 survey, the minimum age for eligible respondents was twenty-one years, whereas in the 1979 and 1984 surveys, the minimum respondent age was eighteen years. Given that the youngest respondents are known to be the heaviest drinkers, this inconsistency in age would be expected to exaggerate the size of a trend increase between 1964 and 1979, but not affect the comparison between 1979 and 1984.

Included in the Johnson et al. series were five surveys conducted by Louis Harris and Associates between 1971 and 1974, two surveys conducted by the Opinion Research Corporation in 1975, and one survey conducted by the Response Analysis Corporation in 1976. Clark and Midanik added their findings to this sequence from the same 1979 survey to be used here. Wilsnack et al. (1986) added data from a 1981 National Opinion Research Center survey that included questions on alcohol use.

As indicated above, both the 1964 and the 1984 surveys used a set of indentical questions about alcohol consumption. These asked respondents how frequently they had consumed wine, beer, and liquor during the past year. Respondents had a choice of ten answers, ranging from "three or more times per day" to "less than once a year or never." The frequency of consuming various amounts was measured somewhat differently. Respondents were asked how often they drank "one or two· drinks," "three or four drinks," and "five or more drinks." The response choices here represented *proportions* rather than true frequencies, ranging from "nearly every time" to "once in a while" or "never." Based on answers to the above questions, volume of drinking was estimated according to the system described in Appendix I of Cahalan et al. (1969). This procedure requires that number of assumptions[1] be made in order to translate responses into volume estimates, so that, for example, an average daily beer consumption volume of 4.0 drinks would be assigned to a respondent who reported drinking beer "once a day," and "five or six drinks" of beer once in a while, and "three of four drinks of beer" nearly every time, (Cahalan et al. 1969, p. 214).

The 1979 questions were quite different. They asked "About how often did you drink any wine (beer, liquor) in the past month?" and "When you drank wine (beer, liquor), how much did you usually have at one time, on the average, during the past month?" Volume was estimated according to a technique employed by Clark et al. (1981), which multiplies a usual quantity per occasion by the frequency of drinking and sums over the three types of alcohol (wine, beer, liquor).[2] Both the usual quantity and the frequency were asked for the past month rather than the past year. This "usual amount" method was also used by the surveys in the Johnson series.

Aside from volume, the following consumption variables were used: proportion of abstainers, frequency of drinking, frequency of drinking five or more drinks per occasion, frequency of drinking enough to feel "high," and frequency getting drunk (as self-defined). Abstention was defined as drinking less often than once per year in the 1964 and 1984 surveys, and as not having consumed any alcohol during the past twelve months in the 1979 survey. Frequency of drinking and frequency of drinking five or more per occasion were estimated using the same set of assumptions described in Appendix I of Cahalan et al. (1969) for the 1964 and the 1984 data. For 1979, frequency was obtained by summing the frequency of drinking each beverage (wine, beer, and liquor). In contrast to their general incomparability, the 1979 and 1984 surveys were comparable in asking the frequency of intoxication. Both asked "How often in the past year did you drink enough to feel drunk?" In regard to getting high, the 1979 survey asked, "About how often in the past year did you drink enough to feel high?" while the 1984 survey asked, "About how often (do/did) you get high or tight, on the average?" The 1964 survey did not ask about either getting drunk or getting high, so only 1979–1984 comparisons can be made on these points.

RESULTS

Figure 8.1 shows the trend in apparent consumption over the past two decades. Apparent consumption figures, based on NIAAA's analysis of state-reported sales and tax data, express the total value of absolute ethanol consumed in the country, divided by the population aged fifteen years and older (U. S. Doernberg and Stinson, 1985; Doernberg et al. 1986). Of course not all people aged fifteen years and older are drinkers, and any trend comparison based on these data implicitly assumes a constant rate of abstention (which is generally the case; see Hilton, 1986). Also, such data tell us little about how this consumption is divided among drinkers. Despite these shortcomings, figure 8.1 shows a steady rise in apparent consumption from the mid-1960s through the late 1970s, after which consumption peaked and then began a small decline in the early 1980s. Of special interest are the three survey years. In 1964 apparent consumption stood at 2.23 gallons per capita, by 1979 this had increased to 2.75 gallons per capita—an increase of 19%. But by 1984 consumption had fallen to 2.65 gallons per capita. On the basis of these figures, the expectation would be that survey data will show an increase in the prevalence of heavy drinking between 1964 and 1979 but stability (or possibly a slight decline) between 1979 and 1984 (Skog, 1982a; 1983).

The survey data for 1964, 1979, and 1984 appear on table 8.1. The reader should keep in mind that the comparison between 1964 and 1984 is the more precise since exactly comparable items were used. Comparisons involving the 1979 data are much less precise due to incomparability between the items used there and in the other two surveys.

TABLE 8.1
Selected Measures of Alcohol Consumption in
1964, 1979, and 1984 (in percents)

	1964	1979	1984
1. *Abstainers*			
Men	23	25	24
Women	40	40	36
2. *Frequency of Drinking*			
Men			
Daily[a]	13	17*	12
Weekly[b]	35	35	37
Monthly[c]	20	13*	16
Yearly[d]	10	10	10
Abstainer	23	25	24
Women			
Daily	5	6*	4
Weekly	18	25*	21
Monthly	19	15*	20
Yearly	18	14*	19
Abstainer	40	40	36
3. *Monthly Volume Consumed*			
Men			
More than 60 drinks	17*	14*	21
30.1–60 drinks	15	15	15
15.1–30 drinks	11	15*	10
0–15 drinks	34	32	30
Abstainer	23	25	24

(continued)

TABLE 8.1 *(continued)*

	1964	1979	1984
3. *Monthly Volume Consumed (continued)*			
Women			
More than 60 drinks	4	4	5
30.1–60 drinks	7	6	9
15.1–30 drinks	6	9	8
0–15 drinks	43	40	42
Abstainer	40	40	36
4. *Frequency of Drinking Five or More Drinks on an Occasion*			
Men			
Weekly	18*	14*	24
Monthly	12	16	12
Less than once per month or never	48*	45*	40
Abstainer	23	25	24
Women			
Weekly	4*	3*	6
Monthly	4*	7	6
Less than once per month or never	53	50	52
Abstainer	40	40	36
5. *Frequency of Getting High*			
Men			
Weekly	—	9	9
Monthly	—	10*	14
Less than once per month or never	—	56	52
Abstainer	—	25	24
Women			
Weekly	—	3	3
Monthly	—	6	8
Less than once per month or never	—	51	53
Abstainer	—	40	36
6. *Frequency of Getting Drunk*			
Men			
Weekly	—	2*	5
Monthly	—	5	6
Less than once per month or never	—	69	65
Abstainer	—	25	24
Women			
Weekly	—	1	1
Monthly	—	2	2
Less than once per month or never	—	58	61
Abstainer	—	40	36

(continued)

TABLE 8.1 *(continued)*

	1964	1979	1984
N *(unweighted)*			
Men	*(1,169)*	*(762)*	*(2,093)*
Women	*(1,577)*	*(1,010)*	*(3,128)*

* Significantly different from 1984 figure by difference of proportions test at 0.05 level.

ᵃ Once per day or more often.

ᵇ At least once per week but less often than once per day.

ᶜ At least once per month but less often that once per week.

ᵈ At least once per year but less than once per month.

Abstention rates have been roughly constant across the period, as is consistent with several previous studies (Johnson et al. 1977; Clark and Midanik, 1982; Hilton, 1986). The proportion of respondents reporting daily drinking appears to have risen and then fallen over the three survey years for both sexes. But given that the estimates of the frequency of drinking are especially vulnerable to the incomparability in the measurement techniques that were used, one must be cautious that this trend may not be genuine. Comparing only the first and last surveys, there is little evidence that Americans have changed their frequency of drinking. Volume of drinking did change, however, at least for men. There was quite a noticeable increase in the proportion of men who drank more than sixty drinks a month, most of it occurring between 1979 and 1984. This finding is limited to men, however; data for women showed little evidence of change. One important reason that this volume change was not detected in earlier work is that the previous study (chapter 7) employed a relatively low cut off point for its top intake category (forty-five drinks per month). It could be that most of the increase is due to change in the proportion (or behavior) of those who drink very heavily. Although the proportion of very heavy drinkers diminishes at higher volume levels, the impact of these drinkers on the total amount of alcohol consumed can be substantial given a sharply skewed distribution of consumption. If change occurs only at the higher end of the spectrum, our ability to detect it may be swamped out if we look with cutpoints that are too low.

Since, among men, the volume seems to have risen but the frequency to have remained unchanged, one suspects that the amount consumed per occasion must have risen. The data on frequency of drinking five or more drinks per occasion supports this conclusion. Again, rather noticeable differences are found in the most frequent category (once a week or more often). Also, the differences seem to have occurred primarily between 1979 and 1984. Perhaps even more interesting is that this time the differences are found among women as well as men.

Unfortunately, only the latter two surveys (1979 and 1984) contained questions on the frequency of getting "high or tight" and of getting drunk. The reported frequency of getting high or tight does not show much change between 1979 and 1984, but the frequency of getting drunk does. Reported weekly drunkenness was clearly more widespread among men in 1984 than it was in 1979; among women there was no corresponding increase.

As mentioned earlier, 1964–1984 comparisons are open to error insofar as the 1964 survey did not include respondents between the ages of eighteen and twenty while the 1984 survey did. To take this into account, the 1964–1984 comparisons on table 8.1 were recalculated after excluding eighteen to twenty years olds from the 1984 data set. This recalculation caused only minor changes in the substantive conclusions. All comparisons which were significant in the original table 8.1 remained significant in the recalculated table. In addition, two borderline comparisons emerged as significant when recalculated: the proportion of men who drank monthly fell significantly from 19.5% in 1964 to 15.6% in 1984 and the proportion of men who consumed zero to fifteen drinks per month fell significantly from 33.8% in 1964 to 29.5% in 1984. (Note that in both cases, the percentage figures would round to the same values as appear in table 8.1.) The first difference is not a strong indication of much change in the frequency of men's drinking and the second difference is consistent with the observed increase in the proportion of men drinking at the high volume level.

In sum, an analysis of a broad set of consumption measures shows that there have been measurable changes according to some indicators. Change seems to be most noticeable among men and for measures of the proportion who drink sixty or more drinks per month, who drink five or more drinks per occasion at least once a week and the proportion who get drunk at least once per week (according to self-definition of drunkenness).

Tables 8.2 through 8.4 place the 1984 and the 1964 data within the context of the Johnson et al. series of collected results. The consumption categories used were:

Abstainer Drinks less often than once per year. (Or did not drink in the past 12 months—1979 survey.)
Lighter Drinks less than 0.22 ounces of ethanol per day.
Moderate Drinks between 0.22 and 1.0 ounces of ethanol per day.
Heavier Drinks more than 1.0 ounces of ethanol per day.

The reader should remember, however, that although this uniform categorization of average volume is employed across all of the studies, the questions from which these volumes are calculated were quite different among the various surveys, and therefore the reporting format exaggerates the level of comparability in these data. In conformance with the original Johnson et al. tables, different table formats are used for men and for women.

Table 8.2 indicates that among all men and among all women, there has been little change over the period studied. The abstention rate among women was measured at a relatively low 36% in 1984, and fluctuated between 40% and 45% for most of the other survey years. Among men there was little difference between the 23% abstention rate recorded in 1964 and the 24% rate recorded in 1984. Similarly, the proportion of women who were heavier drinkers changed only slightly: 4% in 1964 to 5% in 1984. Among men the proportion of heavier drinkers was somewhat higher in 1984 than in previous years (21%). Looking across the table within each sex/drinking-category group, there were no cases where a significant linear trend (at the 0.05 level, one tailed) was detected—none had been detected in earlier studies either (Johnson et al. 1977; Clark and Midanik, 1982; Wilsnack et al. 1986). Turning from statistical tests to a simple perusal of the data, there is no clear suggestion that heavier drinking grew more rapidly during the first half of the series than the second half. Thus, known changes in apparent consumption are not paralleled by corresponding changes in the prevalence of heavy drinking according to these data.

Table 8.3 contains similar data broken down by age for women; table 8.4 presents the similar for men. When age categories are examined separately, some interesting trends emerge. Among women aged twenty-one to thirty-four years, there were increases in the proportion who reported heavier drinking (from 4% to 7%).[3] There was also an increase in light drinking among women aged eighteen to twenty years. Presumably, women in the eighteen to twenty year age group are increasingly likely to experiment with light drinking at the same time that women in the slightly older twenty-one to thirty-four year category are more likely to indulge in heavier drinking. An increase in the proportion of women who were drinkers was also noted among women aged fifty to sixty-four.

Among men (table 8.4), there was only one series that exhibited a linear trend across the period, but as with women, that trend was an increase in heavier drinkers among those in the twenty-one to thirty-four age category. However, the data contain an extreme score at one end of the series, the 15% estimate for heavier drinkers in 1964. Had this data point been excluded as an outlier, the linear trend would not have been significant.

TABLE 8.2

Alcohol Consumption in Collected Surveys, 1964–1984 (in percents)

Type of Drinker	SRG 1964	Harris 1971	Harris 1972	Harris 1973a	Harris 1973b	Harris 1974	ORC 1975	RAC 1976	SRG 1979	UND 1981	ARG 1984
Men
Abstainer	23	30	28	25	26	24	27	26	25	24	24
Lighter	31	29	29	24	29	24	27	33	29	29	28
Moderate	30	26	28	29	26	34	26	24	31	29	27
Heavier	17	15	15	22	19	18	20	18	14	18	21
N	(1,169)	(1,084)	(767)	(783)	(783)	(776)	(505)	(1,230)	(755)	(358)	(2,093)
Women
Abstainer	40	42	44	42	47	42	45	39	40	39	36
Lighter	42	40	34	35	32	32	35	44	38	38	41
Moderate	15	13	18	17	17	21	15	15	18	17	18
Heavier	4	5	4	6	4	5	4	3	4	6	5
N	(1,577)	(1,111)	(770)	(796)	(821)	(803)	(566)	(1,340)	(1,003)	(901)	(3,128)

Adapted from Johnson et al. (1977), Clark et al. (1981), and Wilsnack et al. (1986).
Abbreviations: SRG, Social Research Group; ORC, Opinion Research Corporation; RAC, Response Analysis Corporation; UND, University of North Dakota; ARG, Alcohol Research Group (formerly Social Research Group).

* Linear trend, p ≤ .05, one tailed.

TABLE 8.3

Alcohol Consumption in Collected Surveys, 1964–1984, Women Only by Age (in percents)

Age Groups	SRG 1964	Harris 1971	Harris 1972	Harris 1973a	Harris 1973b	Harris 1974	ORC 1975	RAC 1976	SRG 1979	UND 1981	ARG 1984
18–20											
Drinkers	—	65	54	60	66	53	—	70	69	—	66
Lighter Drinkers	—	42	35	31	36	32	—	52	47	—	49*
Moderate Drinkers	—	18	15	18	24	19	—	16	20	—	14
Heavier Drinkers	—	5	4	11	6	2	—	3	4	—	3
N		(57)	(52)	(44)	(65)	(63)		(103)	(52)		(171)
21–34											
Drinkers	70	71	67	62	65	71	68	71	77	70	73
Lighter Drinkers	50	47	37	46	40	36	44	51	46	41	44
Moderate Drinkers	16	18	26	21	22	29	19	15	26	24	22
Heavier Drinkers	4	6	4	5	3	6	5	4	5	6	7*
N	(410)	(360)	(276)	(295)	(223)	(229)	(176)	(396)	(336)	(356)	(1159)
35–49											
Drinkers	68	64	56	63	55	65	57	73	65	72	64
Lighter Drinkers	46	45	38	36	32	34	25	50	39	43	39
Moderate Drinkers	17	14	14	19	17	26	28	19	19	20	19
Heavier Drinkers	5	5	4	8	5	6	3	3	8	9	6
N	(523)	(307)	(210)	(215)	(207)	(207)	(106)	(306)	(242)	(243)	(721)

50-64

Drinkers	51	47	44	43	50	49	48	50	49	52	62*
Lighter Drinkers	33	32	28	24	28	27	40	36	30	37	42
Moderate Drinkers	13	10	13	13	18	18	16	11	16	10	16
Heavier Drinkers	4	5	4	5	4	4	1	3	3	4	4
N	(374)	(224)	(139)	(140)	(186)	(174)	(116)	(312)	(197)	(190)	(519)

65 and over

Drinkers	39	26	42	29	28	36	32	37	40	33	44
Lighter Drinkers	29	19	29	19	22	26	23	28	31	25	31
Moderate Drinkers	7	6	8	8	3	7	7	9	7	7	11
Heavier Drinkers	3	0	5	2	2	2	1	0	2	2	2
N	(260)	(155)	(83)	(94)	(132)	(127)	(111)	(222)	(161)	(111)	(515)

Adapted from Johnson et al. (1977), Clark et al. (1981), and Wilsnack et al. (1986).

Abbreviations: SRG, Social Research Group; ORC, Opinion Research Corporation; RAC, Response Analysis Corporation; UND, University of North Dakota; ARG, Alcohol Research Group (formerly Social Research Group).

People aged 18–20 were not included in the SRB 1964, ORC 1975, or UND 1981 surveys.

*Linear trend, $p \leq .05$, one tailed.

TABLE 8.4

Alcohol Consumption in Collected Surveys, 1964–1984 (in percents)

Age Groups	SRG 1964	Harris 1971	Harris 1972	Harris 1973a	Harris 1973b	Harris 1974	ORC 1975	RAC 1976	SRG 1979	UND 1981	ARG 1984
18–20											
Drinkers	—	77	78	86	77	78	—	82	95	—	84
Heavier Drinkers	—	18	22	31	18	28	—	20	10	—	21
N		(85)	(58)	(71)	(67)	(66)		(104)	(37)		(112)
21–34											
Drinkers	85	84	88	85	84	86	89	85	84	88	83
Heavier Drinkers	15	20	17	26	20	21	28	21	19	25	23*
N	(321)	(280)	(241)	(268)	(230)	(226)	(163)	(401)	(235)	(146)	(787)
35–49											
Drinkers	81	73	76	78	82	80	75	75	73	70	81
Heavier Drinkers	20	18	19	25	22	21	20	19	16	11	24
N	(394)	(231)	(174)	(161)	(207)	(210)	(125)	(293)	(178)	(98)	(529)
50–64											
Drinkers	72	65	64	68	65	72	67	69	69	68	71
Heavier Drinkers	20	16	13	14	20	15	21	22	11	14	23
N	(276)	(234)	(165)	(157)	(166)	(168)	(114)	(256)	(181)	(83)	(343)
65 and over											
Drinkers	62	54	45	46	53	54	36	51	59	69	53
Heavier Drinkers	9	6	6	14	12	5	6	2	8	20	9
N	(172)	(252)	(126)	(122)	(106)	(101)	(68)	(175)	(118)	(58)	(299)

Adapted from Johnson et al. (1977), Clark et al. (1981), and Wilsnack et al. (1986).

Abbreviations: SRG, Social Research Group; ORC, Opinion Research Corporation; RAC, Response Analysis Corporation; UND, University of North Dakota; ARG, Alcohol Research Group (formerly Social Research Group).

People aged 18–20 were not included in the SRG 1964, ORC 1975, or UND 1981 surveys.

* Linear trend, p ≤ .05, one tailed.

Overall, these findings from the expanded Johnson series suggest that if there has been an increase in heavier drinking, as some of the data suggest, this increase has been most pronounced among younger drinkers. Table 8.5 searches further for evidence of change among this group by restricting the analysis to the twenty-one to thirty-four age group and repeating the comparisons previously given in table 8.1. The results confirm that heavy drinking has increased among this age group by showing increases on several measures. Between 1964 and 1984 the proportion of respondents who drank sixty or more drinks per month increased among both men (15% to 23%) and women (4% to 7%). Increases were also detected in the proportions who drank five or more drinks per sitting as often as once a week or more. These increased from 19% to 31% among men and 3% to 8% among women. Self-reported drunkenness showed an increase among men only. The proportion of respondents reporting weekly drunkenness rose from 3% in 1979 to 6% in 1984. As in table 8.1, the results regarding frequency of drinking are confusing. Again they seem to show that among men daily drinking rose very sharply between 1964 and 1979 and fell again by 1984, but again the figures are suspect because of item incomparability.

TABLE 8.5
Selected Measures of Alcohol Consumption in
1964, 1979, and 1984 (in percents)
Ages 21–34 only

	1964	1979	1984
1. *Abstainers*			
Men	15	17	17
Women	30	23	27
2. *Frequency of Drinking*			
Men			
Daily[a]	7	17*	10
Weekly[b]	44	46	47
Monthly[c]	28*	15	18
Yearly[d]	7	5	7
Abstainer	15	17	17
Women			
Daily	3	3	3
Weekly	21	34*	26
Monthly	24	18*	26
Yearly	22	22	18
Abstainer	30	23	27
3. *Monthly Volume Consumed*			
Men			
More than 60 drinks	15*	19	23
30.1–60 drinks	17	17	19

(continued)

TABLE 8.5 (continued)

	1964	1979	1984
3. *Monthly Volume Consumed (continued)*			
Men			
15.1–30 drinks	16	19*	12
0–15 drinks	38*	29	28
Abstainer	15	17	17
Women			
More than 60 drinks	4*	5	7
30.1–60 drinks	6	12	9
15.1–30 drinks	9	11	11
0–15 drinks	51	49	46
Abstainer	30	23	27
4. *Frequency of Drinking Five or More Drinks on an Occasion*			
Men			
Weekly	19*	24	31
Monthly	16	20	18
Less than once per month or never	50*	39	34
Abstainer	15	17	17
Women			
Weekly	3*	4*	8
Monthly	6*	12	12
Less than once per month or never	61*	61*	54
Abstainer	30	23	27
5. *Frequency of Getting High*			
Men			
Weekly	—	14	11
Monthly	—	18	23
Less than once per month or never	—	52	49
Abstainer	—	17	17
Women			
Weekly	—	5	5
Monthly	—	10	14
Less than once per month or never	—	62*	55
Abstainer	—	23	27
6. *Frequency of Getting Drunk*			
Men			
Weekly	—	3*	6
Monthly	—	9	10
Less than once per month or never	—	72	86
Abstainer	—	17	17
Women			
Weekly	—	1	2
Monthly	—	4	3
Less than once per month or never	—	73	68
Abstainer	—	23	27

(continued)

TABLE 8.5 *(continued)*

	1964	1979	1984
N *(unweighted)*			
Men	*(321)*	*(235)*	*(787)*
Women	*(410)*	*(336)*	*(1,159)*

*Significantly different from 1984 figure by difference of proportions test at 0.05 level.

ª Once per day or more often.

ᵇ At least once per week but less often than once per day.

ᶜ At least once per month but less often that once per week.

ᵈ At least once per year but less than once per month.

DISCUSSION

This study has widened the analysis of trends in American drinking patterns by analyzing a larger set of consumption variables than were used in a the previous paper (chapter 7), and by making comparisons against a broader set of survey results than was offered earlier. In doing so, it has been necessary to substantially relax the standards of comparability, and the results must therefore be viewed with appropriate caution. Many of the results show a picture of stability in drinking patterns as is consistent with the earlier study. However, some results suggest that there have been increases in alcohol consumption over the past twenty years. Specifically, the data point to increases in the proportion of the population who drink sixty or more drinks per month (among men), who drink five or more drinks per sitting as often as once per week (among both men and women), and who got drunk as often as once per week (among men). Contrary to the conclusion reached earlier, these findings do suggest that there have been increases in heavy drinking.

Why weren't these findings apparent in the earlier analysis? In that analysis, the cutpoints that were selected to define heavy drinking ("high volume-high maximum") drinking were rather low: consumption of at least forty-five drinks per month and consumption of five or more drinks on *any* occasion during the past year. Apparently, changes have been taking place at the higher end of the drinking spectrum, and these are better seen when higher cutpoints are used.

Given that there have been known increases in apparent consumption, these increases would seem consistent with the single distribution theory of alcohol consumption (Skog, 1982a; 1983). Yet the timing of the increases found in the survey data is problematic. In the three variables where increases are most apparent (volume of sixty drinks or more, weekly consumption of five or more drinks per occasion, and weekly drunkenness) increases appear between 1979 and 1984, a period when apparent consumption was relatively stable. In addition, the data from the Johnson series, as now expanded, do not consistently indicate that the prevalence of heavy drinking grew between 1964 and the mid-1970s and stabilized thereafter.

The Johnson series data suggest that the increases in heavy drinking were concentrated among people in the twenty-one to thirty-four age group. Additional investigation of this age group shows that increases in heavy drinking are measurable on a number of variables. It would be premature to speculate from these cross-sectional data whether heavier drinking in relative youth will be followed by heavier drinking as these cohorts age, but the question should be pointed out as a topic for future longitudinal research.

We know that the prevalence of heavy drinking and the prevalence of drinking problems are linked. Given this, it would seem desirable that future analysis should search for trends in drinking problem prevalences. The earlier Hilton and Clark study found some evidence for increased problem rates, although this finding was based on a rather small set of comparable problem indicators. Again, more substantial results might be achieved through an expanded investigation of the issue. The ability to further explore this issue, however, will be constrained by the lack of comparable items in existing data sets.

MICHAEL E. HILTON

9

Trends in Drinking Problems and Attitudes in the U.S., 1979–1984

INTRODUCTION

Recent findings about trends in American drinking practices contain some evidence that there has been an increase in heavy drinking in recent years, but there is some ambiguity surrounding this conclusion. Apparent per capita consumption statistics show a gradual rise from 2.23 gallons per person aged fifteen and older in 1964 to 2.75 gallons per capita in 1979, after which they leveled off and declined slightly to 2.65 gallons in 1984 (Doernberg and Stinson, 1985; Doernberg et al. 1986). Research based on survey data initially showed no change in the prevalence of heavy drinking between 1967 and 1984 (chapter 7 in this volume), but further analysis was later able to find some signs that the prevalence of heavy drinking had increased between 1964 and 1984, especially for men (chapter 8). The timing of this increase, however, was problematic. There was evidence of an increase occurring between 1979 and 1984, but (a) measures used in those two years are not really comparable and, (b) this increase is inconsistent with the relatively stable behavior of apparent consumption statistics during that period.

These findings lead one to ask whether there has been an increase in drinking related problems between 1979 and 1984. One comparison of 1967 and 1984 data has shown increases in some problems (chapter 7), especially in indicators of dependence, but that comparison was restricted to fourteen comparable items (only four of which were dependence indicators). A comparison of 1967, 1969, 1979, and 1984 data based on eleven common items demonstrated increases in problem rates over the entire period, especially for lifetime problems, but its evidence for increases in current problems between 1979 and 1984 was considerably weaker (Hasin et al., in press). This paper examines data taken over a shorter period (1979–1984) in order to take advantage of the greater number of problem items that are comparable between these two surveys.

In addition to the practical issue of whether U.S. alcohol-related problems are on the rise, there are interesting theoretical issues at stake here as well. Theories of how apparent consumption levels are related to problem levels can be divided into two general perspectives, which might be called the "consumption response" view and the "cyclical" view. The consumption response view predicts that problem prevalences will rise and fall in more or less direct response to changes in per capita consumption (although a time lag is sometimes specified between increases in consumption and the consequent development of certain problems; Skog, 1984). Under this view, one would expect to find a relatively stable rate of problems between 1979 and 1984.[1] Extrapolating the theory from problems to attitudes, one might hypothesize that attitudes toward alcohol should have also remained relatively stable between 1979 and 1984.

A somewhat more complex view is Room's theory of long wave cycles in drinking patterns (see chapter 10). According to this view, consumption gradually rises and falls in cycles whose periodicity is roughly seventy years. At the low point of a cycle, a rejection of anti-alcohol norms coupled with a social forgetting of the problems associated with high consumption levels may propel an upward rise in consumption along with a general liberalization of attitudes and norms around drinking. In time, and as consumption rises, alcohol-related problems also increase, though at a lag. Eventually, mounting problems become a burden to which the society responds by becoming more sensitive to the costs of alcohol use, by strengthening social sanctions against excessive drinking, and by shifting the normative climate toward less permissiveness around drinking. These forces impart an opposite momentum, slowing down the rise in consumption and turning it into a decline. In time, consumption levels fall again to relatively low levels, where the cycle begins again.

Under this theory, the 1979–1984 period represents the crest of a cycle. One would expect to find rising reports of alcohol related problems during this period. This would be more true for drinking related consequences than for dependence measures since the former, being often rooted in objections by others toward the drinker's behavior, are more sensitive to shifts in the public's views about alcohol. If the society is in the crest phase of the cycle, second parties who are aware of or affected by the drinker's behavior might be more sensitive to the existence of problems or more vociferous in bringing their objections to the attention of the drinker.

The cyclical view has implications for attitudes toward drinking as well as for problem rates. During the crest phase, the public's attitudes are hypothesized to become less permissive toward alcohol use and moral sensitivities hypothesized to rise. In order to investigate these hypotheses, data on changes in attitudes toward alcohol use will also be examined in this paper.

METHODS

As reported elsewhere (chapter 2 and Appendix), the 1984 data were collected through a survey in which face-to-face interviews of about one hour's length were completed with 5,221 respondents representative of adults over the age of eighteen years living in households within the forty-eight contiguous United States. The survey was designed to provide samples of Blacks and Hispanics of sufficient size to analyze alcohol use in these minority populations. Accordingly, Blacks and Hispanics were oversampled so that 1,947 Blacks and 1,433 Hispanics were surveyed in addition to 1,841 non-Black, non-Hispanic respondents. A weighting scheme was devised to compensate for these unequal selection probabilities. Weighted data will be used for all percentages and statistical calculations presented here. Sample sizes will be reported using unweighted data.

Details of the 1979 national alcohol survey appear in Clark and Midanik (1982) and Clark et al. (1981). This was also a national probability sample of adults aged eighteen years and over living in households within the forty-eight contiguous states. Interviews were completed with 1,772 respondents.

Nine dependence items and twelve drinking consequences items were common to both surveys. They are reprinted in figure 9.1. Simple summative scales were constructed for both areas, and each index had an acceptable reliability. For the dependence scale, the alpha coefficient of reliability was 0.74 in the 1979 data and 0.76 in the 1984 data. For the consequences scale, the alphas were 0.56 in 1979 and 0.69 in 1984.

FIGURE 9.1
Questionnaire Items Measuring Dependence, Consequences,
and Attitudes toward Drinking

DEPENDENCE ITEMS
1. I have skipped a number of regular meals while drinking.
2. I have often taken a drink the first thing when I got up in the morning
3. I have taken a strong drink in the morning to get over the effects of last night's drinking.
4. I have awakened the next day not being able to remember some of the things I had done while drinking.
5. My hands shook a lot the morning after drinking.
6. Once I started drinking it was difficult for me to stop before I became completely intoxicated.
7. I sometimes kept on drinking after I had promised myself not to.
8. I deliberately tried to cut down or quit drinking, but I was unable to do so.
9. I was afraid I might be an alcoholic.

CONSEQUENCES ITEMS
1. Now I'm going to read you a list of some other people who might have liked you to drink less or act differently when you drank. Did a spouse or someone you lived with ever feel this way?
2. Did your mother ever feel this way?
3. Did your father ever feel this way?
4. I have lost a job, or nearly lost one, because of drinking.
5. Drinking may have hurt my chances for promotion, or raises, or better jobs.
6. People at work indicated that I should cut down on drinking.
7. I have been arrested for driving after drinking.
8. A policeman questioned or warned me because of my drinking.
9. A physician suggested I cut down on drinking.
10. I felt that my drinking was becoming a serious threat to my physical health.
11. My drinking contributed to getting hurt in an accident in a car or elsewhere.
12. My drinking contributed to getting involved in an accident in which someone else was hurt or property, such as an auto, was damaged.

ATTITUDE ITEMS
Now I'll describe situations that people sometimes find themselves in. For each one, please tell me how much a person in that situation should feel free to drink. Just tell me the number that describes your answers.
1. At a party, at someone else's home.
2. As a parent, spending time with small children.

(continued)

FIGURE 9.1 *(continued)*

---

3. For a husband having dinner out with his wife.
4. For a man out at a bar with friends.
5. For a woman out at a bar with friends.
6. For a couple of co-workers out to lunch.

Answer Categories and Coding Values for the Above.
  No drinking. (1)
  One or two drinks. (2)
  Enough to feel the effects but not drunk. (3)
  Getting drunk is sometimes all right. (4)

Attitudes were measured by a series of six items that asked about the acceptability of drinking in a series of social situations. Questions and coding values for the responses are also given in figure 9.1. These coding values were summed to achieve an index score, which again demonstrated a suitable reliability (alpha of 0.83 in 1979 and 0.84 in 1984). The technique is the same as that used in another paper in this volume (although fewer common items are use here than were available there) (chapter 17).

RESULTS

Changes in the mean scores on the dependence index are shown on table 9.1. For all men, the mean dependence score rose from 0.298 in 1979 to 0.406 in 1984. Though small, this increase was significant at the 0.05 level. When age subcategories were examined separately (with consequent reduction in sample sizes) a significant difference emerged for only one group, those aged sixty and over. This difference does not seem terribly important since this group had an exceptionally low mean score (0.047) in 1979 and because drinking problems play so small a role among the elderly.

Among women, there were no indications of significant change in mean dependence scores between 1979 and 1984. Among all women, the mean score increased from 0.145 in 1979 to 0.168 in 1984, which was not a statistically significant change. Furthermore, no significant changes were found for any of the age subcategories that were examined.

Because so few respondents experienced any of the problems asked about, drinking problems scores were heavily skewed, as is typical in research of this kind. Therefore it was thought advisable to also analyze these data by establishing an arbitrary cutpoint (two or more problems experienced) and analyzing changes in the proportion reporting scores above this cutpoint.[2] These results appear in table 9.2.

TABLE 9.1
Mean Dependence Scores in 1979 and 1984 by Age and Sex

	1979			1984		
	Mean Score	Standard Deviation	N	Mean Score	Standard Deviation	N
Men						
18–29	0.547	0.963	180	0.670	1.365	610
30–39	0.361	1.137	149	0.396	1.007	499
40–49	0.215	0.822	106	0.424	1.306	300
50–59	0.157	0.690	119	0.193	0.756	230
60 and over	0.047	0.265	169	0.151*	0.706	410
All ages	0.298	0.857	723	0.406*	1.114	2,049
Women						
18–29	0.203	0.563	277	0.313	0.844	890
30–39	0.202	0.735	212	0.226	0.912	759
40–49	0.272	1.354	136	0.146	0.643	400
50–59	0.100	0.627	139	0.032	0.269	352
60 and over	0.002	0.048	222	0.019	0.278	677
All ages	0.145	0.712	986	0.168	0.694	3,078

* Significant difference of means at 0.05 level; two tailed t test.

This second analysis confirmed that there had been an increase in dependence among men of all ages; the proportion of men reporting scores of two or more rose from 6.2% to 9.6%. Again, however, differences proved hard to detect when the age subcategories were examined individually. The only significant increase among these subcategories was that among men aged forty to forty-nine, the proportion rose from 1.7% (an exceptionally low figure) to 8.4%.

Among women there were again no significant changes in dependence scores. In 1979, 3.1% of all women reported scores of two or more while in 1984, 3.8% of all women reported such scores, a nonsignificant difference. Nor were significant differences found among the age subcategories that were examined.

Consequences scores are presented in a similar manner, with comparisons in mean scores given in table 9.3 and proportions of respondents reporting mean scores of two or more given in table 9.4. Only one significant difference is found on these two tables. In table 9.3, the mean consequences score for men aged thirty to thirty-nine decreased from, 3.84 in 1979 to 0.183 in 1984. Otherwise there were no significant changes. For all men, the mean consequences score was 0.263 in 1979 and 0.227 in 1984. For all women, the mean score was 0.070 in 1979 and 0.066 in 1984. The proportion of men with scores of two or more was 6.4% in 1979 and 5.7% in 1984. The proportion of women with consequences scores of two or more was 1.9% in 1979 and 1.5% in 1984.

TABLE 9.2
Proportion of Respondents with
Dependence Scores of Two or More (in percents)

	1979		1984	
	Percent Reporting	*N*	*Percent Reporting*	*N*
Men				
18–29	11.6	180	16.9	610
30–39	8.8	149	8.5	499
40–49	1.7	106	8.4*	300
50–59	3.9	119	5.6	230
60 and over	1.3	169	3.4	410
All ages	6.2	723	9.6*	2,049
Women				
18–29	4.1	277	7.6	890
30–39	6.0	212	4.2	759
40–49	4.3	136	4.0	400
50–59	2.4	139	0.3	352
60 and over	0.0	222	0.2	677
All ages	3.1	986	3.8	3,078

* Difference of proportions significant at 0.05 level.

TABLE 9.3
Mean Consequences Scores in 1979 and 1984 by Age and Sex

	1979			1984		
	Mean Score	*Standard Deviation*	*N*	*Mean Score*	*Standard Deviation*	*N*
Men						
18–29	0.394	0.856	177	0.401	1.107	603
30–39	0.384	0.898	152	0.183*	0.665	488
40–49	0.169	0.662	110	0.265	0.834	290
50–59	0.162	0.605	116	0.107	0.470	225
60 and over	0.116	0.485	173	0.070	0.335	406
All ages	0.263	0.742	728	0.227	0.796	2,012
Women						
18–29	0.120	0.420	275	0.130	0.563	880
30–39	0.082	0.346	210	0.079	0.410	749
40–49	0.095	0.450	134	0.059	0.344	395
50–59	0.022	0.149	138	0.018	0.140	349
60 and over	0.021	0.204	220	0.004	0.076	675
All ages	0.070	0.337	977	0.066	0.386	3,048

* Significant difference of means at 0.05 level; two tailed t test.

TABLE 9.4
Proportion of Respondents with
Drinking Consequences Scores of Two or More (in percents)

	1979		1984	
	Percent Reporting	*N*	*Percent Reporting*	*N*
Men				
18–29	11.5	177	10.3	603
30–39	7.2	152	4.0	488
40–49	1.7	110	6.2	290
50–59	4.3	116	2.3	225
60 and over	3.6	173	2.3	406
All ages	6.4	728	5.7	2,012
Women				
18–29	3.0	275	2.9	880
30–39	2.2	210	2.2	749
40–49	2.9	134	1.1	395
50–59	0.0	138	0.1	349
60 and over	1.1	220	0.0	675
All ages	1.9	977	1.5	3,048

* Difference of proportions significant at 0.05 level.

Summing up the results of tables 9.1 through 9.4, we would say that there appears to have been a small increase in the prevalence of dependence symptoms among men, though not among women, and that there has not been an increase in the prevalence of drinking-related consequences among either sex. The increase in dependence among men was so small that it is hard to detect when age subcategories are examined separately, with consequent reduction in sample size and statistical power. It is quite important that no parallel increases in the prevalence of drinking-related consequences were found. If changes in problem prevalence are reflective of changes in popular opinion about and sensitivity to drinking, there should have been a greater increase in consequences scores than in dependence scores.

Table 9.5 contains results regarding attitude scores. While reviewing these figures, readers should remember that a higher score indicates attitudes more favorable toward alcohol while a lower score indicates less favorable attitudes. Since these attitude scores are not as skewed as drinking problem scores, it was not thought necessary to add a comparison table showing the proportion with scores above some arbitrary cut-off.

For men of all ages, the change from a mean score of 11.64 in 1979 to 11.19 in 1984 was a significant decrease. Significant decreases were also found for two age subgroups. Among men aged eighteen to twenty-nine, the mean score fell from 12.86 to 12.10, and among men aged fifty to fifty-nine, the mean score fell from 11.12 to 10.44.

TABLE 9.5
Mean Attitude Scores in 1979 and 1984 by Age and Sex

	1979			1984		
	Mean Score	*Standard Deviation*	*N*	*Mean Score*	*Standard Deviation*	*N*
Men						
18–29	12.86	3.06	174	12.10*	2.93	616
30–39	11.79	3.25	149	11.73	2.47	503
40–49	11.35	2.60	108	11.06	2.59	298
50–59	11.12	2.57	114	10.44*	2.49	225
60 and over	10.30	2.66	162	9.82	2.78	402
All ages	11.64	3.02	707	11.19*	2.85	2,044
Women						
18–29	11.96	2.72	272	11.23*	2.58	885
30–39	11.26	2.48	207	10.55*	2.60	754
40–49	10.32	2.84	130	9.91	2.41	397
50–59	10.30	2.54	124	10.10	2.29	353
60 and over	9.21	2.46	193	9.24	2.46	659
All ages	10.69	2.81	926	10.30*	2.60	3,048

* Significant difference of means at 0.05 level; two tailed t test.

Among women of all ages, mean attitude scores decreased from 10.69 in 1979 to 10.30 in 1984. This decrease appears to be concentrated in the younger age categories. Among women aged eighteen to twenty-nine there was a significant decrease from a mean of 11.96 to 11.23, and among women aged thirty to thirty-nine there was a significant decrease from a mean of 11.26 to 10.55.

Overall, then, there is clear evidence of a change in attitude scores. Attitudes seem to have become less permissive toward the acceptability of alcohol, and this is particularly true among the younger respondents of both sexes.

DISCUSSION

The results of this examination of problem and attitude scores in 1979 and 1984 do not seem to satisfy either the consumption response theory or the cyclical theory of how the levels of drinking problems and attitudes toward drinking will correspond to changes in the aggregate consumption of alcoholic beverages. Most of the evidence regarding drinking problems shows stability in problem prevalences between 1979 and 1984. However, there were increases in dependence levels among men. This is inconvenient for the consumption driven view, under which problem rates are expected to be a simple reflection of consumption rates.

However the evidence does not fully support the more complex cyclical view either. The most troublesome finding here is the absence of an increase in the prevalence of drinking related consequences. Such consequences should be quite sensitive to changes in popular attitudes toward alcohol, and should therefore increase during the crest period. Yet, we find little evidence in these data of an increase in consequences scores.

An important caveat must be mentioned. Five years is a fairly short period of time for detecting change in the prevalence of alcohol related consequences. Although no changes have been detected, proponents of the cyclical view might argue that they are nonetheless underway and require a little more time to become evident.

One aspect of the cyclical view did find some support. This was the expectation that attitudes toward alcohol would turn less permissive during the crest period. It is particularly noteworthy that the observed decrease in permissiveness was concentrated among younger respondents. This could signal any of a number of things. First, it could be merely another indication of the greater conservatism of younger Americans in the 1980s as compared to earlier cohorts. But the fact that it was among the youngest respondents that changes toward less permissive attitudes were found, taken in conjunction with the fact that drinking is always heaviest among younger adults is consistent with the view that attitudes are shifting because of an increased experience with and sensitivity to heavy drinking—a crucial moment in the dialectic of the cyclical view. Given this, the lack of an increase in reported consequences to correspond with the decrease in permissiveness is problematic for the theory, and the situation bears watching to see whether consequences rates do eventually rise. Another point that bears watching is whether the less permissive attitudes of younger adults will spread through the process of imitating young "trend setters" or through the replacement of more permissive cohorts with less permissive ones.

10

Cultural Changes in Drinking and Trends in Alcohol Problems Indicators: Recent U.S. Experience

The observation that there has been a change in the American cultural climate on drinking is by now a commonplace in the United States. This perception, however, is not of long standing. As recently as 1982, the general media consensus emphasized an upward trend in "America's boozing" (e.g., San Francisco Chronicle, 1982; Jacobs, 1982). The first signs of a shift in media perceptions appeared in the form of interpretative articles in the urban "alternative press" weekly newspapers in 1983 and 1984, emphasizing the emergence of "public health" interests into public debates on alcohol policies (Fager, 1983; Miller, 1984). At roughly the same time, writers in the business press started to note the effects on production and sales interests of a perceived shift away from alcoholic and towards nonalcoholic beverages (Moskowitz, 1983; Hall, 1984; Business Week, 1985). In the course of 1984, the plight of the liquor industry began to be noticed also in the general news columns of major newspapers (e.g., Leary, 1984; Kleinfeld, 1984). Finally, the major newsweeklies set their seal on the idea of the shifting cultural climate concerning drinking. A three-page article appeared in *Newsweek* on the last day of 1984, and the cover story for the *Time* magazine issue of May 20, 1985 was a five-page spread entitled "Water, Water Everywhere: At Work and at Parties, Americans Are Drinking Less and Enjoying It More," along with associated articles on campaigns against drunk driving and on the fiftieth anniversary of Alcoholics Anonymous (Dentzler, 1984; Reed, 1985). The Time cover carried the legend, "Cocktails '85: America's New Drinking Habits," with an illustration of a filled cocktail glass labeled "Water," "Ice," and—pointing to the lemon slice—"The Fun"). In general, the perception of a "new temperance" spirit has continued to the present (e.g., Butler, 1987; Hock, 1987).

A variety of evidence has been offered in the media concerning the shift in the cultural climate. One strong empirical support, certainly, is the data on per capita consumption of alcohol. Computed on a base of the population aged fourteen and over, the per capita consumption topped out at 2.76 gallons in both 1980 and 1981, and declined in each of the four following years, reaching 2.58 gallons in the most recent year reported, 1985. (Doernberg et al. 1986; *The Bottom Line on Alcohol In Society*, 1986.) Per capita consumption showed a further fall in 1986—recalculated from figures in *Jobson's Liquor Handbook, 1987*. In the statistical series extending back to the end of Prohibition in 1934, there had been no previous sequence as long as four years in which overall per capita consumption consistently fell.

On this basis, one could argue there was a point of inflection for the country as a whole in 1980–1981. But it could be argued that there was also an earlier point of inflection, in terms of a significant slowing of the rising trend, in the early 1970s; around 1971 the gradient changed from a total rise of 23% in 1962–1971 to a rise of 7% in 1971–1980. (Doernberg and Stinson, 1985). In comparison, if the 1981–1985 rate of decline continues, by 1990 the fall from 1981 will be about 15%.

The overall per capita figures mask some significant differences in detail. The flattening-off of spirits consumption came as early as 1969, and since 1979 spirits sales have actually fallen as per capita consumption fell faster than the growth in population (*Jobson's Liquor Handbook*, 1987) The point of inflection for per capita consumption of beer came in 1980–1982, while wine consumption has not clearly stopped growing, buoyed most recently by the advent of "wine coolers." In the traditionally "driest" part of the country—the two South Central regions, stretching from Kentucky to Alabama to Texas—overall consumption went on rising in the early 1980s, while it was falling in the traditionally "wettest" regions—the New England, Mid Atlantic and Pacific regions (Hilton, chapter 17 of this volume). This regional convergence continued a long-term pattern already well established by 1960 (Room, 1974). In the 1984–1985 comparisons, however, the downturn had reached all parts of the country; of the fifty states, only a scattered minority of seven showed an increase between 1984 and 1985, while the figures for two remained steady (*The Bottom Line on Alcohol in Society*, 1986).

Viewed in a broader perspective, these changes in the United States in the last few years are not unique. A few years ago, researchers from seven countries participated in the International Study of Alcohol Control Experiences, studying trends and interrelations in alcohol controls, alcohol consumption levels, and alcohol-related problems in the postwar period (Mäkelä et al. 1981). In all seven societies, which historically had all had a substantial temperance tradition, we found in the period 1950–1975 a loosening of alcohol controls, an increase in consumption levels, and an increase also in at least some alcohol-related consequences, including health problems such as cirrhosis mortality. Writing in 1980, we found evidence that all of the societies were moving into a new era, an era of greater attention to alcohol problems and of stable or declining consumption. Looking at the longer sweep of history in the last two centuries, we began to talk of the "long waves of consumption." By this we meant that in a number of industrialized societies there appeared to be a regular pattern of rises and falls in consumption levels, to some extent linked across societies, and not explainable simply in terms of economic cycles. The periodicity of these waves seems to be about three generations—seventy years or so. In the United States for instance, consumption levels fell in the 1830s from the very high levels of what might be called the corn whiskey epidemic of the preceding years. After building up, they fell again after the turn of the century, reaching a low point early in the period of national Prohibition. With some hesitations and blips, the general trend from the 1930s through the early 1970s was of increasing consumption. That Australia and Britain, which did not experience Prohibition, show roughly the same trends across decades of the twentieth century suggests that what we are considering cannot be explained by any particularistic factor such as Prohibition.

We might propose that these waves of consumption reflect a kind of dialectic social learning process. The increases may partly reflect material changes in alcohol availability: improved production or distribution practices, rising affluence, the shift to a consumer society. They may also partly reflect a societal process of forgetting: when the problem to which a control law or social norm responded diminished two generations ago, it is easy to forget its rationale and to regard it as an anomalous vestige. And there is good evidence that a dialectic of generational revolt may become involved. Psychoactive drugs make a wonderful arena for such symbolic action, and American middle-class youth of the late 1920s and early 1930s, for instance, took heavy drinking as a badge of revolt and of emancipation from the constraints and (as they viewed it) the hypocrisy of Victorian bourgeois morality (Room, 1984b).

As the consumption level increases in any given society; the rates of problems related to drinking also tend to rise, although often with a considerable lag. At the individual level, it takes some years of heavy drinking to destroy a liver, for instance, and perhaps some years for a family or employer to get fed up with the role failures of a heavy drinker. The society's response to the increased problems tends to lag still further behind. For one thing, the build-up of production and distribution will have created vested interests which tend to operate as a ratchet mechanism pushing the trend in only one direction.

In my view, what we are seeing around us every day in the United States are the myriad of small steps by which an open society with a strong tradition of social movements responds to an objectively increased rate of alcohol problems, and eventually reduces them. Whereas the drinking age was lowered in many states in the early 1970s, in every state it has now been raised to twenty-one; teenagers, perhaps as surrogates for the rest of us, are now experiencing a mini-prohibition as a matter of national policy. In the last ten years, alcohol treatment agencies and their caseloads have grown by leaps and bounds, against the general trend of shrinking health and social services during the period. Some 1.3% of respondents to our 1984 national alcohol survey reported having been in treatment or in Alcoholics Anonymous for their drinking in the preceding year (Room, chapter 12 in this volume). The Gallup Poll reports that the proportion reporting that anyone in their immediate family had "ever sought professional help or counseling to overcome a drinking problem" rose from 9% in 1984 to 20% in 1987 (Gallup Poll, 1987). Federal spirits taxes, which had been unchanged since the early 1950s, were increased in 1986, and there is talk of increased so-called "sin taxes" including all alcoholic beverages in the near future. A notable difference between the "antidrug war" rhetoric of 1986 and 1988 and that of the early 1970s is that alcohol is now included in the rhetoric. These are just some of the straws in the changing wind of societal concerns about drinking. At the ideological level, we have moved from an era of "problem deflation" concerning alcohol problems in the 1950s to an era of "problem amplification" (Room, 1984a).

The most visible parts of such a change appear at the level of politics and public discourse. A discussion of alcohol tax levels, the pressure politics of Mothers Against Drunk Driving (MADD), public warning campaigns against the Fetal Alcohol Syndrome, Nancy Reagan's "Just Say No" campaign—all of these easily claim our attention. But in these periods there is also a quieter process of change, of change going on in the hearts and minds of women and men, and eventually— often with backsliding and anguish—in their behavior. We can see this process at work today for cigarette smoking: the decreasing rate of smokers reflects not only social pressures but also personal struggles, often over a considerable part of a lifetime. The "slips" of AA's thought, the "relapse prevention strategies" of cognitive behavioral psychology, reflect how hard it often is to change ingrained behaviors.

Part of this process of change at the individual level is a process of recognition and sensitization. The threshold for noticing untoward effects of drinking drops; one may begin to notice and question norms and behaviors that were previously taken for granted. In a climate of focus on self-control and addiction issues, even relatively light drinkers may begin to wonder if their drinking is really under control.

The present climate has thus brought a renewed growth of mutual-help groups like AA and of other therapies. The rising proportion of women in such groups and other treatment reflects, according to the available data, that men remain less amenable than women to health-seeking concerns and self-control issues, since survey data does not show disproportionate increases in women's drinking. The last five years or so have also brought a remarkable new and rapidly growing phenomenon into the arena of popular concepts of self-control—that is, the Adult Children of Alcoholics (ACA) movement.

Although books related to the ACA movement have been prominent on best-seller lists and at local bookstores for some time, there has been as yet little scholarly attention to the movement. The movement starts from the idea of "co-dependency," an idea which arose from the paraprofessional therapeutic practice in the early 1970s (Martin, 1988). People are recruited to the movement on the premise that everyone in an alcoholic's family has a disease, that problems in the adult life of the child of a parent with alcohol problems are due to unresolved issues from the co-dependency instilled in childhood. As recruits move deeper into the movement, the dependency paradigm is applied to their current life-problems, alcohol-related or not, as is the AA paradigm of twelve steps to recovery.

Although both genders are represented in the ACA movement, women probably predominate in it, just as fathers certainly predominate among the alcoholic parents. Like MADD (it is, after all, not "Parents Against Drunk Driving"), the ACA movement thus carries a cloaked feminist critique of men's drinking and its impact on women. Since much of the initial membership of ACA was in their thirties and forties, it can also be seen as in part a generational phenomenon: these are the children of the "wet generation" of the college kids of the 1930s, a generation who themselves came to adulthood in the period of rising consumption in the 1960s. As ACA movement members turn from their initial reinterpretation of their childhood to the issues of the present-day life, a "fearless and searching inventory" of their own current-drinking patterns is thus high on their agenda. Even those with relatively modest drinking habits by traditional standards may decide that their drinking is not under control.

My hypothesis, then, is that we are living at a historic moment when the rate of dependence as a cognitive and existential experience is rising, although the rate of alcohol consumption and of heavy drinking is falling (A recent comparison of proportions of heavy drinkers in 1979 and 1984 surveys found in the 1984 rates higher; but the comparison is complicated by the differences in the underlying drinking questions in the studies. See Hilton, chapter 8, in this volume). Cirrhosis mortality has been falling in North America for considerably longer than alcohol consumption (A recent Canadian analysis argues that increased treatment provision plays a part in this drop; see Mann et al. 1988), and the rate of alcohol-related driving casualties has also fallen slightly in the 1980s (Zobeck, et al. 1986). Along with these trends, we might expect the prevalence of the physical side of dependence—of withdrawal symptoms and of tolerance—to be falling. More generally, we may hypothesize that, in periods of increased questioning of drinking and heavy drinking, the trends in the two forms of dependence, psychological and physical, will tend to run in opposite directions. Conversely, in periods of a "wettening" of sentiments, with the curve of alcohol consumption beginning to rise, we may expect the rate of physical dependence—of withdrawal and tolerance symptoms—to rise while the rate of dependence as a cognitive experience falls.

What might we expect to be happening at times like the present to the rate of survey-reported "consequences" of drinking, (originally called "tangible consequences" in Cahalan and Room, 1974)—in particular, the social consequences of drinking, which reflect the interaction between the respondent's problematic behavior and the reaction of a family member, friend, or official to the behavior? A conventional "social control" hypothesis would suggest that in the short run they would rise—that part of the societal change of consciousness would be an increased sensitization to others' drinking behavior, which in turn would act as a major mechanism to depress heavy drinking. (Compare the argument in Hilton, chapter 9, in this volume) From observation, we might expect to find such an increase in rates of consequences of tobacco smoking in recent years. But an alternative perspective on processes of social change might put less emphasis on the coercive dimension in change, particularly in the early stages of a cultural turnabout. Blocker (1988) has recently interpreted American temperance history in terms of a series of cycles, with an earlier stage of voluntaristic moral reform and a later stage of coercive reform. In this view, around the point of inflection in behavior we might see a rise in phenomenological experiences of dependence and loss of control without a concomitant rise in external social controls. It might, in fact, be argued that cigarette smoking had this status for well over a decade between the 1960s and 1980s. Of course, such a hypothesis has to set aside coercive movements of the 1980s such as Mothers Against Drunk Driving as not being directed against heavy drinking per se, but only against its specific manifestation in drinking-driving.

Let me turn now to the rather limited and distal quantitative data I can bring to bear on these various hypotheses. It should be clear that the data cannot be said to test the hypothesis of the short-term contrary motion of psychological dependence indicators and other alcohol problems indicators, but only to bear on its plausibility.

Table 10.1 shows the trends in three questions asked repeatedly in the postwar era by the Gallup Poll. While there are some sampling difficulties and other issues with this data, it is useful in showing broad trends in sentiment. The first column shows that acceptance of drinking as "here to stay" in American life has risen in the postwar period, and shows no sign of declining. The second column shows that the proportion of adults who drink at all has varied within a fairly narrow range; consumption levels meanwhile rose by over 30%, particularly in the 1960s. Drinkers thus on the average drink more than thirty years ago. The proportion of drinkers has fallen modestly in the 1980s. The third column shows that there was a sharp rise in the late 1970s in the proportion of respondents perceiving drinking as a cause of trouble in their family, which may be taken as in part an index of the population's sensitization to drinking. This indicator is if anything rising again in the most recent survey.

Table 10.2 shows for selected years changes by demographics in the latter two indicators of table 10.1, and in a question Gallup has asked a few times which is more directly related to self-perceived dependence, "do you sometimes drink more than you think you should?" It will be noted that the increase in perception of drinking causing trouble in their family has been particularly marked for women and for respondents under fifty. The increase also seems particularly marked among the less educated and those with lower income. Broadly speaking, on the other hand, it is those with more education and income who have shown

TABLE 10.1

Gallup Poll Trends, 1947–1987

	Would you favor or oppose a law forbidding sale of all beer, wine and liquor through-out the nation? Oppose	Do you (ever)* have occasion to use alcoholic beverages such as liquor, wine, or beer, or are you a total abstainer? Drinker	Has drinking/liquor ever been a cause of trouble in your family?** Yes
1946	69***	67	—
1947	—	63	15
1948	62	—	—
1949	62	58	—
1950	—	60	14
1951	—	59	—
1952	67	60	—
1954	66	—	—
1956	65	60	—
1957	72	58	—
1958	—	55	—
1959	73	55	—
1960	74	62	—
1963	—	63	—
1964	—	63	—
1966	78	65	12
1969	—	64	—
1974	—	68	12
1976	81	71	17
1977	—	71	—
1978	—	71	22
1979	81	69	—
1981	—	70	22
1982	—	65	—
1983	—	65	—
1984	83	64	18
1985	—	67	21
1987	83	March 66	24
	—	July 65	—

* "Ever" dropped in 1966 and later surveys.

** Wording changed from "liquor" to "drinking" for 1984 and later. (1987 test of each wording with half sample showed no difference in result.)

*** "If the question of national prohibition should come up again, would you vote wet or dry?"

Sources: *Alcohol Use and Abuse in America*, Gallup report No. 265, October 1987; George Gallup, Jr., "Americans are Drinking about as Much as Ever," *San Francisco Chronicle* August 24, 1987, p. 19; George Gallup, *The Gallup Poll: Public Opinion 1935–1971*, New York: Random House, 1972.

the greatest increase in worries about their own drinking. The historical precedents would suggest that this segment of the population often sets trends; we might expect a wider diffusion of this increase in worrying in the future. Although the overall trend for this indicator is confused, there is some tendency for it to have risen since the 1970s.

In table 10.3, we turn to data from the 1967 and 1984 national alcohol surveys on drinking practices and drinking problems. In 1967, the U.S. population was in the middle of the steepest sustained rise in consumption levels in the postwar period, while in 1984, it was in the middle of the longest sustained fall. Results are shown for three indicators: What is sometimes called "frequent heavy drinking," that is, drinking at least five drinks on an occasion at least once a week; a measure of consequences of drinking in the last year composed from nine mainly social problems items; and a measure of dependence symptoms based on four items. Maintaining comparability between the two samples limited the selection of items; the four dependence items used are: skipping meals while drinking, waking up in the morning after unable to remember the night before, having been unable to stop drinking until intoxicated, and having stayed drunk or high for more than a day at a time.

From Table 10.3 it will be seen that for both men and women the proportion reporting a dependence symptom rose between 1967 and 1984 much more steeply than the proportion reporting frequent heavy drinking or consequences. (The comparison in trends between social consequences and dependence symptoms can be seen at the item level for 1967, 1979, and 1984 in the same data-set series in Hasin, Grant, and Harford, in press). So far, at least, the rise in self-perceived problems with drinking has not been overshadowed or even matched by the rise in others' complaints about the drinking. The ratio of those reporting dependence symptoms per frequent heavy drinker is higher for women than for men; this implies that for a given level of drinking, women are more likely than men to notice and report dependence symptoms. In general, all three indicators have risen more among the younger than the older age groups, but the rise is particularly steep in the younger age groups for dependence symptoms. Table 10.4 shows that this is true for both genders. Dependence symptoms have also increased particularly disproportionately in the Western region (table 10.3), and somewhat disproportionately among those with less income and less education.

The overarching conclusion from tables 10.3 and 10.4 is that while frequent heavy drinking rose somewhat for men and women under fifty, and consequences rose slightly for men under fifty, respondents aged less than fifty reported sharply increased rates of dependence

TABLE 10.2
Gallup Poll Questions by Demographics

	Drinks at all					Has drinking/liquor ever been a cause of trouble in your family?				Do you sometimes drink more than you think you should? (drinkers only)		
	1966	1974	1985	March 1987	July 1987	1966	1974	1985	1987	1974**	1985	1987
National	65	68	67	66	65	12	12	21	24	26	32	29
Gender												
Men	70	77	72	72	72	11	10	19	19	35	38	38
Female	61	61	62	62	57	14	14	24	29	16	25	19
Age												
18–29	76*	79	74	68	72	15*	13	24	27	30	43	43
30–49	70	75	74	74	70	11	11	24	26	27	33	29
50+	57	54	54	58	53	12	13	15	22	22	16	17
Education												
College graduate	75 }	83 }	80	86	79	14 }	8 }	17	19	25 }	32	28
Some college			74	68	73			21	26		29	34
High school graduate	70	70	69	64	64	12	14	22	22	27	30	28
Less	51	45	49	50	44	12	13	24	33	29	38	24

Region												
East	83	78	72	74	71	8	8	18	19	23	25	25
Midwest	65	75	70	74	70	8	13	22	22	27	35	33
South	38	51	56	52	52	19	14	22	27	25	34	27
West	77	70	73	68	69	17	15	23	29	34	34	29
Income												
Higher	81	c.80	c.80	86	80	10	c.10	c.18	16	c.27	c.28	31
Upper middle	70	64	73	70	68	10	11	19	24	17	32	32
Lower middle	46	58	61	68	58	16	16	22	28	33	34	22
Lower	41	c.46	50	52	54	5	c.18	28	30	c.28	37	30

* Age 21-29.

** Recalculated from 1974 report on base of drinkers only.

c. Approximately; interpolated from figures for two or three categories.

Sources: *Alcohol Use and Abuse in America*, Gallup Report no. 265, October 1987; George Gallup, Jr., "Americans Are Drinking About as Much As Ever," *San Francisco Chronicle*, August 24, 1987, p. 19; *Alcohol Use and Abuse in America*, Gallup Report no. 242, November 1985; Gallup Opinion Index Report no. 108, June 1974; 1966 Drinking Audit, Gallup Poll.

TABLE 10.3

Heavy Drinking, Consequences of Drinking, and Dependence Symptoms by
Demographics, in Percent, 1967 and 1984 National Surveys

	Weekly 5+ Drinks		Consequences		Dependence Symptoms	
	1967	1984	1967	1984	1967	1984
National	16	20	9	12	7	15
Gender						
Male	26	31	11	14	8	20
Female	7	9	8	9	5	10
Age						
20s	15	25	11	16	12	25
30s	19	22	10	12	7	14
40s	18	23	10	10	6	15
50s	17	17	7	5	5	5
60+	10	8	8	6	3	5
Education						
College graduate	14	21	6	7	6	12
Some college	21	21	11	9	9	13
High school graduate	15	20	7	15	5	16
Less	16	17	12	15	8	19
Region						
East	21	16	8	11	8	12
Midwest	14	23	7	9	5	16
South	13	19	14	13	9	14
West	18	24	10	16	4	20
Income						
Upper	18	22	7	11	6	13
Lower	14	12	12	14	7	17

symptoms—for men under fifty, the rates at least doubled (table 10.4). This effect could result from the dependence measure tapping a different and heavier-drinking segment of the "curve of consumption" than the other two measures. But the fact that the cut-points used for the different measures yield population segments of much the same size makes this unlikely. A more likely interpretation is phenomenological: that people in 1984 are better attuned to recognizing the symptoms in themselves, and to resonating with the language of the questions. On the evidence of these data, the lowering of the threshold for noticing problematic drinking is so far turned mostly inward, rather than being directed at others' drinking behavior; while dependence symptom indicators have risen much more sharply than the proportion of heavy drinkers, consequence scores have not done so.

TABLE 10.4

Change in Three Drinking Measures, 1967–1984, by Age and Gender,
Percentaged on Base of Drinkers Only

	Weekly 5+ Drinks		Consequences		Dependence Symptoms	
	1967	1984	1967	1984	1967	1984
Men						
21–29	30	40	15	20	15	31
30–39	28	29	10	14	8	18
40–49	28	34	11	14	8	22
50–59	28	29	8	11	9	9
60+	14	14	8	7	3	9
Total	26	31	11	14	8	20
Women						
21–29	5	9	8	11	10	18
30–39	9	14	10	9	6	9
40–49	8	12	10	7	5	8
50–59	6	5	3	2	1	1
60+	5	2	7	4	3	1
Total	7	9	8	7	5	10

This paper is of course only a first essay in charting and interpreting the changes and trends in American drinking in a period of flux. One implication is the potential importance for analysis of separating indicators of physical dependence from indicators of psychological dependence. To analyze societal trends only at the level of aggregated measures of "alcohol dependence" or the "alcohol dependence syndrome," as is commonly done in epidemiological work following the current diagnostic categories of psychiatric nosology, risks averaging together dimensions which might well, as we have hypothesized, move in contrary directions at turning-points in the history of alcohol consumption.

Future work is needed to expand on this line of work in several directions. Thoughtful efforts should be undertaken to expand our repertory of drinking-related indicators, and particularly of indicators of the structure and strength of popular beliefs and attitudes concerning drinking and problematic drinking. These efforts, which might usefully involve cross-national collaboration, should be directed both at coding archival and documentary materials, to allow a more sophisticated retrospective analysis, and at defining new indicators which can be collected from now on. Attention should be paid also to the theoretical level: what are the competing theories we can bring to bear on the interpretation of changes in alcohol-related indicators, and changes in the cultural position of alcohol? The simple passage of time will also put us in a better position to understand what is happening. In the limited inventory of full-scale U.S. adult national drinking practices and problems surveys, the most recent data-points are presently 1979 and 1984—dates which bracket the 1980–1982 point of inflection in consumption level. A new national survey sample, to be interviewed in 1989, will allow a more precise charting of trends in a five year period that seems likely to be marked by a steady downward drift in the overall level of alcohol consumption.

PART V. PROBLEMS

WALTER B. CLARK

11

Conceptions of Alcohol Problems

There is no agreed upon operational definition of alcoholism or alcohol dependence, although many have been proposed and no doubt there will be more to come. The choice of one or another of these competing definitions has consequences for epidemiological research because differing criteria yield differing apparent rates of alcohol problems in a given population. Further, the "positive cases" screened out by the use of one set of criteria too often will not be the same ones screened out by others (Clark, 1981). This in turn may mean that the correlates of alcohol problems defined by one set of criteria may differ from those found when using another set. It is not the case that alcohol problems are rare in general populations; quite the opposite is true, as the discussions in this section will document. However, these alcohol-related problems differ in kind, in recency, and in severity, perhaps forming a rough continuum of troubles due to drinking. Researchers have long sought a means of distinguishing between those alcohol problems which will abate and those which are likely to accumulate and worsen with the passage of time—only the latter to be designated alcoholism or alcohol dependence. To date, no theoretically compelling and empirically acceptable set of criteria has come to light, and in fact there may be no distinction to be made except that of degree. A considerable body of epidemiological work, often called the "drinking problems approach," has raised this possibility (Cahalan, 1970; Cahalan and Room, 1974, contain useful discussions of these matters). This introductory note recalls some of the events which led to the current lack of agreement on these conceptual and theoretical questions, and it also provides a sketch of three current, quite different, competing views of the nature of severe alcohol problems.

Following this note, all the separate research reports in this section are concerned with measuring alcohol problems in general populations. The researchers are using the same set of data, but it will be apparent that their views on the appropriate conceptual tools to use are not identical. Researchers with differing views selectively choose among available indicators of alcohol problems, and those selected are given alternative interpretations in their conceptual frameworks. The 1984 national alcohol survey included a broad range of questions about possible problems related to alcohol use, including some which were asked on earlier national surveys. Happily, there is more agreement on the kinds of questions that should be asked in surveys on alcohol problems than there is on the ways in which the resulting data should be used in operational definitions of dependence or alcoholism or problem drinking. Thus, researchers who disagree on conceptual questions, or who construct differing definitional schemes, can still make some use of the same data sets in their work, as they have in the chapters in this section.

The beginnings of the current controversies concerning the nature of alcoholism (or alcohol addiction or dependence) are not to be found in scientific works, but in the views of people concerned with alcohol use and its associated problems (Levine, 1978). Convenience alone suggests that the views of Alcoholics Anonymous be taken as a starting point here. In the Big Book of AA (1939) are contained the early views of this organization, and these views have had great influence on members and nonmembers alike. Trying to make sense of a bewildering inability to drink alcoholic beverages in moderation, they formulated a model that seemed to fit their common experiences. It was obvious to them that they were in some way different from the majority of drinkers who "can take it or leave it" and they suggested that alcoholics differed even from habitual drunks in having been born to lose control over drinking if their life circumstances brought them into contact with alcohol. That inborn trait, which they sometimes referred to as an allergy, implied also that alcoholism was not curable; a nondrinking alcoholic was still an alcoholic, and if he resumed drinking he would continue to experience worsening problems due to drinking. Craving alcohol was thought to be the subjective indication of the objective, underlying condition of alcoholism, and it was this that was thought to compel the alcoholic to drink ruinously. Craving was construed as evidence of a lack of control over alcohol use. The AA organization, then as now, was dedicated to helping its members to permanent abstinence, which was seen as the only alternative to self-destructive drinking.

Jellinek's writings on the nature of alcohol problems has had enormous influence on research and on public policy and popular opinion as well. At the request of AA, he undertook an analysis of some data from questionnaires distributed by AA to its members by means of their newsletter. From this admittedly poor sample and from data from clinical studies, he described the nature and course of alcohol problems as these were represented in his data (Jellinek, 1946; 1952). In 1960 he published "The Disease Concept of Alcoholism" which discussed his thinking at that time. His argument was that some "species" of alcoholism involved loss of control over drinking (although he did not say that this tendency was inborn). Loss of control was marked by unintended and unwanted drunkenness; it was seen as marking a phase in the drinking histories of alcoholics who had developed the "Gamma" species of alcoholism thought to be relatively common in North America. Heather and Robertson's (1981) analysis of Jellinek's thought quotes the following: "anomalous forms of the ingestion of narcotics and alcohol, such as drinking with loss of control and physical dependence, are caused by physiopathological processes and constitute diseases" (p. 12). In this connection, it is important to note that in Jellinek's view, as in AA's, one either was or was not alcoholic.

The great service of Jellinek's work was that what he proposed as the natural history of the disease species of alcoholism led to empirical testing of the characteristics of this hypothesized disease state. This period of the 1960s also marks the beginning of studies of alcohol use and alcohol problems in scientific samples of the general population. In general, the results of research cast doubt on the adequacy of Jellilnek's model. For one thing, the hypothesized fairly regular phases through which alcoholism was thought to develop did not match the results of research, which found relatively little order in their occurrence. For another, the symptoms that were expected to mark the "prodromal phase" preceding the crucial loss of control over drinking did not occur in the expected middle age range. Instead, such things as blackouts, tremors after drinking, and so forth, were most commonly reported by young, heavy drinking men, and this did not match well the experiences of AA members or results from clinical studies of diagnosed alcoholics. Reports of craving alcohol and associated loss of control over drinking were not as stable as expected; instead, these things, like other alcohol problems, tended to come and go over relatively brief periods of time. This, of course, posed a problem for the view that one either was or was not alcoholic.

In short, the expected regularities which would have supported this model of alcohol problems could not be found in general population studies (Room, 1977; Heather and Robertson, 1981). Further, if one counted as "alcoholic" only those cases which closely resembled the alcoholics in clinical populations (or in Jellinek's description of Gamma alcoholism), then there were altogether too few alcoholics in the general population (Room, 1980b, 1977; Polich, 1980). Conversely, if one counted as alcoholic all those who reported any serious alcohol problems, then there were far too many. In general, the indicated rate of alcohol problems in the general population could be made to appear to range from over a third of male drinkers to very nearly zero depending upon which indications of alcohol problems were selected by the researcher, and there was no clear rationale for selecting one set of indicators rather than another.

A further serious problem emerged in more recent years. Loss of control over drinking is a nebulous idea. For instance, if it means only that a drinker began to drink or continued to drink despite a desire not to, then the only evidence that he could not control drinking is that he did not, which is not a helpful observation. Further, as Heather and Robertson (1981) detail, there was accumulating experimental evidence that diagnosed alcoholics often did exercise control over drinking to suit the needs of their circumstances; they could remain sober when necessary, they could limit the amounts they drank in order to make their circumstances more pleasant or convenient. However, that was not always the case among such drinkers or clearly they would not have been in treatment for alcohol problems. The idea of "lost control" came to be replaced by "impaired control" in the thinking of some researchers. Note that this change removes the hypothetical dividing line between alcoholics and nonalcoholics; it is now a case of more or less. Further, as Heather and Robertson point out, there is as yet no objective way to measure impaired control over drinking directly, and thus its correspondence to the physical world cannot be confirmed or refuted.

The idea of a craving for alcohol which presumably underlies lost or impaired control over drinking was similarly subject to experimental trial, although it was and is a difficult concept to operationalize. For one thing, a report of craving alcohol by an abstinent alcoholic which could lead to his taking the first drink is not easily linked to a physiological state of alcohol dependence; it may as easily be attributed to a learned response as to alcohol-altered physiology, and thus does not differentiate between alcoholics and non-alcoholics in any clear way.

Another idea was to see whether a priming dose of alcohol given to diagnosed alcoholics resulted in subjectively experienced craving for more alcohol. If so, a drinker who was able to abstain from alcohol might not be able to control the amount of intake if he began to drink (in AA's phrase, "one drink, one drunk"). However, it is possible that craving following a priming drink might be a psychological effect rather than a physiological one; therefore it was necessary to contrive circumstances where some diagnosed alcoholics would be led to believe they had taken alcohol when in fact they had not, and that others be given alcohol who thought they had none. The nature and outcomes of many such research designs again have been summarized by Heather and Robertson. At best, the results were seen as mixed. For instance, in some studies, diagnosed alcoholics who were duped into believing they had received alcohol were as likely to report craving as others who had received alcohol but who were duped into believing they had not. However, in another, somewhat similar experimental study using alcoholics classified as severely alcohol dependent versus others classified as moderately dependent, and using speed of drinking as a measure of craving as well as subjective reports of craving, there were indications that the severely dependent alcoholics were influenced to drink more rapidly by a priming dose of alcohol, independently of any psychologically induced craving due to the mistaken belief that they had been given alcohol when they had not. However, subjectively experienced craving did not seem to be affected by the real or phony priming dose of alcohol.

Work in this area is still inconclusive, and the debate over the usefulness of such concepts as lost or impaired control continues. As noted, Heather and Robertson's review (1981) provides an overview of these materials. Edwards et al. (1977), Pattison et al. (1977) also contain useful discussions.

Note that in all this, no one is arguing that alcohol problems are not real and serious. Regular, heavy drinking is demonstrably linked to all kinds of physical, psychological and social problems. What is open to question is whether there is an underlying, recognizable condition of individuals which leads them to persist in destructive drinking, and, if so, what its nature may be. As sketched above, by the middle 1970s, the earlier ideas of alcoholism had encountered serious problems from research in both clinical and general population samples. The operational definitions of alcoholism were not capable of clearly delimiting a condition which could reasonably be called alcoholism. Today it is at least fair to say, as Fingarette (1988) has, that researchers no longer accept as useful the disease model of alcoholism as proposed by Jellinek.

In recent years several more modern models of alcoholism have been proposed. Each has its supporters, and research continues, but as yet there is no compelling reason to prefer one over the others. The Alcohol Dependence Syndrome (ADS) was devised in the light of the shortcomings of earlier formulations (Edwards, 1977; Edwards and Gross, 1976). Dependence on alcohol is its focus, and this dependence is seen as existing in degree. Similarly, the mainstay of Jellinek's formulation, loss of control over drinking, is seen as "impaired control" in the ADS. These are important changes; in the new conception there is no longer a division between alcoholics and non-alcoholics, but a continuum of greater to lesser dependence upon alcohol. Of course, this means that in epidemiological research the choice in a cutting point in the distribution will affect both the apparent number of dependent drinkers, and quite possibly the correlates of the now defined alcohol dependence.

In an attempt to limit the concept of dependence to physiological correlates, such things as interpersonal, occupational, or legal difficulties due to drinking were eliminated from the diagnostic criteria (although they are not ignored in the treatment of drinkers). The reasoning behind this change was that such troubles as these will be affected by the drinker's milieu; perhaps what is tolerated in one society will not be tolerated in another. Beyond such variations in responses to drinking behavior, it is thought that there is a core of alcohol dependence that exists in recognizable form in quite different societies (Caetano, 1985).

The ADS was provisionally proposed as a device to stimulate and guide empirical research, which it has done. The lively debate concerning ADS's conceptual and operational usefulness is far from over (Caetano, 1985; 1987e). However, in one form it has been incorporated into the Ninth International Classification of Diseases, and that is a great step toward wide acceptance for purposes of epidemiological research.

A second, competing potential replacement for the older medical model of alcoholism has roots in psychiatric research in the United States. Its most recent formulation can be seen in the Diagnostic and Statistical Manual of the American Psychiatric Association. There are two recent formulations (DSM-III and DSM-III-R) which differ from each other; both differ greatly from the earlier DSM-II. The particular concern here is with the diagnostic criteria for "alcohol dependency"— which is not to be confused with the Alcohol Dependence Syndrome's operationalized definition mentioned above.

In fact, the differences between DSM-III and ADS are important and striking. First, DSM-III conceptualizes dependence as being either present or absent, while, as noted, ADS sees dependence as being a continuous variable. Also, the DSM-III requires there to be a drink-induced impairment of social functioning for a diagnosis of dependence to be made, while, as noted, ADS would exclude such problems from consideration in assessing dependence.

Even greater differences between these two approaches can be seen when the comparisons are made between specific questions asked of respondents in the application of these research instruments. Questionnaire items found in the one are missing from the other, and similar items are categorized differently and assigned different meanings. Despite recent attempts to reconcile differences between the two conceptual frameworks, (that is, with the introduction of DSM-III-R) one reviewer convincingly demonstrates that no bridge has been built (Caetano, 1985; 1987e).

A very different conception of alcoholism can be seen in the work of George Vaillant. His medical model differs from those above chiefly by not making a measure of alcohol dependence its central concern. Vaillant (1983) reports the results of a long-term prospective study of alcohol use and alcohol problems among two groups of men. One study group consisted of men from the central areas of a city; many of these men were boys of disadvantaged circumstances when in their early teens the study began. The other group was drawn from young men students in a university who were doing well in their studies, and who were judged to have no serious physical or mental impairments at the time. Thus, these study groups were not representative of any population, but were quite diverse in their backgrounds and economic circumstances. However, these study groups did provide the great advantage of prospective study of the emergence and course of drinking problems, and a rare advantage that is. Members of both groups were interviewed periodically from adolescence through middle age, thus to provide information on alcohol problems as these emerged, developed or were remitted over the years.

Vaillant, both researcher and clinician, found reason to dismiss as oversimplified the earlier, rigid views of alcoholism as a unitary and progressive disease with identifiable stages. But he also rejects the view that no pattern of progressive alcoholism can be seen. It can be seen, he argues, among those drinkers who are the most troubled with alcohol problems even though these people differ only in degree from those drinkers with fewer alcohol-related problems. A great enough degree of difference may be a difference of kind even if there is no particular dividing line between greater and lesser degree. In his data, patients with many alcohol problems at one time were apt to have alcohol problems at a later time—but not necessarily the same problems. In this finding, he suggests, is a way of making sense of the shifting, here-again-gone-again patterns of alcohol problems seen in general population studies. Reports of alcohol dependence or apparent loss of control over drinking did not reliably separate those drinkers who would continue to have drinking problems from those who would not. Thus, Vaillant's conception of alcoholism is that it is the upper end of a distribution of number of alcohol problems at a given time, and neither dependence nor loss of control are given priority over other problems.

This model of alcohol problems obviously differs as greatly from the two others sketched above as they differ from each other. For the foreseeable future, alcohol researchers will have to choose between these or other competing schemes, or they may incorporate a wide variety of questions about drinking problems in their questionnaires so that the various conceptual models can be compared. To the extent possible, the 1984 survey did include a wide range of such questions. In the separate discussions of the nature and relationships among drinking problems which follow, some of the conceptual questions and problems noted above can be seen. These discussions reflect the differing viewpoints of their authors, made all the more interesting by the fact that all analyses made use of the same data set which is representative of the adult U.S. household population.

12

The U.S. General Population's Experiences with Responses to Alcohol Problems

INTRODUCTION

This paper considers the experiences of the general population with responses to alcohol problems, drawing on the 1984 national alcohol survey of the U.S. adult household population. Our focus here is not on drinking practices, attitudes and problems; the survey's results on these dimensions are conveyed in other papers in this volume (e.g., Hilton, chapters 5 and 6; Hilton & Clark, chapter 7). Rather, we are concerned with interactions where someone's drinking—the respondent's or someone else's—is defined as problematic, and is being responded to as such. In sociological terms, we are concerned with what the respondents can tell us about the processes of social control of drinking and of its labeling.

We may roughly divide these responses to alcohol problems into "formal" and "informal." By formal responses we mean interactions between the drinker and community agencies—for instance, an arrest by the police, a stay in a hospital, counseling sessions in a social work agency, a treatment episode in an alcohol treatment agency. In this paper, we are focusing on those formal responses which may be considered, in a broad sense, to be treatment for alcohol problems. Despite the growth in the treatment system for alcohol problems in the United States, and the partial decriminalization of public drunkenness, treatment responses in the United States are still overshadowed in numbers by police responses—in particular, by arrests for alcohol-specific crimes such as drinking driving and public drunkenness. In recent years, formal responses have increasingly taken the form of an arrest followed by diversion for alcohol treatment (Weisner & Room, 1984).

By informal responses, we mean the responses of the drinker's family, friends or acquaintances. "The troubled drinker exists in a society, and that society will respond to him through the actions of varieties of important noninstitutionalized persons such as his family, his neighbors, his employers, and the man at the bus stop" (Edwards, 1973, p. 133). Such informal responses to others' drinking may be expected to be much more frequent than formal responses by community agencies. There is an enormous range in the intensity of such responses, from a lifted eyebrow to a prolonged interpersonal struggle or a decisive break in relations. Such informal responses can be viewed from a number of different perspectives. The more intensive responses may be viewed as a form of "home treatment" (Mann, 1950; Wiseman, 1976)—responses to which Alanon and other mutual-help groups have long directed their attention. In some perspectives, those reacting to the heavy drinker are seen as themselves having a form of disease, "co-alcoholism" or "co-dependence" (Schaef, 1986). From a sociological perspective, family members and friends may be seen as free-lance agents of social control, endeavoring to exercise control over each other's behavior, and particularly over each other's drinking behavior (Holmila, 1987). An approach attuned to social ideologies might notice that alcohol issues are a readily available discourse for expressing interpersonal complaints in our culture, so that there is potentially some element of convention in complaints within the family about a member's drinking. In the context of studies of "drinking-related problems" in the general population, complaints about drinking or suggestions that the respondent cut down have been a mainstay of "drinking problems" or "tangible consequences" scores; that is, the complaints of others have been taken as in themselves constituting a "drinking problem" for the respondent (see discussion in Cahalan & Room, 1974).

Still rather little is known quantitatively about the dimensions of informal and formal responses to drinking in the population at large, and about the relation between informal and formal responses (see Weisner 1987b for a relevant review). From drinking history studies of clinical populations, we know that coming into treatment often occurs relatively late in a lengthy process, after the drinker has exhausted the patience of and strained connections with relatives and friends. Evidence from clinical settings suggests that drinkers' relatives often play a crucial part in induction into formal treatment; Corrigan's study (1974) is typical in finding that callers to a referral service were more often calling about someone else's drinking than about their own. Studying the role of alcohol-related events in induction into treatment, Weisner (1987a) found that when the event produced treatment suggestions from relatives and friends it was especially likely to play a major role in the respondent's coming into treatment. Relatives often turn to the treatment system, indeed, in search of backing for their definition of the situation and thus for their efforts at social control of the drinker (Wiseman, 1976).

In the light of such studies, we may hypothesize that entry into the alcohol treatment system, at least for those residing in households, usually follows on and reflects the failure of previous attempts at informal social control of the drinker. An exception to this might occur for drinking drivers and others diverted into treatment following arrests, since the arrest will often be unrelated to efforts at informal social control. Even here, however, Weisner's analysis (1987a) suggests that relatives and friends often play a part in the decision to come into treatment.

METHODS

Questions asked in the 1984 national alcohol survey provide a first opportunity to examine from a general population perspective informal and formal responses to drinking and their relationships. Respondents were read "a list of some other people who might have liked you to drink less or to act differently when you drank." For each category of person, they were asked whether "this person ever felt this way," "did that break up your relationship with that person or threaten to break it?," and "did this happen in the last twelve months?" Respondents were next asked, "have you ever talked about an alcohol problem of your own with anyone?" Those answering affirmatively were read a list of categories of people they might have talked to, including "a doctor," "a priest, minister or rabbi," and "your supervisor or any other fellow worker" as well as categories of relatives and friends, and further asked if this had happened in the last twelve months. Respondents were then asked, "have you ever gone to anyone—a physician, AA, a treatment agency, anyone at all—for a problem related in any way to your drinking?" Those answering "yes" were then read "a list of community agencies and professions" and asked if they had "ever gone there about a drinking problem," and if so "how long ago was the last contact?"

Respondents were asked a few further questions elsewhere in the questionnaire about their experiences with informal social control, either at the giving or at the receiving end. Notably, they were asked "some questions about your reactions to other people's drinking. Have you ever said something about their drinking or suggested that they cut down?" Respondents giving a positive answer were asked how such persons were related to them, and whether the respondent had said something to anyone in the last twelve months.

Since the national sample survey of the general population was integrated with national sample surveys of the Black and Hispanic subpopulations of the United States, a large total number of interviews—5,221—were completed, but this total sample includes a heavy overrepresentation of the Black and Hispanic populations (the sampling strategy is discussed in Santos, the Appendix to this volume). Sample weightings were therefore assigned to each respondent to reconstruct a national random sample, with the weighted sample size—2,176—keyed to the numbers which would be in an equivalent simple random sample. For this effective sample size, the margin of sampling tolerance (95% confidence level) is about 2–3% each way: particularly for rare characteristics such as current treatment, thus, the proportion of respondents reporting the characteristic is a best estimate rather than an exact proportion of the population. Percentages in the tables in this paper are based on weighted data, while the base numbers are given unweighted.

The primary emphasis in this paper is on mapping the magnitude and outlines of responses to others' drinking for the society as a whole. While attention is given to patterns in the last 12 months, many of the results are reported on a lifetime basis; this means, of course, that the different events and conditions cross-tabulated may have occurred at different points in the respondent's lifetime.

RESULTS

Experience of Treatment for Alcohol Problems

On a lifetime basis, 3.4% of the sample reported that they had gone to an agency, program or professional for a problem related to their drinking (table 12.1, part A). About equal numbers had been in only one and in more than one type of treatment; those who had been in several types, however, pulled the mean number of types of treatment experienced on a lifetime basis up to 2.1.

TABLE 12.1
Experience of Treatment for Alcohol Problems:
Lifetime and Current (within last year)*

"Have you ever gone to anyone—a physician, AA, a treatment agency, anyone at all—for a problem in any way related to your drinking?"

A. *Number of types of treatment in the time periods:*

	Current	Lifetime
None	98.7%	96.6%
One	0.7	1.7
Two or more	0.6	1.7
Mean number of types of treatment among those treated in the time period	2.6	2.1
(*Unwt.* N *treated*)	(58)	(149)

B. *"I am going to read you a list of community agencies and professions. For each one, please tell me if you have gone there about a drinking problem...":*

	Current	Lifetime
General hospitals	0.3%	0.9%
Health or mental programs	0.4	0.7
Mental hospitals	0.1	0.2
A medical group or private physician	0.4	1.0
Social welfare department	0.2	0.4
Alcoholics Anonymous	0.8	2.0
Some other alcoholism program	0.3	1.0
Vocational rehabilitation program...	0.2	0.4
Some other agency or professional person	0.1	0.5

*Weighted data (unwt. N = 5,221).

A smaller percentage (1.3%) had been to a treatment agency in the last twelve months. It would be interesting to check this proportion reported by respondents against health statistics derived from agency reports, but there is a great deal of guesswork involved in deriving any such comparison figure. Using a series of plausible but arbitrary assumptions from alcohol treatment system patient loads, short stay hospital discharges and visits to doctors for alcohol-related conditions, and Alcoholics Anonymous (AA) censuses (drawing on Sanchez, 1984) yields a period prevalence of about 1.2% of American adults in treatment for alcohol problems around 1984. For large health insurance plans, it is a rule-of-thumb that 0.4% to 0.7% of those enrolled will receive alcohol treatment in any one year (Harold Holder, personal communication). This figure, of course, would exclude Alcoholics Anonymous. The current year prevalence of treatment reported in table 12.1, part A thus appears to be at least in the right range.

Table 12.1, part B shows the prevalences of experience of treatment by different types of agencies or professions. Alcoholics Anonymous is the single most common treatment modality, followed by other alcoholism programs, medical groups or private physicians, and general hospitals. It should be kept in mind that with percentage estimates this small, the size of the sampling variance exceeds the estimate itself, thus obscuring the interpretation. The results underscore that treatment for alcohol problems extends well beyond the bounds of the alcohol-specific treatment system.

Table 12.2 shows the respondent's report of how long ago the last contact occurred with the treatment modality. The percentages in the table are based on those treated by each modality at some point in their life, which is a very small number of cases for some modalities. In general, a strong majority of those who have been in treatment report their last contact with treatment as having occurred less than five years ago. This may reflect a variety of factors: the relatively high rate of relapse in treated populations, the fact that some modalities (AA in particular) emphasize lifelong "aftercare," the relatively recent growth of the alcohol treatment system (Room 1980b, Weisner and Room 1984), and a probable tendency for differential underreporting of long ago treatment episodes. There is some tendency for treatment episodes in the general medical system (general hospitals and medical groups or private physicians) to have occurred longer ago than treatment by alcohol-specific modalities (AA and other alcoholism programs). Again, this probably reflects the growth of the alcoholism-specific treatment system.

There is a good deal of variation between treatment types in the extent of overlap with other treatment types (table not shown). For each other modality, Alcoholics Anonymous is the most reported other treatment, no doubt in part reflecting the use of AA as an adjunct to many institutional therapies. General hospital treatment is generally the next most frequent conjunction for other modalities, followed by alcoholism treatment programs.

Self-recognition of an Alcohol Problem: Talking to Others about It

In table 12.3, we turn our attention to an intermediate area in the response to alcohol problems. When respondents tell us they have "talked" to someone about an alcohol problem of their own, they are

TABLE 12.2
How Long Ago was the Last Contact, for Those with Lifetime Experience of a Type of Alcohol Treatment*

	Unwt. (N)	Less than one year	1–4 years	5–9 years	10+ years
General hospitals	(41)	29%	33%	26%	12%
Health or mental programs	(29)	53	24	23	1
Mental hospitals	(6)	65	33	0	2
A medical group or private physician	(38)	39	20	15	26
Social welfare department	(11)	58	2	40	0
Alcoholics Anonymous	(83)	41	35	15	9
Some other alcoholism program	(40)	34	39	13	14
Vocational rehabilitation program	(19)	48	31	20	1
Some other agency or professional program	(27)	25	32	21	23

*Weighted data.

reporting both their own acknowledgement of having a problem and that someone else was involved in seeking a solution. Those most commonly involved were family members and friends. Somewhat less frequently, it was a doctor or someone at the workplace who was involved. On a lifetime basis, twice as many respondents report having talked to someone about a drinking problem as report experience of treatment. Over a lifetime, those who had talked to some category of person about their problems were more likely than not to have talked to at least one other category of persons. About two-fifths of those reporting having talked to someone in their lifetime reported having done it during the last twelve months.

TABLE 12.3
Alcohol Problem Recognition:
Lifetime and Current (within last year)*

"Have you ever talked about an alcohol problem of your own with anyone? Did you ever talk to (PERSON)?"

A. Number of categories talked to in time period:	Current	Lifetime
None	97.2%	93.2%
One category	1.4	2.6
Two categories	0.7	1.5
Three or more categories	0.6	2.7
Mean number of categories talked to in the time period, of those talking to someone	1.8	2.5
(Unwtd. N who talked to someone)	(133)	(313)

(continued)

TABLE 12.3 *(continued)*

B. *"Did you ever talk to (PERSON)?"*	*Current*	*Lifetime*
Your husband/your wife/someone you were living with	1.4%	3.8%
An ex-spouse	0.0	0.6
A relative	0.9	2.6
Someone you were dating	0.6	1.3
Any other friend or acquaintance	1.0	3.2
A neighbor (not counting the friend you just told me about)	0.1	0.5
Your supervisor or any other fellow worker	0.4	1.6
A priest, minister or rabbi	0.1	0.9
A doctor	0.4	1.8
Anyone else	0.3	0.9

*Weighted data (unwt. N = 5,221)

Overlap with other categories of people talked to is most common for the spouse (table not shown). While a primary clustering among primary relations—relatives and friends—can be discerned, there also seems to be some clustering among secondary relationships—between neighbor, work supervisor, minister, and doctor.

Other's Pressures on Respondent's Drinking

In table 12.4 we turn to social controls at the level of primary relations—to a list of people or categories "who might have liked you to drink less or to act differently when you drank." On a lifetime basis, three times as many respondents reported this was true for someone as reported they had talked to someone about a problem with their drinking. Many more respondents, thus, are willing to acknowledge that someone else has defined their drinking as problematic than are willing to say that they defined themselves as having had a problem to talk over with someone else. About one-third of those acknowledging someone else would have liked them to drink less reported that it had happened in the previous twelve months. However, the twelve-month rate may have been depressed by confusion resulting from the interposition of another question, on whether their drinking had ever broken up or threatened to break up their relationship with the person involved.

On a lifetime basis, more respondents reported pressure from their mother than from anyone else, although the spouse ran a close second. Other relatives and friends were also fairly frequent sources of pressure. In terms of the last twelve months, the spouse was the most frequent source of pressure, with the girl/boyfriend moving into third position after the mother. Although parents were a substantial source of pressure, the respondent's drinking was relatively unlikely to have broken or threatened to break his or her relation with them; the most likely relations to have been threatened or broken were with the spouse and the girl/boyfriend.

TABLE 12.4
Others' Pressures on Respondent's Drinking: Lifetime and Current*

"Now I'm going to read you a list of some other people who might have liked you to drink less or to act differently when you drank."

A. Number of persons/categories who felt that way in the time period:

	Current	Lifetime
No one	92.9	77.7
One person/category	4.1	11.7
Two persons/categories	1.7	4.8
Three persons/categories	0.9	3.5
Four or more persons/categories	0.3	2.4
Mean number of persons/categories pressuring in time period, among those pressured	1.6	1.9
(Unwt. N who were pressured)	*(371)*	*(942)*

B. a. "Did this person every feel this way?" b. (IF YES TO a.) "Did that break up your relationship with that person or threaten to break it?" c. (IF YES TO b.) "Did this happen in the last 12 months?"

	Current	Lifetime	
		Felt That Way	Threatened Relationship
A spouse or someone you lived with	3.3	11.7	3.3
Your mother	2.8	12.3	0.7
Your father	1.2	5.3	0.4
A girl or boyfriend	1.9	4.5	1.3
Any other relative	1.3	4.4	0.7
Anyone else you lived with	0.3	1.3	0.6
Any other friend	0.7	2.9	0.7
Anyone else	0.2	0.7	0.1

*Weighted data.

In terms of overlaps of pressure from different sources (table not shown), the mother is consistently the most likely person to have also pressured respondents who were pressured by any other category. This is particularly true for pressure from the father; relatively few respondents have been pressured by their father without being pressured also by their mother. Many respondents are pressured by their parents or spouse without coming under other pressures; on the other hand, there is some clustering of pressures among more distal relationships—between other relatives, housemates and friends.

Rather small proportions of those whose relation with a spouse has been threatened by their drinking have also had other relationships threatened. In general, the overlap among threats to relationships is lower than among pressures concerning drinking. An exception is for the relatively small numbers of respondents whose relationship with a parent has been threatened. These cases show a somewhat greater tendency for a cumulation in the threatened breaks.

Stages of Response: Interrelations of Treatment,
Recognition and Pressure

Table 12.5 examines, on a lifetime and on a current basis, the interaction of the three summary variables we have been considering so far: experience of treatment, having talked to someone about the respondent's drinking problem, and pressure from others about the respondent's drinking. Table 12.5 shows that the three dimensions in fact scale hierarchically (like a Guttman scale): very few respondents reach treatment without having talked to someone about their problem, and very few talk to anyone without having been pressured about their drinking.

Given these findings, a hierarchical measure was constructed for each time period, with those having been in treatment as the "top" category, the remainder who have talked to someone as the next category, and the remainder who have been pressured as the third category. A fourth category of "other drinkers" was composed of those who had not experienced any of the three responses. Table 12.6, part A shows the distributions by age and gender on this measure on a lifetime basis. Experience of treatment is over three times as common among men as among women. Treatment experience is more common among younger than among older women, while the proportions do not vary much by age among men. For men and women, both talking to others about a problem and being pressured by others are somewhat more common at younger than at older ages. In both genders, older people seem less likely than younger people to talk to someone about a problem if they have been pressured about their drinking. On a proportional basis, women who have been pressured (including those in the "ever talked" and "ever treated" categories) are slightly less likely to receive treatment for an alcohol problem.

TABLE 12.5
Experience of Treatment by Alcohol Problem Recognition by Others'
Pressure on Respondent's Drinking, Lifetime and Current Basis,
Corner Percentaging*

A. *Lifetime basis:*

Lifetime experience of treatment:		Yes		No	
Lifetime alcohol problem recognition ("talked to others"):		Yes	No	Yes	No
Lifetime others' pressure on respondent's drinking	Yes	2.5%	0.3	3.6	15.6
	No	0.3	0.0	0.2	77.1
					/100%

B. *Current Basis (last 12months)*

Current experience of treatment:		Yes		No	
Current alcohol problem recognition ("talked to others")		Yes	No	Yes	No
Current others' pressure on respondent's drinking:	Yes	1.0%	0.0	1.4	5.1
	No	0.2	0.1	0.6	91.4
					/100%

* Weighted data (unwt. N = 5,221).

Table 12.6, part B shows the distribution of the "stage of response" measure by lifetime drinking summary categories, excluding lifetime abstainers. Respondents were asked if at any time in their life they had been drinking five or more drinks at a sitting as often as once a week, and positive responses to this item are used here as the heaviest drinking category. Those who did not report this, but who either reported having been "high or tight" or having had seven or more drinks on an occasion at some time in their life form a second category, with other drinkers as the third category. Among the heaviest drinking category, women are as likely as men to have been in treatment, more likely to have talked to someone, but less likely to have been pressured about their drinking. In both genders, almost three-quarters of those who report having drunk five or more drinks at a sitting at least once a week report having been pressured or otherwise responded to about their drinking at some point in their life.

As Table 12.7 part A shows, in terms of patterns in the last year, treatment is if anything more common among middle-aged than among younger men, although younger men are somewhat more likely to have been pressed or to have acknowledged drinking problems. The few females who report current treatment are mostly under forty, and

TABLE 12.6
Lifetime Stage of Response Sumary, by Age and Gender and by Lifetime Drinking Patterns Summary‡

A. Lifetime Stage of Response Summary, by Age and Gender*

	Male				Female			
	18–39	40–59	60+	Total	18–39	40–59	60+	Total
Ever treated	5.6%	5.8%	5.2%	5.5%	2.0%	1.4%	0.4%	1.5%
Ever talked	7.0	5.2	3.1	5.7	3.5	2.1	0.2	2.4
Ever pressed	31.2	28.7	16.1	27.3	17.1	7.3	5.9	11.9
Other drinkers	49.2	52.0	60.5	52.3	64.1	70.3	60.1	64.9
Lifetime abstainer	7.0	8.3	15.3	9.1	13.2	19.0	33.3	19.3
Unwt. (N)	(1,132)	(540)	(413)	(2,085)	(1,660)	(764)	(679)	(3,103)

*Excluding 8 males and 25 females with no answer on age.

B. Lifetime Stage for Response Summary, by Lifetime Drinking Patterns Summary (lifetime abstainers excluded):

	Male			Female		
	Ever 5+ Weekly	Ever 7+ or High/Tight	Other Ever Drinker	Ever 5+ Weekly	Ever 7+ or High/Tight	Other Ever Drinker
Ever treated	14.5%	2.0%	1.0%	14.8%	0.5%	0.4%
Ever talked	15.2	2.3	0.0	20.3	2.0	0.0
Ever pressed	42.6	31.9	6.4	37.3	19.6	4.5
Other drinkers	27.6	63.8	92.6	27.6	78.0	95.1
Unwt (N)	(561)	(788)	(472)	(215)	(917)	(1,092)

‡Weighted data (unwt. N = 5,221).

TABLE 12.7
Current Stage of Response Summary, by Age and Gender, and by Current Drinking Pattern Summary‡

A. Current Stage of Response Summary, by Age and Gender:*

	Male				Female			
	18–39	40–59	60+	Total	18–39	40–59	60+	Total
Current treated	2.1%	3.0%	1.4%	2.2%	1.0%	0.1%	0.2%	0.6%
Current talked	4.2	1.3	1.1	2.8	2.0	1.5	0.2	1.5
Current pressed	13.4	10.9	3.2	10.6	8.5	2.3	0.5	4.9
Other drinkers	64.7	60.1	53.5	61.1	60.3	58.4	47.8	56.8
Other current Abstainer	15.5	24.7	40.7	23.3	28.2	37.7	51.2	36.2
unwt. (N)	(1,132)	(540)	(413)	(2,093)	(1,660)	(764)	(679)	(3,128)

*Excludes 8 males and 25 females with no answer on age.

B. Current Stage of Response Summary, by Current Drinking Pattern (current abstainers excluded)*

	Male			Female		
	Ever 5+ Weekly	Ever 7+ or High/Tight	Other Ever Drinker	Ever 5+ Weekly	Ever 7+ or High/Tight	Other Ever Drinker
Current treated	2.9%	1.7%	1.1%	3.5%	1.7%	0.0%
Current talked	9.7	2.9	0.8	14.0	3.4	0.7
Current pressed	32.2	13.6	4.0	28.8	11.9	4.1
Other drinkers	55.2	81.8	94.1	53.7	83.0	95.2
unwt. (N)	(377)	(505)	(645)	(135)	(379)	(1,161)

*Excludes 4 males and 6 females unclassified on current drinking pattern. "Current treated" includes 10 males and 3 females classified as current abstainers.

"5+ at least weekly": reports drinking five or more drinks on an occasion in a pattern implying at least once a week (Room, chapter 3).

"5+ or high or tight": not the above, but has five or more drinks on an occasion or is "high or tight" at least once in a while.

‡Weighted data (unwt. N = 5,221).

pressure from others about their drinking is also largely limited to this age group. In table 12.7, part B, results are shown for a summary measure of current drinking patterns, with a heaviest drinking category of those reporting drinking five or more drinks on an occasion at least once a week, and a middle drinking category of those reporting drinking five drinks on an occasion or getting high or tight at least once in a while. When level of drinking is controlled, the genders are roughly equally likely to experience some reaction to their drinking, although women seem slightly more likely to have been treated or to acknowledge a problem within the last year.

Respondents' Experiences of Pressures on Others' Drinking

As the analysis so far suggests, efforts at informal control of others' drinking are quite a common part of the American scene. The respondents gave further evidence on this when asked both about witnessing such efforts and about their own efforts in this direction. Part C of table 12.8 shows that 42.5% of the sample reported overhearing someone's drinking criticized to their face in the course of the last year, and that only minorities of the sample agreed with statements disclaiming the responsibility to be concerned about others' drinking.

TABLE 12.8
Respondent's Pressure on Others' Drinking, Lifetime Basis*

"Now some questions about your reactions to other people's drinking. Have you ever said something about their drinking or suggested that they cut down?"

A. Number of categories/persons involved:

None	44.5%
One	39.7
Two	11.1
Three	2.9
Four or more	1.6
Mean number of persons/categories involved:	*1.4*

B. "How was that person related to you? Who else?"

Husband or wife, significiant other or spouse equivalent, Ex-husband or ex-wife	10.0%
Mother	2.6
Father	5.5
Brother	8.9
Sister	3.2
Son	3.7
Daughter	1.0
Other relative: cousins	1.6
generation above respondent	3.9

(continued)

TABLE 12.8 *(continued)*

Other relative: same generation as respondent	3.8
generation below respondent	1.3
generation indeterminate	0.7
Friend or acquaintance	29.5
Other	1.9

C. Events and beliefs concerning controls on others' drinking:
  a. Respondent said something about the drinking of someone
  named above in the last 12 months. — 31.4%
  b. "During the past year, I've heard someone criticize
  someone else's drinking to his face."–True — 42.5%
  c. "It's not my place to comment on my friends' drinking, no
  matter how they behave."–True — 30.1%
  d. "A man's drinking is his own business and no concern of
  the community."–True — 24.5%

*Weighted data (unwt. N = 5,221).

On a lifetime basis, indeed, a majority of the sample claim to have said something to someone else about their drinking or to have suggested that they cut down (table 12.8, part A), and over three in ten report doing this in the last twelve months (table 12.8, part C). The most common category of recipients of this advice is friends, with the spouse and family members (particularly male family members) also fairly likely to have received advice.

There is only a modest overlap between a respondent's pressuring one person category and pressuring another (table not shown). There seems to be a conditional relation between pressuring a man and pressuring a woman in any given family generation; respondents are more likely to have pressured fathers than mothers, brothers than sisters, sons than daughters; but if they have pressured a woman of a particular generation they are substantially more likely to have also pressured a man of the same generation.

The Balance of Pressures on and from Others

In table 12.9 we examine the balance of pressures, on a lifetime basis, on and from particular relationship categories. It should be kept in mind, in interpreting this table, that more respondents are "at risk" of putting pressure on others than of receiving pressures, since lifetime abstainers cannot be pressured to reduce their drinking. Part A of the table shows that respondents are slightly more likely to report pressure from a spouse than to report having pressured a spouse. On the other hand, that the reported pressures in each direction on this item are roughly equal lends some convergent validation to the responses. Respondents are about twice as likely to have received pressure from their parents as to have pressured them. With respect to both spouse and parents, it is relatively rare for the pressure to have been reciprocal.

TABLE 12.9
Pressures On and From Others, Lifetime Basis*

A. *Pressures on and from others by category:*

	Spouse	Parents	Family	Friends	Family and Friends
On and From	1.2%	1.3%	7.0%	3.9%	13.9%
From	10.5	11.5	13.5	2.8	8.5
On	8.8	5.9	20.1	25.6	35.7
Neither	79.5	81.3	59.4	67.6	42.1

B. *Pressures on family and friends, and from family and friends:*

	Pressures On	Pressures From
Family and friends	7.5%	5.2%
Family only	19.8	15.5
Friends only	22.3	1.7
Neither	50.6	77.8

"Pressure from": "people who might have liked you to drink less or act differently when you drank."
"Pressure on": "said something about their drinking or suggested that they cut down."
"Family" includes spouse, parents, brother, sister, son, daughter.
"Friend" includes (explicitly for "pressures from") girl/boyfriend and nonrelatives the respondent lived with.
Sample includes 14.6% lifetime abstainers.

*Weighted data (unwt. $N = 5{,}221$).

In the broader frame of reference of family relationships, adding in pressures on and from children and siblings, the balance of pressures is reversed; in this larger frame of nuclear family relationships, more respondents report applying than report receiving pressure. In this larger frame, it is also not so uncommon for the same respondents to have both received and applied pressure.

As reported by respondents, pressures among family members are not greatly imbalanced. In contrast, many more respondents report having pressured friends than report having been pressured by friends about their drinking. Respondents are more likely, in fact, to report having said something about a friend's drinking than to report having said something about a family member's drinking; but rather few respondents report having been pressured by friends.

How are we to make sense of these results, since our sample should equally well represent those applying and those receiving pressure? One answer, of course, is that respondents may be reluctant to admit pressures from friends—although, against this, they seem fairly ready to admit pressure from a spouse or parent. Another answer may be that advice from different friends piles up on a relatively small number of heavier drinkers: in this view, each heavy drinker under pressure would have been pressed at some time by an average of ten friends. A third possibility is that advice from a friend may be easier to avoid hearing than advice from a spouse or mother—either because of diffidence in the friend's choice of words, or because of a diplomatic deafness on the part of the drinker.

The last column of table 12.9, part A shows the balance of pressures on and from family and friends taken together. Overall, pressure on others is reported substantially more commonly than pressure from others. On a lifetime basis, a solid majority of the sample has been involved in pressure on or from others concerning drinking.

Part B of the table summarizes the distribution of pressures in a different fashion, underlining that, while respondents are roughly equally likely to have pressured family and friends, they are much more likely to report having been pressured by family than by friends.

Table 12.10 shows the balances of pressures on and from others for parents, spouse and friends by age and gender. Reported pressures from parents are less likely among older than among younger respondents; since the questions here are on a lifetime basis, there is a likelihood that there has been some forgetting of long ago events by older respondents. Sons are substantially more likely than daughters to have been pressed by parents; daughters, in fact, are slightly more likely to have pressed parents than to have been pressed by them. In conjunction with previous tables, we can see from the results here that the dominant directions of pressure are from older generations to younger ones, and from females to males. The distributions in table 12.10, part A suggest that the flow of pressure across gender is somewhat stronger than the flow across generations. However, table 12.11, part A, cross-tabulating the balance of pressures by the respondent's lifetime drinking patterns, shows that the gender differences in the flow of pressure are in considerable part explained by gender differences in drinking pattern: the balance of pressures for relatively heavy-drinking women and their parents is closer to that for heavy-drinking men than to that for light-drinking women.

TABLE 12.10

Pressures On and From Others, by Age and Gender, Lifetime Basis

	Male				Female			
(unwt. N)	18-39 (1,132)	40-59 (540)	60+ (413)	Total (2,085)	18-39 (1,660)	40-59 (764)	60+ (679)	Total (3,103)
A. *Pressures on and from parent(s):*								
Both on and from	2.3%	0.5%	0.0%	1.3%	1.9%	1.6%	0.0%	1.4%
From parent(s)	23.0	17.0	7.4	18.1	9.1	3.7	1.7	5.9
On parent(s)	6.9	5.3	0.7	5.1	8.8	6.8	1.8	6.6
Neither	67.8	77.2	91.9	75.5	80.2	88.0	96.5	86.1
B. *Pressures on and from spouse(s):*								
Both on and from spouse	0.8%	0.1%	1.8%	0.8%	2.22%	1.9%	0.0%	1.6%
From spouse	16.4	25.2	14.4	18.2	5.0	3.5	1.6	3.8
On spouse	2.1	4.1	1.7	2.5	14.0	16.6	12.9	14.5
Neither (includes never married)	80.7	70.6	82.0	78.4	78.9	78.0	85.4	80.1
C. *Pressures on and from friend(s):*								
Both on and from	8.7%	4.4%	1.4%	6.0%	3.1%	1.7%	0.2%	2.1%
From friend(s)	6.1	3.1	1.5	4.3	2.2	1.1	0.5	1.5
On friend(s)	32.0	29.6	23.8	29.6	28.3	19.5	13.7	22.6
Neither	53.3	62.9	73.3	60.1	66.4	77.7	85.5	73.9

*Weighted data (unwt. $N = 5,221$).

TABLE 12.11
Pressures On and From Others, by Lifetime Drinking Pattern Summary and Gender*

	Male				Female			
	Ever 5+ Weekly	Ever 7+ or High/Tight	Other Ever Drinker	Lifetime Abstainer	Ever 5+ Weekly	Ever 7+ or High/Tight	Other Ever Drinker	Lifetime Abstainer
(unwt. N)	(561)	(788)	(472)	(272)	(215)	(917)	(1,092)	(904)
A. *Pressures on and from parent(s):*								
Both on and from	3.7%	0.4%	0.0%	0.0%	8.4%	1.9%	0.0%	0.0%
From parent(s)	40.9	11.1	3.3	0.0	31.4	8.0	1.1	0.0
On parent(s)	4.8	6.2	4.8	1.6	6.9	9.1	4.8	4.8
Neither	50.7	82.2	91.9	98.4	53.4	81.1	94.0	95.1
B. *Pressures on and from spouse(s):*								
Both on and from	1.7%	0.7%	0.0%	0.0%	13.0%	1.2c	0.4%	0.0%
From spouse	35.0	16.4	2.8	0.0	23.1	4.7	0.5	0.0
On spouse	1.2	3.7	2.2	2.2	16.4	17.4	13.1	9.7
Neither (includes never married)	62.0	79.2	95.0	97.8	47.6	76.7	85.9	90.3
C. *Pressures on and from friend(s):*								
Both on and from	13.9%	3.8%	0.4%	0.0%	12.9%	2.0%	0.8%	0.0%
From friend(s)	9.6	3.0	0.2	0.0	12.7	1.1	0.3	0.0
On friend(s)	34.7	27.0	22.9	35.0	26.1	23.6	22.0	19.2
Neither	41.9	66.1	76.5	65.0	48.3	73.3	77.0	80.8

*Weighted data (N = 5,221).

The results for spouses in table 12.10, part B dramatically underline the gender imbalance in pressures among family members. Men and women agree, whatever their age level, that women are much more likely to pressure men than vice-versa. Unlike the results for pressures from parents, the results here are fairly consistent across age groups. Still, that the data are on a lifetime basis implies that some forgetting of long-ago events is going on, and/or that there is more pressure of wives on husbands in cohorts which are now young than there was in those now older. Again, the results of table 12.11, part B show that controlling by drinking level partially mutes the results. Even so, relatively heavy-drinking women, unlike relatively heavy-drinking men, are often involved in pressuring their spouse to drink less.

From table 12.10, part C it can be seen that younger respondents of both genders are more likely to report pressures both on and from friends than older respondents. Except among older respondents, those who have been pressed are more likely than not themselves in turn to have pressed others. While women in particular seem to bear the burden of social control of drinking within the family, men are somewhat more likely than women to have pressed friends about their drinking. Table 12.11, part C shows that this remains true at all levels of drinking. In both genders, the heaviest drinkers are the most likely to report having pressed friends about their drinking, although the differences by level of drinking are relatively modest.

DISCUSSION

In the U.S. adult population, we have shown, informal social controls over drinking, where a family member or friend expresses disapproval of someone's drinking, are widespread; almost half of respondents have overheard such efforts at control in the previous year, and over 30% report having done it themselves in the same period. There is little evidence that such control efforts are heavily clustered in a few "control specialists": having pressed one category of persons about their drinking is not a very strong predictor of having pressed other categories of persons.

Smaller but still quite substantial proportions of respondents report having been on the receiving end of such pressures—7% within the last year, and 22% sometime in their life. That these proportions are smaller may in part reflect underreporting, although the rough balance of reported pressures on and from spouses (table 12.9, part A) gives us some confidence that reports of applying and receiving pressure are equally valid. Very likely, the main explanation of the smaller proportion receiving than applying pressure is that one heavy drinker usually attracts advice from several quarters. Thus, the average number of pressuring person categories for respondents receiving pressures (1.9 on a lifetime basis) is greater than the average number of person categories pressured by those applying pressures (1.4). And lighter drinkers, we have seen, are relatively infrequent recipients of pressure on their drinking (they may attract pressures to drink more—Room, 1971a, p. 103).

Attempts at the social control of drinking, at least within the family, flow predominately in predictable directions—from older to younger generations, and (in particular) from women to men. As studies in other countries have begun to suggest (Gullestad, 1984, pp. 214, 256; Holmila, 1987), women bear a double burden of control of drinking—they are supposed to control not only their own drinking, but also their men's.

By and large, the results suggest that in the United States general population, informal efforts to control drinking are far more widespread than such formal efforts as alcoholism treatment. Informal control efforts seem indeed to be a precondition for formal treatment: few people enter treatment, it seems, without having been pressured by family or friends about their drinking.

The results presented here pose a number of issues for future research and analysis. A variety of methodologies need to be brought to bear in future studies of efforts to control others' drinking, including more qualitative work on how the control is attempted and what the outcome is, and studies of the interaction of informal and formal control efforts. Studies of attempts at control and pressure over drinking might well also be set in a broader context of efforts to influence each others' behavior in families and among friends. It would also be illuminating to put the results found here in a cross-cultural context; would the relatively dense network of control efforts found in this study also be found, for instance, in a southern European viticultural society, where less power is ascribed to alcohol, and drinking is a less socially "visible" activity?

Such questions are of substantial theoretical interest. They also have a practical significance. Strengthening the informal community responses to heavy drinking is a major strategy for reducing the toll of alcohol problems in a society (Rootman and Moser, 1984).

13

Demographic Characteristics and the Frequency of Heavy Drinking as Predictors of Self-Reported Drinking Problems

INTRODUCTION

The demographic distributions of drinking problems in the U. S. population are fairly well known, having been documented by a number of surveys (Cahalan, 1970; Cahalan and Room, 1974; Clark and Midanik, 1982). We know that these problems are more prevalent among those who are male, young, single, residents of the wet regions of the country, urbanites, less educated, and of lower socioeconomic status than among those of contrasting demographic characteristics. Not surprisingly, these distributions of drinking problems match the distributions of heavy drinking, which have also been well studied (Clark and Midanik, 1982; Cahalan et al. 1969). This match obviously reflects the fact that heavy drinking is the primary risk factor for drinking problems. But few studies have attempted to find out whether demographic variables are associated with a higher risk for drinking problems after controlling for alcohol intake (some exceptions are Mäkelä and Simpura, 1985;

Knupfer, 1984). For example, we know that greater proportions of men than women report experiencing drinking problems and also that men tend to drink more than women. But we do not know whether men at any given level of drinking are more likely to report problems connected with drinking than are women. Some might expect this to be the case, arguing that women who drink heavily are often hidden within the family and protected from many adverse consequences of their drinking (Sandmaier, 1980; Ferrence, 1980). Others might counterargue that the greater opprobrium against women's drinking would lead to a greater likelihood of experiencing an adverse consequence at a given level of drinking. The present study investigates this and related issues by examining (through a multiple regression analysis) whether selected demographic characteristics are associated with higher or lower drinking problem scores after controlling for the frequency of drinking at specified levels of intake.

There are several reasons to expect that people with certain demographic characteristics would be at greater risk to experience drinking problems at a given level of intake. To begin with, in some social environments temperance traditions and antialcohol sentiments are stronger, and therefore heavy drinkers in those environments more readily encounter social disapproval (see Hilton, 1986 on variations in abstainer militancy). Along these lines, Room (1982) argued that heavy drinkers in rural areas and in the dry region of the country are more likely to experience sanctions than are heavy drinkers living in areas where more liberal norms prevail. A somewhat different approach is Mäkelä's thesis of differential social control, which posits that the drinking behavior of subordinate groups in society is more heavily monitored, restricted, and sanctioned (1978). Thus, women, younger people, and those of lower socioeconomic status are more likely than men, older people, and the better-off to experience sanctions at a given level of drinking. With regard to socioeconomic status, Mäkelä also noted that the poor have fewer resources to insulate themselves from adverse reactions to their drinking (see also Park, 1983). Knupfer (1984) proposed a theory that predicts effects which are the opposite of those predicted by Mäkelä. In her view, heavy drinking is less tolerated for those who hold positions of greater imputed responsibility. Thus, the relative risk of experiencing a problem is expected to be greater among the middle-aged than among the young, among the married than among the single, and among those of higher socioeconomic status than among those of lower socioeconomic status. Finally, characteristics of the drinking itself, beyond simply its amount, may be different for different groups in ways that are more likely to trigger a social reaction. In this regard Room noted that "intermittent potentially 'explosive' drinking did seem more prominent in the mix of drinking styles in dryer regions and in the more and in the more rural parts, at least, of the wetter areas." (Room, 1982; p. 569). Mäkelä (1978) made a similar argument about the drinking of the young, noting that its public and often provocative character invites greater disapproval.

Existing studies suggest a number of demographic variables that might be profitably studied in this regard. In the existing literature on the subject, it has been suggested that women will be at greater risk to experience a problem related to drinking than men (Polich and Orvis, 1979; Knupfer, 1982, though contrary evidence is found in Knupfer, 1984 and Robins et al. 1962), that younger people will be at greater risk than older people (Mäkelä, 1978 though Knupfer, 1984 found little difference), that married people will be at greater risk than single people (Knupfer, 1984), that residents of the dry regions will be at greater risk than residents of the wet regions (Room, 1982; Polich and Orvis, 1979), that both big city and rural dwellers will be at greater risk than suburban and small town residents (Room, 1982), and that lower income and less educated people will be at greater risk than better educated people (Mäkelä, 1978, Park, 1983; and Robins et al., 1962, although Knupfer, 1984 disagrees).

By and large, these expectations focus on the consequences of drinking. They are theories about why some kinds of heavy drinkers are more likely than others to experience troubles with the law, arguments with spouses, disaffections of friends, losses of employment, illnesses, and the like. But measures of drinking problems have traditionally distinguished between these consequences of drinking and indicators of dependence (here taken to include loss of control) (Cahalan et al. 1970; Cahalan and Room, 1974; Clark and Midanik, 1982; Room, 1977). Simply because measures of dependence are available in the 1984 data set, one might want to include them along with measures of consequences in an analysis of drinking problems. However, the conceptual meaning of such an analysis is much less clear.

Surely dependence and heavy consumption are not the same thing. Seldon Bacon's classic statement that "Alcoholics Do Not Drink" emphasizes the distinction using an older rhetoric of alcoholism (Bacon, 1958; see also Mann, 1958). The point is further underscored by the finding that not all clinically diagnosed alcoholics drink heavily (Room, 1968). Yet the typical problem drinker or dependent drinker is expected to drink repeatedly in large quantities, and thus there should be some substantial subset of persons among whom both dependence and high intake are present. Among these cases, dependence and heavy consumption are thought to be two pieces of the same whole, and it is therefore not quite meaningful to ask whether certain demographic groups are more likely to exhibit dependence once the amount of alcohol consumption is taken into account. However an alternate view (Clark and Midanik 1982; Room 1977) is that many of these indicators, in particular such dependence symptoms as tremors, blackouts, night sweats, and the like, are not, in fact, indicators of an underlying dependence, but instead are short-term, physiological consequences of bouts of very heavy drinking. While it is not our intention to settle this debate here, it should be noted that under the latter view, the issue of what kind of drinkers are more likely to experience such events at a given level of drinking becomes a reasonable and indeed the obvious question to pose. We might expect, for example, that younger drinkers, who are more physically vigorous, might be less likely to report such occurrences than older drinkers (Polich and Orvis, 1979). For the most part, however, current research supplies us with few expectations as to the outcome of such an analysis.

Up to this point, the crucial control variable, drinking intake, has been left unspecified. Following Knupfer (1984), we have chosen to use the frequency of heavy drinking occasions as the measure of drinking intake (a four country Scandinavian survey also favored this approach; see Hauge and Irgens-Jensen, 1986). Specifically, we shall use two indicators: the number of times per month that the respondent consumed five or more drinks at a sitting and the number of times per month that the respondent consumed eight or more drinks in a day.[1] These selections were made both for the theoretical reason that it is usually intoxication rather than drinking per se that places an individual at risk for various drinking problems (an exception being health problems) and for the practical reason that the intake items in the 1984 national alcohol survey are not well suited to estimate the respondent's volume of consumption—the leading competitor as an intake measure.

METHODS

As discussed in an earlier paper (Hilton, chapter 4 in this volume), two scores for drinking problems were computed, one for what is called dependence and the other for what is called consequences of drinking. Items under the heading of dependence included such things as whether the respondent had tried to cut down on drinking but had been unable to do so, had experienced such things as memory loss or tremors after drinking, or had engaged in morning or binge drinking. Consequences included such things as problems with spouse, problems on the job, problems with the police, and health problems. Only current problems (those experienced in the past twelve months) were counted.

As indicated in the introduction to this chapter, the present analysis concentrates on the frequency of consuming five or more drinks at a sitting and the frequency of consuming eight or more drinks in a day. The frequency of having five or more drinks at a sitting was estimated from the responses to questions A, B, C, E, H, and K in figure 13.1. Responses to questions A, B, C, E, H, and K were assigned the values appearing on figure 13.1. Multiplying the proportion by the corresponding beverage frequency and summing across all three beverages produced the estimates of the monthly frequency of drinking five or more drinks at a sitting that are used here. The frequency of consuming eight or more drinks in a day was estimated from the responses to questions N and O. The coding system for these questions is also indicated on figure 13.1. The codes for questions N and O were summed to estimate the monthly frequency of consuming eight or more drinks in a day. Both frequencies (five or more at a sitting and eight or more per day) were capped at maximum values of thirty times per month in order to limit the influence of extreme values.

FIGURE 13.1
Alcohol Intake and Drinking Problems Items

ALCOHOL INTAKE ITEMS. (Parentheses indicate values used in scoring).
   A.   How often do you usually have wine (or a punch containing wine)?
   B.   How often do you usually have beer?
   C.   How often do you usually have drinks containing whiskey or any other liquor, including scotch, bourbon, gin, vodka, rum, etc.?
   D.   How often do you usually have any kind of beverage containing alcohol, whether it is wine, beer, or whiskey, or any other drink?
        Response choices for Questions A through D.
           Three or more times a day. (90)
           Two times a day. (60)
           Once a day. (30)
           Nearly every day. (22)
           Three or four times a week. (15)
           Once or twice a week. (7)
           Two or three times a month. (2.5)
           About once a month. (1)
           Less than once a month but at least once a year. (0.5)
           Less than once a year. (0)
           I have never had wine (beer or liquor). (0)
   E.   When you drink wine, how often do you have as many as five or six glasses?
   F.   When you drink wine, how often do you have three or four glasses?
   G.   When you drink wine, how often do you have one to two glasses?
   H.   When you drink beer, how often do you have as many as five or six glasses or cans?

(continued)

FIGURE 13.1 (continued)

I. When you drink beer, how often do you have three or four glasses or cans?

J. When you drink beer, how often do you have one to two glasses or cans?

K. When you drink whiskey or liquor, how often do you have as many as five or six drinks?

L. When you drink whiskey or liquor, how often do you have as many as three or four drinks?

M. When you drink whiskey or liquor, how often do you have one or two drinks?

Response Choices for Questions E through M
Nearly every time. (0.80)
More than half the time. (0.60)
Less than half the time. (0.40)
Once in a while. (0.20)
Never. (0)

N. During the past year, how often did you have 12 or more drinks of any kind of alcoholic beverage in a single day, that is, any combination of cans of beer, glasses of wine, drinks containing liquor of any kind?

O. During the past year, how often did you have at least eight, but less than 12 drinks of any kind of alcoholic beverage in a single day, that is, any combination of cans of beer, glasses of wine, drinks containing liquor of any kind?

Response Choices for Questions N and O
Every day or nearly every day. (30)
Three to four times a week. (15)
Once or twice a week. (7)
Once to three times a month. (2)
Seven to eleven times in the past year. (0.75)
Three to six times in the past year. (0.38)
Twice in the past year. (0.17)
Once in the past year. (0.08)
Never in the past year. (0)

DRINKING PROBLEM ITEMS (Parentheses indicate values used in scoring.)

I. *Dependence.*

1. Once I started drinking it difficult for me to stop before I became completely intoxicated.

2. I sometimes kept on drinking after I had promised myself not to.

3. I deliberately tried to cut down or quit drinking, but I was unable to do so.

4. I was afraid I might be an alcoholic.

5. Sometimes I have needed a drink so badly that I couldn't think of anything else.

6. I have skipped a number of regular meals while drinking.

7. I have often taken a drink the first thing when I got up in the morning.

8. I have taken a strong drink in the morning to get over the effects of last night's drinking.

(continued)

FIGURE 13.1 *(continued)*

9. I have awakened the next day not being able to remember some of the things I had done while drinking.
10. My hands shook a lot the morning after drinking.
11. I need more alcohol than I used to, to get the same effect as before.
12. Sometimes I have awakened during the night or early morning sweating all over because of drinking.
13. I stayed intoxicated for several days at a time.

II. *Consequences.*
14. I have gotten in a fight while drinking. (2)
15. I have gotten in a heated argument while drinking. (1)
16. Did your spouse's feelings about your drinking break up your relationship with him/her or threaten to break it up? (3)
17. A spouse or someone I lived with threatened to leave me because of my drinking. (3)
18. A spouse or someone I lived with got angry about my drinking or the way I behaved while drinking. (2)
19. Was there a ever a time when you felt that your drinking had a harmful effect on your home life or marriage? (2)
20. Did your spouse or someone you lived with ever feel that you should drink less or act differently when you drank? (1)
21. Did your mother's feelings about your drinking threaten to break up your relationship with her? (3)
22. Did your father's feelings about your drinking threaten to break up your relationship with him? (3)
23. Did any other relative's feelings about your drinking threaten to break up your relationship with him or her? (3)
24. Did your mother ever feel that you should drink less or act differently when you drank? (1)
25. Did your father ever feel that you should drink less or act differently when you drank? (1)
26. Did any other relative ever feel that you should drink less or act differently when you drank? (1)
27. Did a girlfriend's or boyfriend's feelings about your drinking threaten to break up your relationship with him or her? (3)
28. Did a any other friend's feelings about your drinking threaten to break up your relationship with him or her? (3)
29. Was there ever a time when you felt that your drinking had a harmful effect on your friendships or social life? (2)
30. Did your girlfriend's or boyfriend ever feel that you should drink less or act differently when you drank? (1)
31. Did any other friend ever feel that you should drink less or act differently when you drank? (1)
32. I have lost a job, or nearly one, because of drinking. (3)
33. Drinking may have hurt my chances for promotion, or raises, or better jobs. (2)

(continued)

FIGURE 13.1 *(continued)*

34. Was there ever a time when you felt that your drinking had a harmful effect on your work and employment opportunities. (2)
35. People at work indicated that I should cut down on drinking. (1)
36. I had trouble with the law about drinking when driving was not involved. (2)
37. I have been arrested for driving after drinking. (2)
38. A policeman questioned or warned me because of my drinking. (1)
39. I had an illness connected with drinking which kept me from working on my regular activities for a week or more. (3)
40. A physician suggested I cut down on drinking. (2)
41. I felt that my drinking was becoming a serious threat to my physical health. (1)
42. Was there ever a time when you felt that your drinking had a harmful effect on your health? (1)
43. My drinking contributed to getting hurt in an accident in a car or elsewhere. (2)
44. My drinking contributed to getting involved in an accident in which someone else was hurt or property, such as an auto, was damaged. (2)
45. Was there ever a time when you felt that your drinking had a harmful effect on your financial position. (2)

RESULTS

Table 13.1 shows the univariate distributions of frequent heavy drinking occasions, measured at both the 5 or more and the 8 or more levels and the distributions of reported drinking problems at both the moderate and high levels. Only current drinkers are included in the table. As expected, men were more likely than women to report both frequent heavy drinking occasions and drinking problems of both types (dependence and consequences). Greater proportions of younger respondents than older respondents reported both frequent heavy drinking occasions and the occurrence of both types of problems. (One exception to this was that the differences in dependence at the higher level among age groups were not statistically significant, though they were in the expected direction). Marital status exhibited the expected pattern, with much larger proportions of single respondents reporting frequent heavy drinking occasions and both types of problems.

When one looks at the entire adult population, rather than just drinkers, one finds that there were proportionally fewer frequent heavy drinkers in the dry region than in the wet region;[2] however, most of this difference disappears when only current drinkers are counted. Thus table 13.1 shows little regional difference in the proportions reporting

TABLE 13.1
Percentage of Current Drinkers Reporting Frequent Heavy Drinking or Drinking Problems

	5 or More per Occasion at Least Once per Week	8 or More per Day at Least Once per Week	Moderate Level Dependence	Moderate Level Consequences	High Level Dependence	High Level Consequences	N
1. Sex							
Male	31.0	9.9	8.9	13.9	5.7	7.4	769
Female	9.0	2.5	4.4	6.1	2.6	2.3	727
	$X^2 = 110.5^{**}$	$X^2 = 33.5^{**}$	$X^2 = 11.7^{**}$	$X^2 = 24.2^{**}$	$X^2 = 8.1^{**}$	$X^2 = 20.2^{**}$	
2. Age							
18–29	25.5	10.0	10.1	16.0	5.4	8.1	497
30–39	22.4	6.6	6.9	8.5	4.8	3.9	357
40–49	22.8	5.6	6.5	11.0	4.8	6.1	211
50–59	16.5	3.0	2.8	5.0	1.4	2.3	175
60 and over	7.9	1.6	2.6	3.7	2.3	0.9	254
	$X^2 = 35.7^{**}$	$X^2 = 24.3^{**}$	$X^2 = 20.3^{**}$	$X^2 = 36.4^{**}$	$X^2 = 7.9$	$X^2 = 23.3^{**}$	
3. Marital Status							
Married	17.5	3.9	4.1	7.7	2.6	3.1	903
Single	24.5	10.0	10.6	13.7	6.6	7.6	593
	$X^2 = 10.4^{**}$	$X^2 = 21.2^{**}$	$X^2 = 22.7^{**}$	$X^2 = 13.4^{**}$	$X^2 = 13.5^{**}$	$X^2 = 14.2^{**}$	
4. Region							
Wet	20.7	6.0	6.6	8.7	3.8	3.8	893
Dry	19.7	6.8	6.7	12.2	4.6	6.6	603
	$X^2 = 0.2$	$X^2 = 0.3$	$X^2 = 0.0$	$X^2 = 4.5^{*}$	$X^2 = 0.4$	$X^2 = 5.3^{*}$	

5. Urbanicity

							N
Metropolitan cities 50,000 and over	23.5	7.1	7.9	12.6	4.9	6.8	523
Metropolitan towns under 50,000	18.4	6.2	5.5	8.3	3.5	4.1	608
Nonmetropolitan areas	18.9	5.3	6.9	9.5	4.3	3.5	365
	$X^2 = 5.0$	$X^2 = 1.1$	$X^2 = 2.6$	$X^2 = 5.9$	$X^2 = 1.5$	$X^2 = 6.6$*	

6. Family Income

							N
$0–10,000	17.5	6.7	10.4	15.5	6.9	9.3	279
$10,001–20,000	20.0	7.3	7.5	8.4	4.6	4.6	335
$20,001–30,000	17.5	6.7	4.0	8.8	2.3	3.2	303
$30,001–40,000	23.9	5.8	6.6	7.9	3.7	3.2	226
Over $40,000	26.0	4.9	5.1	9.7	3.5	4.6	261
	$X^2 = 9.7$*	$X^2 = 1.7$	$X^2 = 11.0$*	$X^2 = 11.6$*	$X^2 = 8.1$	$X^2 = 14.4$**	

7. Education

							N
Less than high school graduate	21.2	7.1	9.7	14.6	5.0	7.0	288
High school graduate	21.3	9.2	9.0	11.6	6.4	6.3	561
Some college	20.4	4.3	3.7	7.9	2.1	2.6	344
College graduate and beyond	17.4	2.5	2.8	5.5	1.6	2.9	303
	$X^2 = 2.1$	$X^2 = 17.8$**	$X^2 = 21.4$**	$X^2 = 16.9$**	$X^2 = 16.4$**	$X^2 = 11.7$**	

* Significant at 0.05 level.
** Significant at 0.01 level.

dependence (at either level). However, drinkers in the dry region were more likely than drinkers in the wet region to report consequences of drinking at either the moderate or the high level. In contrast to Room's data (1982), differences in reported problem rates were not very large across the three levels of urbanicity. Although drinkers living in metropolitan cities of over 50,000 were more likely than drinkers living in metropolitan towns of under 50,000 or drinkers living in non-metropolitan areas to report both frequent heavy drinking occasions and the occurrence of problems, differences were significant only for the proportions reporting consequences at the high level.

Those with lower incomes reported higher problem rates than those with higher incomes. (An exception to this was the data for dependence at the high level, where the results were not significant, although they were in the expected direction.) Similarly, those with less education reported higher problem rates than those with more education. However, this fairly consistent pattern in regard to drinking problems was not matched by similarly consistent results in regard to intake. The frequency of consuming eight or more drinks per day did vary with education, with the less educated reporting greater intake. However, the frequency of drinking five or more drinks per occasion was not significantly related to education nor was the frequency of drinking eight or more drinks per day significantly related to income. Most interestingly, the relationship between intake at the five or more level and income ran in the opposite direction of the relationship between problems and income. Those with higher incomes were *more* likely to report frequent heavy drinking at this level even though they were *less* likely to report drinking problems. Although this finding is curious, we should guard against reading too much into it, especially given that it is not reproduced in the eight or more data nor in the data for heavy intake by education.

In sum, the univariate distributions suggest that among drinkers: (1) sex, age, and marital status are related to both heavy drinking and drinking problems; (2) region is not related to heavy drinking or dependence, but is related to consequences of drinking; (3) urbanicity is not related to either heavy drinking or drinking problems; and (4) income and education are related to drinking problems but the relationship of these variables to the frequency of heavy drinking is unclear.

It is often heavy drinkers, and not simply all drinkers, who are the focus of attention in discussions of the likelihood or the distribution of drinking problems (Robins et al. 1962). Accordingly, in table 13.2, the analysis is restricted to those who reported consuming five or more drinks at a sitting as often as once per week ($N = 302$; and here called "frequent heavy drinkers"). Note that this group of frequent heavy drinkers is largely male (79%) and overrepresents the young (42% were between eighteen and twenty-nine and another 26% were between thirty and thirty-nine).

In this analysis, differences between the sexes were not significant, indicating that gender may not be an influence on the likelihood of experiencing drinking problems among frequent heavy drinkers. Likewise, age differences were not statistically significant, although there was some suggestion that frequent heavy drinkers in the eighteen to twenty-nine age group were more likely to report problems. Marital status was significant for all four problem comparisons. Greater proportions of single frequent heavy drinkers than married frequent heavy drinkers reported both types of problems at both levels of severity, despite the fact that single drinkers would have been ineligible to report problems with spouses.

Region was not associated with the occurrence of problems among frequent heavy drinkers. Although drinkers residing in the dry region were much more likely than those residing in the wet region to report consequences at either the moderate or the high level, these differences were not statistically significant. This appears to contradict the regional results shown in table 13.1, where there were significant regional differences in the occurrence of consequences in the absence of corresponding differences in frequent heavy drinking and dependence. One possible explanation is that drinkers in the dry region who do *not* frequently drink large amounts per occasion may nevertheless encounter adverse social reactions, thereby increasing the degree of regional divergence in problem prevalences when all drinkers rather than simply all frequent heavy drinkers are examined (see Cahalan and Room, 1974 for additional evidence of this). Urbanicity had no significant impact on the proportion of frequent heavy drinkers who reported problems.

Income was strongly associated with the occurrence of problems. In all four problem comparisons, low income frequent heavy drinkers were more likely to report problems than high income frequent heavy drinkers. Both the lowest (0–$10,000 annually) and the highest ($40,000 and over annually) income groups were of particular note. A larger proportion of frequent heavy drinkers in the lowest group and a smaller proportion of those in the highest group reported problems than in the middle income categories. Education, the other social class variable, produced similar results. For all four comparisons, less educated frequent heavy drinkers were more likely to report problems than were more educated frequent heavy drinkers.

In sum, for this group of frequent heavy drinkers, the univariate distributions of drinking problems measures suggest that marital status,

TABLE 13.2

Percentage of Current Drinkers Reporting Drinking Problems among Drinkers Who Consume Five or More Drinks per Occasion as Often as Once a Week or More

	Moderate Level Dependence	Moderate Level Consequences	High Level Dependence	High Level Consequences	N
1. Sex					
Male	21.6	31.2	14.4	18.5	238
Female	26.1	36.4	21.8	13.3	64
	$X^2 = 0.4$	$X^2 = 0.4$	$X^2 = 1.5$	$X^2 = 0.6$	
2. Age					
18–29	28.9	38.7	18.8	22.3	126
30–39	16.7	25.2	12.6	12.1	80
40–49	22.8	39.4	18.6	21.4	47
50–59	13.3	18.3	7.0	12.5	29
60 and over	19.4	24.1	19.1	4.5	20
	$X^2 = 5.9$	$X^2 = 8.5$	$X^2 = 3.5$	$X^2 = 7.0$	
3. Marital Status					
Married	13.7	26.2	10.5	12.1	158
Single	32.3	39.0	22.0	23.1	144
	$X^2 = 13.9^{**}$	$X^2 = 5.0^*$	$X^2 = 6.5^*$	$X^2 = 5.6^*$	
4. Region					
Wet	21.4	28.6	13.9	14.0	185
Dry	24.5	38.0	19.4	22.6	117
	$X^2 = 0.2$	$X^2 = 2.5$	$X^2 = 1.2$	$X^2 = 3.1$	

5. *Urbanicity*

Metropolitan cities 50,000 and over	25.2	34.2	17.0	20.1	121
Metropolitan towns under 50,000	19.8	29.7	14.8	18.0	112
Nonmetropolitan areas	22.5	33.2	16.2	11.4	69
	$X^2 = 1.0$	$X^2 = 0.5$	$X^2 = 0.2$	$X^2 = 2.4$	

6. *Family Income*

$0–10,000	37.5	50.7	27.9	34.0	48
$10,001–20,000	28.4	32.0	18.9	17.0	66
$20,001–30,000	15.5	34.5	11.5	12.5	53
$30,001–40,000	22.8	24.0	15.6	13.4	54
Over $40,000	10.7	22.2	7.9	12.0	68
	$X^2 = 14.5^{**}$	$X^2 = 12.5^*$	$X^2 = 9.7^*$	$X^2 = 12.2^*$	

7. *Education*

Less than high school graduate	26.8	37.5	14.7	14.9	61
High school graduate	32.3	39.8	26.4	27.0	120
Some college	14.7	27.6	9.3	9.1	68
College graduate and beyond	6.1	15.5	2.7	9.2	53
	$X^2 = 17.7^{**}$	$X^2 = 11.4^{**}$	$X^2 = 19.0^{**}$	$X^2 = 13.7^{**}$	

* Significant at 0.05 level.
** Significant at 0.01 level.

income, and education might be related to drinking problems. In this group, drinking problems do not appear to be related to gender, age, region, or urbanicity, but in many of these cases low *Ns* prevented relationships that were suggested by the data from being statistically significant.

In the multivariate analysis of drinking problems, four regression models were developed — called Models A, B, C, and D. Model A predicts the *dependence* score on the basis of the demographic variables discussed above and the monthly frequency of consuming *five* or more drinks at a sitting. Model B predicts the *consequences* score on the basis of the demographic variables and the monthly frequency of drinking *five* or more at a sitting. Model C predicts the *dependence* score on the basis of the demographic variables and the monthly frequency of drinking *eight* or more drinks in a day. Model D predicts the *consequences* score on the basis of the demographic variables and the monthly frequency of drinking *eight* or more in a day.[3] The distributions for the problem scores and the frequencies of heavy intake occasions were highly skewed, necessitating the use of log transformations for both of these variables. The transformation $\ln(x + 0.01)$ was used. For Models A and B, the analysis was restricted to those who drank five or more drinks at a sitting at least once in the past year ($N = 612$). For Models C and D, the analysis was restricted to those who drank eight or more drinks in a day at least once in the past year ($N = 425$). This was done to prevent the large numbers of respondents who never drank in such quantities from distorting the results (see Cahalan and Room, 1974; Mäkelä, 1981).

The results of the multiple regression analysis appear in table 13.3. None of the four models was able to provide a strong prediction of drinking problems; the R^2s indicated only 16% to 23% of the total variance was explained. However, it should not come as a surprise that our ability to predict complex phenomena such as problems with drinking on the basis of a single drinking intake variable (with no correction for body weight or metabolism) and a handful of demographic characteristics is limited.

In all four models, the frequency of heavy drinking occasions was clearly the best predictor of problems. Using the higher standard of heavy drinking (eight or more drinks per day rather than five or more drinks per occasion) produced somewhat stronger associations between intake and problems, as expected (Knupfer, 1984). The coefficients for some of the other predictors were statistically significant but were very small in magnitude. Taking the strongest case as an example, in Model A marital status accounted for less than 3% of the variance in the dependent variable, even though the relationship was statistically significant due to the large N. The magnitudes of the other demographic coefficients were similarly unimportant. Thus, the substantive conclusion of this investigation must be that none of the demographic variables had a substantial impact on the reported problem level at a given frequency of heavy drinking. Nevertheless, the patterning of the remaining coefficients does bear some discussion.

TABLE 13.3
Multiple Regression Analyses of Problem Scores
Betas
(Unstandardized Coefficients in Parentheses)

	Model A Dependence Score[t]	Model B Consequences Score[t]	Model C Dependence Score[t]	Model D Consequences Score[t]
Independent Variables				
Monthly frequency of 5+ drinking occasions[t]	0.36** (0.65)	0.31** (0.61)	n.i.	n.i.
Monthly frequency of 8+ drinking days[t]	n.i.	n.i.	0.40** (0.64)	0.41** (0.75)
Sex (effect of female)	0.02 (0.14)	0.004 (0.03)	0.02 (0.12)	0.04 (0.29)
Age in years	-0.10* (-0.02)	-0.15** (-0.04)	-0.03 (-0.01)	-0.06 (-0.02)
Marital status (effects of single)	0.17** (0.90)	0.12** (0.69)	0.15** (0.84)	0.10* (0.61)
Region (effect of dry region)	0.01 (0.07)	0.04 (0.26)	-0.02 (-0.13)	0.03 (0.21)
Urbanicity (effect of large city)	0.03 (0.16)	0.02 (0.16)	0.04 (0.23)	0.01 (0.05)
Urbanicity (effect of non-metro)	0.04 (0.27)	-0.004 (-0.03)	0.06 (0.42)	-0.04 (-0.27)
Family income	-0.06 (-0.01)	0.006 (-0.001)	-0.005 (-0.001)	0.04 (0.01)
Years of education	-0.04 (-0.04)	-0.15** (-0.17)	-0.05 (-0.06)	-0.11* (-0.14)
Constant	(-2.31)**	(-0.08)	(-1.42)	(0.12)
N	612	613	425	425
R²	0.195	0.167	0.217	0.228
F	16.2**	13.5**	12.8**	13.6**

[t] Transformed ln (x + 0.01).
* Significant at 0.05 level.
** Significant at 0.01 level.
n.i. Not included in model.

Despite the expectation that women are more likely than men to encounter adverse consequences if they drink heavily, sex was not a significant predictor in any of the four models. Though there were large gender differences in the frequency of heavy drinking and in the occurrence of problems, there appeared to be no association between gender and problems once the frequency of heavy drinking was controlled. Age had a weak association with both the dependence score (Model A) and the consequences score (Model B) when the five or more standard of heavy drinking was used but no association when the eight or more standard was used. The direction of the relationship was that younger respondents reported higher problem scores, which is consistent with the views of Mäkelä (1978). Marital status emerged as a significant (though weak) factor in all four models and was the only demographic factor to do so. The direction of the relationship was that single respondents tended to report higher problem scores, as expected. Note that it was not clear whether being single placed a person at greater risk for experiencing drinking problems or whether those with greater problems were more likely to become divorced or remain single.

Neither region nor urbanicity were associated with greater problem scores once the frequency of heavy drinking was taken into account. Regarding both variables, these findings show a continuation of trends noted in Room's (1982) comparison of 1964 and 1979 data. In that comparison, both regional and urban/rural differences in heavy drinking and in consequences were shown to be diminishing over time. As the present findings indicate, the trend seems to have continued until the importance of either factor has disappeared. Of the socioeconomic status indicators, education had a small association with consequences (Models B and D) but not with dependence (Models A and C). But given the findings on education, it was surprising that no effects were associated with the income variable.[4]

DISCUSSION

The results of this analysis indicate that the frequency of heavy drinking occasions is related to drinking problem scores, but that none of the demographic variables analyzed seems to be strongly associated with problem scores in multivariate analyses in which the frequency of heavy drinking is included as an independent variable. That intake should be the primary predictor only reconfirms common sense — that people experience drinking problems because they drink too much. But the negative results regarding the demographic variables were unexpected given that the literature includes so much discussion of demographic characteristics which presumably put people at greater risk for experiencing adverse consequences should they drink heavily.

With regard to dependence, as distinct from consequences, these results perhaps could have been anticipated. It is easy to imagine that both excessive intake and the various behaviors tapped by the dependence items are manifestations of the same underlying condition, and therefore both should be present in the same subset of individuals regardless of sex, age, social position, and the like. Or, under an alternate view (Clark and Midanik, 1982; Room, 1977) those who indulge in bouts of heavy drinking might be expected to experience tremors, blackouts, and similar short term physiological consequences regardless of their demographic characteristics. The findings would support either of these expectations, although this segment of the analysis was exploratory, as noted above. However, with regard to the consequences of drinking, the findings require some reflection. How should they be interpreted and what implications do they have?

First, the findings indicate the kinds of explanations that we should seek for the relatively high prevalence of drinking problems in certain demographic groups. These results suggest that we should put more emphasis on explanations that focus on why some groups drink more than others and less emphasis on explanations that stress the greater relative impropriety of drinking for some groups (and therefore the greater likelihood that members of those groups will suffer negative consequences if they do drink heavily.) The former kinds of explanations may seem more prosaic and less sociologically rich than the latter, but a fascination for apparent sociological richness should not draw us away from propositions that have stronger empirical support. In the same vein, one notes that arguments explaining why certain demographic groups face greater consequences for their heavy drinking than others have been offered rather often whereas empirical investigations of this issue have been rather few. And this is not for lack of appropriate data; data similar to those used here have been available from a number of surveys for several years. This research should caution us that we have been too willing to entertain and accept such notions in the absence of an adequate empirical foundation.

Second, what was previously an unremarkable finding has now come to pose a dilemma. It is generally known that it is more acceptable for some kinds of people to drink than for others. Surveys have shown, for example, that people generally have stronger objections to drinking and drunkenness by women than by men and by the elderly than by other adults (Knupfer, 1982; Knupfer, 1964; Clark, 1977; Roizen, 1981; Caetano and Medina-Mora, 1986). There is nothing remarkable, or in need of explanation, about these observations so long as it is imagined that these differences in social opprobrium are accompanied by differences in problem rates. When it is discovered, however, that there are not substantial differences in problem rates between groups after controlling for consumption, there is suddenly very much to explain. How is it that known differences in popular objections to drinking and drunkenness are not translated into differences in the relative rates of consequences of drinking, after controlling for consumption? Although it is premature to offer an answer on the basis of the present analysis, it is clear that future research should grapple with this dilemma.

A similar conclusion surrounds the more "environmental" observations that norms against drinking are stronger in the dry region and in rural areas. Again, known differences in public norms are not matched in these results by differentials in problem prevalences. Perhaps heavy drinkers in dry environs are better able to withdraw into social circles peopled by other heavy drinkers and to thereby insulate themselves from opprobrium far better than we had previously expected. Again, something that needs explaining, and further study, emerges from the present findings.

Finally, the results afford a methodological comment. It has been claimed that the inclusion of consequences items in drinking problems indices is undesirable because the differential propensity for society to react against drinking by certain types of people, such as women, biases a problem index with regard to those groups (Homiller, 1980; although this view is discounted by Ferrence, 1980). The present results should not be interpreted as showing that no such bias does or could exist in such indices, but they do weaken the presumption that such bias necessarily exists whenever consequences indicators are used.

THOMAS C. HARFORD
BRIDGET F. GRANT
DEBORAH S. HASIN

14

The Effect of Average Daily Consumption and Frequency of Intoxication on the Occurrence of Dependence Symptoms and Alcohol-Related Problems[1]

INTRODUCTION

An impressive body of evidence is now available on the exact nature of the relationship of alcohol consumption to physical abnormalities, such as liver cirrhosis (Lelbach, 1974; Pequignot et al. 1974; Skog, 1982b; Tuyns, Pequignot and Esteve, 1983). Much less is known about how alcohol consumption is related to alcohol dependence and other consequences of drinking. The scientific and practical need to determine the effect of consumption levels on a broader range of negative consequences has not yet been matched by a sustained research effort.

There are several conceptual and methodological reasons for the lack of direct evidence on the association between levels of intake and alcohol-related problems. In the psychiatric literature, actual drinking behavior and dependence symptoms are often considered equivalent manifestations of the entity alcoholism. Consistent with this view, definitions of alcohol abuse and dependence as described in major psychiatric nomenclatures have traditionally highlighted symptoms of pathological use of alcohol rather than levels of alcohol consumption per se. Consequently, structured and semi-structured diagnostic interviews used to operationalize clinically derived criteria (Endicott and Spitzer, 1973; Robins et al. 1981) have not included assessment of drinking levels, preventing the quantification of the ethanol intake-dependence association. In sociological research, dependence symptoms are considered alternate indicators of heavy alcohol intake (Room, 1977). For example, tremors and night sweats are conceptualized as short-term physiological consequences of bouts of heavy drinking, and thus as alternative ways of measuring heavy drinking (Clark and Midanik, 1985). The belief in the equivalence of dependence symptoms and heavy alcohol intake has had an equally disinhibiting effect on research in this area.

Problems in operationalizing both alcohol consumption and drinking consequences have contributed to our lack of information concerning the link between the two areas. For instance, psychiatric and sociological researchers have grouped diverse consequences of drinking into global classifications of abuse and dependence or into composite measures of problematic and symptomatic drinking. This obscures the specificity of associations and provides for premature closure of research questions that are best resolved empirically. Also, several investigators (Ashley and Rankin, 1979; Popham and Schmidt, 1978; Room, 1977; Turner, Mezey and Kimball, 1977a, 1977b) have highlighted the difficulties of measuring consumption as average or typical daily ethanol intake. A different type of consumption measure (i.e., frequency of drinking to intoxication) might be more informative when considering the relationship between consumption and certain types of drinking problems. As Knupfer (1984) has pointed out, average daily consumption may be important with regard to the development of certain consequences of excessive alcohol use, such as liver cirrhosis. However, frequency of intoxication may be more closely related to other alcohol-related problems including driving accidents and legal entanglements due to drinking. In addition to these issues, few studies have used appropriate statistical strategies to describe the risk of adverse drinking consequences at various levels of intake. The usual presentation of data bearing on the amount of alcohol intake and drinking consequences consists of a cross-tabulation of both factors sometimes controlling for levels of a third (e.g., sociodemographic) variable thought to influence the relationship (Clark and Midanik, 1985; Hilton, chapter 13 in this volume). Typically, the association is expressed as either first-order or partial correlations. This procedure is straightforward, but the interpretation of such stratified analyses becomes more and more difficult as the number of variables to be controlled increases. Additional consideration of more than one or two control variables is usually precluded by the small numbers that result. Recent studies examining the relationship between several socio-demographic variables and alcohol-related consequences while controlling for levels of intake represent improvements over earlier analyses. However, these applications have either disregarded the potential for interaction in their data (Hilton, chapter 13) or have not used appropriate modeling procedures to ensure that confounding has been adequately controlled (Hauge and Irgens-Jensen, 1987; Mäkelä and Simpura, 1985).

In other studies (e.g., see Kreitman and Duffy, 1988), a forward stepwise algorithm in conjunction with logistic regression analysis was used to determine if drinking pattern variables (e.g., maximum intake, rate of drinking) modified the relationship between total ethanol intake and alcohol-related consequences. Although this research question required that ethanol intake be specified as the exposure variable of interest, the stepwise procedure ensured that total consumption and the presumed drinking pattern or confounder/modifier variables would be treated on equal footing as independent variables. Thus, these independent variables were selected for inclusion in the model solely on the basis of their association with the outcome measure. Unfortunately, the adequate assessment of confounding and interaction requires regression models and ancillary algorithms that take into account the relations of confounders and modifiers to both exposure and to outcome variables. Another shortcoming of using the forward stepwise algorithm to arrive at the "best" regression model is that the results are often dependent on the order in which the undifferentiated independent variables are entered into the analysis.

Given the state of knowledge on the above issues, the purpose of the present study was to evaluate more precisely the risk of various consequences of drinking at different levels of ethanol intake. The quantification of the consumption-problem associations required mathematical modeling techniques that allowed for the simultaneous control of several extraneous factors and the assessment of potential interaction. Linear logistic regression analysis (Breslow and Day, 1980; Breslow and Powers, 1978; Cox, 1978; Prentice, 1976) was selected as the most suitable multivariate technique to achieve this purpose. In the model we selected, a backward elimination algorithm was used to avoid the pitfalls of the forward stepwise procedure. To ensure that the confounding and interaction features of our data were adequately addressed, ethanol consumption was treated as the major risk factor or exposure variable of interest. Based on numerous theories and empirical research, several sociodemographic factors were identified as putative confounders and/or modifiers of the consumption-problem associations.

Given our concerns that the use of aggregate measures of alcohol problems might obscure differences in the relationships between consumption and different types of alcohol-related problems, we performed separate logistic regression analyses for six categories of drinking problems. These included (1) dependence symptoms, (2) belligerence, (3) social/family problems, (4) work/financial problems, (5) legal problems, and (6) physical health problems. By examining each consumption-problem association separately, we allowed for the identification of putative risk factors modifying the relationships in ways that could reveal underlying social or biological processes. Moreover, separate analyses of alcohol-related problem groups might redefine high risk groups identified in investigations that use more global classifications of alcohol abuse, dependence, or problematic drinking as outcome measures.

Because various aspects of alcohol consumption can relate in entirely different ways to the various drinking problems, we examined the relationship of each alcohol-related problem to the frequency of intoxication as well as to average daily ethanol intake.

METHODS

Respondents

The data for this study were drawn from the 1984 National Alcohol Survey conducted by the Alcohol Research Group under a grant from the National Institute on Alcohol Abuse and Alcoholism. This multistage area probability survey was designed to provide samples of Blacks and Hispanics large enough for cross-ethnic analyses (see Appendix). Due to the oversampling of Blacks and Hispanics, these respondents were downweighted to allow analyses generalizable to the U.S. population as a whole. Weights were also calculated to account for sample selection within households, and for varying completion rates by sex, age, and the four census regions of the country. The downweighting procedure produced an N of 2,167 cases, representing the actual number of non-Black, non-Hispanic respondents who were interviewed in addition to an approximately proportional number of Blacks and Hispanics.

Alcohol Consumption

Consumption questions used in the 1984 survey included beverage-specific quantity items related to typical amount of drinking on recent occasions. Additional questions using the past year time frame assessed beverage-specific frequency and the frequency of heavier drinking occasions (i.e., eight to eleven drinks or twelve or more drinks). Employing the responses to all of these items, we computed an estimate of the average amount of ethanol in ounces consumed per day during the past year. More detail on the algorithm used to arrive at this measure is presented elsewhere (Harford and Grant, 1988).

A measure of monthly frequency of intoxication was constructed by converting responses to the question, "How often during the past year did you drink enough to feel drunk?" to a monthly time frame (i.e., dividing by twelve). Coded values for this continuous exposure variable ranged from twenty-seven days representing drinking to intoxication every day or nearly every day on a monthly basis to zero days or never drinking enough to feel drunk.

Sociodemographic Characteristics

Age (A) in years, sex (S: 0 = female, 1 = male), ethnicity (ET: 0 = white, 1 = nonwhite), education (ED: 0 = high school graduate and beyond, 1 = less than high school graduate), and marital status served as extraneous variables in the present study. Current marital status was entered into the analyses as two dummy variables, one representing never married (NM) and the other representing widowed, separated, or divorced (W) status. Married or living with someone was the contrast category in each case.

Dependence Symptoms and Alcohol-Related Problems

Figure 14.1 lists the items that measured alcohol dependence and alcohol-related problems. Items traditionally used as indicators of alcohol dependence in the sociological literature included such symptoms as impaired control over drinking and memory loss or tremors after drinking (twelve items). Drinking problem or consequence items from the questionnaire were divided into five groups: belligerence (two items); social/family (twelve items); work/financial (five items); legal (four items); and physical health (three items) problems. For the purpose of defining our dependent variables, two scoring systems were used. For the dependence items, the number of positive symptoms were totalled, and respondents with a score of three or more symptoms during the past year were classified as dependent on alcohol while persons affirming two symptoms or less were classified as nondependent. For each of the remaining alcohol problem groups, persons experiencing at least one consequence within the past year were contrasted with those persons who had not reported any. For example, persons reporting at least one social/family problem over the course of the past year were compared to those persons who had not experienced social/family problems during this time.

FIGURE 14.1
Alcohol Dependence Symptoms and Alcohol-Related Problems

I. ALCOHOL DEPENDENCE SYMPTOMS
    1. I have awakened the next day not being able to remember some of the things I had done while drinking.
    2. I have skipped a number of regular meals while drinking.
    3. I sometimes kept on drinking after I had promised myself not to.
    4. I need more alcohol than I used to, to get the same effect as before.
    5. My hands shook a lot the morning after drinking.
    6. Once I started drinking it was difficult for me to stop before I became completely intoxicated.
    7. I deliberately tried to cut down or quit drinking, but was I unable to do so.
    8. I have often taken a drink the first thing when I got up in the morning.
    9. Sometimes I have awakened during the night or early morning sweating all over because of drinking.
    10. I have taken a strong drink in the morning to get over the effects of last night's drinking.
    11. I stayed intoxicated for several days at a time.
    12. Sometimes I have needed a drink so badly that I couldn't think of anything else.

II. ALCOHOL-RELATED PROBLEMS
    Legal
    1. A policeman questioned or warned me because of my drinking.
    2. I had trouble with the law when driving was not involved.
    3. I have been arrested for driving after drinking.
    4. Have you driven a car when you had drunk enough to be in trouble if the police had stopped you?
    Belligerence
    1. I have gotten in a heated argument while drinking.
    2. I have gotten into a fight while drinking.
    Physical Health
    1. I had an illness connected with my drinking which kept me from working on my regular activities for a week or more.
    2. Was there a time when you felt that your drinking had a harmful effect on your health?
    3. I felt that my drinking was becoming a serious threat to my physical health.

(continued)

FIGURE 14.1 *(continued)*

4. People at work indicated that I should cut down on drinking.
5. Drinking may have hurt my chances for promotion, or raises, or better jobs.

Work/Financial

1. Was there a time when you felt that your drinking had a harmful effect on your work and employment opportunities?
2. Was there a time when you felt that your drinking had a harmful effect on your financial position?
3. I have lost a job, or nearly lost one, because of drinking.
4. People at work indicated that I should cut down on drinking.
5. Drinking may have hurt my chances for promotion, or raises, or better jobs.

Social/Family

1. Was there a time when you felt that your drinking had a harmful effect on your friendships or social life?
2. Was there a time when you felt that your drinking had a harmful effect on your home life or marriage?
3. A spouse or someone I lived with got angry about my drinking or the way I behaved while drinking.
4. A spouse or someone I lived with threatened to leave me because of my drinking.
5. My drinking had interfered with my spare time activities or hobbies.
6. Did your mother's feelings about your drinking break up your relationship with her or threaten to break it up?
7. Did your father's feelings about your drinking break up your relationship with him or threaten to break it up?
8. Did your girlfriend's or boyfriend's feelings about your drinking break up your relationship with him/her or threaten to break it up?
9. Did any other relative's feelings about your drinking break up your relationship with him/her or threaten to break it up?
10. Did the feelings about your drinking of anyone else you lived with break up your relationship with him/her or threaten to break it up?
11. Did any other friend's feelings about your drinking break up your relationship with him/her or threaten to break it up?
12. Did your anyone else's feelings about your drinking break up your relationship with him/her or threaten to break it up?

Statistical Analysis

Linear logistic regression analyses were conducted to separately examine the association between average daily ethanol consumption or frequency of intoxication with each of the six alcohol-related problem areas. Daily ethanol intake, measured in ounces per day, or monthly frequency of intoxication was designated as the exposure variable and sociodemographic factors were included as potential confounders or modifier variables. Operationally, a sociodemographic variable is considered an actual confounder if its control results in a substantial change in the estimate of the effect of consumption on the outcome measure, conditional on all other potential confounders. A statistically significant cross-product term (i.e., interaction) is indicative of nonuniformity across strata of another risk factor, or what is usually referred to as effect modification.

Our data analytic strategy consisted of two stages. In the first stage, we identified important modifiers by allowing for interaction effects up to second-degree product terms involving the exposure variable, either average daily ethanol intake (e.g., ethanol intake x age) or frequency of intoxication (e.g., intoxication x sex). Using a backward elimination process, all nonsignificant cross-product terms (p ≥ .05) were eliminated from the model while at the same time all main effects were retained. We included only second-degree interaction terms because cross-product terms involving higher levels of interaction are: (1) rarely statistically significant; (2) usually uninterpretable, and (3) often questionable due to induced multicollinearity.

Stage Two entailed the identification of confounders, or alternatively, the deletion of nonconfounders from the reduced model resulting from Stage One (i.e., a model containing all main effect and significant cross-product terms). In the case of no interaction, the elimination of nonconfounders consists of removing all main effects except the primary exposure variable to produce a further reduced model. If the main effect coefficient of the exposure variable, ethanol consumption, does not materially change, the use of this model can lead to a gain in precision. On the other hand, if the exposure-involved coefficient does show substantial change upon refitting, the main effect terms for the confounders should be retained in the model. In the presence of interaction, main effect terms involved in the model as modifiers are not candidates for deletion. Under these conditions, the main effect exposure coefficient and all exposure-related cross-product coefficients must be monitored for change upon refitting to determine if confounders should be retained in the model.

Twelve sets of logistic regression analyses were conducted: six for each alcohol-related consequence with daily ethanol intake as the exposure variable and six for each alcohol-related consequence with intoxication as the exposure variable. All analyses were performed on weighted data and restricted to those respondents who drank five or more drinks at a sitting at least once during the past year ($N = 1,384$). This was done to prevent the large number of respondents in this survey who never drank in such amounts from distorting the results (Cahalan and Room, 1974; Hilton, 1987; Mäkelä, 1978).

RESULTS

Prevalence of Alcohol-Related Consequences

The twelve month prevalence of alcohol dependence was 14.2% among respondents included in these analyses. The percentage of respondents reporting at least one drinking consequence during the past year varied by problem category: nearly 40% for legal problems (including drinking and driving); 26.8% for social/family problems; 20.9% for belligerence; and approximately 10% each for work/financial and physical health problems.

The majority of the respondents who reported three or more dependence symptoms were heavier drinkers, males, whites, high school graduates, under thirty years of age, currently married or living with someone, and drank to intoxication at least once a month during the past year (table 14.1). The percentage distributions of respondents reporting each type of alcohol-related problem showed similar patterns across sociodemographic subgroups (table 14.2).

TABLE 14.1
Percent Distribution of Respondents
Reporting Three or More Dependence Symptoms*

Characteristic	Percent	N
Ethanol (ounces per day)		
0.01–.50	17.9	29
0.51–1.00	16.1	34
1.01–1.50	10.5	21
1.51.2.00	8.2	18
2.01–2.50	6.3	10
2.51–3.00	5.3	10
3.01–3.50	2.9	10
3.51+	32.8	72
Intoxication (frequency)		
2 times/year or less	16.3	42
3–11 times/year	21.4	44
1–3 times/month	23.5	49
1–2 times/week or more	38.8	70
Sex		
Male	69.2	145
Female	30.8	60
Age		
18–29	51.9	84
30–39	24.6	61
40–49	12.3	31

(continued)

TABLE 14.1 *(continued)*

Characteristic	Percent	N
Age (continued)		
50–59	4.9	17
60+	6.3	12
Marital Status		
Married/living together	47.2	85
Widowed/separated/divorced	15.5	48
Never married	37.3	71
Ethnicity		
White	84.2	68
Hispanic	4.3	54
Black	11.5	83
Education		
Less than high school	28.6	14
High school graduate	51.8	31
Some college	12.1	72
College graduate and beyond	7.5	87

* Percentages based on weighted figures; *Ns* based on unweighted figures.

Average Daily Ethanol Intake and Alcohol-Related Consequences

The results of the logistic regression analyses for the full and reduced model associated with average daily ethanol intake and alcohol dependence are shown in table 14.3. Table 14.4 summarizes similar results for the reduced models when each of the five remaining types of drinking consequences served as the outcome measure. In all six analyses, the simultaneous removal of all eligible main effect terms for potential confounder variables did not result in meaningful changes in exposure coefficients, exposure-involved cross-product terms, or the corresponding estimated adjusted odds ratios. Thus, the deleted extraneous variables (e.g., sex, ethnicity, age) were not likely to be actual confounders.

With regard to alcohol dependence, age was the single discernible modifier (table 14.3). The negative coefficient for this interaction indicates that the ethanol intake-dependence relationship was strongest among the younger as opposed to older respondents. The estimated odds for dependence decreased from 1.67, exponent [0.675—0.008 (20)], among twenty year olds to 1.21 for sixty year olds (table 14.5). That is, for twenty year olds, the risk for dependence is estimated to increase by 0.51, [0.675—0.008 (20)], for each additional ounce of ethanol consumed daily while the corresponding increase in risk is 0.19 for sixty year olds. Alternatively, sixty year olds have an odds of dependence that is approximately 70% of the odds for twenty year olds.

TABLE 14.2
Percent of Respondents Reporting Alcohol-Related Problems

Characteristic	Belligerence		Social/Family		Work/Financial		Legal		Physical	
	Percent[a]	(N)[b]	Percent	(N)	Percent	(N)	Percent	(N)	Percent	(N)
Ethanol (ounces per day)										
0.01–0.21	7.4	(20)	11.9	(43)	9.2	(9)	8.8	(30)	12.1	(28)
0.22–0.99	26.8	(74)	25.3	(109)	24.9	(29)	38.0	(130)	30.4	(67)
0.99	65.8	(168)	62.8	(243)	65.9	(101)	53.2	(209)	57.5	(130)
Intoxication frequency)										
2 times/year or less	21.8	(69)	27.8	(133)	20.2	(30)	31.3	(107)	34.4	(76)
3–11 times/year	28.2	(67)	30.4	(104)	15.8	(29)	34.3	(118)	21.1	(54)
1–3 times/month	23.9	(57)	19.6	(74)	24.6	(32)	15.3	(66)	21.4	(46)
1–2 times/week or more	26.1	(59)	22.2	(84)	39.4	(48)	19.1	(78)	23.1	(49)
Sex										
Male	66.4	(169)	73.7	(283)	60.8	(104)	74.5	(275)	56.9	(90)
Female	33.6	(93)	26.3	(112)	39.2	(35)	25.5	(94)	43.1	(135)
Age										
13–29	54.5	(124)	49.0	(177)	66.2	(61)	49.3	(161)	42.1	(79)
30–39	26.2	(84)	24.5	(114)	13.9	(37)	27.9	(115)	26.6	(66)
40–49	11.5	(35)	15.9	(59)	14.1	(27)	14.3	(63)	19.0	(48)
50–59	5.9	(15)	5.4	(31)	3.9	(9)	5.1	(19)	4.9	(20)
60+	1.9	(4)	5.2	(14)	1.9	(5)	3.4	(11)	7.4	(12)

(continued)

TABLE 14.2 (continued)

	Alcohol-Related Problem									
	Belligerence		Social/Family		Work/Financial		Legal		Physical	
Characteristic	Percent[a]	(N)[b]	Percent	(N)	Percent	(N)	Percent	(N)	Percent	(N)
Marital Status										
Married/living together	53.5	(123)	54.3	(188)	51.5	(61)	54.4	(182)	57.3	(96)
Widowed/separated/divorced	11.0	(54)	13.6	(88)	9.7	(31)	11.8	(72)	17.8	(65)
Never married	35.5	(85)	32.1	(118)	38.8	(47)	33.8	(115)	24.9	(64)
Ethnicity										
White	88.2	(106)	85.5	(134)	86.3	(44)	93.1	(201)	79.7	(64)
Hispanic	3.4	(69)	4.5	(124)	3.5	(39)	3.3	(95)	5.8	(65)
Black	8.4	(87)	10.0	(137)	10.2	(56)	3.6	(73)	14.5	(96)
Education										
Less than high school	21.6	(103)	24.7	(167)	22.6	(59)	15.5	(106)	21.1	(20)
High school graduate	49.7	(100)	43.7	(131)	54.4	(49)	41.9	(127)	47.2	(36)
Some college	16.1	(40)	18.5	(70)	18.6	(24)	26.1	(88)	15.6	(80)
College graduate and beyond	12.6	(18)	13.1	(27)	4.4	(6)	16.5	(47)	16.1	(89)

[a] Percentages based on weighted figures.
[b] Ns based on unweighted figures.

TABLE 14.3
Results of Logistic Regression Analysis of Alcohol Dependence

Variable	All Main Effect Variables Included[a]				All Irrelevant Effect Variables Excluded[b]			
	β	Standard Error (β)	P Value	R[c]	β	Standard Error (β)	P Value	R
Intercept	−2.362	0.544	0.0000	0.0000	−2.150	0.458	0.0000	0.000
Ethanol (ounces per day)	0.689	0.143	0.0000	0.198	0.675	0.142	0.0000	0.194
Age	−0.008	0.014	0.5705	0.000	−0.008	0.012	0.5066	0.000
Sex (effect on male)	−0.172	0.264	0.5153	0.000				
Ethnicity (effect on non-white)	−0.069	0.354	0.8449	0.000				
Education (effect of less than high school)	0.687	0.286	0.0163	0.083				
Marital Status (effect of widowed/separated/divorced)	0.479	0.359	0.1830	0.000				
Marital Status (effect of never married)	0.326	0.309	0.2916	0.000				
Ethanol x Age	−0.088	0.033	0.0063	−0.100	−0.008	0.003	0.0106	−0.091

[a] Model Chi Square = 75.1 with 8 df, p < .0000.
[b] Model Chi Square = 66.6 with 3 df, p < .0000.
[c] R = A measure of the contribution of each variable independent of sample size.

TABLE 14.4

Results of Logistic Regression Analysis of Alcohol-Related Problems[a]

| | Alcohol-Related Problem | | | | |
Characteristic	Belligerence[b]	Social/Family[f]	Work/Financial[d]	Legal[e]	Physical[f]
Intercept	-2.076	-2.015	-2.689	-0.924	-2.315
	(0.0000)	(0.0000)	(0.0000)	(0.0000)	(0.0000)
Ethanol (ounces per day)	0.479	0.563	0.216	0.279	0.510
	(0.0000)	(0.0000)	(0.0000)	(0.0000)	(0.0001)
Age					
Sex (effect of male)					-0.265
					(0.4156)
Race (effect of non-white)					
Education (effect of less than high school)	0.626	0.824			
	(0.0387)	(0.0047)			

Marital Status (effect of never married)		0.854 (0.0021)	
Marital Status (effect of widowed/separated/divorced)		0.179 (0.5504)	
Ethanol x Sex			−0.314 (0.0212)
Ethanol x Education	−0.355 (0.0005)	−0.315 (0.0105)	
Ethanol x Marital Status (effect of never married)		−0.312 (0.0097)	

[a] Numbers in parenthesis are p values.
[b] Model Chi-square = 66.9 with 3 df, p < .0000.
[c] Model Chi-square = 74.4 with 6 df, p < .0000.
[d] Model Chi-square = 19.5 with 1 df, p < .0000.
[e] Model Chi-square = 38.2 with 1 df, p < .0000.
[f] Model Chi-square = 38.1 with 3 df, p < .0000.

TABLE 14.5
Estimated Adjusted Odds Ratios for the
Ethanol Intake-Dependence Association at Various Ages

Age	Odds Ratio[a]
20	1.674 (1.400, 1.999)
30	1.545 (1.339, 1.782)
40	1.426 (1.256, 1.619)
50	1.316 (1.141, 1.519)
60	1.215 (1.017, 1.452)

[a] Figures in parentheses are 95% confidence intervals.

The estimated adjusted odds ratios for ethanol intake-problem associations that were modified by at least one extraneous sociodemographic variable are shown in table 14.6. The relationships between ethanol intake and belligerence and social/family problems were both modified by education, as the adjusted odds ratios for both were greater among high-school graduates than among those who had not completed high school. Persons with at least a high school education had an odds of demonstrating belligerent behavior as a result of their drinking that was approximately 1.5 times the odds for respondents who did not complete high school. The association between ethanol intake and social/family problems was also modified by marital status. The effect of the ethanol intake x education and ethanol intake x marital status interactions were primarily concentrated among the married respondents. The confidence intervals for the underlying odds ratios related to the never-married status included or quite nearly included 1.0 (the value indicating no association).

Sex was identified as a significant modifier of the ethanol intake-physical problem association. The risk of experiencing physical problems due to drinking was greater for women than men. Among women, the risk for health problems increased by 0.51 for each additional ounce of ethanol consumed daily, while the corresponding increase in risk for men was 0.20.

Age, sex, ethnicity, marital status, and education were not found to modify or confound the relationships between levels of intake and work/financial or legal problems. A one ounce increase in daily ethanol consumption was accompanied by an increase of 0.22 in the risk for work/financial problems and a 0.28 increase in the risk for legal consequences (table 14.4). Equivalently, the odds for work/financial problems are increased 25% with each additional ounce of ethanol consumed on a daily basis while the odds for legal problems are increased by 32% for an equal amount of ethanol intake.

TABLE 14.6

Estimated Adjusted Odds Ratios for the Ethanol Intake-Problem
Associations at Various Levels of Sex, Education, and Marital Status[a]

		Alcohol-Related Problem		
Effect	*Physical*	*Belligerence*	*Social/Family*	
Sex				
Male	1.216			
	(1.094, 1.353)			
Female	1.665			
	(1.300, 2.132)			
Education			*Marital Status*	
			Married	*Never Married*
Less than high school	1.312		1.281	0.938
	(0.983, 1.303)		(1.075, 1.537)	(0.787, 1.117)
High school and beyond	1.614		1.756	1.285
	(1.409, 1.849)		(1.458, 2.115)	(1.068, 1.537)

[a] Figures in parentheses are 95% confidence intervals.

Frequency of Intoxication and Alcohol-Related Consequences

The results of the logistic regression analyses for the reduced models associated with frequency of intoxication and each alcohol-related problem are presented in table 14.7. When legal problems served as the outcome measure, the removal of all eligible main effect terms resulted in substantial changes in the exposure coefficient, the exposure-involved cross-product term (intoxication x marital status), and more importantly the corresponding adjusted odds ratios. Because of this, sex and ethnicity were retained in the reduced model as confounders of the intoxication-legal problem association.

The relationship between frequency of intoxication and alcohol dependence, physical health, and work/financial problems were nearly identical to those in which average daily ethanol consumption served as the exposure variable of interest (table 14.8). That is, the risk for dependence decreased with age, physical problems were more closely associated with intoxication among females, and none of the sociodemographic variables were found to confound or modify the intoxication-work/financial problem association. Moreover, the magnitude of the associations between intoxication and these problem areas were similar to those observed when average daily consumption was specified as the exposure variable.

Associations between intoxication and belligerence, social/family, and legal problems due to drinking were dependent on at least one

TABLE 14.7

Results of Logistic Regression Analyses of Alcohol Dependence and Alcohol-Related Problems[a]

	Problem					
Variable	Alcohol Dependence[b]	Belligerence	Social/Family[c]	Work/Financial[d]	Legal[e]	Physical[f]
Intercept	-2.807 (0.0000)	-2.299 (0.0000)	-1.442 (0.0003)	-2.680 (0.0000)	-1.323 (0.0000)	-2.105 (0.0000)
Frequency of Intoxication	0.703 (0.0000)	1.405 (0.0000)	0.741 (0.0000)	0.205 (0.0000)	0.397 (0.0000)	0.349 (0.0006)
Age	0.009 (0.4385)		-0.002 (0.8408)			
Sex (effect of male)		0.468 (0.1103)			0.594 (0.0022)	-0.264 (0.3590)
Ethnicity (effect on non-white)					-1.352 (0.0000)	
Education (effect of less than high school)		0.328 (0.2514)				
Marital Status (effect of widowed/separated/divorced)			0.241 (0.4200)		0.580 (0.0467)	

Marital Status (effect of single)		0.279 (0.3220)	0.384 (0.0685)
Intoxication x Age	−0.009 (0.0001)	−0.009 (0.0039)	
Intoxication x Education	−0.250 (0.0028)		
Intoxication x Marital Status (effect of widowed/separated/divorced)		−0.263 (0.0326)	−0.349 (0.0001)
Intoxication x Marital Status (effect of never married)			
Intoxication x Sex	−1.067 (0.0002)		−0.246 (0.0234)

a Numbers in parenthesis are p values.
b Model Chi-square = 107.9 with 3 df, p < .0000.
c Model Chi-square = 101.3 with 5 df, p < .0000.
d Model Chi-square = 78.0 with 6 df, p < .0000.
e Model Chi-square = 35.6 with 1 df, p < .0000.
f Model Chi-square = 102.8 with 6 df, p < .0000.
g Model Chi-square = 30.9 with 3 df, p < .0000.

sociodemographic variable not shown to modify the corresponding daily ethanol intake-problem relationships (table 14.8). Similar to the ethanol intake-belligerence relationship, the association between intoxication and belligerence was stronger among high school graduates. However, unlike the ethanol intake-belligerence association, the intoxication-belligerence relationship was also modified by sex. Females, regardless of educational attainment, were at higher risk of demonstrating belligerent behavior while intoxicated.

The association between intoxication and social/family problems was dependent on levels of both age and marital status, but not education, similar to the case when average daily ethanol intake served as the exposure variable. The negative coefficient for age (table 14.7) indicated that the intoxication-social/family association was stronger among younger respondents. For example, married twenty year olds had a 75% increased risk of experiencing a social/family problem compared to a 22% increase among sixty year olds. Risk rose more slowly among the never married respondents: corresponding increases in the odds for twenty year olds was 35% with no significant increase in risk for sixty year olds. The intoxication x marital status interaction was primarily concentrated among the married respondents. In contrast to the increased risk of experiencing social/family problems in this marital status group, confidence intervals surrounding the underlying odds ratios of the never married group included or nearly included 1.0, a value indicative of no association.

Unlike the results of the ethanol intake-legal problem analysis, the risk of encountering legal problems as the result of intoxication was approximately 1.5 times greater for married respondents compared to those respondents who were currently widowed, separated, or divorced.

DISCUSSION

Sex, ethnicity, marital status, and education were not identified as important confounders of the relationship between dependence and either average daily consumption or frequency of intoxication. However, age did modify both relationships. Alcohol dependence was more closely related to average daily ethanol consumption and frequency of intoxication among young adults than in those at later stages of life. The greater magnitude of the consumption-dependence association among the younger age groups may reflect the fact that young people drink more on the average and become more frequently intoxicated than older persons and thus tend to report more symptoms associated with

TABLE 14.8

Estimated Adjusted Odds Ratios for the Intoxication-Dependence and Intoxication-Problem Associations at Various Levels of Sex, Education, Age and Marital Status[a]

Effect:	Dependence	Physical	Belligerence (Education) High School	Belligerence (Education) High School	Legal — Married	Legal — Separated/Divorced	Social/Family — Married	Social/Family — Never Married
Sex								
Male		1.108 (1.023, 1.201)	1.092 (0.968, 1.232)	1.402 (1.221, 1.594)				
Female		1.418 (1.165, 1.725)	3.174 (1.788, 5.635)	4.075 (2.323, 7.149)				
Marital Status					1.487 (1.298, 1.704)	1.049 (0.881, 1.249)		
Age								
20	1.687 (1.462, 1.946)						1.752 (1.369, 2.243)	1.347 (1.129, 1.606)
30	1.542 (1.377, 1.725)						1.602 (1.299, 1.974)	1.231 (1.020, 1.486)
40	1.409 (1.280, 1.551)						1.464 (1.214, 1.765)	1.125 (0.904, 1.401)
50	1.288 (1.162, 1.428)						1.338 (1.111, 1.611)	1.028 (0.791, 1.338)
60	1.177 (1.037, 1.336)						1.223 (0.996, 1.501)	0.940 (0.685, 1.289)

[a] Figures in parentheses are 95% confidence limits.

alcohol dependence. Alternatively, there may be something different about the circumstances or experiences of these young persons which leads them to report subjectively experienced impaired control more often than older respondents. Younger respondents might also experience greater risk for alcohol dependence due to differences in drinking habits. That is, younger persons may achieve intoxication more frequently than do older persons, even at the same level of alcohol consumption. In contrast, older persons may be less at risk for dependence as the result of reduced participation in social and occupational activities accompanying increasing age.

In contrast to the findings on age and dependence, age was only found to be an influential modifier of one of the remaining ten relationships. These results are inconsistent with those of Fillmore (1974) who found that the occurrence of drinking problems tended to be less closely related to the frequency and amount of drinking among younger adults than in the later stages of life. This discrepancy probably reflects methodological differences between the two studies. Fillmore analyzed data from the same individuals at two points in time compared to the cross-sectional design of the present investigation. She also used a drinking problem measure that did not differentiate between the various types of drinking consequences.

It is not entirely clear why persons with higher levels of education should show a stronger relationship between average daily ethanol and belligerence and social/family problems or frequency of intoxication and social/family problems. It may be that heavy drinking is less tolerated for those who hold positions of greater imputed responsibility (Knupfer, 1984). This explanation may also account for the elevated risk of social/family and legal problems among respondents who were currently married or living with someone. The results do not appear to support Mäkelä's (1978) thesis of differential social control which posits that drinking behavior in subordinate groups in society is more heavily restricted and sanctioned. In contrast to this thesis and similar formulations (Park, 1983; Robins, Bates and O'Neil, 1962), the risks of belligerence and social/family consequences were not shown to be greater among the less educated and the never married, who presumably have fewer social and financial resources to insulate themselves from such adverse reactions to their drinking.

Women were at higher risk for experiencing physical health problems than were males for equivalent levels of daily average ethanol consumption. For women, the odds for physical health consequences increased by 66% for each additional ounce of ethanol consumed daily while the corresponding increase in the odds for men was 21%. Similarly, there was an 84% increase in the risk of experiencing health problems among women reporting intoxication once a week compared to those reporting drinking to intoxication once a month during the past year. The corresponding increase in risk for males was 36%. That women may be more susceptible to the adverse physical consequences of drinking has been corroborated in numerous case-control studies focusing on the development of liver cirrhosis (Bhattacharyya and Rake, 1981; Krasner et al. 1977; Levi and Chalmers, 1978; Saunders et al. 1982). In these studies, lower levels of consumption were reported among women with severe forms of liver disease compared to men with equally severe forms of liver damage. Differences in body weight, distribution of adipose tissue, and hormonal influences on alcohol metabolism have been hypothesized to account for increased female susceptibility to several adverse physical consequences of drinking. However, the exact mechanisms underlying increased risk of health problems in women are not yet clear.

Regardless of whether we examined average daily consumption or frequency of intoxication, the magnitude of the associations between each of these exposure variables and alcohol dependence, physical health, and work/financial problems were strikingly similar across levels of identical sociodemographic (i.e., modifier) variables. However, the configuration of confounding and modification of the associations between intoxication and social/family, belligerence, and legal problems was quite different from those observed for average daily consumption. It appears that certain negative drinking consequences such as legal problems, belligerence, and social/family problems are more closely related to intoxication than to average daily ethanol intake. Relationships between intoxication and the occurrence of these consequences also tended to be more dependent on and confounded by sociodemographic characteristics than the corresponding associations with average daily consumption.

The key to interpreting these results lies in understanding the different meanings attached to the various negative drinking consequences. In this regard, Mäkelä's (1978) classification of adverse effects of drinking provided a helpful first step. According to Mäkelä, legal problems and belligerence can be classified as behavioral concomitants of drinking while the social/family problems examined in our study reflect environmental reactions. Alcohol withdrawal (a component of dependence) and physical health problems can be characterized as physiological consequences of drinking and work/financial problems can be interpreted as behavioral aftereffects of drinking. Each of these subtypes of adverse effects can be further categorized as proximal or distal to the origin of consumption as well as acute or chronic as shown in table 14.9.

TABLE 14.9
Classification of the Adverse Consequences of Drinking

	Adverse Physiological Effects of Drinking	*Behavioral Aftereffects of Drinking*
Distal Consequences	Alcohol dependence	Work/financial
(Chronic Effects)	Physical health problems	
	Behavioral Concomitants of Drinking	*Environmental Reactions*
Proximal Consequences	Legal problems	Social/family problems
(Acute Effects)	Belligerence	

This classification of the negative effects of drinking provides a framework for organizing some of the major findings of this investigation. Both the behavioral concomitants of drinking and environmental reactions would be expected to be closely linked to acute effects of alcohol consumption that results in intoxication. Conversely, the more chronic, distal effects of drinking (e.g., alcohol dependence, physical health problems) relate similarly to average daily consumption and intoxication, suggesting that such effects are more likely for individuals whose consumption is excessive over prolonged periods of time. Presumably, among drinkers with high levels of average daily consumption, we can anticipate more frequent episodes of intoxication as well. Like the other chronic, distal problems, work/financial effects related similarly to both average daily consumption and intoxication. This finding suggests that work problems may be manifestations of cognitive dysfunction that often accompanies prolonged, excessive drinking rather than the product of societal reaction as has been presumed in the past.

The behavioral concomitants of drinking and environmental reactions have a strong interactional or, more appropriately, reactional component not shared by the more chronic, distal effects. This may account for the finding that these acute, proximal consequences of drinking are more strongly determined by one's social position, sex, and ethnicity when intoxication is the exposure variable than when average daily consumption was used. It is intoxicated behavior that evokes a societal response and not merely the amount of alcohol consumed. Apparently, it is also important who is doing the consuming.

Although one strength of the present study lies in examining alcohol dependence and other adverse consequences of drinking in relation to both levels of intake and frequency of intoxication, limitations inherent in the exposure variables should be noted. First, similar to even the most complex and detailed indexes of consumption, our measure of the average amount of ethanol consumed daily did not operationalize the duration component. Second, reports of frequency of intoxication are subject to under- and over-estimation, and to varying conceptualizations of the experience of being drunk or high. Third, neither consumption variable tapped all potentially important drinking styles and patterns including steady daily drinking, regular heavy drinking limited to weekends, and binge drinking (i.e., continuous vs. episodic drinking). The possibility exists that alcohol consumption may relate to drinking problems in entirely different ways depending on duration or styles of heavy drinking not examined in this study.

There are also several reasons why the estimates of the effect of consumption on alcohol dependence and associated disabilities should be considered preliminary. First, the precise quantification of these relationships should not depend on a single test based on one set of observations. Second, the process of inferring that a given factor is a risk factor for dependence or other drinking problems is always a complex process, as demonstrated by the number of variables in our study that were not shown to confound or modify the associations of interest. Third, our estimates of effect are obviously related to the method in which alcohol-related problems were aggregated. To date, theoretical disagreements about the selection of appropriate operationalizations have not been resolved and will not likely be resolved in the near future.

We look forward to future research that will refine our description of the risks associated with alcohol dependence and drinking consequences at different levels of drinking and frequencies of intoxication. The quantification of risk in various populations using conceptually different definitions of dependence and alcohol-related problems, specification of extraneous risk factors, and measures of consumption that tap duration and various other drinking styles should help to address the issues raised in our study. Our research would also benefit from demonstrations by other researchers of the relative variance or invariance of the estimates of effect across different mathematical modeling techniques.

15

Higher and Lower Levels of Self-Reported Problems among Heavy Drinkers

INTRODUCTION

Knupfer's recent editorial on current practice in alcohol research surveys included a number of important criticisms that researchers would be well-advised to heed. Among the points made is that heavy drinking has been defined poorly:

> Consider the minimum amount of drinking that would qualify a respondent as a heavy drinker in a few of these surveys: five drinks once in the last year plus forty-five drinks in thirty days (United States); one and one-half pints of beer every day (Scottish towns); get drunk four times in the last year (Montreal): three and one-half pints of beer once a week (London); one pint of beer twice a week (Iowa); five drinks once in the last year (Ontario); five drinks once a month (Western New York State); one drink five days out of seven (Sydney). Are the researchers so naive, are they

so ignorant of the real world out there, that they consider those patterns to be 'heavy drinking'? (Knupfer 1987b: p. 583)

In my view, this criticism is correct and deserves a response.

I also find merit in Knupfer's suggestion that we should compare heavy drinkers who report many drinking-related problems to those with few problems. Hence, a subset of very heavy drinkers is selected from the respondents in a 1984 national alcohol survey; this subset is divided between those reporting higher and lower levels of drinking problems, and differences between these groups, as measured by both demographic and personality variables, are investigated.

Knupfer suggested that there might be demographic differences between those who reported greater and lesser amounts of problems, indicating that some social groups were relatively more exposed to the negative consequences of drinking. Yet a previous analysis using these same data was not able to find such differences (Hilton, chapter 13 in this volume). Perhaps as important as demographic differences are differences in the psychological domain. A long-standing theory is that ascribed statuses (reflected by demographic variables) are important determinants of how much a person drinks but that personality characteristics are more determinant of drinking problems among those who drink heavily:

> This pattern does provide some modest support for a two-stage model where social differentiations are the primary predictors of heavy drinking behavior per se — behavior which at least conceptually is necessary but not sufficient for drinking problems—while personality variables are the best predictors of tangible consequences of drinking emerging among those who have put themselves "at risk" by heavy drinking. (Cahalan and Room, 1974, p. 125; see also Robins, Bates and O'Neal 1962)

Numerous studies have found a relationship between depression and problem drinking (Midanik, 1983; Neff and Husaini, 1982; Schuckit, 1979; Weissman and Myers, 1980). The 1984 national alcohol survey included the CES-D depression scale, which will be used to further investigate this link. Another relevant set of personality variables are those studied by Cahalan and Room (1974); these include impulsivity, intrapunitiveness (elsewhere called "guilt feelings"), alienation, and sociability. Risk taking was also included in the 1984 survey, which makes it a convenient candidate for analysis as well. While this list of variables is only a fraction of those whose association with drinking problems has been of interest (see Cox, 1987, for a review), they should be helpful in illustrating the relative importance of the psychological domain.

METHODS

Respondents who drank were asked the following two questions: "During the past year, how often did you have twelve or more drinks of any kind of alcoholic beverage in a single day, that is, any combination of cans of beer, glasses of wine, or drinks containing liquor of any kind?" and, "During the past year, how often did you have at least eight, but less than twelve drinks of any kind of alcoholic beverage in a single day, that is, any combination of cans of beer, glasses of wine, or drinks containing liquor of any kind?" The response choices along with their assigned coding values (in the metric of days per month) are shown in table 15.1 The coded frequencies for both questions were summed to arrive at a frequency of drinking eight or more drinks in a day. Knupfer has suggested that a reasonable definition of heavy drinking is drinking eight or more drinks per day as often as three times a week (Knupfer, 1984). Accordingly, all drinkers with scores of twelve or higher were defined as heavy drinkers in this analysis.

TABLE 15.1
Response Choices for Alcohol Consumption Questions

Response Choice	Coding Value in Drinks per month
Every day or nearly every day	30
Three to four times a week	15
Once or twice a week	6
Once to three times a month	2
Seven to eleven times in the past year	0.75
Three to six times in the past year	0.38
Twice in the past year	0.17
Once in the past year	0.08
Never in the past year	0

In most reports on this data set, weighted results have been reported. However, since the present analysis focuses on a small subset of the original 5,221 respondents, it is necessary to use and report unweighted results.

One hundred eighteen of the 5,221 respondents qualified as heavy drinkers by this criterion. Given the nature of the 1984 national sample, this subgroup heavily overrepresented Blacks and Hispanics. Forty percent (47) of these heavy drinkers were Black and 35% (41) were Hispanic. The socioeconomic characteristics of these one hundred eighteen respondents also reflected this bias. Forty-five percent (51) reported family incomes of $10,000 or less while another 29% (33) reported family ncomes between $10,001 and $20,000. Forty-three percent (51) had not graduated from high school. The heavy drinking subsample was 81% (96) male and had the following age breakdown: eighteen to twenty-nine years, 36% (43); thirty to thirty-nine years, 31% (37); forty to forty-nine years 15% (18); fifty to fifty-nine years 10% (12); sixty years and older 7% (8).

It is unfortunate that the oversampling of Blacks and Hispanics produced such an unrepresentative subgroup of heavy drinkers. The results must be assumed to exaggerate relationships that occur among minority drinkers, and the analysis is only offered as provisional until a more representative sample is available. Nevertheless, the study does contribute to the field since there are so few studies that include a comparison group of very heavy drinkers who do not experience many drinking-related problems.

Respondents who drank were asked thirty-two questions about negative consequences of drinking. These respondents were divided into high and low problem groups according to whether they scored eight or more on an index composed of these items.[1] Fifty-six cases fell into the high problem group and sixty-two cases fell into the low problem group. It is important to recognize that "high problem" and "low problem" are relative terms here.

Measures of alcohol consumption were the same as used in other papers in this volume. These included the monthly volume of consumption, the frequency of drunkenness, and the frequency of consuming eight or more drinks per day.

The depression scale (CES-D) was taken from Radloff (1977). Fourteen items reflective of selected personality traits were selected from previous surveys on the basis of their relatedness to drinking problems (Cahalan and Room, 1974; Social Research Group, 1974). Added to these were items indicative of risk taking.

RESULTS

The first analytic task was to see whether the difference between the two groups was due simply to more drinking among the high problem group. Comparisons were made along three dimensions: the frequency of consuming eight or more drinks per day, the monthly volume of drinks consumed, and the frequency of self-reported intoxication (table 15.2). There was some difference in the mean frequency of drinking eight or more drinks per day (28.1 times per month vs. 23.0 times per month), but given a wide variance about both means, the difference was only of borderline significance, accounting for only about 2.6% of the overall variance according to the Eta squared statistic. Similarly, the difference between a mean of three hundred forty drinks per month consumed in the high problem group and two hundred seventy per month consumed in the low problem group was substantial in absolute terms, but failed to be of statistical significance or to account for much of the overall variation. Differences in the frequency of self-reported intoxication were significant (9.75 times per month vs. 4.71 times per month), and this accounted for a small part (8.7%) of the overall variance. In sum, the difference between groups in the amount of drinking was relatively small and accounted for a limited portion of the variance in the data. Thus, other factors must be sought to explain why some heavy drinkers reported more problems than others. At the same time, it seems advisable to control for the amount of drinking while searching for other differences between groups.

TABLE 15.2
Analysis of Variance for Measures of Drinking
between High and Low Problem Groups

Measure	Mean, High Problem Group	Mean, Low Problem Group	F	Significance of F	Eta Squared
Frequency of eight or more drinks per day (days per month)	28.1	23.0	3.07[a]	0.082	0.026
Volume of consumption (drinks per month)	340	271	2.09[b]	0.151	0.018
Frequency of self-reported intoxication (days per month)	9.75	4.71	11.06[a]	0.001	0.087

[a] N = 118; d.f. = 1,116.
[b] N = 115; d.f. = 1,113.

Logistic regression was used to analyze the impact of selected demographic variables on problem status (high versus low; table 15.3). The independent variables were: the frequency of consuming eight or more drinks per day; sex; marital status, dichotomized as married or living together vs. single; race, dichotomized as Black vs. White (all of the one hundred eighteen heavy drinkers were either Black or White); Hispanic ethnicity, dichotomized as Hispanic vs. other; urbanicity, dichotomized as residents of metropolitan area cities of 50,000 or more vs. others; family income; and years of education completed.

TABLE 15.3

Logistic Regression of Intake and Demographic Variables on
High Problem versus Low Problem Status

Variable	Coefficient	Standard Error	Coefficient /S.E.
Frequency 8+ drinks	0.014	0.0069	2.00*
Sex	0.192	0.263	0.73
Age	−0.016	0.0082	−1.93
Marital status	0.026	0.224	0.12
Urbanicity	0.250	0.229	1.09
Race	0.186	0.245	0.76
Hispanic ethnicity	−0.061	0.268	−0.23
Family income	0.002	0.0087	0.26
Years of education completed	−0.044	0.043	−1.03
Intercept	5.262	0.675	7.79

* Significant at 0.05 level.
$N = 113$.
$X^2 = 113.2$.
d.f. = 103.
Model: $1/2 \ln (P/(1-P)) + 5 = \beta_0 + \beta_1 X_1 + \beta_2 X_2 \ldots$
PROBIT procedure, SPSSX

The results showed that none of the demographic variables were related to problem status, although the frequency of heavy drinking was weakly related. Consistent with the above, the frequency of consuming eight or more drinks per day was found to have a barely significant effect at the 0.05 level (ratio of coefficient to standard error = 2.00). Age had the strongest impact of any of the demographic variables, but it fell slightly short of significance (ratio = 1.92). Sex, marital status, urbanicity, race, Hispanic ethnicity, family income, and years of education completed all failed to have a significant relationship with problem status.

In contrast to the demographic variables, the CES-D depression scale was strongly related to group status in a one-way analysis of variance. The mean depression score in the high problem group was 17.7 (SD = 12.7) contrasted against a mean of 8.5 (SD = 9.8) in the low problem group. This difference was highly significant (F = 19.4; p less than 0.001). Using the standard cut off of sixteen or more points on the scale, 55% of the high problem group would be classified as depressed according to these results while 20% of the low problem group would be classified as depressed.

Intergroup findings regarding the other personality items included in the questionnaire are depicted on table 15.4. For most of the fourteen items, no differences were found between the high and low problem groups. The item "I often change my mind rather quickly" was the only one of four impulsivity items where significant differences emerged. Similarly, "I often feel left out of things" showed a significant difference that was not corroborated by the other alienation item. In neither case was this strong evidence for a genuine difference between groups. For intrapunitiveness, however, there was stronger evidence of a difference. For both "I have not lived the right kind of life" and "I do many things which I regret afterwards," significantly more high problem respondents affirmed the item. This suggests a higher level of intrapunitiveness among the high problem drinkers.

TABLE 15.4
Personality Items

| | % Responding "True" | | |
Item	High Problem Group	Low Problem Group	Chi Square
Impulsivity			
I often change my mind rather quickly.	71	46	6.80*
I often spend more money than I think I should.	82	67	2.68
I don't let the risk of getting hurt a little stop me from having a good time.	64	56	0.57
I often act on the spur-of-the-moment without stopping to think.	61	48	1.54
Risk Taking			
I think that people who don't take any risks must have pretty dull lives.	68	56	1.34
I get a kick out of doing things that are a little dangerous.	45	41	0.05

(continued)

TABLE 15.4 *(continued)*

| | % Responding "True" | | |
Item	High Problem Group	Low Problem Group	Chi Square
Risk Taking *(continued)*			
I like to test myself every now and then by doing something a little chancey.	62	57	0.14
Sociability			
I would like to belong to as many clubs and social organizations as possible.	20	25	0.18
I like to take part in many social activities.	52	51	0.00
I like to be with people.	91	87	0.15
Intrapunitiveness			
I have not lived the right kind of life.	54	18	14.86*
I do many things which I regret afterwords.	62	34	8.13*
Alienation			
I often feel left out of things.	34	15	4.89*
I often feel that the people I am around are not too friendly.	32	20	1.77
N	58	62	

* Significant at 0.05 level.
N = 117.

DISCUSSION

The operational definition of "heavy drinking" is usually set too low by survey researchers in the alcohol studies field. The reason for this has often been that far too few cases for a reliable analysis would remain if more realistic criteria were used. In the present analysis, the use of a more realistic criterion for heavy drinking has reduced the number of eligible cases from 5,221 to 118, thereby leaving the analysis to depend on the unweighted data from a sample that heavily over-represented Black and Hispanic respondents. The caveat must be given that these results overrepresent relationships as they occur in these minority respondents and that the findings should be taken as provisional until replicated on a more representative sample. Despite this, the findings are generally consistent with earlier work.

It was determined that demographic factors had no association with high vs. low problem status. Thus, Knupfer's expectation that one could identify groups of heavy drinkers who are particularly vulnerable to the consequences of their drinking was not born out. This negative finding is consistent with an earlier finding that demographic factors had little impact on problem status net of the influence of drinking variables (Hilton, chapter 13 in this volume). The major difference between the present study and the former one is that the former examined a broader spectrum of drinkers while the present study examined only the heaviest drinking tip of the distribution. While frequency of heavy drinking had an effect on problem scores in the previous study, it was a less important factor here, where all respondents drank enough to be at substantial risk.

The finding that depression was more widely prevalent among the high problem drinkers also replicates previous work (Midanik, 1983; Neff and Husaini, 1982; Weissman and Myers, 1980). In addition, the finding that intrapunitiveness showed a strong association with problem status is very similar to Cahalan and Room's finding of a relationship between intrapunitiveness and tangible consequences in a 1969 survey (Cahalan and Room, 1974).

The findings with regard to both depression and intrapunitiveness are clouded by issues of interpretation. As was pointed out earlier (Cahalan and Room, 1974), much of the reported intrapunitiveness may represent an internalization of external criticisms of the respondent's drinking, some of which is picked up by the consequences items (problems with spouse, problems with employer, problems with family, etc.). This means both that the direction of causality cannot be taken for granted and that the measures may not be strictly independent of each other. In regard to depression, the direction of causality is also problematic, since one would expect drinkers who experience substantial problems to be depressed about these experiences.

Nevertheless, the fact that some personality variables did discriminate between the high and low problem groups while no success in this regard was achieved with the demographic variables does support the "two stage" conception of drinking problems articulated by Cahalan and Room (1974). Variables in the personality domain were related to differences in problem status whereas variables in the demographic domain were not.

PART VI. CONTEXTS

WALTER B. CLARK

16

Introduction to Drinking Contexts

Bruun et al. (1975), among others, have argued that the per capita consumption of a nation is strongly related to the death rate due to portal cirrhosis for that population. Research in many nations has indicated that generally there is indeed a strong positive correlation between the cirrhosis rate and the mean quantity of absolute alcohol per population member. The link has to do with the distribution of alcohol consumption among the members of that population. Ledermann (1956), and others since, have shown that a log normal distribution describes reasonably well the proportion of the population who drink any given amount; that is, the proportion of the population drinking any given amount are close to the proportion predicted by the appropriate member of the log-normal family of distributions. Given the mean per capita consumption, one can estimate the proportion of the population whose typical alcohol consumption exceeds a given amount, and one can also estimate the rate of alcoholic cirrhosis for the population, since continued, heavy alcohol use contributes much to the development of portal cirrhosis. Whether the statistical assumptions necessary for the application of log normal curve are reasonably well met, and whether that particular family of curves is the most appropriate to use are matters of continued dispute. Nevertheless, for the industrialized nations, and perhaps for others, if one knows the mean per capita consumption of alcohol one can estimate the cirrhosis rate as well.

Why should it be so? One can imagine two populations with identical mean per capita consumption figures, one of which contains many heavy drinkers and many very light drinkers, while the other contains relatively few heavy drinkers but a generous number of moderate drinkers. However, there are now a sizable number of studies which suggest that these imaginary examples have not been found in experience. Rather, a higher mean alcohol consumption seems always to imply a higher proportion of heavier drinkers. Skog (1982a, 1983) critically examines the literature connected with this phenomenon. He argues persuasively that the link between per capita consumption in a given year and the proportions of people in that population whose drinking sums to each given level of yearly consumption of absolute alcohol is due to the circumstances affecting drinkers in that population. It is a probability distribution expressing the net effect of factors affecting consumption. Within the population such effective factors "work on" people to a greater or lesser extent, but the net effect is a strong relationship between the mean and the proportions around the mean. Many studies have pointed out factors affecting overall consumption; cost, availability, and so forth, are among them. However, it is at least as interesting to focus on another level of possible explanation for the observed regularity: alcoholic beverages are much used in social settings, and there are common practices, common understandings, common values which underlie such drinking. And, within actual groups, there are norms which influence the amounts drunk either upwardly or down, as circumstances dictate. Thus it can be argued that drinking customs widespread in a society work an influence on individuals, and that this underlies the observed regularity. The drinking patterns of individuals in a population will vary greatly, but cannot be expected to vary independently of the norms of the population.

Two of the papers in this chapter are especially concerned with matters related to the social circumstances in which drinking may take place. Hilton's paper on regional variation in drinking patterns (chapter 17) shows that the United States is composed of diverse populations in its various regions, and that the people in these areas differ greatly in terms of alcohol use. Certainly it is the case that individual differences in drinking patterns can be found in all the regions of the United States, but it is also the case that certain common tendencies can be found in the various regions which set them apart from others. In a second paper (chapter 18) Hilton shows that the conventions and under-standings which influence drinking in a few social settings have changed over the course of twenty years. If, as we suspect, total amount of drinking is decreasing for the nation as a whole, some future study may well demonstrate that amount of drinking has declined in the four social settings with which Hilton is concerned.

The discussions in this section have to do with the places or settings or contexts of alcohol use. Such settings are not just physical spaces; rather they are social events which are influenced by the expectations of participants concerning what is right and proper in a event. There are individual differences in these matters as in most others, of course, but there are also "average expectations" which can be seen in statistical analyses such as are included here. The regularities that Ledermann found are thought to be the sum of these individual quirks and social regularities, and these have turned out to be quite regular and predictable phenomena.

The results from two analyses of alcohol use in various settings illustrate both such individual and situational variations. We would expect to find that some situations are sites for drinking for more people than are others. We would expect to find that heavier drinking is more often reported for some sites than others. Beyond this, we would expect to find individual variation; some people will drink more in a given setting than will others. The following data illustrate how this works out. The national surveys of 1979 and 1984 included a few questions on drinking in various places (Clark, 1985, 1988). Taverns, parties, club meetings, restaurants, and sporting events were among those asked about as were "spending a quiet evening at home," and "when friends drop over and visit." For each setting in the list respondents were asked:

1. How often they went to such a setting—whether or not they had alcoholic drinks while there.
2. How often while in that setting they did have a drink—never, less than half the time, about half the time, more than half the time, all or almost all the time.
3. When they did drink in that setting, how many drinks they typically had.

Thus we can describe what our respondents have said about the "wetness" of some common situations and settings. Among situations asked about were three that had to do with one's home, "spending a quiet evening at home," "watching TV," "have friends drop over and visit in your home." As would be expected, almost all respondents reported that they did find themselves in these situations. About half the men reported they that sometimes had a drink while spending an evening at home, and about half also sometimes had a drink while watching TV. Among women the proportions reporting ever drinking during a quiet evening at home or while watching TV were 39% and 27% respectively, which figures are significantly lower than those for men. Friends dropping in to visit more often calls for a drink; fully 57% of women said they sometimes drank in some situations, and 8% said that they almost always had a drink when friends visited them. For the men, the figures were higher; 71% said they sometimes drank when friends visited them, and 13% reported they almost always drank then.

There is nothing surprising in these figures, but a quantitative measure enables us to compare these at home settings to some other common situations, some of which are thought to be more appropriate settings for alcohol use. For instance, about 60% of men said they ever went to lunch in a restaurant and 37% of those who do go sometimes have a drink while there. Among women, 69% sometimes go to lunch in a restaurant, but a significantly lower 27% report drinking when there. Compare these figures to having an evening meal in a restaurant: 86% of men and 92% of women do go to restaurants in the evening, and a much higher 72% or 73% of men and women sometimes have a drink while there. About a quarter of both men and women almost always have a drink when out for an evening meal.

The figures for movies, concerts, and plays are quite different. Seventy percent of men and 73% of women do sometimes go there, but only 30% of men and an even lower 22% of women ever drink when they do go there. Going to clubs or organizational meetings is less common; only about 40% of men and women alike go to such, but of those who do, 47% of men sometimes have a drink while there, and 32% of women say the same. Thus the relative wetness of situations varies considerably, and where there is a difference between the sexes in the proportion drinking while there, it is always relatively more men than women who report having a drink in a given setting.

Going to parties and visits to taverns are sure to be settings where drinking is more common. But going to taverns is much less common than going to some other settings asked about. Only 54% of men and a significantly smaller 42% of women in our national population ever go to taverns or bars. Among men, the same proportion, 54%, report they give parties in their homes, but among women, giving parties is 58%—higher than the figure for men, and much higher than the 42% of women who ever go to bars or taverns. As might be expected, higher proportions of both men and women report going to parties in others' homes. Seventy five percent of men and 78% of women do. When at parties (theirs or others) over 80% of women who ever drink sometimes have a drink when there; fully 96% of women drinkers sometimes have a drink when in a tavern. Among men who ever drink, over 90% report they sometimes have a drink while at parties, and 96% drink when in taverns.

In considering the proportions of drinkers of each sex who report they ever drink in a given setting, we can see that those situations such as parties and taverns are indeed among the wettest, with other situations ranking much lower. Women and male drinkers alike tended to report similar patterns in terms of who drinks where, but wherever a difference exists at all, it is male drinkers who report the higher proportions of drinking in a given situation. Interestingly, going out to restaurants for dinner and out to lunch as well are the only settings where more women than men reported that they sometimes go. Given that bars and taverns are not equally open to both sexes, one might wonder whether the restaurant provides for women some of the functions that the bar provides for men. We suggest that the similar ranking of settings by men and women expresses the common understandings concerning where it is appropriate to use alcohol. However, it may still be the case that alcohol use is thought more appropriate for men than for women. At least there is nothing in these data to contradict these notions, and the process can be carried a little further.

As noted, we also asked those respondents who drank at all, about the typical number of drinks they had in a given setting on the occasions when they did drink while there. Again one would expect variation across settings in terms of amount of drinking, and that is what was found. Drinkers who ever drink in taverns reported they typically had 3.1 drinks per visit. The figures for parties are only slightly lower; 2.9 drinks on the average for parties at others' homes and 3.0 drinks for parties at their own homes. Mean numbers of drinks in other settings are much lower. For instance, 1.89 drinks per occasion when friends drop in is the average among those who ever drink on such occasions, while evening meals at restaurants typically are accompanied by only 1.5 drinks. Again, where there is a difference between the sexes, it is males who report the higher amounts typically drunk in each setting.

These same data can be looked at in a slightly different way. Drinking at parties is common, but parties are not such frequent events. Evenings at home are frequent for most respondents, but amounts drunk on such occasions are not so large. To quantify these matters for all situations, we can multiply the frequency of going to each setting for each respondent by the proportion of times in each setting that a drink is taken and by the typical quantity of drinks taken per such occasion. Thus for all respondents we can provide a rough measure of how alcohol is distributed across these social settings, taking into account the frequency of attending such settings and the frequency and quantity of drinking while there. The results from the 1979 and 1984 surveys were nearly identical. About 30% of all drinks taken in the settings asked about were drunk in bars and taverns. Another 16% of drinks were drunk at parties, and about the same percent "when friends drop in to visit" and about the same percent of drinks were reportedly taken when spending quiet evenings at home. Fourteen percent of all drinks were taken while having an evening meal in a restaurant, three percent while having lunch there. Other settings accounted for the additional small amount of the reported drinking. Thus we can see quite clearly that the tavern looms quite large in alcohol consumption in our society, even though many respondents report they never go there.

One final step can be taken, this to illustrate the effects of individual differences on patterns of consumption in the various settings asked about. If we divide respondents into categories of amount of drinking overall (not just the amount drunk in the settings discussed here) we find the following. Lighter drinkers and heavier drinkers alike report that they drink their largest amounts of drinks per occasion in the "wet situations" which include taverns and while at parties, and that they drink lesser amounts while at home, etc. Those drinkers whose overall consumption of alcohol falls between these extremes follow the same pattern in proportion; each heavier category of drinker reports somewhat higher amounts of drinking in each setting than the next lighter category of drinker, but each ranks the "relative wetness" of the settings about the same as all others. That is, lighter and heavier drinkers agree on where they drink their most and least, but heavier drinkers take somewhat more alcohol in each setting, thus nicely illustrating both individual variation and social understanding.

We would expect that frequency of attendance at wetter situations would be related to the total amount of alcohol consumed. This source of variability, the frequency of going to the various settings, is the one which sets the heavier drinkers far apart from those who drink less overall. In almost every case, respondents in each category of amount of drinking report that they go to each drinking situation more often than those respondents in the lower drinking category to one side of them, and that they go less often than the heavier drinkers on the other side of them. Very sizeable differences in amount of drinking are shown to be accounted for by the combined effect of frequency of going to wetter settings and by individual propensities to drink while there. For instance, the lightest drinkers in the sample reported a mean of about 2.6 drinks per month drunk in a bar in a typical month; the heaviest drinkers in the sample reported 12.6 drinks per month in that setting. The heavier drinkers go more often and they typically drink more per occasion. The same pattern of differences between lighter and heavier drinkers obtains for all the different drinking situations asked about in the two surveys. That is, lighter and heavier drinkers seem to agree on where heavier than usual drinking should take place, and in general both lighter and heavier drinkers do drink more in those settings than in others. But there is still much room for individual variation in terms of what "the usual" amount of drinking includes, and in terms of how often one goes to a particular setting.

In summary, these data on who drinks how much where add a little to our knowledge of alcohol use by giving a rough quantitative view of the interrelations among drinking settings and overall amount of drinking. The survey findings would be in accord with the expectations of psychologists of the behaviorist tradition who suggest—and who present evidence to back the suggestion—that elements of situations commonly found at bars and at parties can strongly influence drinking toward heavier consumption. Sociologists would stress the importance of the agreed upon definitions of various settings as being more or less appropriate places for drinking various amounts. The papers which follow in this section have more to say about such matters.

17

Regional Diversity in
U.S. Drinking Practices

INTRODUCTION

Abstention rates vary widely across regions of the United States; they are much higher in the Southern and Mountain states than elsewhere.[1] These higher abstention rates give evidence of the "dryness" of these regions, a condition that is commonly taken to include lower levels of apparent per capita consumption, attitudes unfavorable toward alcohol, greater legal restrictions, and stronger traditions of temperance and prohibition. However, a recent study showed that when alcohol consumption statistics are computed on a *per drinker* rather than a *per capita* basis, consumption is higher in the drier regions of the country than in the wetter ones (Room, 1983). This conjoint presence of high abstention and high consumption per drinker seems contradictory. As such, it begs for an explanation and prompts speculation about many aspects of dry region drinking culture. This paper presents some recent survey findings about: whether the regional trends in abstention rates and apparent consumption noted by Room have continued, whether differences in per drinker consumption are matched by differences in the prevalence of heavy drinking, whether differences in heavy drinking are in turn matched by differences in alcohol-related problems—and if so which kinds of problems, whether there are regional differences in attitudes toward drinking, and whether there are regional differences in drinking contexts.

There are two issues specific to Room's paper that need to be addressed at the outset. The first is whether his scheme of distinguishing between the wetter and the drier regions continues to be a useful classification system. It is always possible that conditions have changed so that previous regional classification schemes are no longer valid. The second issue is whether the trends noted by Room continue to exist. These were: (1) Abstention rates were roughly stable from 1964 to 1979, preserving a marked difference between the wetter and the drier regions; (2) Per capita apparent consumption had converged; (3) Per drinker apparent consumption, however, had diverged, with rates in the drier regions rising above those in wetter regions; (4) Prevalence rates for heavy drinking ("High Quantity" or "High Frequency-High Quantity" drinking), when converted to a per drinker basis, had become as high in the drier regions as in the wetter regions; (5) The prevalence of consequences of drinking, when converted to a per drinker basis, had become higher in the drier regions than in the wetter ones. Consequences ("tangible consequences" in Room's discussion) refers to such problems due to drinking as disputes with family, friends, employers, or officials as well as accidents, and so on. The present analysis can confirm whether these trends have continued into the early 1980s.

These findings have a clear implication under the single distribution theory of alcohol consumption (Ledermann, 1956; Skog, 1982a, 1983; de Lint, 1978; Schmidt and Popham, 1978). The prevalence of heavy drinking *among drinkers* should be higher in the drier regions of the country than the wetter ones since apparent per drinker consumption is higher in the former. The notion that heavy drinking may be more widespread among drinkers reared in dry environments is certainly not a new one (Skolnick, 1958), but empirical findings have not always been able to show that heavy drinking is indeed more prevalent in the dry regions (Clark and Midanik, 1982).

Regardless of its prevalence, heavy drinking in the drier regions is said to be of a more explosive character (Cahalan and Room, 1974). This suggests that problematic consequences of drinking are more prevalent among drinkers in the drier regions (Room, 1971a, 1983). We would want to investigate not only regional differences in the overall level of problems but also differences in the *kinds* of problems that are more or less prevalent. There is some reason to expect that the more "explosive" drier-region drinking style would include higher rates of aggression and belligerence. It may also be the case that less tolerant, drier-region views toward alcohol make it unacceptable to engage in drinking-related behaviors that might be allowable elsewhere. Hence, we would expect to find regional variations in interpersonal problems.

Attitudinal differences are also of interest. According to the "sociocultural" view of drinking problems, those who are reared in an abstinence-oriented subculture but who nonetheless become drinkers are more likely to drink heavily or problematically (Bales, 1946; Skolnick, 1958; Pittman, 1967; Globetti, 1978; Frankel and Whitehead, 1981; critiqued by Mäkelä, 1975). The theory is rather difficult to demonstrate empirically, although there have been creative efforts in this direction (Linsky et al. 1986). However, one piece of the theory that is amenable to analysis is that drinkers in the dry regions have different attitudes toward drinking and drunkenness than have drinkers elsewhere. Among the former there should be a greater prevalence of attitudes favorable toward drinking and drunkenness.

The mix of drinking contexts may also differ regionally. Drier-region states tend to have alcohol control policies more restrictive of public drinking (see for example Holder and Blose, 1986, on liquor by the drink in North Carolina). Also, in areas where temperance sentiment is strong, there is a greater tendency for drinking to become a public rather than a private issue (Gusfield, 1981). This suggests that there might be substantial regional differences in the social contexts of drinking.

METHODS

This paper uses the same indices of amount of drinking, dependence, and adverse consequences of drinking as do most other papers in this volume. These and their subsets are discussed in the Introduction. Essentially these measures are the same as those used in earlier surveys by the Alcohol Research Group, thus permitting comparisons with earlier analyses and some trend studies. Cahalan and Room (1974) contains a discussion of these and other indices together with the rationale underlying their construction. Occasionally these measures have been called by other names; for instance, Cahalan and Room referred to "Problematic Drinking" and "Tangible Consequences" while these same measures in this volume are called "dependence" and "consequences."

Four drinking attitude scales were formed from the items listed in the figure 17.1. Each index was a simple summative scale of the coding values listed. Scores were then indexed to a mean score of one hundred for all respondents.[2] The first two scales reflect attitudes about how much alcohol it is appropriate to consume. The first was formed by asking a series of questions about how much alcohol would be appropriate to drink in a variety of situations; hence, it is called the Appropriateness-Contexts scale. The second scale was formed from a set of similar items that asked how much alcohol would be appropriate for people of varying age and gender statuses to drink; it is called the Appropriateness-Persons scale. Both scales are thought of as measurements of favorability toward drinking. The third scale assesses favorability toward drunkenness as distinct from favorability toward drinking. The fourth scale measures the extent to which subjects endorse the notion of disinhibition. Most of the questions asked whether misbehavior is more likely to occur when a person has been drinking or if that misbehavior is easier to forgive when a person has been drinking. Since heavy drinking in the drier regions may be more explosive and more rebellious against prevailing norms, it was thought especially pertinent to examine possible regional differences in the endorsement of disinhibition. Presumably, rowdier drinking behavior within a milieu which is relatively less tolerant of drinking would be accompanied by a greater belief that rowdy misbehavior either doesn't count or is to be expected when one is drunk.

FIGURE 17.1
Questionnaire Items Used in this Paper

I. Appropriateness-Contexts Items

Now I'll describe situations that people sometimes find themselves in. For each one, please tell me how much a person in that situation should feel free to drink.

At a party, at someone else's home.
For a husband having dinner out with his wife.
For a man out at a bar with friends.
For a woman out at a bar with friends.
When with friends at home.
When getting together with friends after work before going home.
When getting together with people at sports events or recreation.

Answer Categories and Coding Values

1. No drinking.
2. 1 or 2 drinks.
3. Enough to feel the effects but not to feel drunk.
4. Getting drunk is sometimes all right

(continued)

FIGURE 17.1 *(continued)*

II. Appropriateness-Persons Items

In your opinion, what is the most that each of the following kinds of people should drink at one time? Just tell me the appropriate number.

A young man about 21 years old.
A man about 30 years old.
A man about 40 years old.
A man about 60 years old.
A young woman about 21 years old.
A woman about 30 years old.
A woman about 40 years old.
A woman about 60 years old.

> *Answer Categories and Coding Values*
>
> Same as for Appropriateness-Contexts items.

III. Favorability Toward Drunkenness Items

Now please tell me whether you agree or disagree with each of these statements.

Getting drunk is just an innocent way of having fun.
A man who is always drunk should be punished. (scored inversely)
It does some people good to get drunk once in a while.
I would feel ashamed if anyone in my family got drunk. (scored inversely)
A drunk person is a disgusting sight. (scored inversely)
People who get drunk can be very amusing.

> *Answer Categories*
>
> The above were dichotomous agree/disagree items. Some items were inversely scored, as indicated.

IV. Belief in Disinhibition Items

Now please tell me whether you agree or disagree with each of these statements.

Drinking is one of the main causes of people doing things they shouldn't.
If someone says something mean when they've been drinking, it doesn't really count.
The main point of drinking is to loosen up and be able to do things you wouldn't do otherwise.
If a person has been drinking, I think you have to make some allowances for rowdy behavior.
Someone who is drunk and punches someone else should be punished just as hard as if you were sober.

> *Answer Categories*
>
> The above were dichotomous agree/disagree items.

(continued)

FIGURE 17.1 *(continued)*

V. Drinking Contexts Included in the 1984 Survey

How often do you:

Go out for an evening meal in a restaurant not including fast-food places and luncheonettes

Go out for lunch in a restaurant not including fast-food places and luncheonettes

Go to club or organizational meetings

Go to bars, taverns, or cocktail lounges

Go to a party in someone else's home

Spend a quiet evening at home

Have friends drop over and visit in your house

Hang around with friends in a public place such as a park, street, or parking lot.

Answer Categories

Discussed at length in Clark, 1985.

Respondents were also asked about their drinking in eight different contexts (listed in figure 17.1). The question formats were the same as those discussed by Clark (1985) although the list of contexts was slightly different. Respondents were asked how often they went to (or participated in) each context, how often they had something to drink when they did attend (or participate), and how many drinks they usually had on such occasions. From their responses a rough indicator of the number of drinks per month typically consumed in each context was constructed according to the procedure described by Clark (1985). Readers should be aware that the system only provides a rough approximation that is useful for determining relative difference between contexts but does not serve as an accurate estimate of the actual amounts consumed in each setting.

RESULTS

Table 17.1 repeats the 1964–1979 comparisons of regional drinking patterns offered by Room (1983) and extends these to include 1984 data. The results show that abstention rates continue to be distinctly higher in the drier regions than in the wetter regions. An exception is the West North Central region, where declining abstention rates have caused us to reclassify the region as a wetter region rather than a drier region; this will be further discussed below. The proportion of heavy drinkers among the adult population is correspondingly higher in the wetter regions than in the drier ones, with the exception of an unusually high prevalence in the Mountain states. Otherwise, regional differences along this dimension have generally persisted. It needs to be noted, however, that the definitions of heavy drinking used in the three years are quite different. In 1964 heavy drinking was defined as drinking "Nearly every day with five or more per occasion at least once in a while, or about once weekly with usually five or more per occasion" (Cahalan, Cissin, and Crossley, 1969, p. 19); in 1979 heavy drinking was defined as the consumption of sixty or more drinks per month; and in 1984 heavy drinking was defined as drinking five or more drinks per occasion once a week or more.

An important trend between 1964 and 1979 was the closing of the regional gap in per capita consumption (a factor on which Smith and Hanham's claim of regional convergence in drinking patterns is based; Smith and Hanham, 1982). The 1983 data shows that it continues to be difficult to distinguish between regions on the basis of per capita consumption. Given similar levels of per capita consumption but quite different abstention rates, the per drinker consumption levels are different among regions. This was, perhaps, Room's most significant finding: that apparent per drinker consumption had diverged sharply between the mid-1960s and the late-1970s, leaving much higher levels of per drinker consumption in the drier regions than in the wetter ones. The 1984 data shows that this continues to be the case. Although differences are smaller than they used to be, drier regions tend to have higher levels of per drinker consumption than wetter ones.

An important difference in the 1984 data as compared to earlier years is that the West North Central region has "migrated" from the drier group to the wetter group. In 1964, the abstention rate of the West

TABLE 17.1

Regional Distribution of Alcohol Consumption and Abstention (in percents)

	Percent Abstainers			Percent Heavy Drinkers		
	1964[b]	1979[c]	1984	1964[d]	1979[e]	1984[f]
Wetter Regions						
New England	21	18	28	16	16	15
Mid Atlantic	17	25	18	19	12	12
East North Central	25	29	27	13	14	18
West North Central[a]	34	38	20	8	11	16
Pacific	27	16	26	15	14	17
Drier Regions						
South Atlantic	42	50	38	9	5	11
East South Central	65	66	56	5	9	5
West South Central	38	38	42	9	14	12
Mountain	42	38	38	9	19	17

(continued)

TABLE 17.1 (continued)

	Apparent Per Capita Consumption[g]				Apparent Per Drinker Consumption[h]			Survey Reported Per Drinker Consumption[i]
	1940[j]	1964[k]	1979[k]	1984[l]	1964[m]	1979[m]	1984[n]	
Wetter Regions								
New England	1.72	2.48	3.14	3.08	3.14	3.78	4.28	1.72
Mid Atlantic	1.78	2.41	2.67	2.57	2.92	3.53	3.13	1.43
East North Central	1.75	2.26	2.67	2.57	3.04	3.75	3.52	1.96
West North Central	1.22	1.82	2.45	2.32	2.77	3.95	2.90	1.67
Pacific	1.87	2.55	3.38	3.09	3.47	3.99	4.18	2.27
Drier Regions								
South Atlantic	1.11	1.89	2.81	2.68	3.27	5.44	4.32	1.66
East South Central	0.57	1.01	1.95	1.93	2.87	5.48	4.39	1.39
West South Central	0.88	1.71	2.62	2.58	2.76	4.21	4.45	1.82
Mountain	1.33	2.08	3.29	2.96	3.58	5.31	4.77	3.36

a Previously categorized among the Drier Regions.

b Cahalan, Cisin, and Crossley, 1969, p. 38.

c Room, 1983, p. 574.

d Drinks nearly every day with five or more per occasion at least once in a while, or about once weekly with usually five or more per occasion. 1964 data from Cahalan, Cisin, and Crossley, 1969, p. 19.

e Sixty or more drinks per month. Calculated from Clark and Midanik, 1982, p. 33.

f Drinks five or more drinks per sitting once per week or more often.

g Gallons of absolute alcohol annually per population aged 15 or 14 (as indicated) and over. Based on sales and taxation records.

h Based on sales and taxation records, as in previous columns, but divided by survey-reported abstention rates.

i Based on survey results.

j Based on population aged 15 and over. Cahalan and Room, 1974, p. 80.

k Based on population aged 14 and over. Room, 1983, p. 578.

l Based on population aged 14 and over. Calculated from Doernberg et al. 1986, p. 6.

m Room, 1983, p. 578. Also see note n below.

n Calculated from Doernberg et al. 1986, p. 6 and the "Percent Abstainers" figure given earlier in the table. Note that all persons aged 14 and over appear in the consumption figure, but abstention is based on percentage of adults 18 and over (21 and over in 1964). This age mismatch probably overstates the number of drinkers and hence underestimates per capita consumption.

North Central region, though the lowest in the drier states, was on a par with that found in the Southern and Mountain regions, but in 1984, the West North Central had the second lowest abstention rate in the country. The proportion of heavy drinkers in the West North Central population also seems to have shifted during the 1970s, to a rate closer to the rates found in other wetter regions. In summary, the West North Central region seems to have experienced significant changes since the 1960s, and today has a statistical profile that better justifies counting it among the wetter regions than among the drier regions.

Because the West North Central region can be counted among the wetter regions, it is best to present the results in a five-region system: Northeast, Midwest, South, Mountain, and Pacific. Northeast, Midwest, and Pacific can be collapsed into the Wetter Regions while South and Mountain can be collapsed into the Drier Regions. This presentation is much like the familiar system of dividing the United States into four quadrants (Northeast, Midwest, South, and West), except that it keeps the Mountain and Pacific states separate so as to preserve the wet/dry distinction between them.

An important qualification to these results appears in the last column of table 17.1, where per drinker consumption based on the 1984 survey results, rather than on sales and taxation data, are given. As is usual in alcohol consumption surveys, the reported consumption is far lower than the actual consumption. More to the point, however, is the existence of regional differences in the coverage rates (survey reported consumption divided by sales and taxation recorded consumption); these are generally higher in the Wetter Regions than in the Drier Regions. The effect of this bias would be to exaggerate differences for comparisons where consumption is heavier in the Wetter Regions. Unfortunately, it is not known whether similar biases exist in the regional reporting of alcohol problems or alcohol-related attitudes.

Table 17.2 shows the distribution of heavy drinking in the 1984 data. Since no one measure of heavy drinking is optimal, a set of six indicators is used: consumption of sixty or more drinks per month, consumption of one hundred twenty or more drinks per month, daily drinking of any amount of alcohol, consumption of five or more drinks at a sitting twice a week or more often, consumption of eight or more drinks per day once a week or more often, and self-reported drunkenness once a week or more often. Figures show the percentages of respondents or drinkers reporting each behavior. Generally, there are few important indications of regional differences in these data. Mountain states respondents reported an unusually high prevalence of heavy drinking. This was especially notable among women but was also true for men. Given the small numbers of Mountain respondents,

TABLE 17.2
Distribution of Heavy Intake (in percents)

	Volume 60+ per Month	Volume 120+ per Month	Daily Drinking	5+ Twice a Week or More	8+ Once a Week or More	Weekly "Drunk"	N
All Respondents							
Men							
Northeast	20.1	7.6	12.7	11.6	8.1	3.3	400
Midwest	26.5	8.6	12.8	18.0	5.1	3.2	348
Pacific	22.3	11.0	12.0	14.4	9.6	5.3	339
Wetter Regions	23.2	8.8	12.5	14.8	7.2	3.7	1,087
South	17.1	7.4	8.8	10.9	6.9	5.6	900
Mountain	26.2	16.3	17.3	19.5	14.1	11.9	106
Drier Regions	18.5	8.7	10.1	12.2	8.0	6.6	1,006
	*		**			*	
Women							
Northeast	4.8	1.6	6.1	2.3	1.0	0.9	590
Midwest	5.5	1.4	4.1	3.8	1.7	0.6	535
Pacific	7.3	2.9	3.7	5.2	3.2	3.0	476
Wetter Regions	5.7	1.8	4.7	3.6	1.8	1.2	1,601
South	2.8	1.6	2.0	1.8	0.6	0.7	1,422
Mountain	9.0	3.4	3.4	9.0	5.1	0.0	105
Drier Regions	3.6	1.8	2.2	2.7	1.2	0.6	1,527
	*			*	*	*	

Drinkers Only

Men

Northeast	23.9	9.1	15.0	13.8	9.6	3.9	300
Midwest	31.8	10.4	15.3	21.6	6.1	3.8	283
Pacific	28.6	14.0	15.3	18.5	12.2	6.9	266
Wetter Regions	28.1	10.6	15.2	18.0	8.7	4.5	849
South	26.4	12.0	13.6	17.0	10.7	8.7	607
Mountain	37.9	24.3	25.1	28.3	20.4	17.2	75
Drier Regions	28.3	14.0	15.5	18.8	12.3	10.1	682
				*		*	
					**	**	

Women

Northeast	6.3	2.1	8.1	3.0	1.3	1.2	357
Midwest	8.3	2.2	6.1	5.7	2.6	0.9	336
Pacific	10.3	4.1	5.2	7.4	4.5	4.3	276
Wetter Regions	8.0	2.6	6.6	5.1	2.6	1.8	969
South	5.5	3.1	3.9	3.4	1.2	1.3	649
Mountain	16.4	6.3	6.3	16.4	9.3	0.1	63
Drier Regions	7.0	3.5	4.3	5.2	2.3	1.1	712
				*	*		

* Chi square test indicates significant difference among the five regions listed at $p \leq .05$.

** Chi square test indicates significant difference between wetter and drier regions at $p \leq .05$.

one is inclined to be cautions about the importance of these findings; however, other studies have also found unusually high rates of heavy drinking in the region (Clark and Midanik, 1982). In comparisons involving all five subregions, significant differences are found in several cases, but these appear to be caused by the very high rates in the Mountain region. Otherwise, differences do not appear noteworthy. In comparisons of the wetter region versus the drier region, there are significant differences among women for daily drinking, however these differences disappeared when the data were recalculated for women drinkers only. A much clearer finding was the higher prevalence of weekly drunkenness among drier region men than among wetter region men. This means that there was unambiguous evidence of regional differences among drinkers for only one of the six indicators examined, for the most subjective of those six indicators, and for only the male sex. This is weak, if any, support for the notion that heavy drinking is more prevalent among drinkers in the drier regions.

Table 17.3 presents regional differences in the percentage who reported various problems related to drinking. There are some indications of regional differences when all respondents are considered, but these were more pronounced when only the drinkers were examined. Most readers will be more interested in the data given in the "drinkers only" half of the table, since only these respondents are at risk to experience a problem related to drinking. An important finding is that regional differences are apparent in the consequences area but not in the dependence area. This is consistent with earlier findings (Room, 1971a, 1983; Clark and Midanik, 1982). However, earlier findings have not contained finer breakdowns of problem types, as are presented here. Among men, there are two general areas where regional differences in drinking related problems exist. First, drier region male drinkers are more prone to belligerence, accidents, and problems with the police. This seems consistent with the interpretation that drier-region drinking is more often aggressive or explosive. Second, there are regional differences in problems with spouses and friends—that is, significant others. To some extent, this may be a piece of the explosive drinking pattern. Presumably spouses and close friends are the most likely victims of belligerent and aggressive drunken comportment and therefore the most likely to complain or break off a relationship with the drinker. At the same time, spouses and friends in the drier regions are likely to hold less tolerant views about drinking and are therefore more likely to object to the drinker's behavior.

Substantial gender differences are also apparent in the table. While regional differences are, in many instances, apparent among male drinkers, there are no cases where there are significant regional

TABLE 17.3
Regional Distribution of Drinking Problems (in percents)

	Men		Women	
	Wetter Regions	*Drier Regions*	*Wetter Regions*	*Drier Regions*
All Respondents				
Loss of Control	3.6	3.4	1.9	1.2
Symptomatic Behavior	3.5	4.1	1.3	0.5
Binge Drinking	0.7	2.2	0.6	0.4
Dependence	6.7	6.8	3.5	1.6*
Belligerence	3.0	4.8	2.0	0.8
Problems with Spouse	8.2	12.3*	3.5	2.7
Problems with Relatives	0.7	0.2	0.1	0.1
Problems with Friends	4.4	7.4	2.8	1.7
Job Problems	2.3	3.0	1.1	0.5
Problems with Police	1.5	3.0	0.1	0.0
Health Problems	1.5	1.6	0.6	0.6
Accidents	0.5	2.9*	0.2	0.5
Financial Problems	3.0	2.7	1.4	1.5
Consequences	8.5	13.7*	4.5	3.0
N	1,087	1,006	1,601	1,527
Drinkers Only				
Loss of Control	4.4	5.2	2.7	2.3
Symptomatic Behavior	4.2	6.3	1.9	0.9
Binge Drinking	0.9	3.3	0.8	0.8
Dependence	8.1	10.5	4.9	3.1
Belligerence	3.7	7.3*	2.8	1.5
Problems with Spouse	9.9	18.8*	5.0	5.2
Problems with Relatives	0.9	0.3	0.1	0.1
Problems with Friends	5.3	11.3*	3.9	3.2
Job Problems	2.8	4.6	1.6	1.0
Problems with Police	1.8	4.6*	0.2	0.0
Health Problems	1.8	2.4	0.8	1.2
Accidents	0.6	4.5*	0.3	0.9
Financial Problems	3.6	4.2	2.0	2.9
Consequences	10.3	21.0*	6.3	5.7
N	849	682	969	712

* Proportions for wetter and drier regions significantly different at p ≤ .05.

differences in problem rates among female drinkers. Thus, when we speak of regional differences in drinking problems it is important to recognize that only male drinking patterns show such differences. If drier-region drinking is said to be more explosive, violent, or belligerent, then this is evident only among men.

Table 17.4 shows regional differences in four scales of attitudes toward drinking: two scales measuring the appropriateness of drinking (Appropriateness-Contexts and Appropriateness-Persons), a scale measuring favorability toward drunkenness, and a scale measuring the belief in disinhibition. Given the differences in problems relating to aggressive or violent drunken comportment, it was felt especially important to see if there were accompanying differences in the degree to which drier region drinkers endorsed the concept of disinhibition as an explanation for drunken behaviors. It is likely that their higher level of aggressive and violent behavior is accompanied by a greater tendency to excuse such behavior by attributing it to the disinhibiting effects of alcohol. Thus, we expect to find stronger endorsement of disinhibition in the drier regions. Higher scores represent greater favorability toward drinking or drunkenness or a greater adherence to the disinhibition idea. Among all respondents, residents of the wetter regions registered more favorable opinions toward alcohol on three of the four scales. Wetter region respondents felt that higher levels of drinking were appropriate as measured by either the Appropriateness-Contexts or the Appropriateness-Persons scale, and they were also more favorable toward drunkenness. However, there were no apparent differences in the degree to which respondents endorsed the disinhibition concept. It is, therefore, quite interesting that the elevated levels of violent and aggressive drunken behavior, as occur in the drier regions, are not accompanied by a stronger belief in disinhibition, which would excuse that behavior.

In the drinkers only data, these attitudinal differences largely disappear among men. The only exception is the extremely high score for favorability toward drunkenness among men in the Mountain states, and this is consistent with the especially high levels of heavy drinking and intoxication that occur in that region (table 17.2) Thus, among men, regional differences in drinking attitudes appear to be entirely attributable to regional differences in the proportion of abstainers (Hilton, 1986). Among women drinkers significant regional differences exist for the first three attitude scales and these differences seem particularly focused on the South rather than on the wetter regions as a whole. Thus, while female drinkers in the South are equally likely to drink heavily or to report drinking problems as female drinkers elsewhere, they are less likely to express attitudes favorable toward drinking and drunkenness. At the same time, women drinkers in the Mountain states show a particularly strong favorability toward alcohol across all four measures (though not significant for Belief in Disinhibition). Though not always significant, the same elevated attitude scores are found among men drinkers in the Mountain states, also suggesting again a particularly strong favorability toward drinking as well as a particularly strong cultural tension between these drinkers and their dry social environment.

Finally, in table 17.5 we examine regional differences in the amount of alcohol consumed in various contexts. Again, the index used—the average number of drinks typically consumed per month in each context—is a crude indicator that should be taken only as an approximation of the relative wetness of different settings rather than an accurate representation of actual consumption. The patterns here are somewhat more complicated than those shown in the earlier tables but they can generally be summarized as showing that there is more public drinking in the wetter regions and that this is somewhat compensated by more private drinking in the drier regions. This is as expected since both the legal restrictions on public drinking and the greater relative social impropriety of drinking in the drier regions were expected to push drinking out of public contexts and into private ones. Looking at the wetter versus drier comparisons, we find that for men and women, for all respondents and drinkers only, dinnertime drinking in restaurants was greater in the wetter regions than in the drier regions (the regional difference being more marked among men than among women). Contrary to expectations these were not matched by regional differences in the amount of drinking in bars and lounges. Male drinkers in the dry region, or more precisely in the South, had higher levels of consumption while "hanging out," which is another public, though not commercial, drinking context, and this context of drinking perhaps compensates for the greater restrictions on bar and restaurant drinking that exist in many Southern states. Conversely, drinking at home was more popular among all men and among male drinkers in the drier regions than it was in the wetter regions. Again we may speculate that drinking at home in the drier region compensates somewhat for the more restricted opportunities to drink in public. Drinking at parties was greater among all women and women drinkers in the wetter regions than the drier regions.

DISCUSSION

It has been recently argued that drinking practices and problems in the United States are heading toward a regional convergence (Smith and Hanham, 1982). If this view were correct there would be little point in studying regional variations in drinking patterns. These, at best, would be vestigial remains of historical differences, only of interest as grist for a case study in the process of cultural diffusion. The evidence

TABLE 17.4
Regional Distribution of Drinking Attitude Index Scores
Mean Index Scores

	Appropriateness-Contexts	Appropriateness-Persons	Favorability Toward Drunkenness	Belief in Disinhibition	N
All Respondents					
Men					
Northeast	137	128	129	101	400
Midwest	132	133	119	96	348
Pacific	126	131	127	86	339
Wetter Regions	133	131	124	95	1,087
South	95	92	96	103	900
Mountain	114	118	164	102	106
Drier Regions	98	96	106	103	1,006
	*	*	*		
	**	**	**		
Women					
Northeast	99	100	96	105	590
Midwest	95	90	89	97	535
Pacific	100	103	97	91	476
Wetter Regions	97	97	93	98	1,601
South	56	62	64	106	1,422
Mountain	85	93	112	106	105
Drier Regions	60	66	70	106	1,527
	*	*	*		
	**	**	**		

Drinkers Only

Men

Northeast	150	142	141	97	300
Midwest	150	152	128	91	283
Pacific	146	151	144	86	266
Wetter Regions	149	148	136	92	849
South	148	134	129	99	607
Mountain	160	163	210	103	75
Drier Regions	149	139	142	99	682
			*		
	*	*			
	**	**			

Women

Northeast	118	120	109	93	357
Midwest	136	128	115	93	336
Pacific	131	131	119	93	276
Wetter Regions	128	125	114	93	969
South	104	106	89	101	649
Mountain	143	160	124	113	63
Drier Regions	110	114	94	102	712
			*		
	*	*			
	**	**	**		

* F test indicates significant difference among the five regions listed at p ≤ .05.
** F test indicates significant difference between wetter and drier regions at p ≤ .05.

TABLE 17.5

Regional Distribution of Typical Quantity Consumed per Month in Various Contexts

Mean Number of Drinks per Month

	Restaurant Dinners	Restaurant Lunches	Club Meetings	Bars & Lounges	Parties	At Home	When Friends Drop In	Hanging Out	N
All Respondents									
Men									
Northeast	2.2	0.5	0.5	4.1	3.0	1.8	1.9	0.8	400
Midwest	2.0	0.2	0.9	4.1	2.5	2.6	2.9	0.3	348
Pacific	2.0	0.4	0.8	3.9	2.2	3.1	2.6	1.1	339
Wetter Regions	2.1	0.4	0.7	4.1	2.6	2.4	2.5	0.7	1,087
South	1.4	0.4	0.7	4.3	3.2	3.2	2.4	1.4	900
Mountain	1.0	0.6	0.6	4.8	2.8	2.6	2.0	0.6	106
Drier Regions	1.4	0.5	0.7	4.4	3.2	3.1	2.3	1.3	1,006
	*					*			
	**					**			
Women									
Northeast	1.4	0.2	0.1	1.4	1.3	1.2	1.2	0.1	590
Midwest	1.4	0.2	0.2	2.6	2.2	1.4	1.6	0.2	535
Pacific	1.6	0.7	0.2	2.8	1.4	1.2	1.3	0.3	476
Wetter Regions	1.4	0.3	0.2	2.2	1.6	1.3	1.4	0.2	1,601
South	1.0	0.1	0.2	1.4	1.0	1.4	1.2	0.0	1,422
Mountain	1.4	0.7	0.3	3.9	0.9	2.0	1.7	0.1	105
Drier Regions	1.1	0.2	0.2	1.7	1.0	1.5	1.3	0.06	1,527
		*		*	*				
	**				**				

All Drinkers

Men

									N
Northeast	2.2	0.5	0.5	4.1	3.0	1.8	1.9	0.8	300
Midwest	2.0	0.2	0.9	4.1	2.5	2.6	2.9	0.3	283
Pacific	2.0	0.4	0.8	3.9	2.2	3.1	2.6	1.1	266
Wetter Regions	2.1	0.4	0.7	4.1	2.6	2.4	2.5	0.7	849
South	1.4	0.4	0.7	4.3	3.2	3.2	2.4	1.4	607
Mountain	1.0	0.6	0.6	4.8	2.8	2.6	2.0	0.6	75
Drier Regions	1.4	0.5	0.7	4.4	3.2	3.1	2.3	1.3	682
	*		*			*		*	
	**		**			**		**	

Women

									N
Northeast	1.4	0.2	0.1	1.4	1.3	1.2	1.2	0.1	357
Midwest	1.4	0.2	0.2	2.6	2.2	1.4	1.6	0.2	336
Pacific	1.6	0.7	0.2	2.8	1.4	1.2	1.3	0.3	276
Wetter Regions	1.4	0.3	0.2	2.2	1.6	1.3	1.4	0.2	969
South	1.0	0.1	0.2	1.4	1.0	1.4	1.2	0.04	649
Mountain	1.4	0.7	0.3	3.9	0.9	2.0	1.7	0.1	63
Drier Regions	1.1	0.2	0.2	1.7	1.0	1.5	1.3	0.06	712
	**				**	**		**	

* F test indicates significant difference among the five regions listed at $p \leq .05$.

** F test indicates significant difference between wetter and drier regions at $p \leq .05$.

given here, however, contradicts the convergence thesis. According to the latest national survey data, the wetter and the drier sections of the country continue to have markedly different rates of abstention and per drinker consumption.

The northeastern and midwestern states share a similar profile on most of the drinking measures discussed here. Taken together they set the normative standard for wetter region drinking and by implication for the nation as a whole. This wetter region pattern is characterized by low abstention rates, high per capita prevalences of heavy drinking and alcohol problems, plus relatively favorable attitudes toward drinking and drunkenness. The Pacific states have similar characteristics, although these states seem to have even higher levels of consumption and heavy drinking. In the southern states, abstention rates are quite high and show no signs of changing. The per capita consumption in the South is similar to that elsewhere in the country, but when this measure is calculated on a per drinker rather than a per capita basis, the consumption is actually higher in the South than elsewhere. Among the general population of the South, attitudes tend to be much more unfavorable toward both alcohol and drunkenness. The Mountain states roughly share the same characteristics, although they differ in some intriguing ways. Mountain states drinkers, both male and female, reported especially high rates of heavy drinking and attitudes particularly favorable toward drinking and drunkenness. The small number of cases in the region makes it difficult to draw solid conclusions, yet continued findings of widespread heavy drinking suggest that Mountain states drinking patterns merit further investigation.

Another important finding is that gender has a profound influence on regional patterns. Regional differences in the rates of drinking problems were only apparent among men and not among women. And unlike male drinkers, female drinkers exhibited regional differences in their attitudes toward drinking and drunkenness. Gender influences such as these indicate that regional patterns of drinking-related behaviors and attitudes are bounded by the stronger influences of gender. Thus, gender establishes a context in which regional factors are placed and indicates something about the limits of regional influences.

Differences between regions are not simply static, and trends in regional patterns have also been noted in the above data. Three general comments regarding the dynamics of regional differences bear some discussion here. First, the wettening of the drier regions between the mid-1960s and the end of the 1970s has run its course, in the sense that most drinking indicators have stabilized since 1979. Second, there seems to have been a "migration" of the West North Central region from the drier to the wetter group of regions. While one must remain cautious of the possibility that this finding reflects only sampling factors unique to this data set, the result is significant insofar as it may represent a process by which this particular region adopted the "dominant" or northeastern drinking pattern. If this is correct, then the West North Central region would be particularly important as a case study of the cultural diffusion of drinking practices (which gives added significance to the work of Fitzgerald and Mulford on trends in Iowa; Fitzgerald and Mulford, 1978; Mulford and Fitzgerald, 1983). Third, the data for the drier regions may be taken as a cross-sectional snapshot of the processes that are at work when a previously dry region undergoes a pronounced wettening. It would appear that the wettening of the drier regions has not necessarily been accompanied by increases in the prevalence of heavy drinking. One might speculate that the drier regions' high rate of interpersonal problems or the relatively less favorable attitudes toward alcohol held by women drinkers in that region might be temporary reactions to the upsurge in consumption, which might therefore decline as the drier regions adjust to their increased level of consumption. While such notions cannot be founded on the kind of data presented here, these results do provide a benchmark for future studies.

The findings which have been presented in this paper have, in several cases, given empirical support to existing theses about regional drinking patterns. In other cases, however, theoretical expectations were not supported by the evidence. Consumption per drinker remains substantially higher in the dry region than in the wet region, and given the single distribution thesis, this should mean that the prevalence of heavy drinking is higher in the drier regions (among drinkers). This, however, did not appear to be the case in the evidence examined. Several previous studies suggested that drinking is more problematic in the drier regions and the data has supported that view. In particular, problems related to aggression or violence are more prevalent among drier region drinkers, as are interpersonal problems. The former of these findings supports the idea that drier region drinking is more explosive. The latter finding was unanticipated and seems to open a new line of inquiry. The gender issue, as discussed above, is another unresolved problem. More needs to be known about why regional factors influence one gender but not the other and about what the interplay between gender based and region based drinking phenomena are.

As expected, attitudes among the general population are less permissive about alcohol in the drier regions than the wetter ones. It was also expected in terms of well-known differences in the cultural climates of the regions. But contrary to what might be inferred from

FIGURE 17.2

Census Regions and Geographic Divisions of the United States

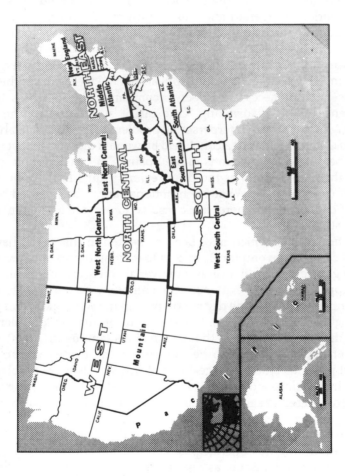

Source: U.S. Bureau of the Census, County and City Data Book, 1987.
U.S. Government Printing Office: Washington, D.C., 1983.

a sociocultural view of the causes of drinking problems, those who do choose to drink among the drier region population do not have noticeably more favorable attitudes toward drinking or toward drunkenness. Why this is the case is not clear, since those who abandon abstinence norms in subcultures where drinking is not well integrated into the society are supposed to have a lower likelihood of internalizing moderate drinking norms. At the same time it was unexpectedly found that drier region people do not believe in the disinhibition notion any more strongly than wetter region people. This raises the question of what account drier region drinkers give for their relatively more rowdy behavior.

Finally, as expected, there was some evidence that drier region drinkers were less likely than wetter region drinkers to drink in some public settings. Among male drinkers in the South, there appeared to be a compensating tendency to do more drinking at home or while hanging out. This suggests that alternative drinking locales play a more important role in the mix of drinking contexts in places where alcohol control policies limit the availability of public drinking opportunities.

18

The Presence of Alcohol in Four Social Situations: Survey Results from 1964 and 1984

INTRODUCTION

The period since the 1960s has been one of sweeping cultural change, so much so that "the late sixties" has become a catchphrase denoting normative transformation in a variety of areas. Marijuana use, for example, changed from a relatively rare and deviant act to a common-place behavior which is socially if not legally tolerated. To alcohol researchers, an interesting question has been whether these broad changes about the acceptability of drug use have been accompanied by corresponding changes in the normative acceptability of alcohol use. Such normative changes, while often used as explanations for social trends, are very difficult to verify empirically. However, in this case there is a small and rather imperfect window through which such changes can be viewed. This window is provided by a short set of questions that were asked in both the 1964 and 1984 national alcohol surveys. The questions asked whether alcohol was served at social get-togethers involving four types of participants: people met at work, people in the neighborhood, people met at church, and close friends. The present paper presents an analysis of these items, focusing both on trends between the two survey years and on cross-sectional relationships.

In the cross-sectional analysis, three hypotheses can be offered. These can be called the intimacy hypothesis, the selectivity hypothesis, and the composition hypothesis. The intimacy hypothesis states that alcohol will more often be present among close friends than among distant acquaintances. Glynn et al. (1983) found that drinking was more likely to occur among friends than among acquaintances or strangers. However, Harford (1983) found that drinking was most common among friends for men but not for women. The selectivity hypothesis states that heavier drinkers will report wetter situations than will light drinkers. Cahalan and Room (1974) found substantial evidence that heavier drinkers were more often enmeshed in "heavy drinking contexts," that is, friendship circles where drinking is heavier and more frequent, than were moderate drinkers. Clark's (1977, 1982b) findings that bars and parties are settings where heavier drinkers are concentrated exemplify the phenomenon. The composition hypothesis states that respondents from demographic groups that contain greater proportions of heavy drinkers will correspondingly report wetter situations. The demography of drinking patterns has been repeatedly studied, and the results are well known (Cahalan et al. 1969; Cahalan and Room, 1974; Johnson et al. 1977; Clark and Midanik, 1982). On the basis of this work, we expect that wetter reports of social situations will be given by respondents who are male, young, single, of Catholic or Liberal Protestant background, and who live in the "wet" regions (Room, 1983).

All three hypotheses describe expectations about the relative frequency of serving alcohol in various social situations. For the sake of brevity, I will refer to the reported frequency of serving alcohol in various situations as the "wetness" of these situations. In order to avoid confusion, readers should note that a relatively wet situation by this definition is not necessarily one where large amounts of alcohol are consumed or where the respondent consumes more than his or her usual amount.

METHODS

Data from two national alcohol surveys are compared here. One was conducted in 1964 (see Cahalan et al. 1969), the other in 1984. Both surveys consisted of face-to-face interviews with respondents chosen as a probability sample of the adults living in households in the coterminous United States. In 1964 only persons aged twenty-one or older were interviewed, but in 1984, persons above the age of eighteen were interviewed. To correct for this difference, 1984 survey respondents under the age of twenty-one have been excluded from this analysis. Also, the analysis was conducted on the weighted data from both surveys.

Two questions were asked about each of the four social situations. These were: "Please think about the people you have met *at work or through (your husband's/your wife's/your living mate's) work*. How often do you get together socially with people you have met through *work?*" and "When you get together socially with people *from work*, how often are drinks containing alcohol served?" (The italicized words varied to indicate each of the four situations.) The response categories were as shown in tables 18.2 and 18.3.

RESULTS

The rate of participation in each of the four social situations mediates between the wetness of that situation and the exposure of individuals to it. Data on participation rates are contained in table 18.1. Socializing with close friends was the most frequently occurring of the four situations in the 1984 survey; but the same question was not asked in 1964. Participation in the other three situations occurred with a lower frequency, but the rates were roughly the same for all three. Differences between the sexes were small, although women more often socialized with friends from church than did men. Regarding the changes over time, there were small but consistent decreases in socializing with workmates and neighbors. There was a much smaller decrease in socializing with church friends.

Table 18.2 shows the frequency of serving alcoholic beverages in the four situations according to those respondents who reported that they did attend them. Although the intimacy hypothesis predicts that alcohol would be most often served among close friends, these data show that gatherings involving workmates were actually the wettest settings. The composition hypothesis states that men would report wetter situations than women, and this occurred in three of the four situations. (Although the differences were quite small in the very dry "friends from church" situation.) It is notable, however, that women did not give much drier responses than men to the "people at work" item, especially in the 1984 data.

The trend comparison shows that three of the four settings have become noticeably wetter. Only among people from church, a very dry group to begin with, has there been no increase in perceived wetness. This pattern was the same for both genders. It can also be noted that the situations that were already relatively wet were those where the increases in perceived wetness were greatest.

TABLE 18.1
Frequency of Attending Various Social Occasions (in percent)

	Total		Men		Women	
	1964	*1984*	*1964*	*1984*	*1964*	*1984*
People from work						
Fairly often	19	12	21	14	17	10
Once in a while	35	35	37	38	33	33
Almost never	46	53	42	49	49	57
N	(2,746)	(1,891)	(1,216)	(886)	(1,530)	(1,005)
Neighbors						
Fairly often	22	13	20	13	24	13
Once in a while	36	29	38	31	34	28
Almost never	42	57	42	56	42	59
N	(2,746)	(2,011)	(1,216)	(942)	(1,530)	(1,069)
Church						
Fairly often	21	20	18	17	24	23
Once in a while	36	28	39	29	33	27
Almost never	43	52	43	54	43	50
N	(2,170)	(1,613)	(897)	(724)	(1,273)	(890)
Close friends						
Fairly often	x	44	x	41	x	46
Once in a while	x	44	x	45	x	43
Almost never	x	13	x	14	x	11
N		(2,010)		(941)		(1,069)

x Not asked in 1964

TABLE 18.2
Reported Presence of Alcohol in Various Social Situations (in percent)

	Total		Men		Women	
	1964	*1984*	*1964*	*1984*	*1964*	*1984*
People from work						
Nearly every time	24	37	26	39	22	36
More than half the time	12	18	15	18	9	18
Less than half the time	9	11	11	12	7	10
Once in a while	30	18	28	16	33	20
Never	25	16	20	16	29	16
	(1,477)	(888)	(703)	(460)	(774)	(428)

(continued)

TABLE 18.2 *(continued)*

	Total		Men		Women	
	1964	*1984*	*1964*	*1984*	*1964*	*1984*
Neighbors						
Nearly every time	9	17	13	20	7	14
More than half the time	7	9	10	11	4	7
Less than half the time	9	9	12	10	7	8
Once in a while	26	24	29	22	23	26
Never	49	41	36	36	59	45
	(1,584)	(856)	(702)	(418)	(882)	(438)
People from your church						
Nearly every time	3	3	4	4	2	2
More than half the time	2	2	4	2	1	1
Less than half the time	7	5	9	5	5	6
Once in a while	20	19	22	18	20	19
Never	67	71	60	70	72	72
	(1,231)	(775)	(507)	(331)	(724)	(444)
Close friends						
Nearly every time	14	20	17	26	11	14
More than half the time	9	15	13	18	6	12
Less than half the time	11	14	14	14	8	14
Once in a while	32	25	30	22	33	28
Never	35	27	27	21	41	32
	(2,736)	(1,756)	(1,210)	(810)	(1,526)	(946)

Table includes only respondents who reported having participated in each setting.

Table 18.3 shows the relationship between situational wetness and the drinking habits of the respondents. Respondent drinking was categorized into: abstainers (no alcoholic beverages within the past year), infrequent drinkers (neither wine, beer, nor liquor as often as once a month), light volume (not infrequent but less than 17.5 drinks per month), medium volume (between 17.5 and 45.0 drinks per month) and high volume (45.0 drinks or more per month.) The cutpoints are the same as those used by Cahalan et al. (1969; Appendix 1).

The wide differences between drinker types are a striking feature of this table. High volume drinkers reported much more wetness than did abstainers. This should be taken as strong support for the selectivity hypothesis. In terms of trends between surveys, there was a general tendency for respondents in all consumption categories to report increases in the wetness of get togethers involving people from work, neighbors, and close friends. However, the data for abstainers, and to a lesser extent for infrequent drinkers, contain additional points of note.

Among abstainers, increasing wetness was far more strongly noted in the workmates situation than in the other situations. This was also true of infrequent drinkers. On the other hand, abstainers have been generally successful at insulating themselves from increased wetness when getting together with close friends, many of whom are presumably also abstainers.

TABLE 18.3
Percentage of Respondents Reporting that Alcohol is Served
at Least Half the Time by Respondent Drinker Type (in percent)

	People from Work		Neighbors		People from Church		Close Friends	
	1964	*1984*	*1964*	*1984*	*1964*	*1984*	*1964*	*1984*
Abstainer	10	27	2	8	1	1	3	5
Infrequent	20	40	10	15	3	1	8	15
Light Volume	38	51	16	25	7	4	23	33
Medium Volume	59	68	31	41	9	13	45	62
High Volume	69	84	46	62	21	24	66	78
	(1,477)	(888)	(1,584)	(855)	(1,231)	(774)	(2,736)	(1,755)

Table 18.4 continues the analysis by presenting the data by various demographic categories. As already noted, men gave wetter reports of all four settings than did women. This difference was especially large among "close friends." Changes over time were noted by both sexes, the greatest increases occurring among workmates for women but among close friends for men. For the work and close friends situations, younger people reported the greater wetness. However, with regard to neighbors and people from church respondents in their twenties reported somewhat drier situations than did respondents in their thirties and forties. Trend increases were fairly uniform across the age categories, although greater increases in perceived wetness among close friends were reported by younger respondents.

Cross-sectional differences with regard to education were noticeably large, with the more educated reporting much wetter occasions than the less educated. One might speculate that serving alcohol at social occasions is much more a middle and upper class ritual than a working class one. This educational gap may be narrowing, since trend increases are strongest in the least educated category.

As expected, respondents from the Wet Regions of the country (the New England, Mid Atlantic, East North Central, and Pacific states; see Room, 1983), gave wetter reports than did respondents from the Dry Region (the southern, West North Central, and Mountain states).

TABLE 18.4
Percentage of Respondents Reporting that Alcohol is Served at Least Half the Time by Selected Demographic Categories (in percent)

	People from Work		Neighbors		People from Church		Close Friends	
	1964	1984	1964	1984	1964	1984	1964	1984
Total	36	55	16	26	5	4	23	35
N	(1,477)	(888)	(1,584)	(856)	(1,231)	(775)	(2,736)	(1,756)
Sex								
Men	41	56	22	31	9	7	30	44
Women	32	53	11	22	3	3	17	26
Age								
21–29	41	64	15	29	4	4	28	43
31–39	41	56	20	31	8	4	28	39
41–49	41	57	20	33	7	9	25	34
51–59	32	56	17	31	5	6	20	35
60 and over	17	32	8	14	1	2	13	20
Education								
Some high school	19	38	8	17	2	1	14	23
High school graduate	40	53	17	23	5	3	25	34
Some college	48	58	24	31	9	5	33	36
College graduate	56	66	34	38	13	12	41	46

Region								
Wet	45	61	23	32	9	7	29	42
Dry	25	47	9	19	2	2	14	25
Marital Status								
Married	38	54	18	27	6	5	24	33
Never married	34	58	6	33	5	5	24	47
Divorced and separated	15	56	5	28	2	4	10	38
Widowed	35	45	14	11	8	1	25	15
Religion								
Catholic	45	68	24	40	11	10	33	49
Jewish	60	56	37	58	15	6	30	38
Liberal Protestant	49	61	20	32	8	11	30	41
Conservative Protestant*	23	43	9	14	1	1	13	20

* Conservative Protestant includes the following denominations: Baptist, Methodist, United Brethren, Pentecostal, Assembly of God, Church of God, Nazarene, Holiness, Apostolic, Evangelical, Sanctified, Disciples of Christ, United Church of Christ, Christian Reformed, Jehovah's Witness, Congregational, Seventh Day Adventist, Latter-Day-Saint (Mormon), Brethren, Spiritual, Mennonite, Moravian, and Salvation Army.

In 1964, never married and divorced and separated respondents reported levels of wetness at or below the levels reported by married respondents for the workmates, neighbors, and close friends situations, but in 1984 these groups reported levels that were either comparable or greater than those reported by marrieds. Thus, much larger trend increases were experienced by the never married and the divorced and separated groups than were experienced by the married, except for the people from church situation. As expected, the greatest degree of wetness was reported by Catholics while the least degree was reported by Conservative Protestants.

In sum, the demographic findings support the composition hypothesis. Among demographic groups where drinking is known to be relatively heavier, larger numbers of respondents reported that drinks were served. Trend comparisons did not reveal substantial changes in this pattern.

DISCUSSION

The analysis of changes in the reported presence of alcohol at four social situations between 1964 and 1984 has shown a broad trend toward increasing wetness. To the extent that attitudes are consistent with practice, this trend is supportive of the generally but loosely held notion that norms about the acceptability of drinking have become more liberal since the 1960s. The evidence for this trend must be regarded as suggestive rather than conclusive, however, since it rests on only a handful of questions from two surveys.

Cross-sectionally, these data generally support all three of the hypotheses offered at the outset. The intimacy hypothesis was supported by the substantial differences in the reported wetness across these four settings. However, the greater wetness of situations involving workmates as opposed to those involving close friends was a surprise. Selectivity was also well documented; heavier drinkers gave substantially wetter reports of all four situations than did abstainers or lighter drinkers. The composition hypothesis was also supported. Greater wetness was reported by demographic groups that are known to have higher consumption levels.

Get-togethers among workmates emerged at several points in the analysis as the most interesting of the four situations, often yielding unexpected results. This suggests that further research on drinking among workmates should be undertaken. Such research could usefully begin by a diary study of recent drinking occasions in which the following variables are included: (1) whether the workmates with whom the respondent drinks are regarded as close friends or merely acquaintances; (2) the extent to which the drinking event is regarded as related to work duties (e.g., entertaining clients); (3) whether the group of co-workers is a mixed sex or a same sex group; and (4) whether the participants are of equal or unequal status.

PART VII. BLACKS AND HISPANICS

RAUL CAETANO

19

Findings from the 1984 National Survey of Alcohol Use among U.S. Hispanics

INTRODUCTION

This paper reviews findings from the 1984 national alcohol survey of drinking practices and alcohol problems among U.S. Hispanics. It involved interviewing 1,453 individuals of Hispanic ethnicity (selected after self-identification) in the coterminous United States. These individuals were selected at random and formed a multistage probability sample of U.S. Hispanics eighteen years of age and older. Interviews were conducted by trained interviewers at respondents' homes with help of a standardized questionnaire. Besides English, respondents could also be interviewed in Spanish (there were bilingual interviewers and a Spanish version of the questionnaire), and 43% chose to do so. The response rate for the survey was 72%.

This survey was conducted for a number of reasons. By 1984 there had been several studies of drinking and alcohol problems in the U.S. general population, but none had been specifically designed to study Hispanics. The number of Hispanics interviewed in these studies was small and, consequently, the analysis of their alcohol use was superficial (see Caetano, 1983, for a detailed description of this topic). Studies focusing on the drinking patterns and the consequences of alcohol abuse among Hispanics were few and also dealt with small samples of respondents—mostly Mexican Americans in the Southwest. Studies with a larger number of respondents and more detailed analyses also had methodological limitations, given that they were based on the analysis of combined samples from a number of local surveys.

However, results from these studies were somewhat consistent. In general, they showed that Hispanic men had a high rate of heavy drinking and alcohol problems, while Hispanic women were mostly abstainers. One particular study also showed that the patterning of drinking and alcohol problems by age among Hispanic men was different from that described for men in the U.S. population. Hispanic men had higher rates of heavy drinking and alcohol problems during their thirties, while among men in the U.S. population this occurred at an earlier age, during the twenties (for reviews of this literature see Alcocer, 1982, Caetano, 1983, Gilbert and Cervantes, 1987). When compared to Whites and Blacks, Hispanics in this study also had more liberal attitudes toward alcohol use and intoxication, and this could perhaps explain their higher rate of problems. Given these findings and the methodological limitations of the existing research, it was hoped that a national survey would help explain the characteristics and correlates of alcohol use and abuse among U.S. Hispanics. By interviewing respondents across the country, the survey would allow for a test of results from local studies at the national level. By interviewing a large enough number of individuals, the survey would allow a sophisticated analytical treatment of the data, something which was lacking in the literature.

In this review the findings from the 1984 survey are loosely organized in three groups: comparison with other ethnic groups and populations, sociodemographic correlates of drinking and problems and the relationship between acculturation to U.S. society and drinking.[1] In the conclusion, the implications of these results for future research and the planning of a response to alcohol problems among Hispanics are discussed.

ALCOHOL USE AMONG HISPANICS AS COMPARED TO WHITES, BLACKS AND THE U.S. GENERAL POPULATION

The 1984 survey also collected alcohol-related data on representative samples of the Black and U.S. general population, therefore allowing for cross-ethnic analyses among Whites, Blacks, and Hispanics and comparisons with the U.S. general population as a whole. Abstention is higher among Black men (30%) than among Whites (23%) and Hispanics (22%). Frequent heavy drinking is similar across the three ethnic groups: Whites, 15%; Blacks, 19%; and Hispanics, 17%. The patterning of drinking by age is also different across the three ethnic groups. Among White men, frequent heavy drinking is more common during the twenties, decreasing thereafter (figure 19.1). Among Black men the rate of frequent heavy drinking is similar in the twenty to twenty-nine, thirty to thirty-nine and forty to forty-nine age groups, being higher in the fifty to fifty-nine age group and lower in the oldest age group. For Hispanic men there is yet a third pattern. Frequent heavy drinking is more common in the thirty to thirty-nine age group, less common in older age groups. Although the pattern described for Blacks does not reproduce that previously described for Blacks in California (Caetano, 1989a), the results agree with previous findings for Hispanics and Whites, confirming results of a local survey in Northern California (Caetano, 1984a).

Drinking patterns and alcohol problems among White, Black, and Hispanic women have been described by Herd and Caetano (1987). Abstention is higher among Black and Hispanic women (45% and 46%, respectively) than among those who are White (34%) ($p < 0.05$, test of proportions). Most women who drink are infrequent drinkers, independent of ethnicity (White, 19%; Black, 17%; Hispanic, 25%). Frequent heavy drinking is lowest among Hispanic women (2%), but is also low among Blacks (4%) and Whites (5%) (but not significantly so). The patterning of drinking by age shows that abstention is more common among older age groups, while heavier drinking is more common among younger women (those in their twenties and thirties). However, Hispanic women in their fifties show relatively high rates of frequent high maximum drinking (White and Black, 4%; Hispanic, 20%) and frequent heavy drinking (Whites, 1%; Blacks, 2%; Hispanic, 8%).

All alcohol problems are relatively rare among women. Problems with highest prevalence are: salience of drinking behavior (White, 5%; Black, 4%; Hispanic, 3%); impaired control over drinking (White, 4%; Black, 3%; Hispanic, 3%); belligerence (White, 6%; Black, 3%; Hispanic, 3%); health problems (White, 5%; Black, 4%; Hispanic, 3%).[2] In a previous comparison among White, Black and Hispanic women in California, problem rates were also low and similar to those in the national study. Among White women, results from logistic regression of education, income, marital status and age on alcohol problems (problem vs. no problem) show that those who are less educated, those who are single and those who are younger have a greater chance of

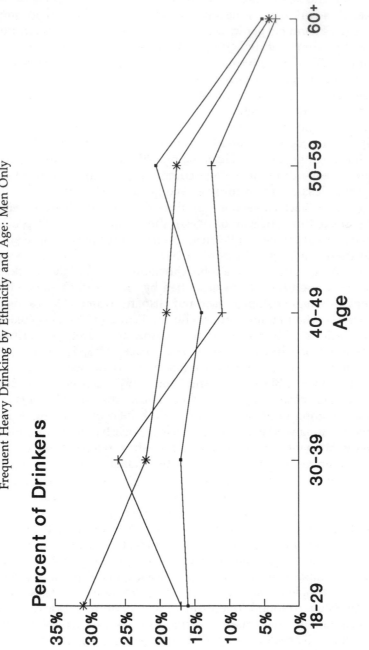

FIGURE 19.1
Frequent Heavy Drinking by Ethnicity and Age: Men Only

having an alcohol problem than other White women. Among Hispanic women those who are single and those who are younger have a greater chance of having problems than other Hispanic women, while among Black women the analysis failed to show any significant association of education, income, marital status, or age with problems.

Alcohol use in different social contexts (restaurants, clubs, bars, parties, homes, with friends at home, in parks, and streets) among White, Black, and Hispanic men have been described by Caetano (1987). Results show that drinking is generally uniform in the social contexts under consideration. Analyses by Trocki (1987) and Herd (1985c) have similar findings. However, some differences in drinking exist, and these are as follows: White men go more frequently and drink more frequently at restaurants, in clubs and in bars, than men in the two other ethnic groups, a possible reflection of income differences across the three groups. Black men go more frequently than White and Hispanic men to parks, streets, and parking lots (Blacks, 35%; Whites, 25%; Hispanics, 26%). However, the mean number of drinks consumed in these public places is higher among Hispanics than among Whites and Blacks (Hispanics, 4.0; Whites, 3.1; Blacks, 2.5). The proportion of men who drink five or more drinks in these public settings is also higher among Hispanics (Hispanics, 7%; Whites, 2%; Blacks, 7%). This is in accordance with other findings showing that Mexican Americans, who are the majority of Hispanics in the United States and in this sample, have a relatively high proportion of people who consume large amounts of alcohol per sitting (see Caetano, 1988 and commentary below).

The settings where heavier drinking is most common in all three ethnic groups are bars and parties. Men who go at least three times a month to bars or public places such as parking lots and parks tend to be single and younger than other men. These men also have a higher rate of heavy drinking and drunkenness than other men. These findings are in general agreement with previous research on contexts of drinking among men (see Clark, 1984; Fisher, 1979; Glynn et al. 1983).

Alcohol use among Mexican Americans ($N = 945$) and individuals in the U.S. general population interviewed in the 1984 ($N = 4,272$) survey has been analyzed by Caetano (1988). Results show that relatively more Mexican American women are abstainers than women in the U.S. general population (46% vs. 36%), and that drinking five or more drinks at a sitting is more common among Mexican American men than among their counterparts in the U.S. general population (54% vs. 42%). When data are examined separately by state of residence— California versus Texas—Mexican American men still have higher rates of drinking five or more drinks than the general population in each state. However, there are differences between Mexican Americans in

Texas and California. Mexican American men in California have a lower rate of abstention (22% vs. 34%) and a higher rate of frequent heavy drinking (20% vs. 13%) than their counterparts in Texas. Mexican American women in California have a rate of abstention similar to those in Texas (51% vs. 55%), but have a higher rate of frequent high maximum drinking (16% vs. 4%).

These findings seem to reflect differences in alcohol use between the populations of Texas and California, which suggests that Mexican Americans are following norms regulating drinking in each of their respective states. Previous analyses of drinking in a California community and a district of Mexico city (Roizen et al. 1988; Caetano et al. 1986), as well as comparison of drinking among Mexican Americans in this sample and Mexicans in Michoacan (Caetano and Medina Mora, 1988) also suggest that this increased rate of drinking five or more drinks at a sitting may be linked to a pattern of drinking which is common in Mexico. However, given the differences in drinking between Mexican Americans in these two states, this reasoning applies more to Mexican Americans in California than in Texas. A number of reasons why this is so can be put forward. For example, differences in Mexican populations migrating to Texas and California may result in different patterns of acculturation to the surrounding drinking norms.

The patterning of drinking by age shows that among Mexican American men frequent heavy drinking is more common in the twenties and fifties. Among all men in the United States sample frequent heavy drinking is highest during the twenties.

The analysis of alcohol problems shows that the proportion of men among Mexican Americans and in the U.S. general population reporting any alcohol problem is 22% and 24%, respectively. Among women these percentages are 7% and 11%, respectively. Compared to Mexican American men, men in the U.S. sample report more salience of drinking behavior, (10% vs. 7%; $p < 0.05$, test of proportions), belligerence (10% vs. 7%; $p < 0.05$, test of proportions) and problems with people other than the spouse (7% vs. 4%). Mexican American men have a higher rate of job problems (4% vs. 1%). Data by age show a lesser rate of problem prevalence among men in the U.S. sample who are in their thirties compared to those who are in their twenties, while most rates among Mexican Americans are equal across age groups. During middle age years, Mexican American men report relatively more problems than men in the U.S. sample. Among women, problem prevalence is similar in both samples (prevalence rates range between 0% and 4%).

In summary, the comparisons between Hispanics, Whites, and Blacks do not show striking differences in the overall distribution of drinking patterns. However, when these data are examined by age, one of the most important predictors of drinking, important differences in the patterning of drinking and the prevalence of problems appear. Something similar occurs in the comparison of drinking among Mexican Americans and the U.S. general population. The overall distribution of drinking patterns for these two groups is somewhat similar. However, when drinking patterns are examined by age, or divided into those who ingest larger quantities per sitting and those who do not, the differences are highlighted and easier to understand in the light of drinking patterns common in Mexico. In these two groups of comparisons the similarities are only skin deep. Beneath the surface of each group the undertow pulls in different directions, and it is only by learning about these hidden currents that a meaningful understanding of alcohol use is achieved.

SOCIODEMOGRAPHIC CORRELATES OF DRINKING AND ALCOHOL PROBLEMS

A number of papers on the 1984 international alcohol survey have examined the association between drinking, heavier drinking, alcohol problems, and sociodemographic factors (Caetano, 1989, 1988, 1987a, 1987b, 1987c). In this section a summary of the findings from these papers is given, again with an emphasis on Hispanic respondents.

Caetano (1989, 1988) describes the relationship between sociodemographic attributes, including Hispanic national survey, and drinking patterns and problems. Drinking has a direct inverse relationship with income and education, independently of sex. This result confirms previous findings among Hispanic women in California (Caetano, 1984b) and in the U.S. general population (Clark and Midanik, 1982). Hispanic men and women in higher income and higher education groups have lower rates of abstention than other respondents. The rate of abstention among men reporting a family income equal to $30,000 or more is 4%, while among those with income less than $6,000 the rate is 24%. Among women, the rates are 22% and 67%, respectively. Men in the highest income bracket also have a high rate of frequent heavy drinking (30%), but this relationship is not linear, and the rate of frequent heavy drinking is approximately equal in all other income groups. Among Hispanic women, those in the highest income bracket, as compared to all other women, have higher rates of frequent high maximum drinking (20%), something which is also observed among those with annual income between $10,001 and $15,000.

With regard to education, Hispanic men with some college education have a rate of abstention only one third of that of men with less than nine years of schooling (11% vs. 32%). At the same time these college educated men have a rate of frequent heavy drinking twice that of the less educated men (32% vs. 16%). Similar differences for abstention rates are observed among Hispanic women. About 59% of the women in the lowest education group do not drink, while only 26% of those who have at least some college education are abstainers.

Among Hispanics, employment status could only be examined for women; few men were unemployed or retired. Women who are in the work force, whether they work full or part-time, have lower rates of abstention than other women, especially homemakers (full-time, 33%; part-time, 32%; unemployed, 57%; homemaker, 68%; retired, 65%) (Caetano and Herd, 1987). Hispanic women who are working full-time also have a higher rate of frequent high maximum drinking than other women (full-time, 14%; part-time, 5%; unemployed, 8%; home-maker, 3%; retired, 0%). When women who are employed are compared with homemakers, the effect of employment on abstention is independent of age and education. Income may certainly play a part in these differences, but the Hispanic woman who works is breaking away from traditions as well as from behaviors, such as abstention, that may be associated with it.

Respondents' birthplace and national origin were also examined in the 1984 national survey (Caetano, 1985; 1988). However, these analyses should be seen as tentative for there are few respondents who identified themselves as Cuban Americans ($N = 95$) and Puerto Ricans on the mainland ($N = 219$). Results by birthplace show that U.S. born Hispanic men who have at least one parent born in a Latin American country have low rates of abstention (17% vs. 30% for other U.S. born Hispanic men), and high rates of frequent heavy drinking (33%). Of men born in Mexico, in Cuba or in Puerto Rico, Mexicans have the highest rate of frequent heavy drinking (19%, 3%, and 3%, respectively). About 40% of these men born in Mexico drink at least once a week. In contrast, most of the men born in Puerto Rico (41%) or in Cuba (41%) report drinking one to three times a month. Results do not differ much when respondent classification is based on self-identification rather than birthplace.

Among women, Mexican Americans have an abstention rate similar to that of Cuban Americans (46% and 42%, respectively) and higher than that of Puerto Ricans (33%). However, Mexican American women have a rate of frequent high maximum drinking (12%), higher than that of women in the other two groups (Puerto Ricans, 3%; Cuban Americans, 7%). Dividing Mexican American women into those born in the United States but with at least one parent born abroad, other U.S. born women, and those born in Mexico shows three different drinking patterns: U.S. born women with at least one parent born abroad have a low rate of abstention compared to other women (22% vs. 44% for other U.S. born women, and 71%, 45% and 48% for women born in Mexico, Puerto Rico and Cuba, respectively); other U.S. born women have a high rate of frequent high maximum drinking (26%); and finally, women born in Mexico have a high rate of abstention (71%).

Turning to alcohol problems, the prevalence of one or more problems is higher among Mexican American men than among other men compared (Mexican Americans, 22%; Puerto Ricans, 8%; Cuban Americans, 4%). The questionnaire gathered information on thirty indicators of symptomatic drinking and social and personal problems related to drinking during the twelve months previous to the study. All these problems are included in these figures. The prevalence rate of four or more problems, a more stringent cutoff point for problem prevalence, is also higher among Mexican Americans than among men in the other national groups (Mexican Americans, 7%; Puerto Ricans, 5%; Cuban Americans, 2%). Data by birthplace show that among Mexican American men problems are more frequent among those who were born in Mexico and among those born in the United States with at least one parent born abroad. Men born in Mexico have a particularly high rate of four or more problems (11% vs. 6% for U.S. born men, 3% for men born in Puerto Rico and 2% for men born in Cuba). This was unexpected because frequent heavy drinking is more common among U.S. born Hispanic men than among those born in Mexico. Previous research comparing drinking and problems in Mexico and U.S. communities have shown this same effect, that is, for a given amount of alcohol there seems to be more reporting of problems in Mexico than in the U.S. (Caetano et al. 1986).

Rates for specific types of problems show that the most common consequences of heavy alcohol use among Mexican American men are: salience of drinking behavior (7%), impaired control over drinking (8%), belligerence (7%), health problems (7%), and problems with spouse (8%). Among Puerto Rican men the most common problems are: salience of drinking behavior (6%), impaired control (6%), health problems (6%), and problems with spouse (6%), and with people other than spouse (6%). Among Cuban American men the most common consequence of heavy drinking is having a problem with people other than the spouse (4%). These rates are lower than those reported by Hispanics, most of whom were Mexican Americans, in a study in Northern California (Caetano, 1984b).

Because they drink little, Hispanic women report few problems in comparison to men. The proportion of women reporting one or more problems by national group is: Mexican Americans, 7%; Puerto Ricans,

3%; Cuban Americans, 2%. About 6% of U.S. born women with at least one parent born abroad report one or more problems. This percentage is 10% for other U.S. born women, and is 4% for women born in Mexico and Puerto Rico, and 2% for women born in Cuba.

United States born Hispanic women with both parents born in the United States, the "other" group, have a rate of four or more problems (7%) which is seven times higher than the rate for any other group of women. As seen above, a higher proportion of these women that the others compared are frequent high maximum drinkers.

Finally, the most common problems among Mexican American women are: salience of drinking (4%), impaired control over drinking (4%), belligerence (4%), health problems (4%), and problems with other people (4%). Among Puerto Rican and Cuban women none of the rates for these specific types of problems is higher than 2%.

Turning to attitudes toward alcohol use, Mexican American and Puerto Rican men have more liberal attitudes toward drinking and drunkenness than Cuban Americans (Caetano, 1988). More men in the former two groups than in the latter agree with items such as "having a drink is one of the pleasures of life" or "it does some people good to get drunk once in a while." Cuban American men seem to value the power of alcohol as a social lubricant more than men in the other two groups. More Cuban American men than Mexican Americans or Puerto Ricans endorse items such as "people who drink have more friends than people who don't" or "people who drink have more fun than people who don't."

Among women attitude patterns are similar to those described for men, with the exception that Cuban American women are *not* more supportive than other women of those items indicating that people who drink have more fun or more friends than people who do not use alcohol. Parallel to these liberal views toward alcohol use, there is also considerable support for items expressing negative views about drinking. More than two thirds of both men and women in each of the three national groups agree with items such as "there is nothing good to be said about drinking" or "drinking is one of the main causes of people doing things they shouldn't."

Norms regulating alcohol use among the three Hispanic national groups considered here are similar. When norms are examined with regard to how much drinking is seen as appropriate for men and women in different age groups, there is considerable agreement that sixteen year olds should not drink, that men may drink more than women, and that those who are thirty or forty years of age may drink more than others. With regard to norms concerned with drinking larger quantities of alcohol ("drinking enough to feel the effects"), more Mexican

Americans express approval of this type of drinking than Puerto Ricans or Cuban Americans. This is in accordance with Mexican Americans' higher rate of heavier drinking and with their attitudes toward drunkenness.

In summary, these results have shown that Hispanics who are in the upper socioeconomic groups drink more than others. Employment and birth in the United States seem particularly important in lowering abstention and increasing rates of heavier drinking among women. Mexican Americans report more drinking than Puerto Ricans and Cubans, and this is particularly so for those who are "first generation," that is, born in the United States but with at least one parent born abroad. Mexican Americans report more problems and also seem to have more liberal attitudes toward drinking and drunkenness than Puerto Ricans and Cuban Americans. The association between drinking and socioeconomic variables is not unexpected, following patterns described for other population groups. The role of employment among Hispanic women deserves further scrutiny, aiming at a better understanding of the relationship between birth in the United States, women's roles among Hispanics and change in alcohol use.

ACCULTURATION AND DRINKING

The role of acculturation to U.S. society and its association with the adoption of different patterns of alcohol use was examined in a series of analyses of the 1984 national alcohol survey data. The first relationship examined was that between drinking patterns and acculturation, and that paper also describes in detail the acculturation scale used in the analysis (Caetano, 1987). Briefly, the scale was built with a series of items assessing daily use and ability to speak, read, and write English and Spanish; preference for media in English or Spanish; ethnicity of the people respondents interacted with in their church, parties, and neighborhood now and when growing up, as well as questions about values thought to be characteristic of the Hispanic way of life. Acculturation is associated with a lower rate of abstention (low, 37%; medium, 27%; high, 17%) and with a higher rate of frequent heavy drinking, though only among men forty years of age and older (low, 9%; medium, 7%; high, 12%). Among men eighteen to thirty-nine years of age, those who are low and high in acculturation have higher rates of frequent heavy drinking than those in the medium category (low, 30%; medium, 13%; high, 21%).

Among Hispanic women, acculturation is associated with a lower rate of abstention, and this is independent of age. Considering only women who are forty years of age or older those who are acculturated have a higher rate of frequent high maximum drinking than other women (low, .5%; medium, 2%; high 42%). However, this finding should be treated with caution because there are only forty-six women in this age group who are high in acculturation. Among foreign born Hispanic women, acculturation does not have an effect on drinking.

Logistic regression was used to establish the independent effect of acculturation and sociodemographic variables on drinking. The model for this analysis used the dichotomy drink versus do not drink as the dependent variable, and age, birthplace, acculturation, education, and work status (for women only) as predictors. Among men, those who are eighteen to thirty-nine years of age, those who are foreign born and those who are high in acculturation include relatively more alcohol users than the other men compared. With regard to heavier drinking (defined as either frequent high maximum or frequent heavy drinking), the predictors of this are being younger and being born in the United States. Among women, those who have completed high school education or more, those who are high on acculturation, and those who are employed are more often drinkers than other women are. Women who are high on the measure of acculturation have nine times greater chance of being heavier drinkers than do women in the low acculturation group.

Acculturation also implies increased social opportunities to drink (Caetano, 1987b). Hispanics who are highly acculturated report more frequent attendance at a number of social settings where alcohol is often consumed (restaurants, clubs, bars, parties, home) as well as greater frequencies of drinking in these places. In general, these relationships are independent of income or work status. Among women, employment and acculturation seem to be particularly strong predictors of drinking in various settings. Women who are employed and who are high on acculturation report frequencies of drinking in settings outside the home which are similar to those reported by men. Finally, Hispanics in the high acculturation group have a pattern of attendance at settings and a pattern of drinking in the settings which are closer to those of the U.S. population than to those of Hispanics in the low acculturation group.

Norms and attitudes toward alcohol use also vary with acculturation (Caetano, 1987c). Hispanics who are in the high acculturation group have more liberal norms and attitudes toward drinking and drunkenness than others. However, the relationship is more consistent for norms than for attitudes. The relationship between acculturation and more liberal attitudes is modified by the amount of drinking in question, the social setting being considered and by the respondent's age and sex. For instance, men are more liberal than women, and among men eighteen to thirty-nine years of age there is no relationship between acculturation and permission to use alcohol at parties, for a husband dining out with his wife and for a man at a bar.

A comparison of alcohol use by Mexican Americans who were interviewed in the 1984 survey and Mexicans in the state of Michoacan has thrown new light on the relationship between acculturation and drinking. Mexicans in Michoacan were interviewed with a Spanish version of the questionnaire used in the United States. These respondents were selected randomly and form a probability sample of the city of Morelia and an adjoining rural county. Details of this survey are in Caetano and Medina Mora (1988). First, patterns of drinking are different between these Mexicans and Mexican Americans. In general Mexicans drink less than Mexican Americans; this is true among both men and women. Abstention rates are similar for men (Mexicans, 26%; Mexican Americans, 27%), but higher for Mexican women than for those in the United States (Mexican women, 66%; Mexican American, 46%). About 50% of the Mexican men are either infrequent or less frequent high maximum drinkers, while only 18% of the Mexican American men are so. In contrast, more Mexican American men than their Mexican counterparts report frequent high maximum drinking or frequent heavy drinking (44% vs. 13%). Among women, 14% of the Mexican Americans are either frequent high maximum or frequent heavy drinkers, compared to 1% of the Mexicans.

The relationship between drinking and acculturation is stronger among women than among men. Mexican American men in the low acculturation group already have a pattern of drinking which is quite different from that of men in the Mexican sample. They have lower rates of infrequent drinking (10% vs. 30%) and of infrequent high maximum drinking (13% vs. 24%), and higher rates of frequent high maximum (12% vs. 7%) and frequent heavy drinking (24% vs. 6%). The differences between men in the low and high acculturation group are best seen in the rate of frequent high maximum and frequent heavy drinking. In the low acculturation group the rate of frequent high maximum drinking is 12%, while in the high acculturation group the rate is 34%. Rates for frequent heavy drinking are: Low, 24%; high, 10%.

For women acculturation is associated with a steady decrease in the rate of abstention (low, 81%; medium, 52%; high, 29%), and increases in the rate of infrequent drinking (low, 8%; medium, 22%; high, 31%). Besides that, Mexican American women in the high acculturation group have a rate of frequent high maximum drinking which is twenty times higher than that for Mexican women and those in the low acculturation group (high, 20%; low, 1%, Mexicans, 0.5%).

The change in drinking patterns associated with acculturation seems to occur more quickly for men than for women. After one to five years of life in the United States, men in the Mexican American group who were born in Mexico already had changed drinking patterns from infrequent drinking of larger amounts to more frequent drinking of such amounts, which made their drinking similar to that of U.S. born men. Among women, the change in drinking patterns described above only occurs among those born in the United States. In other words, immigration from Mexico to the United States does not change these women's drinking patterns; it is only the U.S. born women who seem to be responsible for the lower rate of abstention, and higher rate of infrequent and frequent high maximum drinking described above.

Among Mexican Americans the effect of acculturation on drinking is independent of other sociodemographic variables. Thus, for men the only significant predictors of drinking (abstention vs. drinking) in a model which included age, acculturation, marital status, birthplace, education, income, and attitudes toward alcohol use were: being eighteen to thirty-nine years of age, being highly acculturated, being born in Mexico and having liberal attitudes toward drinking. Among women the predictors were acculturation and liberal attitudes toward drinking. A linear regression of the same predictors mentioned above on number of drinks consumed per month (log 10) suggests that acculturation is not a predictor of number of drinks but only of whether an individual drinks or abstains.

Turning to problems, Mexican men report more problems than Mexican Americans. The rate of four or more problems among Mexicans is 16%, and among Mexican Americans it is 7%. This is in spite of the fact that Mexican men, as seen above, drink less than those in the Mexican American group. Similar findings have been reported in other studies involving comparisons between United States and Mexico (Caetano et al. 1986). Women do not report many problems. Only 7% of the Mexican Americans and 5% of the women in the Mexican sample report any problems due to drinking. Mexican American women in the medium and high acculturation groups have higher rates of four or more problems than other women (medium and high, 4% each; low acculturation and Mexican women, 1% each). Among men the general effect of acculturation seems to be that of diminishing alcohol problems; among women, however, the effect is that of increasing problems. Results from a logistic regression of alcohol problems (problem vs. no problems) shows that the predictors of problems among men who drink are being eighteen to thirty-nine years of age and having less than high school education. Among women the predictors are acculturation and being single.

Among Mexican Americans acculturation is associated with a more neutral view of alcohol, that is, a view where the bad and the good that can be derived from alcohol use are more balanced. Specifically, fewer Mexican Americans in the high acculturation group than in the other two groups believe that alcohol is a facilitator of social life or that it is a source of indiscriminate evil. In Mexico, and among Mexican Americans in the low acculturation group, the attitudes seem to be ambivalent. There is support for alcohol as a social lubricant but there also is considerable support for items expressing negative views about drinking.

Acculturation seems to lead to more liberal views regarding drinking norms. A higher proportion of Mexican American men and women in the high acculturation group than in other groups or than in Mexico would allow any drinking or allow drinking enough to feel the effects of alcohol to most gender-age groups. Norms in the high acculturation group are also more egalitarian. Women and old people are the ones that would be granted more access to alcohol as acculturation to U.S. norms proceeds among Mexican Americans.

In summary, acculturation to U.S. society seems to be a powerful force shaping alcohol use, norms and attitudes toward drinking among Hispanics. The results for drinking patterns among men are not as strong as those for women, but the positive association between acculturation and more liberal norms and a more liberal view of alcohol is independent of sex and other sociodemographic factors. Finally, acculturation has a positive association with problems only among women, a result which once again emphasizes the apparently closer link between this construct and alcohol among women than among men. This difference can be understood by contrasting drinking in Mexico and the United States, the new country to which Mexican Americans are acculturating. While there certainly are differences in norms and patterns of drinking among men in Mexico and the United States, men in both countries live in a "wet" world, a world where, relative to women, there is considerable freedom to drink. For women the picture is different. The United States is a much "wetter" world than Mexico, and coming across the border for women entails a considerable change as far as drinking habits and norms are concerned. There is thus more latitude for change in drinking among women than among men.

20

Drinking Patterns in the Black Population

INTRODUCTION

The 1984 national survey provided a nearly representative sample of black adults living within the forty-eight contiguous states. Further, the sample size was large enough ($N = 1947$) to permit statistical analyses within subsets of the population of blacks—which has rarely been possible in the past national surveys of alcohol use. The explanation for this lies in the oversampling of black adults (as well as Hispanics) in a manner described by Santos in the Appendix to this volume. Thus we are able to present here an overview of black drinking, one which contains some findings at variance with past research.

Herd (1985a) reviewed a range of other social indicators of alcohol problems among the U.S. black population, and these are of interest here. They include psychological consequences such as alcohol related morbidity and mortality as well as psychosocial indicators such as records on hospitalization or treatment for alcohol problems, arrest statistics, and self-reported social problems due to drinking. The findings of the review illustrate that, except for the youth population, blacks are overrepresented on most indirect measures of alcohol problems. However, there is considerable variation in the level of disparity between blacks and whites on different types of problems indicators, and variation in whether indicators of specific problems have been declining or rising in recent years.

Medical problems associated with heavy drinking have increased very dramatically in the black population. Rates of acute and chronic alcohol–related diseases among blacks, which were formerly lower than or similar to whites, have in the postwar years increased to almost epidemic proportions. Currently, blacks are at extremely high risk for morbidity and mortality for acute and chronic alcohol-related diseases such as alcohol fatty liver, hepatitis, liver cirrhosis, and esophageal cancer.

The literature has pointed out that heavy alcohol consumption both in the past and the present are strong predictors of increases in the alcohol–related diseases (Schmidt and DeLint, 1972; Skog, 1980; Bruun et al. 1975). With reference to past alcohol consumption patterns, Herd's research (1985b) has described the shift in black cultural attitudes towards alcohol which has led to alcoholization in many urban communities since the Repeal era. The significance of these historical shifts was affirmed in an epidemiological analysis (Herd, 1985a) which showed the importance of cohort changes in mortality patterns and demographic shifts—such as urban migration—in partially explaining the rise of liver cirrhosis among blacks. An analysis of contemporary black drinking patterns suggests that blacks may be at greater risk for physiological diseases due to a later onset and more prolonged pattern of heavy drinking than whites.

Aside from alcohol consumption level, other factors which may be important in explaining the high rates of alcohol-related diseases have not been specifically explored. These include the possibilities that high hepatitis rates, inferior nutritional status, and low socioeconomic status may be leading to substantial increases in morbidity and mortality among blacks who drink heavily.

In contrast to the rise of medical problems related to alcohol use among blacks reflected in a widening disparity of problem rates between blacks and whites, some social indicators have shown a relative decline in black predominance and a convergence of black and white rates. This has been the case with statistics on arrests for alcohol-related offenses.

Arrests for drunkenness have decreased more substantially for blacks than whites, making the two groups more similar in rates than they were in the 1960s. Although black rates are still significantly higher than white rates, the disparity between the two groups has lessened greatly. Arrest rates for violation of liquor laws have also declined for blacks, but have increased in the white population, making rates between the two groups very comparable. Among both blacks and whites, arrest rates for driving while intoxicated have increased substantially, but the increase in white rates has been twice that of blacks. DUI (Driving Under the Influence) arrest rates for blacks are now almost identical to rates for whites.

The decline in black predominance in arrest statistics seems to be related to general changes in the social and legal responses to alcohol problems. These include the decriminalization of public drunkenness and expansion of alcohol detoxification and treatment centers. Legal responses refer in part to the increases in drinking and driving legislation and rise of grass roots antidrunk driving movements. The changing legal response to alcohol problems have made white drinking drivers more vulnerable to arrest, thus helping to equalize black and white arrest rates.

Black Americans are currently overrepresented in the alcohol treatment system, particularly in the urban areas of the Northeast. The excessive involvement of blacks in the alcohol treatment system is consistent with the high rates of psychiatric hospitalization for alcohol problems described for urban, migrant blacks in earlier decades. Within the current alcohol treatment system, blacks appear to be modestly overrepresented in programs emphasizing voluntary treatment for working or middle-class people such as employee assistance programs. In contrast, they appear greatly overrepresented in programs designed for persons in the lower socioeconomic strata, such as public inebriates.

Survey data, including that reported below, indicate that at the aggregate level, black men and white men appear to have similar drinking patterns. However, despite the similarity in drinking patterns, black men exhibit a higher prevalence of all the kinds of drinking problems asked about in this survey. Black women differ from white women in exhibiting higher rates of abstention and lower rates of frequent drinking. They also report lower rates of problems due to drinking. These findings are detailed below.

RESULTS

The data from the study suggest that at an overall level, black men and white men have very similar drinking patterns (table 20.1). Altogether, 29% of black men were classified as abstainers, compared to 24% of whites, similar proportions of blacks and whites reported drinking infrequently (10% - 11%) and drinking in the less frequent categories (16%) and in the more frequent categories (30%). Slightly more whites than blacks (19% vs. 15%) were considered frequent heavy drinkers.

TABLE 20.1
Drinking Patterns by Sex and Race in Percents (Weighted)

	Males		Females	
	Blacks (715)	*Whites* (743)	*Blacks* (1,221)	*Whites* (1,030)
Abstainers	29	24	46	34
Infrequent drinkers	11	10	16	19
Less frequent low maximum drinkers	8	10	16	14
Less frequent high maximum drinkers	8	6	4	7
Frequent low maximum drinkers	12	12	9	13
Frequent high maximum drinkers	18	18	4	8
Frequent heavier drinkers	15	19	4	5

Among women, there appeared to be greater differences between the races. Nearly half of the black female population (46%) compared to only about a third (34%) of white women were described as abstainers. Similar proportions of black and white women indicated drinking in the infrequent and less frequent drinking categories, but white women appeared to drink more frequently than blacks. Twice as many white as black women (8% vs. 4%) were classified as frequent high maximum drinkers. However, an almost identical proportion of the two groups of women fell into the heaviest drinking category (4% and 5% for blacks and whites, respectively).

In spite of the similarity in aggregate drinking patterns reported for black and white men, important differences between the two groups of men emerge when looking at the association between levels of drinking and some sociodemographic characteristics. For example, the age distribution of drinking patterns showed that among whites frequent heavy drinking is most prevalent among those in the eighteen to twenty-nine year age group. Among blacks however, rates in this age group are very low. For men between thirty to thirty-nine years, blacks showed a sharp increase in rates of frequent high maximum drinking while rates among whites are fairly stable (table 20.2). As will be described later, the increase in frequent high maximum drinking is paralleled by high problem rates for black men in the thirty to thirty-nine year age group.

TABLE 20.2

Drinking Patterns by Age Group and Race among Men in Percents (Weighted)

	18–29		30–39		40–49		50–59		60+	
	Blacks (204)	Whites (201)	Blacks (169)	Whites (165)	Blacks (115)	Whites (97)	Blacks (77)	Whites (90)	Blacks (145)	Whites (187)
Abstainers	23	17	15	13	37	21	29	30	60	41
Infrequent drinkers	10	8	6	10	8	16	23	7	14	12
Less frequent low maximum drinkers	10	11	8	8	9	14	4	6	6	9
Less frequent high maximum drinkers	13	10	7	9	3	2	3	8	1	0
Frequent low maximum drinkers	10	4	15	12	13	10	14	13	7	24
Frequent high maximum drinkers	17	20	33	26	17	17	7	19	6	10
Frequent heavier drinkers	16	31	17	21	14	19	20	17	5	4

TABLE 20.3

Drinking Patterns by Age Group and Race among Women in Percents (Weighted)

	18–29		30–39		40–49		50–59		60+	
	Blacks (336)	*Whites* (236)	*Blacks* (307)	*Whites* (217)	*Blacks* (132)	*Whites* (14)	*Blacks* (147)	*Whites* (120)	*Blacks* (250)	*Whites* (310)
Abstainers	34	22	32	30	56	35	60	35	69	49
Infrequent drinkers	20	20	19	16	11	21	14	20	12	18
Less frequent low maximum drinkers	22	14	18	16	11	12	12	12	8	15
Less frequent high maximum drinkers	4	13	6	10	5	6	2	4	2	0
Frequent low maximum drinkers	9	11	15	7	7	13	7	22	8	15
Frequent high maximum drinkers	6	13	5	13	4	7	4	4	0	1
Frequent heavier drinkers	6	7	5	8	6	7	2	1	1	1

TABLE 20.4
Drinking Patterns by Yearly Income and Race for Men in Percents (Weighted)

	$6,000 or Less		$6,001–$10,000		$10,000–$15,000		$15,001–$20,000		$20,001–$30,000		$30,000 and over	
	Blacks (160)	Whites (62)	Blacks (149)	Whites (70)	Blacks (94)	Whites (84)	Blacks (85)	Whites (97)	Blacks (85)	Whites (150)	Blacks (94)	Whites (233)
Abstainers	34	32	26	40	29	32	32	31	21	22	30	13
Infrequent drinkers	12	10	8	5	10	14	9	8	17	15	9	7
Less frequent low maximum drinkers	8	11	5	4	5	10	3	11	18	8	11	11
Less frequent high maximum drinkers	4	1	6	4	2	6	20	8	6	10	11	6
Frequent low maximum drinkers	8	9	11	14	12	11	11	10	14	13	12	13
Frequent high maximum drinkers	21	14	24	21	19	12	7	13	10	16	22	25
Frequent heavier drinkers	12	22	21	10	23	16	18	19	14	17	6	24

TABLE 20.5
Drinking Patterns by Yearly Income and Race for Women in Percents (Weighted)

	$6,000 or Less		$6,001–$10,000		$10,000–$15,000		$15,001–$20,000		$20,001–$30,000		$30,000 and over	
	Blacks (502)	Whites (153)	Blacks (214)	Whites (140)	Blacks (125)	Whites (129)	Blacks (103)	Whites (109)	Blacks (105)	Whites (190)	Blacks (67)	Whites (241)
Abstainers	53	54	45	44	50	39	28	27	29	28	34	25
Infrequent drinkers	13	17	15	20	16	19	19	22	21	24	17	16
Less frequent low maximum drinkers	10	10	18	12	15	11	31	16	32	15	13	18
Less frequent high maximum drinkers	5	6	7	8	4	8	2	3	3	6	4	6
Frequent low maximum drinkers	9	5	8	7	6	11	8	16	8	13	28	17
Frequent high maximum drinkers	5	4	6	6	3	4	4	10	3	7	3	13
Frequent heavier drinkers	5	4	2	2	6	7	8	7	4	6	2	4

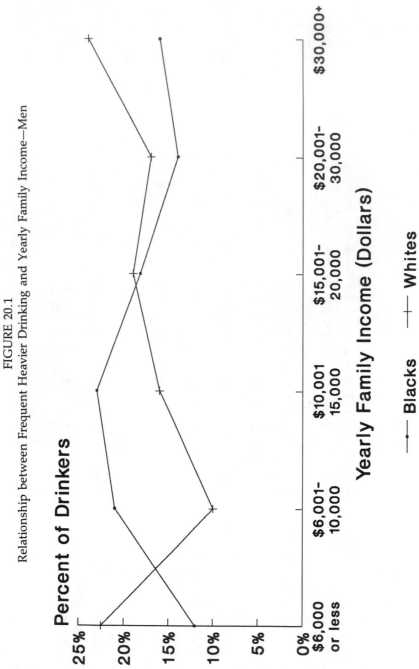

FIGURE 20.1
Relationship between Frequent Heavier Drinking and Yearly Family Income—Men

Among women similar racial differences are observed in the age distribution of drinking (table 20.3). Younger white women (in the eighteen to twenty-nine year age group) are much more likely than young black women to drink at all, to drink frequently, or to drink at high maximum levels. However, similar proportions of both groups of women are classified as frequent heavier drinkers.

Black and white men also differed substantially in the relationship between some indicators of socioeconomic status and frequent heavier drinking. Among white men increasing levels of family income were associated with increases in heavy drinking; however among blacks, as income rose, rates of heavy drinking fell (figure 20.1 and table 20.4). The divergence in the association between income and the two groups of men may be a function of differences in their social backgrounds or in the types of occupations they hold.

In the female population, there were fewer differences between blacks and whites; increases in income were generally associated with decline in abstention and increase in frequent drinking (table 20.5).

In addition, major differences were observed for black and white men in the distribution of drinking patterns by geographical region and the degree of urbanization (table 20.6 and 20.8). Generally, the drinking patterns of whites reflected the traditional split between "wet" and "dry" regions and urban/rural locations. That is among whites, heavier drinking was concentrated in the North and Midwest and in cities. Conversely, in the South and in rural areas, abstention and lighter drinking were prominent. These patterns did not hold for black men. For these men, heavy drinking (combined rates of frequent high maximum and frequent heavier drinking) was highest in the South and in nonmetropolitan areas. Hence, for black men, abstention and lighter drinking patterns were as common in some northern areas and in small cities as in the "drier" southern and rural settings.

Among women, there were fewer differences between the races and both groups showed a positive association between rates of drinking and residing in cities or wetter geographical regions (table 20.7 and 20.9).

The findings for black men differ greatly from the results of previous general population surveys and from epidemiologic analyses on the regional distribution of liver cirrhosis (Barnes and Russell, 1977; Wechsler et al. 1978; Bailey et al. 1965; Haberman and Sheinberg, 1967; Weismann et al. 1980; Robins et al. 1968; Globetti, 1967; Windham and Aldridge, 1965; Warheit et al. 1976; Neff and Husaini, 1984; and Herd, 1985a). These data indicated that rates of heavy drinking and of alcohol-related problems were highest in the urban Northeast and lowest in the South. The contrasting picture in the national data may reflect recent shifts in regional patterns of drinking among black men. Herd's analysis

TABLE 20.6
Drinking Patterns by Yearly Income and Race
for Men in Percents (Weighted)

	Northeast		North Central		South		West	
	Blacks (132)	Whites (174)	Blacks (116)	Whites (195)	Blacks (400)	Whites (231)	Blacks (68)	Whites (141)
Abstainers	34	14	17	16	34	36	20	26
Infrequent drinkers	18	14	9	10	7	1	16	8
Less frequent low maximum drinkers	10	11	8	10	7	9	16	10
Less frequent high maximum drinkers	4	5	21	5	5	7	3	6
Frequent low maximum drinkers	9	15	17	12	10	10	15	13
Frequent high maximum drinkers	8	20	17	23	22	15	15	14
Frequent heavier drinkers	16	20	12	23	15	14	15	22

TABLE 20.7
Drinking Patterns by Yearly Income and Race
for Women in Percents (Weighted)

	Northeast		North Central		South		West	
	Blacks (192)	Whites (230)	Blacks (213)	Whites (281)	Blacks (722)	Whites (343)	Blacks (93)	Whites (177)
Abstainers	38	21	31	33	56	48	38	30
Infrequent drinkers	23	28	15	15	15	20	11	11
Less frequent low maximum drinkers	16	12	24	14	11	10	23	22
Less frequent high maximum drinkers	5	7	5	10	3	5	4	6
Frequent low maximum drinkers	10	17	14	14	7	9	12	10
Frequent high maximum drinkers	4	10	6	9	4	4	5	12
Frequent heavier drinkers	3	4	6	6	4	3	7	9

TABLE 20.8
Drinking Patterns by Degree of Urbanization and Race for Men in Percents (Weighted)

	Metropolitan Cities of 50,000 or More		Metropolitan Cities of Less than 50,000		NonMetropolitan Areas	
	(412)	(226)	(164)	(289)	(140)	(226)
Abstainers	30	18	29	20	28	35
Infrequent drinkers	9	11	16	10	9	10
Less frequent low maximum drinkers	10	5	9	14	5	10
Less frequent high maximum drinkers	3	7	12	4	13	8
Frequent low maximum drinkers	14	19	10	10	8	9
Frequent high maximum drinkers	14	17	14	23	28	14
Frequent heavier drinkers	20	22	10	21	10	14

TABLE 20.9
Drinking Patterns by Degree of Urbanization and Race
for Women in Percents (Weighted)

	Metropolitan Cities of 50,000 or More		Metropolitan Cities of Less than 50,000		NonMetropolitan Areas	
	Blacks (715)	Whites (307)	Blacks (267)	Whites (393)	Blacks (242)	Whites (344)
Abstainers	42	29	41	28	59	46
Infrequent drinkers	18	17	19	21	11	18
Less frequent low maximum drinkers	14	19	22	15	13	9
Less frequent high maximum drinkers	5	8	4	7	2	7
Frequent low maximum drinkers	11	12	8	16	7	9
Frequent high maximum drinkers	6	9	1	9	4	6
Frequent heavier drinkers	5	7	4	3	4	5

(1985a) suggested that the South appeared to be increasingly associated with high rates of cirrhosis mortality—for example, the greatest increase in mortality rates between 1949–1971 occurred the coastal South, and even in the deep South rates were rising although in a lagged fashion. It may be that in recent years alcohol consumption among blacks has rapidly increased in the South, but remained fairly stable among blacks in the North, leading to the blurring of regional differences and the comparatively high rates of heavy drinking in the South.

In general the preliminary findings indicate that although black and white men share roughly similar drinking patterns, there are major differences in the age groups associated with heavy drinking and in the relationship between drinking patterns and some social and demographic characteristics. Hence there may be important racial differences in the etiology of heavy drinking and in the sub-groups at risk for excessive consumption and alcohol-related problems. Among women, there are greater differences in overall drinking patterns, but more similarity in how socioeconomic and geographic factors affect black and white drinking. Although not described in this report, black and white men do differ substantially in the relationship between drinking levels and some social characteristics (e.g., marital and employment status). These findings suggest that there may be important sociocultural and gender differences which affect the distribution of drinking patterns in the black population.

DRINKING PROBLEMS

Table 20.10 presents preliminary data on the prevalence of drinking problems in the past twelve months for respondents classified as current drinkers (consumed one or more drinks of alcoholic beverages over the past year). The percentages are based on the number of respondents reporting one or more items under each problem type.

The findings for males illustrate that for every type of problem, with the exception of drinking and driving, blacks report higher rates of problems than whites. This finding is particularly interesting given the fact that a slightly smaller proportion of blacks were classified as frequent heavier drinkers. It suggests that other factors (e.g., number of times drunk or socioeconomic status), may contribute to high problem levels. The excess in black rates was particularly marked for acute and chronic alcohol-related health problems. Nearly two and a half times as many black men as white men reported binge drinking (4.0% vs. 1.5%) and health problems (15.3% vs. 6.4%). Substantially more black men than white men also indicated experiencing symptoms of alcohol withdrawal (17.1% vs. 9.9%) and loss of control (17.8% vs. 13.7%). There were fewer differences between black and white men in how many reported social and interpersonal problems. These data are consistent with health statistics and arrest figures which show that while racial differences are narrowing on social indicators of problem drinking, the gap is widening for alcohol-related morbidity and mortality.

TABLE 20.10
Prevalence of Current Problems by Sex and Race
among Current Drinkers in Percents (Weighted)

	Males		Females	
	Blacks	*Whites*	*Blacks*	*Whites*
Financial problems	5.4	3.8	1.0	2.6
Accidents	2.0	1.7	0.5	0.6
Binge drinking	4.0	1.5	0.8	0.9
Loss of control symptoms	17.8	13.7	7.6	7.6
Withdrawal symptoms	17.1	9.9	3.9	4.8
Health problems	15.3	6.4	7.7	7.2
Belligerence	15.3	13.1	4.7	8.6
Job problems	6.3	4.9	1.2	1.6
Police problems	6.0	4.2	0.9	1.0
Spouse problems	13.5	11.3	4.3	5.1
People problems	13.8	9.0	3.7	5.3
Total problems	37.6	31.2	15.7	17.8
Proportion frequent				
heavier drinkers	20.8	25.3	8.2	7.4

The distribution of drinking problems shows a different relation-ship between the races among women. In general, black women report fewer alcohol-related problems of any type compared with white women. The differences are especially strong for the proportion of black vs. white women reporting belligerence (4.7% vs. 8.6%) and financial problems (1.0% vs. 2.6%). The low rate of alcohol-related problems for black women in this sample differs from previous studies which suggested that black women exhibit much higher rates of alcoholism than white women. Part of the difference may stem from the different sample bases used—this study includes a large proportion of southern women, while previous surveys have relied almost exclusively on reports from women living in the urban North.

When the relationship between men's drinking problems and age was examined, blacks and whites showed some important differences. Paralleling the relationship between age and frequent heavier drinking described in the previous section, blacks in the youngest age group (eighteen to twenty-nine) were at least risk for experiencing drinking problems, and whites of this age were at highest risk (figure 20.2).

For men reporting one or more alcohol problems, rates among whites over twenty-nine years old declined sharply, then rose in the forty to forty-nine year age group, and rapidly descended for older men. Among blacks, problem rates increased considerably for men in the thirty to thirty-nine age group. After age thirty-nine, rates among blacks decreased, but the decline was much more gradual than it was for whites. In fact the level of problems among blacks remained higher than that of whites throughout middle and old age. For men indicating a more severe level of problems, there were greater differences between blacks and whites. After age twenty-nine, black men experienced sharp increases in problem rates which decreased slightly for men between forty to forty-nine years and rose steeply for those between fifty to fifty-nine years. It is only black men over fifty-nine years old that show considerable decline in rates of severe alcohol problems; in contrast, among whites, drinking problems declined dramatically for men between thirty to thirty-nine, increased considerably in the forty to forty-nine year age group, and then began a consistent decline among the elderly.

The relationship between alcohol problems rates and family income level shows major similarities and differences for black and white men (figure 20.3). In both races, the overall prevalence of alcohol-related problems is highest among men with relatively low incomes. Among blacks, as income increases, rates of problems steadily decline. However, among whites, after taking a steep plunge at the middle income level ($10,000–$15,000 yearly) the proportion of men experiencing problems rises quite dramatically in the next income bracket and continues to increase at higher income levels. Despite the different patterns of association, at every income level blacks appear to be at more risk for alcohol-related problems than whites, except for those with incomes of over $30,000 per year.

For men reporting more severe alcohol-related problems, the proportion of problems at different income levels is very similar for blacks and whites. However, blacks and whites differ somewhat in the way income is associated with level of problems. Among blacks there is strong, steady decline in the proportion of those experiencing problems as income increases. In contrast, among whites the prevalence of problems goes up for men with incomes of $6,000–$10,000 per year and for those with incomes over $30,000 yearly.

In sum, preliminary results from the national survey suggest that black men experience a much higher prevalence of alcohol-related

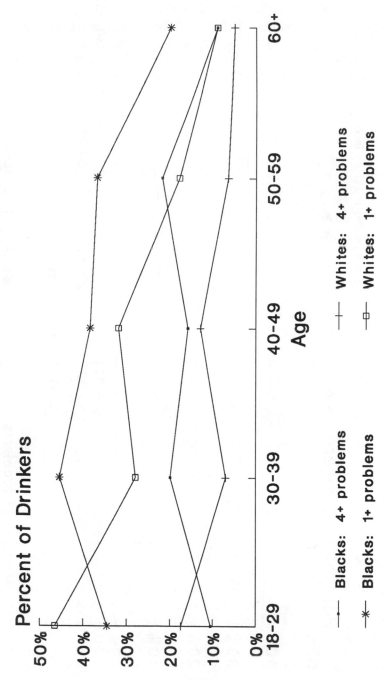

FIGURE 20.2

Alcohol-Related Problems among Current Male Drinkers by Age

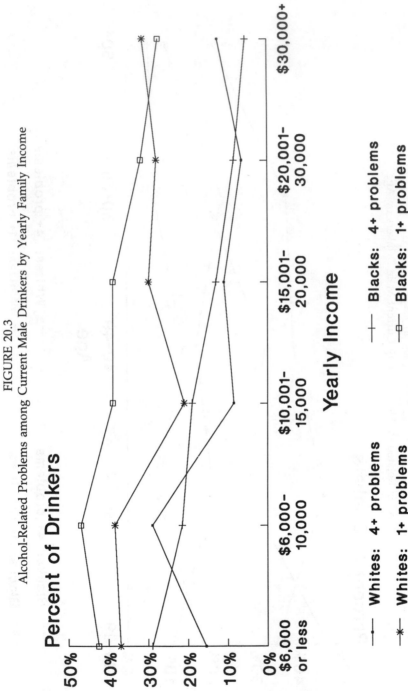

FIGURE 20.3

Alcohol-Related Problems among Current Male Drinkers by Yearly Family Income

health problems than white men despite similar rates of overall alcohol consumption. Important variations in the prevalence of problems for the two groups of men were also described by age, socioeconomic status and geographical region. Among blacks problem rates are highest for men over thirty years old, for men with low incomes, and for men residing in the South. In contrast, the prevalence of alcohol problems for white men is greatest for those aged between eighteen to twenty-nine, at both low and high income levels, and for men residing in the West.

In general, the national survey data suggest that black women exhibit lower rates of alcohol-related problems than white women, particularly in the areas of drinking and driving and some social problems.

DISCUSSION

The data set from the 1984 survey is by no means exhausted by this preliminary analysis; the size and representativeness of the sample call for and permit further work. Planning effective intervention strategies for alcohol-related problems in a special population requires a good knowledge base about the etiology of such problems in the particular population. For the most part, this kind of knowledge is lacking with respect to blacks. There are few in-depth studies which examine alcohol-related problems or diseases among blacks. Most existing analyses rely on studies with very small subsamples of blacks, or on data on blacks gleaned from aggregate statistics.

Research needs to be greatly expanded in the black population. More clinical and epidemiological studies on alcohol-related diseases need to be conducted. These studies are needed to provide insight into the contribution of alcohol consumption and other risk factors for disease. Establishing relative risks for consumption is important for determining safe levels of alcohol beverage use. This is particularly important given the national survey data which suggest that black men are at increased risk for alcohol-related problems despite exhibiting consumption patterns similar to those of white men.

Much more research on the social and cultural factors influencing the etiology of heavy alcohol consumption and alcohol-related problems among blacks should be implemented. For example, the issue of age of transition into heavy drinking is a key problem in the literature on black drinking. Currently, blacks in early middle age appear to be at high risk for social problems related to alcohol use. However, it is not known whether this pattern is related to specific socialization or maturational features in black culture which delay age of drinking, or to "cohort effects" or historical events which make blacks in this age group more vulnerable to drinking. If this phenomenon is more related to cohort effects than to maturational features in black drinking, it may mean that high rates of heavy drinking will persist in older age groups as this cohort ages. Knowledge about the social factors which influence age of drinking and patterns of socialization to drinking thus hold implications for the social forces to be addressed in intervention measures.

A related concern regarding the transition into heavy drinking involves the question of why blacks in alcoholism treatment are so much younger than whites. In contrast to the youthfulness of blacks in alcohol treatment, numerous studies have shown that black youth in the general population are on the whole at much lower risk for drinking, drunkenness, and arrests for alcohol-related offenses. Examining this issue has important implications for determining which youth populations are at risk for developing alcohol problems, and for designing appropriate strategies for intervention.

Appendix

One Approach to Oversampling Blacks and Hispanics: The National Alcohol Survey

INTRODUCTION

The 1984 National Alcohol Survey[1] (NAS) was the first national household survey to study exclusively the drinking attitudes, patterns and problems of Blacks, Hispanics and the general population. The survey objectives called for an area-probability sample of households in the forty-eight contiguous states. In total, 5,000 one hour personal interviews were to be conducted with adults aged eighteen or over. However, 1,500 interviews of Blacks, 1,500 of Hispanics, and 2,000 interviews from the remaining population were desired.

The March 1984 Current Population Survey estimates that about 10.8 percent of all households in the United States are Black households, while only 5.1 percent represent Hispanic households. Thus, the problems of rare element sampling required special consideration. Kish (1965b) and Kalton and Anderson (1984) outline methods suitable for surveys of rare populations. Among such techniques, the NAS employed a multipurpose sample (i.e., selection of Blacks, Hispanics and others), disproportionate stratified sampling of minority strata, large clusters and the supplementation of primary sampling units.

The purpose of this paper is to detail the sampling design employed in the NAS. The results of the NAS are presented and a non-response analysis is conducted. The report closes with an examination of sampling error in the NAS. We shall show that the desired number of interviews was attained or exceeded for Blacks and Hispanics. However, large sampling errors resulted from differential weighting.

SELECTION STRATEGY

Several factors influenced the design strategy of the sample. First, the oversample of Blacks and especially Hispanics posed a formidable problem because of their rare nature. Differential sampling rates for each group would be required, and the implementation of such a design can be rather complex. Secondly, the entire budget available for design, data collection and data reduction was confined to just under $600,000. A per unit cost of $120 for this survey meant that only cost effective sampling plans could be considered. Finally, a third major constraint was time. According to contractual specifications, six months were allotted for sample design, selection, listing, selection of households, and preparation of interviewer assignments.

In reaction to the conditions specified above, the following design features were utilized in the NAS:

1. The Institute for Survey Research (ISR) 100 Primary Sampling Unit (PSU) National Sampling Frame was employed. This reduced both cost and time components in the first stage of a multi-stage design.
2. Ten supplemental PSUs were selected to reduce variances for the Black and Hispanic portions of the survey. The NAS thus comprised a total of one hundred ten PSUs.
3. Secondary Sampling Units (SSUs) were stratified by the density of the Hispanic population and the density of the Black population, and heavier minority strata were oversampled. This reduced the screening costs of the survey.
4. In the third stage of selection, households in minority strata were again oversampled. This further curtailed the costs of identifying Black and Hispanic households, and helped to equalize interviewer workloads and minimize intra-PSU travel costs.

Small interpenetrating replicate "reserve" samples of households were set aside and later allocated in a fashion which ensured that desired subgroup sample sizes were achieved or exceeded. Several features of the sample design of the NAS are somewhat similar to those utilized by Ericksen (1976). However, Ericksen's survey objectives did not include an Hispanic component.

BRIEF DESCRIPTION OF THE SAMPLE DESIGN

The NAS is based on a four-stage area–probability sample of households in the forty-eight contiguous United States. In the first stage of selection, PSUs comprised groups of metropolitan counties representing Standard Consolidated Areas (SCAs) and groups of nonmetropolitan counties. Using 1985 projected population sizes, a total of forty-four self-representing PSU equivalents were determined, while sixty-six noncertainty PSUs were selected with probabilities proportional to measures of size (pps). The final sample of one hundred ten PSUs is essentially a one hundred PSU National Sampling Frame (based on the general population) supplemented with ten PSUs to capture the heterogeneity of the Black and Hispanic populations.

In the second stage of selections, Block Groups (BGs) and Enumeration Districts (EDs) defined SSUs. Within each PSU, SSUs were assembled into three distinct strata:

1. An Hispanic stratum, consisting of all SSUs with 15% or more Spanish Origin population according to 1980 Census data.
2. A Black stratum, consisting of all non-Hispanic SSUs with 10% or more Black population (in 1980).
3. A "balance stratum" of all remaining SSUs.

The Hispanic stratum was oversampled by a factor of eight while the Black stratum was selected at 3.56 times the rate of the balance stratum. Probabilities proportional (within a PSU) to 1980 population counts were used at this stage. In all, five hundred eighty-one SSUs comprised the sample.

Within each SSU, a single tertiary unit called a Listing Area (LA) was selected. A Listing Area is a group of one or more blocks which contain about forty-four housing units (in 1980) on average. Enumerators were sent to each LA so that complete, up-to-date listings of housing units would be available for subselection.

In the final stage of selection, segments of about four contiguously listed housing units were sampled from listing sheets and assigned to interviewers for screening. Segments in Black and Hispanic LAs were selected at twice the rates of those in the balance stratum. In all, 2,844

segments were employed in the sample. A replicate reserve sample 25%
the size of the initial sample was drawn in the event a larger sampling
fraction was desired. Near the end of data collection, the reserve sample
was released into the field for all but the balance stratum. This ensured
that desired minority subgroup sample sizes were attained or exceeded
in the survey, but introduced larger differential weight factors.

In order to control sample sizes and reduce the effects of
differential weighing, white households were subselected in Black and
Hispanic LAs and Black households were subsampled in Hispanic LAs.
Subselection was achieved through the use of randomly assigned
screening forms in predetermined proportions. Three screening form
types were used. The first allowed an interview from a household
regardless of the race/ethnicity of the household head; the second form
permitted an interview only if the household head was reported as Black
or Hispanic. The third form restricted interviews to households with
Hispanic heads. These forms were randomly allocated in fixed proportions in a fashion which yielded (apart from the reserve sample allocation) an equal probability sample of Black households in all but the
balance stratum.

IDENTIFICATION AND ADAPTION OF THE
SAMPLING FRAME OF PSUS

The choice of a sampling frame was an important design issue
in the NAS. Because the survey objectives called for a national area
probability sample of households, the ISR 100 PSU National Sampling
Frame was a natural choice. This frame is based on 1980 Census data
and represents the population in the forty-eight contiguous states plus
the District of Columbia. It is flexible enough to accommodate both
general population surveys as well as studies of special subpopulations
such as Blacks and Hispanics. The ISR National Sampling Frame was
especially convenient because of the existing time restrictions and cost
constraints.

The actual selection of NAS PSUs was composed of two distinct
tasks:

1. The selection of 100 PSUs into the ISR national sample.
2. The adaption of the national frame through the selection of ten
   supplemental PSUs.

ISR NATIONAL SAMPLE OF PSUS

Data from the 1970 and 1980 censuses were employed in gener-
ating 1985 population projections for all PSUs in the ISR national

sample. The projections simply extrapolated the population changes which occurred in the 1970s:

Measure of size (mos) = 1980 population + 1/2 (1980 population − 1970 population). These projections were used as measures of size in the selection of primary areas. These measures approximately equal 235 million when summed across all counties in the geographic area of coverage.

We defined PSUs as follows. First, counties were assembled into two groups: (1) those in "self-representing areas", and (2) the rest of the country. Self-representing areas are Standard Metropolitan Statistical Areas (SMSAs) or Standard Consolidated Areas (SCAs) with projected populations of two million or more. Eighteen self-representing areas satisfy this rule; they contain a total projected population of 84.6 million, 36% of the national total.

For the rest of the country, PSUs were constructed from SMSAs and countries outside SMSAs in one of two ways: if an SMSA or county had a population of 150,000 or more, it was defined as a PSU; if an SMSA or county had a smaller population, it was combined with adjacent counties or a nearby SMSA or from PSUs with populations of 150,000 or more.

The next step involved the construction of thirty-two strata, each with total projected populations ranging 4.2 to 5.2 million. Collectively, these strata contained a projected population of 150.4 million. Strata were created with the goal of increasing their homogeneity. To this end, we employed region and metropolitan/nonmetropolitan status, and within these categories, one or more of the following variables were used: degree of urbanization, economic growth rates, racial composition, and the proportion of the population Hispanic.

Some strata included only a few metropolitan PSUs having populations of 500,000 or more. Other strata were rural in nature, with populations under 200,000 and with individual PSUs which included many counties covering a vast land area. In some cases, a single PSU covered over half the nonmetropolitan area of western or plains states.

Two PSUs were selected from each stratum; this yielded a total of sixty-four non-self representing areas. PSUs were drawn with probabilities proportional to size. Thus, for PSU j in a given stratum,

f_{j*} = (2 x MOS_{j*})/stratum size,
where MOS_{j*} is the measure of size assigned to a given PSU j, and f_{j*} is the PSU selection rate.

The two selections were determined independently, or with replacement.

SUPPLEMENTAL PSU SELECTION

In addition to the 100 PSUs of the ISR National Sampling Frame, ten supplemental PSUs were employed. We supplemented the national frame in order to reduce the average cluster sizes of those PSUs with significant minority populations. Had no PSUs been added, unduly large numbers of interviews would have been taken from minority neighborhoods in non self-representing PSUs. This would occur because the first stage selection probabilities were based on total population projections (rather than minority) and consequently were sometimes small. Moreover, substantial oversampling of minority strata was planned at subsequent stages. In order to yield an overall sampling rate f in the Hispanic stratum, for instance, a within PSU rate of f/p_i is necessary, where p_i is small then f/p_i could be large.

Through contractual agreements, four PSUs were targeted to increase the precision of the Black oversample, and six were designated for the Hispanic sample. Black and Hispanic supplemental PSUs were determined independently. Naturally, their selection necessitated changes in the structure and specification of the national sampling frame. These issues as well as the supplemental PSU selection procedure will now be discussed.

The self-representing PSUs in the ISR frame contain about 45% of the total Black population according to the 1980 Census data. Roughly three quarters of the remaining Black population resides in the South. Thus, Black supplemental PSUs were confined to the Southern states. Three of thirteen Southern nonself-representing PSU strata in the ISR frame were constructed on the basis of high Black population density (25% or more). One stratum comprised rural PSUs while the remaining two contained metropolitan areas. Since the six PSUs representing these strata were most likely to experience large sampling rates within PSUs additional PSU selections were drawn. One selection was drawn from each metropolitan stratum, and two additional PSUs were drawn with pps from the rural PSU stratum.

The advantages of this strategy were twofold. First, the selection of additional PSUs within the existing strata of the ISR frame was the most straightforward method of supplementing the sample. Secondly, time constraints did not permit more elaborate and perhaps more efficient supplementation strategies.

Hispanic supplemental PSUs were determined differently. About 88% of the Spanish Origin population resided within SMSAs in 1980. We therefore restricted PSU supplementation to metropolitan areas. We ranked all SCAs and SMSAs according to 1980 Spanish Origin population and designated those with Spanish Origin populations exceeding 150,000 as self-representing. Table A-1 presents the results of this process. All SCAs and two SMSAs were already self-representing and thus had no effect on the ISR frame. Three SMSAs had been selected into the ISR national sample as non self-representing. Six previously unselected PSUs were added to the national sample as self-representing Hispanic supplements. In total, these self-representing areas contained roughly 66% of the total Spanish Origin population in the United States.

TABLE A-1

Metropolitan Areas with 1980 Spanish
Origin Population Exceeding 150,000

Metropolitan Area	*1980 Spanish Origin Population*	*PSU Status**
Standard Consolidated Areas:		
1. Chicago—Gary—Kenosha, IL, IN, WI	629,801	1
2. Houston—Galveston, TX	447,081	1
3. Los Angeles—Long Beach—Anaheim, CA	2,754,212	1
4. Miami—Fort Lauderdale, FL	620,118	1
5. New York—Newark—Jersey City, NY, NJ, CT	1,997,398	1
6. San Francisco—Oakland—San Jose, CA	632,650	1
Standard Metropolitan Statistical Areas:		
1. Albuquerque, NM	164,224	3
2. Brownsville—Harlingen—San Benito, TX	161,701	3
3. Corpus Christi, TX	158,193	3
4. Dallas—Fort Worth, TX	248,811	1
5. Denver—Boulder, CO	174,405	3
6. El Paso, TX	297,196	3
7. Fresno, CA	150,367	3
8. McAllen—Pharr—Edinburg, TX	230,287	2
9. Phoenix, AZ	199,517	2
10. San Antonio, TX	481,335	2
11. San Diego, CA	274,530	1

* Key to PSU Status Codes:
  1. Self-representing in ISR frame.
  2. Non self-representing selection in ISR frame.
  3. New self-representing Hispanic supplemental PSU.

The ISR national frame was altered to reflect the fact that nonself-representing PSUs were now self-representing. The net effect on the ISR frame was that nine PSUs were deleted from five strata. Stratum population totals were adjusted to their new sizes, and in one case, two strata were collapsed to preserve the paired selections design.

SECOND AND THIRD STAGES OF SELECTION

The second stage of selection was accomplished in three steps: (1) creation of SSUs; (2)stratification of SSUs; and (3) selection of SSUs. SSUs were defined as EDs or BGs which contained a minimum of forty-four housing units in 1980. Whenever an ED or BG did not meet the minimum, it was combined with neighboring units until this criterion was satisfied. Within each PSU, SSUs were assembled into three strata:

1. An Hispanic stratum, consisting of all SSUs with 15% or more Spanish Origin population in 1980.
2. A Black stratum, composed of all non-Hispanic SSUs with 10% or more Black population;
3. A balance stratum of all remaining SSUs.

The Black and Hispanic strata were oversampled at this stage of selection in order to substantially reduce screening costs. Relative to the balance stratum, Hispanic SSUs were oversampled by a factor of eight, while Black SSUs were oversampled by 3.56. This is an important design consideration in the efficiency of oversampling. The efficiency depends on the density of minorities (Black and Hispanic) within the minority SSU strata, as well as the proportion of the minority population in those strata. A full discussion of this topic is furnished in Waksberg (1973). At the time the sampling rates were set, however, these data were not available.

A total of 581 SSUs were drawn, of which 188 were Hispanic, 179 were Black, and 214 were from the balance stratum. A larger number of SSUs was drawn in order to curb the ill effects of intraclass correlations associated with sampling within PSUs. One drawback is that a large number of SSUs increases intra-PSU travel. This lessens the savings from reduced screening costs.

In the third stage of selection, a single sampling unit called a Listing Area was selected from each SSU. The selection was made with pps using 1980 Census data and the SSU selection probability. Each LA contained about forty-four housing units on the average. The resultant sample of LAs comprised an equal probability sample within the Black, Hispanic and balance strata. The overall selection equation may be written as follows: For an LA in non self-representing PSU i, in SSU stratum j:

$$f_j = \frac{(2)PSU_i}{\text{Stratum total}} \quad \times \quad \frac{(K_j)NUMLA}{TOTLA_i} \quad \times \quad \frac{1}{NUMLA}$$

Where

stratum total = 1985 projected population total in that PSU stratum

PSU_i = 1985 projected population total for PSU_i

$$K_j = \begin{cases} 8, \text{ for } j = 1, \text{ the Hispanic stratum} \\ 3.56, \text{ for } j = 2, \text{ the Black stratum} \\ 1, \text{ for } j = 3, \text{ the balance stratum} \end{cases}$$

$TOTLA_i$ = (12,800) PSU_i/(Stratum total)

$NUMLA$ = $TOTLA_i$ x (1980 population in SSU)/(1980 population in PSU_i)

$$f_j = \begin{cases} 1/800 & \text{for } j = 1 \\ 1/1,800 & \text{for } j = 2 \\ 1/6,400 & \text{for } j = 3 \end{cases}$$

For self-representing PSUs, the "first" stage selection probability is one and the "second" stage fraction becomes $(K_j)(NUMLA)/6,400$.

HOUSEHOLD AND RESPONDENT SELECTION

Households were selected using a two phase methodology. In the first phase, segments of about four households were sampled at a constant rate of 6/10 for the Black and Hispanic strata, and 3/10 for the balance stratum. A total of 2,844 segments were employed in the sample. Oversampling by a factor of two helped to equalize interviewer workloads.

Three quarters of selected households were randomly designated for screening and interviewing. The remainder was split into two equal sized replicates and set aside as a reserve sample. It would be used to boost the sampling fraction and meet prespecified numbers of interviews. Midway through the data collection period, we decided to allocate only the reserve samples in the Black and Hispanic strata. This was done in reaction to a lower than expected number of Black and Hispanic interviews gathered by that time. While ensuring that desired numbers of interviews were achieved or exceeded, the reserve allocation yielded an additional differential weighting factor of 4/3 between the minority and balance strata. At this point, the overall household selection probabilities were 1/1,333, 1/1,300 and 1/28,444 for the Hispanic, Black, and balance strata, respectively.

The second phase of household selection consisted of randomly subsampling white households in the Hispanic and Black strata, and subsampling Black households in the Hispanic stratum. The objective was to subsample certain households in minority strata in a fashion which yielded an equal probability sample of white households overall, and an equal probability sample of Black households in the Black and Hispanic strata. To this end, three color coded screening forms were allocated randomly in fixed proportions to all sample households. Yellow, blue and ivory screening forms were used. A yellow form permitted an interview from a randomly selected adult resident if the household head was reported to be Hispanic in origin; otherwise, no interview was conducted at the household. With blue forms, an interview was conducted if the household head was either Black or Hispanic. Ivory forms allowed an interview regardless of the race/ethnicity of the household head.

Within a given SSU stratum, screening forms were distributed to sample households in the percentages shown in table A-2. Apart from the differential weighting due to the allocation (which was unanticipated) of the reserve sample, the form distributions yielded an equal probability sample of white households overall, and the Black households in minority SSU strata. The final household probabilities of selection are presented in table A-3. Note that the selection probability is contingent upon the race/ethnicity of the household head and the SSU stratum. The fractions in table A-3 also incorporate the increased selection probabilities in the minority SSU strata due to the reserve sample allocation. One adult aged eighteen or over was randomly selected within each eligible household. The random selection was realized using standard selection tables outlined in Kish (1949).

SURVEY RESULTS

A total of 10,925 households were selected in the NAS. Table A-4 presents screening response rates by SSU strata. Overall, about 92% of all sample households were screened. Screening response rates varied only slightly across SSU strata, ranging from 89% in the balance stratum to 93% of the Hispanic stratum. Final dispositions of screened households appear on table A-5. The first row of this table shows that about one third of white households were subselected out of the sample in the Black stratum, and roughly half of non-Hispanic households were subsampled in the Hispanic sample. (When a household in the Black or Hispanic stratum was subselected out of the survey on account of the race-ethnicity of the household head, the final disposition was called

TABLE A-2

Percentagewise Distribution of Screening Forms by
Secondary Sampling Unit Stratum (SSU) for the National Alcohol Survey

	Color of Form		
	Yellow	*Blue*	*Ivory*
SSU Stratum			
Hispanic	55.56%	38.19%	6.25%
Black	—	85.94%	44.06%
Balance	—	—	100.00%

TABLE A-3

Household Selection Probabilities in the National Alcohol Survey by
Secondary Sampling Unit (SSU) Stratum and Race/Ethnicity of Household Head

	Race/Ethnicity of Household Head		
	Hispanic	*Black*	*Other*
SSU Stratum			
Hispanic	1/1,333	1/3,000	1/21,333
Black	1/3,000	1/3,000	1/21,333
Balance	1/28,444	1/28,444	1/28,444

TABLE A-4

Screening* Response Rates in the National Alcohol Survey
by Secondary Sampling Unit (SSU) Stratum

	SSU Statrum			
	Black	*Hispanic*	*Balance*	*Total*
Screening Disposition				
Households not screened	378	302	235	915
(column percent)	(9.0%)	(6.6%)	(10.9%)	(8.4%)
Households screened	3,830	4,268	1,912	10,010
(column percent)	(91.0%)	(93.4%)	(89.1%)	(91.6%)
Total	4,208	4,570	2,147	10,925
(column percent)	100%	100%	100%	100%

*This table excludes 1,191 selections which were found not to be in the sample
universe (e.g., outside sample area, vacant, dilapidated, business, etc.)

a designated termination.) The first two rows of table A-5 denote the
successful completion of an interviewer's work. As such, work on about
88% of all screened households was completed.

Interview response rates must be based on the last two rows of
table A-5. The interview response rates were 83% for the Black stratum,

77% for the Hispanic stratum and 82% in the balance stratum. Overall, an interview response rate of 81% was obtained. It is interesting to note that the Hispanic stratum displayed the highest screening response and the lowest interview response, while the screening and interview rates within the Black and balance strata were roughly the same.

Total estimates of survey response may be obtained by multiplying the screening and interview response rates. Doing this, we see that the overall response rate in the Black stratum was 75.9%; the overall response rate for the Hispanic stratum was 72.2%; and the overall response rate in the balance stratum was 73.2%. The total survey attained an overall response rate of 74.2%.

In all, 5,221 interviews were conducted in the NAS. Blacks accounted for 1,947 interviews, Hispanics totaled 1,433 interviews and 1,841 cases represent all others. The distribution of interviews by race/ethnicity and SSU stratum is produced in table A-6. The results of oversampling are clearly revealed in this table. Ninety-two percent of all Black interviews were taken from the Black stratum; similarly, 39% of Hispanic interviews were drawn from the Hispanic stratum. The non-Black, non-Hispanic interviews are more evenly spread across SSU strata, although the balance stratum produced 82% of these cases.

TABLE A-5
Final Disposition of Screened Households by
Secondary Sampling Unit (SSU) Stratum in the National Alcohol Survey

	SSU Stratum			
	Black	Hispanic	Balance	Total
Final Disposition				
Designated Termination*	1,388	2,180	—	3,568
(column percent)	(36.2%)	(51.1%)	—	(35.6%)
Respondent Interviewed	2,036	1,615	1,570	5,221
(column percent)	(53.2%)	(37.8%)	(82.1%)	(52.2%)
Household Member Not Interviewed	406	473	342	1,221
(column percent)	(10.6%)	(11.1%)	(17.9%)	(12.2%)
Total Households	3,830	4,268	1,912	10,010
(column percent)	100%	100%	100%	100%

*Designated Termination denotes those households which were subselected out of the sample on the basis of the race/ethnicity of the household head.

The results of table A-6 can perhaps be put into better perspective by noting the distribution and density of the minority and other

TABLE A-6
Distribution of Interviews by Race/Ethnicity of
Secondary Sampling Unit (SSU) Stratum in the National Alcohol Survey

	SSU Stratum			
	Black	Hispanic	Balance	Total
Race/Ethnicity				
Blacks	1,785	135	27	1,947
(row percent)	(91.7%)	(6.9%)	(1.4%)	(100%)
Hispanics	62	1,338	33	1,433
(row percent)	(4.3%)	(93.4%)	(2.3%)	(100%)
Others	189	142	1,510	1,841
(row percent)	(10.3%)	(7.7%)	(82.0%)	(100%)
Total	2,036	1,615	1,570	5,221
(row percent)	(39.0%)	(30.9%)	(30.1%)	(100%)

populations across the SSU strata. Estimates based on 1980 Census data have been produced for the metropolitan (SMSA) areas of the United States and are presented in tables A-7 and A-8. The first row of table A-7 suggests that SSU stratification was quite successful in isolating 81% of the Black population in the Black stratum while retaining only 18% of the total population. This gives rise to a 56.5% Black population density, as evidenced in the first row of table A-8.

The SSU stratification scheme was not as successful in isolating the Hispanic population. In the second row of table A-7, we see that 63% of the Hispanic population is contained in the Hispanic stratum. The density of Hispanics in this stratum was almost 50% (see table A-7). Unfortunately, 28.5% of Hispanics remained in the Balance stratum. Because this stratum was substantially undersampled, we could expect large sampling errors and design effects for Hispanics.

TABLE A-7
Percentage of the Black, Hispanic, and Total Populations in
Each Secondary Sampling Unit (SSU) Stratum for the
Metropolitan Areas of the United States

	SSU Stratum			
	Black	Hispanic	Balance	Total
Population				
Black	81.0%	9.3%	9.8%	100%
Hispanic	8.6%	62.8%	28.5%	100%
Total	18.1%	9.8%	72.1%	100%

TABLE A–8
Density of Black and Hispanic Population by
Secondary Sampling Unit (SSU) Stratum

	SSU Stratum			
	Black	*Hispanic*	*Balance*	*Total*
Density of Black Population	56.5%	12.0%	1.7%	14.0%
Density of Hispanic Population	3.6%	48.6%	3.0%	7.7%

Average design effects (DEFF), square roots of design effects (DEFT) and intraclass correlation coefficients (ROH) are presented for selected subgroups in tables A-9 and A-10. The design effect is defined as the ratio of the variance of a statistic obtained from a complex sample design to that obtained from a simple random sample of the same size. The intraclass correlation is approximated by the following:

$$ROH \doteq (DEFF\text{-}1)/(\bar{b}\text{-}1)$$

where DEFF denotes the design effect and $\bar{b}$ is the average number of interviews per PSU. A discussion of these statistics may be found in Kish (1965a).

TABLE A–9
Average Design Effects (DEFFs), Square Roots of Design Effects (DEFTS), and Intraclass Correlation Coefficients (ROHs) Based on *Unweighted* National Alcohol Survey Data for the Total Sample and Selected Subgroups

	Sample Size	Average DEFF	Average DEFT	Average ROH*
Total Sample	5,221	2.172	1.160	0.025
Sex				
Males	2,093	1.571	1.247	0.032
Females	3,128	1.940	1.373	0.034
Race/Ethnicity				
Blacks	1,947	1.758	1.315	0.035
Hispanics	1,433	2.056	1.392	0.041
Mexicans	949	1.862	1.809	0.051
Other race/ethnicity	1,841	2.065	1.409	0.067

* Average values of ROH were obtained using (AVE.DEFF-1)/(b-1) where b is the average number of interviews per PSU. The total number of PSUs in b is equal to the number of PSUs with nonzero interviews for that subgroup: 86 for Blacks; 53 for Hispanics and Mexicans; and 110 for all other subgroups.

The average DEFFs, DEFTs and ROHs in tables A-9 and A-10 are based on estimated proportions for eighteen questionnaire items relating to alcohol consumption and abuse. Table A-9 is based on the unweighted data set, while table A-10 was obtained using weighted data. The average DEFFs in table A-9 range from 1.57 for males to 2.17 for the total sample. Average ROHs range from 0.025 for the total sample to 0.067 for non-Blacks/non-Hispanics. Given the substantial efforts to reduce intraclass correlations (e.g., PSU supplementation, many SSU selections) the DEFFs and ROHs most likely reflect the natural intraclass correlations associated with measurement of alcohol related items in a cluster sample.

Table A-10 shows the impact of oversampling on the variances of sample proportions. Average design effects at least doubled for the total sample and sex subgroups. Standard errors for these groups increased by roughly 30%. For the Hispanic and Mexican subgroups, DEFFs based on weighted data are about triple the values obtained from the unweighted data. This represents an increase in standard error of over 80%. Design effects for Blacks and Others increased the least. For Blacks the increase in standard error was 29%, while for the subgroup of other races/ethnicities, the increase was 21%.

TABLE A-10

Average Design Effects (DEFFs), Square Roots of Design Effects (DEFTS), and Intraclass Correlation Coefficients (ROHs) Based on *Weighted* National Alcohol Survey Data for the Total Sample and Selected Subgroups

	Sample Size	Average DEFF	Average DEFT	Average ROH*
Subgroup				
Total Sample	5,221	4.966	2.194	0.085
Sex				
Males	2,093	3.351	1.813	0.130
Females	3,128	4.307	2.048	0.121
Race/Ethnicity				
Blacks	1,947	2.936	1.698	0.089
Hispanics	1,433	6.784	2.533	0.222
Mexicans	949	5.888	2.386	0.289
Other race/ethnicity	1,847	2.584	1.576	0.100

* Average values of ROH were obtained using (AVE.DEFF-1)/(b-1) where b is the average number of interviews per PSU. The total number of PSUs in b is equal to the number of PSUs with nonzero interviews for that subgroup: 86 for Blacks; 53 for Hispanics and Mexicans; and 110 for all other subgroups.

CONCLUSIONS

The design and results of the National Alcohol Survey are useful in illustrating several points regarding rare element sample surveys. First, the economic design and collection of survey data for Black and Hispanic populations is possible, especially in surveys which require Black, Hispanic, and "other" components. Statistically efficient designs for Black oversamples are easier to attain than Hispanic oversamples because the Black population concentrates itself more in higher density minority areas than Hispanics do.

Adequate response rates can be obtained in minority oversamples. The NAS screening response rate was 92% and the interview response rate was 81%.

Disproportionate stratified sampling is the key to economic and efficient surveys. With regard to the NAS, the Hispanic stratum was oversampled by too large a factor. This was the price paid to achieve the survey goal of about 1,500 Hispanic interviews and incur smaller weighting effects.

It is possible that a more conservative definition of the Hispanic stratum could have permitted a more efficient design. For instance, one might employ a minimum criterion of 5% or more 1980 Hispanic population within an SSU (instead of 15%). This could have boosted the percentage of the Hispanic population within the Hispanic stratum substantially. However, this would also lessen the density of Hispanics and therefore increase the per unit cost of Hispanic interviews in that stratum.

Notes

CHAPTER 3

1. Two of these are relatively inaccessible: "Date of Last Purchase Technique", a nine page note with no note of author or date from the Division of Prices and Cost of Living, Bureau of Labor Statistics, U.S. Department of Labor, referenced in Lamale, 1959:137; Anders Ekholm, "Skevheten hos ett speciellt estimat av antalet dryckesganger per ar" (Bias in a certain estimate of the number of drinking occasions per year), Appendix II in Erland Jonsson and Tom Nilsson, *Samnordisk underskning av vuxna mns alkoholvanor* (A joint Nordic study of the drinking habits of adult males), mimeographed, 1969, referenced in Mäkelä, 1971: 7, 31.

2. See also the comparison of Knupfer et al.'s F-Q with what became the Q-F-V index, pp. 10–14 of Cahalan et al., 1965. The report noted that the new measure was adopted because "it was shown to differentiate more sharply between the various groupings for age and family income than was true for the California drinker classifications" (p. 11).

There was also a great deal of unpublished experimentation, comparisons, and correspondence in this period. The few excerpts which follow give the flavor of these discussions between the Washington and Berkeley staffs.

Genevieve Knupfer to Ira Cisin and Don Cahalan, June 2, 1965, responding to the adoption of the Q-F-V index: "I am chagrined at the changes in the definition of the F.Q. index that you have made, as I have been carrying the torch for the importance of 'quantity', and I thought we were all agreed....The essence of the point might be put this way: we want an index that is more related to the blood alcohol level of the drinker than to the profit level of the alcoholic beverages industry. A light drinker as we defined it is one who never gets a high blood alcohol level. One cannot get to be a light drinker in our system by going on a binge once a month, whereas he can in your system. That is what I object to. Being slightly drunk three times a week is *more* drinking, not *less* drinking, than having a glass of wine at each meal, yet the latter type you have called a heavy, for no other reason that that they drink several times a day...."

Don Cahalan to Genevieve Knupfer, June 21, 1965: "I am sure we will agree that no single index will be entirely satisfactory for all purposes. We intend to wring the maximum out of the national data from many standpoints, taking into account frequency, quantity per sitting, and type of beverage. We do intend to use the /Q-F-V/ as one major index on which to report most of the principal group differences. We find it useful primarily because (1) it yields the most linear results for more groupings than any other single index, and (2) because while using the concept of intrapersonal variation, it fits in well with other national and regional studies which use Q-F indices which are familar to the alcohol research fraternity and which permit certain comparisons from one study to another. At the same time, we recognize that it probably is not adequate to differentiate the (probably rare) very occasional binge drinker from the person who has a small amount of alcohol every day. . . ."

Robin Room to Vito Signorile, June 26, 1967, responding to a letter from Signorile concerning a "Rationalized F/Q Typology" Room had proposed in 1965 (Signorile had sent a proposed "Index of Frequent Intoxication" built because "Don Cahalan and I were interested in detecting any tendency toward binge drinking in the Hartford follow-up study"): ". . .when we built the Rationalized F/Q, we did not really intend it as a measure of the frequency of drinking amounts which hold the potential of intoxication. . . .Quite simply our reason for building it was that we had grown dissatisfied with our old F/Q scale. . . .Our basic indicator of drinking patterns provided inadequate means of differentiating the effects of frequency and quantity. . . .[In the new measure] the particular distinctions between levels of quantity were chosen partly with an eye to the possibility of intoxication, and partly to yield a partitioning of a general population with a respectably large N at each level of drinking. The distinction on frequency was made with some idea in mind of distinguishing between 'regular' and 'irregular' patterns, on the assumption that anything that happens less than once a week becomes more a 'special occasion' than a regular part of the respondent's routine. . . .Still, basically, both [indexes] are laboring very hard to overcome difficulties caused by questions on amount of drinking formulated long ago for different purposes. Both of our purposes would be much more simply served by questions of the form, 'how often would you say you drink X amount'."

Don Cahalan to Robin Room, July 27, 1967: "Our own opinion (Ira's, Vito's, and mine) is that the Q-F-V index used in *American Drinking Practices* is already outmoded. (Note the strictures expressed on p. 17 of the book.) We believe that the best single measure thus far is the Volume-Variability Index which we (primarily Ira) developed *after* we had gone too far with the more traditional Q-F-V Index to scrap the whole analysis and start from scratch."

3. Response categories were: usually twice a day, or more often; usually once a day, sometimes twice; only once a day; nearly every day; three or four times a week; once or twice a week; two or three times a month; about once a month; six to eleven times a year; one to five times a year; *never* in the last year (the top response for five or more drinks was "every day"; Cameron, 1981).

CHAPTER 5

1. Readers may notice a discrepancy between consuming five or more drinks as often as once per week—as measured here—and "frequent heavy

drinking," the top category in the typology which is used in some other papers in this volume and which is also interpreted as drinking five or more drinks per sitting once a week or more often. The two differ in making differing assumptions about how the responses should be scored. Respondents who report drinking five or more of a beverage "once in a while" are never counted as frequent heavy drinkers under the typology, no matter how frequently they drink; whereas under the accounting used here drinking a beverage "nearly every day" (coded as twenty-two times a month), or more often, coupled with drinking five or more of that beverage at a sitting "once in a while" (coded as 20% of all occasions) yields 22 x 0.20 = 4.4—or more than once a week. Also the quantity-frequency typology for most cases does not add together occasions across separate beverage types, that is, five or more of any one beverage must be consumed as often as once a week or more, whereas here, drinking five or more beers twice a month plus five or more glasses of wine twice a month would sum to four "five or more" occasions.

CHAPTER 6

1. The more precise definition is places within Standard Metropolitan Statistical Areas but with populations of less than 50,000.

CHAPTER 8

1. In addition to the assumptions made by Cahalan et al., I have also found it necessary to make the assumption that all "infrequent" drinkers (those drinking less often than once per month and therefore not asked any further intake questions in the 1964 survey) should be classified as lighter drinkers (less than 0.22 ounces of absolute alcohol per day). I have done this because if these drinkers had been asked the questions and had replied that they had drunk five or more drinks "nearly every time" for all three beverages (i.e., the wettest response they could have given), they still would not have been counted, under the coding system used, as drinking as much as 0.22 ounces of absolute alcohol per day.

2. Note that there are actually two methods of estimating volume in Clark et al. (1981) and in Clark and Midanik (1982). In addition to the one described here, there was a second that asked how frequently the respondent had consumed specified amounts of beer, wine, or liquor. For example: "About how often in the past twelve months did you have between five and seven glasses or cans (of beer) on one occasion?" Response categories ranged from "every day" to "never" at eleven different levels of frequency. From these questions, volume estimates were constructed according to the discussion in Clark et al. (1981) Appendix I. Although the bulk of the Clark and Midanik (1982) and the Clark et al. analyses used this second technique, both used the above-described "usual amount" technique when constructing comparisons to the Johnson

series. This is because the "usual amount" technique is much more similar to that employed in the surveys collected by Johnson et al. For the same reason, I have chosen to rely on the "usual amount" technique in the 1979 data set although the second technique would have been more appropriate for most other analytical purposes.

3. Again, it seems likely that the reason for not finding similar evidence of change in the Hilton and Clark study (chapter 7) is the relatively low cutpoint for high volume drinking that was used in that study (45 drinks per month).

CHAPTER 9

1. This expectation seems appropriate for survey results of current (within the last year) problems but is more doubtful in the case of cirrhosis rates or other problems where the impact of the lag factor is substantial.

2. Another compensating technique is to perform the analysis on log transformed scores. Such an analysis produed two notable differences from the present results. The difference in logged mean dependence scores for all men, which barely achieved significance (0.05 level) in these results (table 9.1), was not significant in that analysis. Also, the difference in logged mean consequences scores for all men, which was not significant in these results (table 9.3), barely achieved significance (0.05 level) in that analysis. These additional findings underscore the fact that changes in problem prevalences between 1979 and 1984 tend to be of borderline significance and their importance should not be exaggerated.

CHAPTER 13

1. There is a lack of consistency between the "per sitting" format of the 5+ measure and the "per day" format of the 8+ measure. This is regrettable but was unavoidable given the wording of the items that were used.

2. According to Room's (1982) scheme, the wet region consists of the New England, Mid Atlantic, East North Central, and Pacific states while the dry region consists of the South Atlantic, East South Central, West South Central, West North Central, and Mountain states.

3. Marital status and region were represented by dichotomous variables. Urbanization was represented by two dummy variables, one representing metropolitan cities of over 50,000 population and the other representing rural areas. (Metropolitan towns of less than 50,000 was the contrast category). Income was scored at the category midpoints for most categories according to the following scheme: $0-$3,999 = $3,000; $4,001-$6,000 = $5,000; $6,001-$8,000 = $7,000; $8,001-$10,000 = $9,000; $10,001-$15,000 = $12,500; $15,001-$20,000 = $17,500; $30,001-$40,000 = $35,000; $40,001-$60,000 = $50,000; more than

$60,000 = $65,000. Education was measured as years of schooling using the following scheme: no formal schooling = 0; some grammar school (less than 8th grade) = 6; completed grammar school = 8; some high school = 10; completed high school = 12; some college = 14; completed college = 16; graduate study = 18.

4. Since table 2 suggests that very low incomes are more strongly associated with the prevalence of problems, the regression analyses were repeated with a dichotomous poverty variable (under and over $10,000 annually) in place of income. The results, available on request, did not indicate a substantial effect of poverty as measured in this way. The multiple correlation coefficients for poverty were 0.07 (n.s.) in Model A, 0.09 (significant at the 0.05 level) in Model B, 0.06 (n.s.) in Model C, and 0.09 (significant at the 0.05 level) in Model D. The coefficients for the other independent variables did not differ substantively from the results on table 3.

CHAPTER 14

1. Expert technical assistance by Alice Sardone is gratefully acknowledged.

CHAPTER 15

1. Elsewhere in this volume, this has been described as scoring at the "high" level on the consequences scale. See chapter 4.

CHAPTER 17

1. Throughout this paper, the regional classification scheme of the U.S. Census Department will be employed. This scheme divides the American states into the following regions: New England, Mid Atlantic, East North Central, West North Central, South Atlantic, East South Central, West South Central, Mountain, and Pacific. See Figure 17.2 for a map.

2. I.e. Index score = 100 x (1 + Z of raw score).

CHAPTER 19

1. The analysis made use of an index of alcohol consumption which uses quantity and frequency of drinking wine, beer and liquor to classify survey respondents in seven categories, as follows: Abstainer: Drinks less than once a year or has never drunk alcoholic beverages; Infrequent: Drinks less than once a month but at least once a year, may or may not drink five drinks at a sitting (a drink is taken to mean one ounce of spirits, a four ounce glass of

table wine or a 12 ounce can of beer, each of which contains approximately 9 grams of absolute alcohol); Less frequent low maximum: Drinks one to three times a month but never has five or more drinks at a sitting; Less frequent high maximum: Drinks one to three times a month and has five or more drinks at least once a year; Frequent low maximum: Drinks once a week or more often but never drinks five or more drinks at a sitting; Frequent high maximum: Drinks once a week or more often and has five or more drinks at a sitting at least once a year; Frequent heavy drinker: Drinks once a week or more often and has five or more drinks at a sitting also once a week or more often.

2. Salience of drink seeking behavior measures the extent to which drinking has replaced social, familial and recreational activities. Belligerence assesses the extent to which the respondent has been involved in arguments or fights because of drinking.

Appendix

1. An earlier version of this paper was presented at the Annual Meetings of the American Statistical Association in Las Vegas, Nevada, August, 1985.

References

Abelson, H., and R. Atkinson. (1975). *Public Experience with Psychoactive Substances: A Nationwide Study among Adults and Youth*. Princeton: Response Analysis Corp.

Abelson, H. and P. Fishburne. (1976). *Nonmedical Use of Psychoactive Substances: 1975/6 Nationwide Survey among Youth and Adults*. Princeton: Response Analysis Corp.

Abelson, H., P. Fishburne and I. Cisin. (1977). *National Survey on Drug Abuse: 1977*. (DHEW Publ. no. (ADM) 78–618). Washington: USGPO.

Abelson, H., P. Fishburne and I. Cisin. (1980). *National Survey on Drug Abuse: Main Findings 1979*. (DHHS Publ. no. (ADM) 80–976). Washington: USGPO.

Alanko, T. (1984). "An Overview of Techniques and Problems in the Measurement of Alcohol Consumption." *Research Advances in Alcohol and Drug Problems, 8*, 209–226.

Alcocer, A. (1982). Alcohol Use and Abuse among the Hispanic American Population. In *Alcohol and Health Monograph No. 4*: Special Population Issues. DHHS Publication No. (ADM 82–1193. Washington, D.C.: U.S. Government Printing Office.

Alcohol Epidemiology Data System (AEDS). (1984). *Data Catalog, December 1984*. Washington: CSR, Inc.

Alcoholics Anonymous. (1939). New York: Alcoholics Anonymous World Services, Inc.

Armor, D. and J. Polich. (1982). "Measurement of Alcohol Consumption." In E. M. Pattison and E. Kaufman, eds., *Encyclopedic Handbook of Alcoholism*. (pp. 72–80). New York: Gardner Press.

Armor, D., J. Polich and H. Stambul. (1978). *Alcoholism and Treatment*. New York: Wiley.

Armyr, G., A. Elmer and U. Herz. (1982). *Alcohol in the World of the 80s: Habits, Attitudes, Preventive Policies and Voluntary Efforts*. Stockholm: Sober Forlags ab.

Ashley, M. J. and J. G. Rankin. (1979). "Alcohol Consumption and Hypertension—the Evidence from Hazardous Drinking and Alcoholic Populations." *Australia New Zealand Medicine, 9*, 201–206.

Auth, J. and G. Warheit. (1982–1983). "Estimating the Prevalence of Problem Drinking and Alcoholism in the General Population: An Overview of Epidemiological Studies." *Alcohol Health and Research World, 7*, 11–21.

Bachman, J. and P. O'Malley. (1981). "When Four Months Equal a Year: Inconsistencies in Student Reports of Drug Use." *Public Opinion Quarterly, 45,* 536–548.

Bacon, S. (1958). "Alcoholics Do Not Drink." *Annals of the American Academy of Political and Social Science, 315,* 55–64.

Bailey, M. B., P. W. Haberman and H. Alksne. (1965). "The Epidemiology of Alcoholism in an Urban Residential Area." *Quarterly Journal of Studies On Alcohol, 26,* 19–40.

Bales, R. (1946). "Cultural Differences in Rates of Alcoholism." *Quarterly Journal of Studies on Alcohol, 6,* 480–499.

Barnes, G. and M. Russell. (1977). *Drinking Patterns among Adults in Western New York State: A Descriptive Analysis of the Sociodemographic Correlates of Drinking.* Buffalo, New York: Research Institute on Alcoholism.

Barnes, G. and M. Russell. (1978). "Drinking Patterns in Western New York State: Comparison with National Data." *Journal of Studies on Alcohol, 39,* 1148–1157.

Bhattacharyya, D. N. and M. O. Rake. (1983). "Correlation of Alcohol Consumption with Liver Damage in Men and Women." *Alcohol and Alcoholism, 18,* 181–184.

Billings, J. (1903). Data Relating to the Use of Alcoholic Drinks among Brain Workers in the United States. In J. S. Billings, ed., *Physiological Aspects of the Liquor Problem.* (vol. 1, pp. 307–338). Boston: Houghton Mifflin.

Blair, E., S. Sudman, N. Bradburn, and C. Stocking. (1977). "How to Ask Questions about Drinking and Sex: Response Effects in Measuring Consumer Behavior." *Journal of Marketing Research, 14,* 316–321.

Blocker, J. (1988). *American Temperance Movements: Cycles of Reform.* Boston: Twayne Publishers.

The Bottom Line on Alcohol in Society. (1986). "Alcoholic Beverage Consumption in the United States." *The Bottom Line on Alcohol in Society, 7,* 15–29.

Bowman, R., L. Stein and J. R. Newton. (1975). "Measurement and Interpretation of Drinking Behavior." *Journal of Studies on Alcohol, 36,* 1154–1172.

Breslow, N. E. and N. E. Day. (1981). *Statistical Methods in Cancer Research: The Analysis of Case-control Studies.* France: IARC Scientific Publications.

Breslow, N. E. and W. Powers. (1978). "Are There Two Logistic Regressions for Retrospective Studies?" *Biometrics, 34,* 100–105.

Bruun, K. (1969). "The Actual and the Registered Frequency of Drunkenness in Helsinki." *British Journal of Addiction, 64,* 3–8.

Bruun, K. et al. (1975). *Alcohol Control Policies in Public Health Perspective.* Helsinki: The Finnish Foundation for Alcohol Studies, 25.

Business Week. (1985). "The Sobering of America: A Push to Put Drinking in its Place." *Business Week,* February 25, 1985.

Butler, K. (1987). "Boozers Turn to Temperance: Bay Area Baby Boomers." *San Francisco Chronicle,* August 10, 1987, 1.

Caetano, R. (1983). "Drinking Patterns and Alcohol Problems Among Hispanics in the U.S.: A Review." *Drug and Alcohol Dependence, 12,* 37–59.

Caetano, R. (1984a). "Ethnicity and Drinking in Northern California: A Comparison among Whites, Blacks and Hispanics." *Alcohol and Alcoholism*, 19, 31–44.

Caetano, R. (1984b). "Hispanic Drinking Practices in Northern California." *Hispanic Journal of Behavioral Sciences*, 6, 345–364.

Caetano, R. (1985). "Two Versions of Dependence: DSM-III and the Alcohol Dependence Syndrome." *Drug and Alcohol Dependence*, 15, 81–103.

Caetano, R. (1986). Patterns and Problems of Drinking among U.S. Hispanics. In *Report of the Secretary's Task Force on Black and Minority Health*, vol. 7: Chemical Dependency and Diabetes. (pp. 143–186). Washington, D.C.: U.S. Department of Health and Human Services.

Caetano, R. (1987a). "Acculturation and Attitudes toward Appropriate Drinking among U.S. Hispanics." *Alcohol and Alcoholism*, 22, 427–433.

Caetano, R. (1987b). "Acculturation and Drinking in Social Settings among U.S. Hispanics." *Drug and Alcohol Dependence*, 19, 215–226.

Caetano, R. (1987c). "Acculturation and Drinking Patterns among U.S. Hispanics." *British Journal of Addiction*, 82, 789–799.

Caetano, R. (1987d). Alcohol Use among Mexican Americans and in the U.S. Population. Paper presented at the United States - Mexico Conference on Alcohol Related Issues. Los Angeles, California.

Caetano, R. (1987e). "A Commentary on the Proposed Changes in DSM-III Concept of Alcohol Dependence." *Drug and Alcohol Dependence*, 19, 345–355.

Caetano, R. (1988a). "Alcohol Use among Hispanic Groups in the U.S." *American Journal of Drug and Alcohol Abuse*, 14, 293–308.

Caetano, R. (1988b). Alcohol Use among Mexican Americans and in the U.S. Population. In M. Jean Gilbert, ed., *Alcohol Consumption Among Mexicans and Mexican Americans: A Bi-national Perspective*. (pp. 53–84). Spanish Speaking Mental Health Research Center, University of California, Los Angeles.

Caetano, R. (1989). Drinking Patterns and Alcohol Problems in a National Sample of U.S. Hispanics. In D. Spiegler, D. Tate, S. Aitken and C. Christian, eds., *Alcohol Use Among U.S. Ethnic Minorities*. (pp. 147–162). National Institute on Alcohol Abuse and Alcoholism Monograph no. 18. DHHS Publication no. (ADM) 89–1435.

Caetano, R. and D. Herd. (1984). "Black Drinking Practices in Northern California." *American Journal of Alcohol and Drug Abuse*, 10, 571–587.

Caetano, R. and D. Herd. (1988). "Drinking in Different Social Contexts among White, Black, and Hispanic Men." *Yale Journal of Biology and Medicine*, 61, 243–258.

Caetano, R. and M. E. Medina-Mora. (1988). "Acculturation and Drinking among People of Mexican Descent in Mexico and the U.S." *Journal of Studies on Alcohol*, 49, 462–471.

Caetano, R., C. Campillo-Serrand, and M. Medina-Mora. (1986). A Comparison of Alcohol Use and Drinking Problems in Two Communities: Tlalpan, Mexico, and Contra Costa, California. Presented at the meeting on Alcohol

Use in Latin America: Cultural Realities and Policy Implications, Providence, Rhode Island, October 1986.

Caetano, R., R. Suzman, D. Rosen, and D. Vorhees-Rosen. (1982). "A Methodological Note on Quantity-Frequency Categorizations in a Longitudinal Study of Drinking Practices." *Drinking and Drug Practices Surveyor, 18,* 7–12.

Cahalan, D. (1968). *Correlates of Change in Drinking Behavior in an Urban Community Sample over a Three Year Period.* Ph.D. dissertation, The George Washington University, Washington, D.C.

Cahalan, D. (1969). "A Multivariate Analysis of the Correlates of Drinking-Related Problems in a Community Study." *Social Problems, 17,* 234–247.

Cahalan, D. (1970). *Problem Drinkers: A National Survey.* San Francisco: Jossey-Bass.

Cahalan, D. (1987). *Understanding America's Drinking Problem: How to Combat the Hazards of Alcohol.* San Francisco: Jossey-Bass.

Cahalan, D. and I. Cisin. (1968). "American Drinking Practices: Summary of Findings from a National Probability Sample: II. Measurement of Massed Versus Spaced Drinking." *Quarterly Journal of Studies on Alcohol, 29,* 642–656.

Cahalan, D. and R. Room. (1974). *Problem Drinking among American Men.* (Monograph No. 7). New Brunswick, NJ: Rutgers Center of Alcohol Studies.

Cahalan, D. and B. Treiman. (1976a). *Drinking Behavior, Attitudes and Problems in Marin County.* (Report C11). Berkeley: Alcohol Research Group.

Cahalan, D. and B. Treiman. (1976b). *Drinking Behavior, Attitudes and Problems in San Francisco.* (Report C10). Berkeley: Alcohol Research Group.

Cahalan D., I. Cisin, and H. Crossley. (1969). *American Drinking Practices: A National Study of Drinking Behavior and Attitudes.* (Monograph 6). New Brunswick, NJ: Rutgers Center for Alcohol Studies.

Cahalan, D., I. Cisin, A. Kirsch, and C. Newcomb. (1965). *Behavior and Attitudes Related to Drinking in a Medium-Sized Urban Community in New England.* (Report no. 2). Washington, DC: Social Research Group, The George Washington University.

Cahalan, D., R. Roizen, and R. Room. (1976). Alcohol Problems and Their Prevention: Public Attitudes in California. In R. Room and S. Sheffield, eds., *The Prevention of Alcohol Problems.* (pp. 354–404). Sacramento: State Office of Alcoholism.

Cameron, T. (1981). *Alcohol and Alcohol Problems: Public Opinion in California, 1974–1980.* (Report No. C31). Berkeley: Alcohol Research Group.

Cannell, C., K. Marquis, and A. Laurent. (1977). *A Summary of Studies of Interviewing Methodology.* (Vital and Health Statistics, Public Health Service, Series 2, no. 69). Washington: USGPO.

Carman, R. S. (1977). *Patterns of Alcohol Use in Rural Communities.* Final Report on NIAAA grant AA00622-01. Laramie: University of Wyoming.

Celentano, D. D. and D. V. McQueen. (1984). "Alcohol Consumption Patterns among Women in Baltimore." *Journal of Studies on Alcohol, 45,* 355–358.

Clark, W. (1966). "Operational Definitions of Drinking Problems and Associated Prevalence Rates." *Quarterly Journal of Studies on Alcohol, 27,* 648–668.

Clark, W. (1977). *Contextual and Situational Variables in Drinking Behavior.* Unpublished paper (F60). Berkeley: Social Research Group.

Clark, W. (1981). A Very Brief History of Surveys on Alcohol Use and Drinking Problems in General Populations. In W. Clark, L. Midanik, and G. K. Knupfer, eds., *Report on the 1979 National Survey,* (pp. 143–173). Berkeley: Alcohol Research Group.

Clark, W. (1982a). "Frequency of Drunkenness in the U.S. Population." *Journal of Studies on Alcohol, 43,* 1267–1275.

Clark, W. (1982b). Public Drinking Contexts: Bars and Taverns. In T. C. Harford and L. Gaines, eds., *Social Drinking Contexts.* (NIAAA Research Monograph no. 7). Washington: USGPO.

Clark, W. (1985). Alcohol Use in Various Settings. In E. Single and T. Storm, eds., *Public Drinking and Public Policy.* (pp. 49–70). Toronto: Addiction Research Foundation.

Clark, W. (1988). "Places of Drinking: A Comparative Analysis." *Contemporary Drug Problems, 15,* 399–446.

Clark, W. B. and L. Midanik. (1982). Alcohol Use and Alcohol Problems Among U.S. Adults: Results of the 1979 Survey. In *Alcohol Consumption and Related Problems.* (Alcohol and Health Monograph 1). (DHHS Publication No. (ADM) 82–1190). (pp. 3–52). Washington DC: USGPO.

Clark, W., L. Midanik, and G. Knupfer. (1981). *Report on the 1979 National Survey.* Berkeley: Social Research Group.

Corrigan, E. (1974). *Problem Drinkers Seeking Treatment.* (Monograph no. 8). New Brunswick: Rutgers Center for Alcohol Studies.

Cox, D. R. (1970). *The Analysis of Binary Data.* London: Methuen.

Cox, W. (1987). Personality Theory and Research. In H. Blane and K. Leonard, eds., *Psychological Theories of Drinking and Alcoholism.* (pp. 55–89). New York: Guilford Press.

CSR, Inc. (1983). *Final Report: Validity/Reliability Study of Self-Reported Drinking.* (NIAAA contract no. ADM 281–81–0005). Washington, DC: CSR, Inc.

Cutler, R. and T. Storm. (1973). *Drinking Practices in Three British Columbia Cities: I. General Population Survey.* Vancouver: Alcoholism Foundation of British Columbia.

de Lint, J. (1960). *Four Comments on "An Exploratory Survey of Drinking in a Northern Ontario Community".* (Substudy 3–10–60). Toronto: Alcoholism (now Addiction) Research Foundation.

de Lint, J. (1978). "Total Alcohol Consumption and Rates of Excessive Use: A Reply to Duffy and Cohen." *British Journal of Addiction, 73,* 265–269.

Dentzler, S. (1984). "Alcohol on the Rocks: The New Prohibitionists and Health-conscious Consumers Are Sobering up America." *Newsweek,* December 31, 1984, 52–54.

Dight, S. (1976). *Scottish Drinking Habits: A Survey Carried Out for the Scottish Home and Health Department.* London: HMSO.

Doernberg, D., and F. Stinson. (1985). *U.S. Apparent Consumption of Alcoholic Beverages based on State Sales, Taxation, or Receipt Data*. (U.S. Alcohol Epidemiologic Data Reference Manual, Volume 1). Washington, D.C.: National Institute on Alcohol Abuse and Alcoholism.

Doernberg, D., F. Stinson, and G. Williams. (1986). *Apparent Per Capita Alcohol Consumption: National, State, and Regional Trends, 1977–1984*. (Alcohol Epidemiology Data System, Surveillance Report no. 2). Washington, D.C., National Institute on Alcohol Abuse and Alcoholism.

Duffy, J. (1982, July). The Measurement of Alcohol Consumption in Sample Surveys. Presented at the Alcohol Epidemiology Section of the International Council on Alcohol and Addictions, Helsinki.

Duffy, J. (1984, June). Survey Measurement of Drinking Behavior. Presented to the Workshop on Sample Surveys, Epidemiology Section, ICAA, Edinburgh.

Edwards, G. (1973). A Community as Case Study: Alcoholism Treatment in Antiquity and Utopia. In M. Chafetz, ed., *Proceedings of the Second Annual Alcoholism Conference of the National Institute on Alcohol Abuse and Alcoholism*. (DHEW Publication no. (HSM) 73–9083). (pp. 116–136). Washington DC: USGPO.

Edwards, G. (1977). The Alcohol Dependence Syndrome: Usefulness of an Idea. In G. Edwards and M. Grant, eds., *Alcoholism: New Knowledge and New Responses*. (pp. 136–156). London: Croom Helm.

Edwards, G., and M. M. Gross. (1976). "Alcohol Dependence: Provisional Description of a Clinical Syndrome." *British Medical Journal*, 1, 1058–1061.

Edwards, G., J. Chandler, and C. Hensman. (1972). "Drinking in a London Suburb: I. Correlates of Normal Drinking." *Quarterly Journal of Studies on Alcohol*, Supplement 6, pp. 69–93.

Endicott, J., and R. L. Spitzer. (1973). "A Diagnostic Interview: The Schedule for Affective Disorders and Schizophrenia." *Archives of General Psychiatry*, 35, 69–73.

Ericksen, E. (1976). "Sampling a Rare Population: A Case Study." *Journal of the American Statistical Association*, 71, 836–822.

Ewing, J. (1970). "Notes on Quantity Frequency Studies on Alcohol Intake, with a Comment and Response." *Drinking and Drug Practices Surveyor*, 1, 8–15.

Fager, C. (1983). "The New Prohibition." *City Paper* (Washington D.C.), (1983, February 18–25), reprinted in *The Drinking and Drug Practices Surveyor*, 19, pp. 70–73.

Ferrence, R. (1980). Sex Differences in the Prevalence of Problem Drinking. In O. Kalant, ed., *Research Advances in Alcohol and Drug Problems*, vol. 5. (pp. 69–124). New York: Plenum.

Fillmore, K. M. (1974). "Drinking and Problem Drinking in Early Adulthood and Middle Age." *Quarterly Journal of Studies on Alcohol*, 35, 819–840.

Fingarette, H. (1988). *Heavy Drinking: The Myth of Alcoholism as a Disease*. Berkeley, Calif: Univ. California Press.

Fink, R. (1962, August). Survey Method in the Study of Drinking Behavior. Presented at the Annual Meetings of the Society for the Study of Social Problems, Washington, D.C. August 1962.

Fisher, H., (1979). Psychological Correlates of Tavern Use: A National Probability Sample Study. In T. Harford, ed., *Social Drinking Contexts*. NIAAA Monograph no. 7. (pp. 34–53). Washington: USGPO.

Fitzgerald, J., and H. Mulford. (1978). "Distribution of Alcohol Consumption and Problem Drinking: Comparison of Sales Records and Survey Data." *Journal of Studies on Alcohol, 39*, 879–893.

Fitzgerald, J., and H. Mulford. (1981). "The Prevalence and Extent of Drinking in Iowa, 1979." *Journal of Studies on Alcohol, 42*, 38–47.

Fitzgerald, J., and H. Mulford. (1982). "Alcohol Consumption in Iowa 1961 and 1979." *Journal of Studies on Alcohol, 43*, 1171–1189.

Fitzgerald, J., and H. Mulford. (1984a). "Factors Related to Problem-Drinking Rates." *Journal of Studies on Alcohol, 45*, 424–432.

Fitzgerald, J., and H. Mulford. (1984b). "Seasonal Changes in Alcohol Consumption and Related Problems in Iowa, 1979–1980." *Journal of Studies on Alcohol, 45*, 363–368.

Frankel, B., and D. Whitehead. (1981). *Drinking and Damage: Theoretical Advances and Implications for Prevention*. New Brunswick: Rutgers Center for Alcohol Studies.

Fredericksen, L. (1983). Evaluation of Smoking Risk: Some Proposed Minimum Standards. In J. Grabowski and C. S. Bell, eds., *Measurement in the Analysis and Treatment of Smoking Behavior*. (pp. 90–95). (NIDA Research Monograph no. 48, DHHS Publication no. (ADM) 83–1285). Washington: USGPO.

Gabrielli, W., and R. Plomin. (1985). "Drinking Behavior in the Colorado Adoptee and Twin Sample." *Journal of Studies on Alcohol, 46*, 24–31.

Gallup, G. (1972). *The Gallup Poll: Public Opinion 1935–1971*. New York: Random House.

Gallup, G., Jr. (1987). "Americans are Drinking about as Much as Ever." *San Francisco Chronicle*, August 24, 1987, 19.

Gallup Poll. (1987). *Alcohol Use and Abuse in America*, Gallup Report no. 265, October 1987. Princeton: Gallup Poll.

Gerstel, E., R. Mason, P. Piserchia, and P. Kristiansen. (1975). *Final Report: A Pilot Study of the Social Contexts of Drinking and Correlates*. (Project no. 23U–892). Research Triangle Park: Research Triangle Institute.

Gibbins, R., and G. Duda. (1960). *An Exploratory Study of Drinking in a Northern Ontario Community*. (Substudy 1–3 and D–60). Toronto: Alcoholism (now Addiction) Research Foundation.

Gillies, M. (1978a). *The Durham Region Survey: A Preliminary Report*. (Substudy no. 996). Toronto: Addiction Research Foundation.

Gillies, M. (1978b). *The Durham Region Survey: Alcohol Use Characteristics of the Survey Sample*. (Substudy no. 997). Toronto: Addiction Research Foundation.

Glassner B., and B. Berg. (1985). Jewish-Americans and Alcohol: Processes of Avoidance and Definition. In L. Bennett and G. Ames, eds., *The American Experience with Alcohol: Contrasting Cultural Perspectives*. New York: Plenum.

Globetti, G. (1967). *Drinking Patterns of Adults in Two Mississippi Communities*. Report no. 12., Department of Sociology-Anthropology, Mississippi State University.

Globetti, G. (1978). Prohibition Norms and Teenage Drinking. In J. Ewing and B. Rouse, *Drinking: Alcohol in American Society—Issues and Current Research*. (pp. 159–170). Chicago: Nelson Hall.

Globetti, G., W. Bennett, and M. Alsilafki. (1974). Alcohol and Crime: Previous Drinking Careers of Convicted Offenders. Paper presented at Midwest Sociological Society meetings, Omaha, Nebraska, April 3–6, 1974.

Glynn, R., J. Locastro, J. Hermos, and R. Bosse. (1983). "Social Contexts and Motives for Drinking in Men." *Journal of Studies on Alcohol*, 44, 1011–1025.

Grabowski, J. and C. Bell, eds., (1983). *Measurement in the Analysis and Treatment of Smoking Behavior*. (NIDA Research Monograph 48, DHHS Publication no. (ADM) 83-1285). (pp. 90–95). Washington: USGPO.

Greeley, A., W. McCready, and G. Theisen. (1980). *Ethnic Drinking Subcultures*. New York: Praeger Special Studies.

Greenfield, T. (1986). "Quantity per Occasion and Consequences of Drinking: A Reconsideration and Recommendation." *International Journal of the Addictions*, 21, 1059–1079.

Greenfield, T., and C. Haymond. (1980). *Typologies of College Student Alcohol Consumption: Instrument Development, Selected Results, and Application.* (Student Services Research, Report no. 1). Pullman, Wash.: Washington State University.

Greenfield, T., P. Korzmark, C. Haymond, C. Wyatt, and D. Gunns. (1980). *Patterns of Student Drinking: Characteristics, Experiences, Motivations, and Problems in College.* (Student Services Research, Report no. 2). Pullman, Wash.: Washington State University.

Gross, L. (1983). *How Much Is Too Much?: The Effects of Social Drinking*. New York: Random House.

Gullestad, M. (1984). *Kitchen-table Society*. Oslo: Universitetsforlaget.

Gusfield, J. (1963). *Symbolic Crusade: Status Politics and the American Temperance Movement*. Urbana, Ill.: University of Illinois Press, 1963.

Gusfield, J. (1981). *The Culture of Public Problems: Drinking-Driving and the Symbolic Order*. Chicago: University of Chicago Press.

Gwartney-Gibbs, P. (1982). Alcohol Use at the University of Oregon, 1982. Implications for an Alcohol Education Program, working paper.

Haberman, P. W., and J. Sheinberg. (1967). "Implicative Drinking Reported in a Household Survey: A Corroborative Note on Subgroup Differences." *Quarterly Journal of Studies on Alcohol*, 28, 538–543.

Hall, T. (1984, March 14). "Industry Headache: Americans Drink Less, and Makers of Alcohol Feel a Little Woozy: Concerns of Drunk Driving, Health, Sales to Youth Force Producers to Adapt." *Wall Street Journal*, March 14, 1984, 1.

Harford, T. (1979). An Examination of the Consistency of Self-Reports of the Frequency of Drinking and Social Activity. Presented at the 25th International Institute on the Prevention and Treatment of Alcoholism, Tours, France, June 1979.

Harford, T. (1983). "A Contextual Analysis of Drinking Events." *International Journal of the Addictions*, 18, 825–834.

Harford, T., and E. Gerstel. (1979). "The Consistency of Weekly Drinking Cycles." *Drinking and Drug Practices Surveyor, 14*, 7–8.

Harford, T., and B. F. Grant. (1988). *Alcohol Consumption as a Risk Factor in Alcohol Dependence*. Paper presented at the 14th Annual Alcohol Epidemiology Symposium, Kettil Bruun Society for Social and Epidemiological Research on Alcohol, Berkeley, California, June 1988.

Harris, L. and Associates. (1971). *American Attitudes toward Alcohol and Alcoholics*. (Study 2138). New York: Louis Harris and Associates.

Hasin, D., B. Grant, T. Harford, M. Hilton, and J. Endicott. (in press). "Multiple Alcohol-Related Problems in the U.S.: On the Rise?" *Journal of Studies on Alcohol*.

Hauge, R., and O. Irgens-Jensen. (1986). "The Relationship between Alcohol Consumption, Alcohol Intoxication, and Negative Consequences of Drinking in Four Scandinavian Countries." *British Journal of Addiction, 81*, 513–524.

Hauge, R., and O. Irgens-Jensen. (1987). "Age, Alcohol Consumption and the Experiencing of Negative Consequences of Drinking in Four Scandinavian Countries." *British Journal of Addiction, 82*, 1101–1110.

Heather, N., and I. Robertson. (1981). *Controlled Drinking*. London: Methuen.

Herd, D. (1985a). Ambiguity in Black Drinking Norms: An Ethnohistorical Interpretation. In L. Bennett and G. Ames, eds., *American Experience with Alcohol*. New York: Plenum Press.

Herd, D. (1985b). "Migration, Cultural Transformation, and the Rise of Black Liver Cirrhosis Mortality." *British Journal of Addiction, 80*, 397–410.

Herd, D. (1985c). The Social Context of Drinking among Black and White Americans. Read at the Meeting of the International Group for Comparative Alcohol Studies. Helsinki.

Herd, D. (1985d). *The Socio-Cultural Correlates of Drinking Patterns in Black and White Americans: Results from a National Survey*. Ph.D. dissertation, Medical Anthropology, University of California, San Francisco.

Herd, D. (1985e). We Cannot Stagger to Freedom: A History of Blacks and Alcohol in American Politics. In L. Brill and C. Winick, eds., *Yearbook of Substance Use and Abuse*, vol. 3. (pp. 141–186). New York: Human Sciences Press.

Herd, D. (1988). "Drinking by Black and White Women: Results from a National Survey." *Social Problems, 35*, 493–505.

Herd, D., and R. Caetano. (1987). Drinking Patterns and Problems among White, Black, and Hispanic Women in the U.S.: Results from a National Survey. Presented at the Alcohol and Drug Problems Association of North America Conference on Women's Issues, Denver, Colorado, May 3–6.

Hilton, M. (1986). "Abstention in the General Population of the U.S.A." *British Journal of Addiction, 81*, 95–112.

Hilton, M. (1987). "Drinking Patterns and Drinking Problems in 1984: Results from a General Population Survey." *Alcoholism: Clinical and Experimental Research, 11*, 167–175.

Hingson, R., N. Scotch, J. Barrett, E. Goldman, and T. Mangione. (1981). "Life Satisfaction and Drinking Practices in the Boston Metropolitan Area." *Journal of Studies on Alcohol, 42*, 24–37.

Hock, S. (1987). The Grape Debate: Is Wine Hazardous to Your Health? *East Bay Express*, (Berkeley, CA), August 14, 1987, 1.

Hogue, R. C. (1977). *Drinking Behavior and Attitudes: An Alcoholism Needs Assessment for the North Catchment Area of Hillsborough County*. Tampa, FL: Northside Community Mental Health Center.

Holder, H., and J. Blose. (1986). Distilled Spirits Availability, Changes in Drinking Patterns and Alcohol-related Problems: A Natural Experiment Using Both Pre/Post and Longitudinal Designs. Paper presented at the International Group for Comparative Alcohol Studies Conference, Zaborow, Poland.

Holmila, M. (1987). "Young Families and Alcohol Use in Finland and the Soviet Union." *Contemporary Drug Problems, 14,* 649–672.

Homiller, J. (1980). "Alcoholism among Women." *Chemical Dependencies: Behavioral and Biomedical Issues, 4,* 1–31.

Hughes, F., and N. Layne. (1982). Drinking Patterns in Canada: Variations in Drinking Frequencies and Demographic Characteristics of Current Drinkers. Presented at the annual meeting of the ICAA Alcohol Epidemiology Section, Helsinki, June, 1982.

Institute for Survey Research, Temple University (1980). Description of the 1980 National Sampling Frame. unpublished. Philadelphia: Institute for Survey Research, Temple University.

Jacobs, J. (1982). Hard-drinking California Pays the Price. *San Francisco Examiner,* July 25, 1982, A1.

Jellinek, E. (1946). "Phases in the Drinking History of Alcoholics: Analysis of a Survey Conducted by the Official Organ of Alcoholics Anonymous." *Quarterly Journal of Studies on Alcohol, 7,* 1–88.

Jellinek, E. (1952). "Phases of Alcohol Addiction." *Quarterly Journal of Studies on Alcohol, 13,* 673–684.

Jellinek, E. M. (1960). *The Disease Concept of Alcoholism*. New Brunswick, N. J.: Hilhouse Press, 1960.

Jessor, R., T. D. Graves, R. C. Hanson, and S. L. Jessor. (1968). *Society, Personality and Deviant Behavior: A Study of a Tri-Ethnic Community*. New York: Holt, Rinehart and Winston.

Jobson Publishing Corporation (1987). *Jobson's Liquor Handbook 1987*. New York: Jobson Publishing Corporation.

Johnson, P. (1982). "Sex Differences, Women's Roles, and Alcohol Use: Preliminary National Data." *Journal of Social Issues, 38,* 93–116.

Johnson, P., D. Armor, M. Polich, and H. Stambul. (1977). *U.S. Adult Drinking Practices: Time Trends, Social Correlates, and Sex Roles*. Santa Monica: RAND Corporation.

Kalton, G., and D. Anderson. (1984). Sampling Rare Populations for Health Surveys. *Proceedings of the Section on Survey Research Methods, American Statistical Association*.

Keller, M. (1962). The Definition of Alcoholism and the Estimation of Its Prevalence. In D. Pittman and C. Snyder, eds., *Society, Culture, and Drinking Patterns*. (pp. 310–329). New York: Wiley.

Keller, M. (1972). "On Loss of Control Phenomenon in Alcoholism." *British Journal of Addiction, 67*, 53–166.

Keller, M. (1976). "The Disease Concept of Alcoholism Revisited." *Journal of Studies on Alcohol, 37*, 1694–1717.

Keller, M. (1977). A Lexicon of Disablements Related to Alcohol Consumption. In G. Edwards, M. Gross, M. Keller, J. Moser, and R. Room, eds., *Alcohol Related Disabilities*. (pp. 23–60). Geneva: World Health Organization.

Kish, L. (1949). "A Procedure for Objective Respondent Selection within the Household." *Journal of the American Statistical Association, 44*, 380–387.

Kish, L. (1965a). Selection Techniques for Rare Traits. In *Genetics and the Epidemiology of Chronic Diseases*. Public Health Service Publication no. 1163.

Kish, L. (1965b). *Survey Sampling*. New York: Wiley.

Kleinfeld, N. (1984, September 17). Decline in drinking changes liquor industry. *New York Times*, September 17, 1984, 1.

Knupfer, G. (1961). *Characteristics of Abstainers: A Comparison of Drinkers and Abstainers in a Large California City*. (California Drinking Practices Study, report no. 3). Berkeley: California State Department of Public Health.

Knupfer, G. (1964). Female Drinking Patterns. In North American Association of Alcoholism Programs *Selected Papers Presented at the 15th Annual Meeting, September 27–October 1, 1964*. Washington, D. C.: NAAAP.

Knupfer, G. (1966). "Some Methodological Problems in the Epidemiology of Alcoholic Beverage Usage: Definition of Amount of Intake." *American Journal of Public Health, 56*, 237–242.

Knupfer, G. (1967a). "The Epidemiology of Problem Drinking." *American Journal of Public Health, 57*, 973–986.

Knupfer, G. (1967b). The Validity of Survey Data on Drinking and Problems: a Comparison Between Respondents' Self–Reports and Outside Sources of Information. Working Paper, Social Research Group. Berkeley: Univ. California at Berkeley.

Knupfer, G. (1982). Problems Associated with Drunkenness in Women: Some Research Issues. In *Special Population Issues* (Alcohol and Health monograph no. 4). Rockville, MD: National Institute on Alcohol Abuse and Alcoholism.

Knupfer, G. (1984). "The Risks of Drunkenness (or *ebrietas resurrecta*): A Comparison of Frequent Intoxication Indices and of Population Subgroups as to Problem Risks." *British Journal of Addiction, 79*, 185–196.

Knupfer, G. (1987a). "Drinking for Health: The Daily Light Drinker Fiction." *British Journal of Addiction, 82*, 547–555.

Knupfer, G. (1987b). "New Directions for Survey Research in the Study of Alcoholic Beverage Consumption." *British Journal of Addiction, 82*, 583–585.

Knupfer, G., and R. Room. (1964). "Age, Sex and Social Class as Factors in Amount of Drinking in an Urban Community." *Social Problems, 12*, 224–240.

Knupfer, G., and R. Room. (1970). "Abstainers in a Metropolitan Community." *Quarterly Journal of Studies on Alcohol, 31*, 108–131.

Knupfer, G., R. Fink, W. Clark, and A. Goffman. (1963). *Factors Related to Amount of Drinking in an Urban Community*. (California Drinking Practices study, report no. 6). Berkeley: California State Department of Public Health.

Krasner, N., M. Davis, B. Portmann, and R. Williams. (1977). "Changing Patterns of Alcoholic Liver Disease in Great Britain: Relation to Sex and Signs of Autoimmunity." *British Medical Journal*, 1, 1497–1500.

Kreitman, N., and J. Duffy. (1988). Beyond Consumption: The Effect of Drinking Patterns on the Consequences of Drinking. Edinburgh, Scotland: MRC Unit for Epidemiological Studies in Psychiatry, Royal Edinburgh Hospital.

Lamale, H. (1959). *Study of Consumer Expenditures, Incomes and Savings: Methodology of the Survey of Consumer Expenditures in 1950*. Philadelphia: University of Pennsylvania Press.

Leary, K. (1984). Drinkers Going for the Lighter Stuff. *San Francisco Chronicle*, April 9, 1984, 1.

Ledermann, S. (1956). *Alcool, Alcoolisme, Alcoolisation*. Vol. 1. Paris: Presses Universitaires de France.

Lelbach, W. K. (1974). Organic Pathology Related to Volume and Pattern of Alcohol Use. In R. J. Gibbins, Y. Israel, H. Kalant, R. Popham, W. Schmidt and R. Smart, eds., *Research Advances in Alcohol and Drug Problems*. (pp. 93–197). New York: Plenum.

Levi, A. J., and D. M. Chalmers. (1978). "Recognition of Alcoholic Liver Disease in a District Hospital." *Gut*, 19, 251–255.

Levine, H. (1978). "The Discovery of Addiction: Changing Conceptions of Habitual Drunkenness in American History." *Journal of Studies on Alcohol*, 39, 143–174.

Linsky, A., J. Colby, and M. Straus. (1986). "Drinking Norms and Alcohol-related Problems in the United States." *Journal of Studies on Alcohol*, 47, 384–393.

Little, R., F. Schultz, and W. Mandell. (1977). "Describing Alcohol Consumption: A Comparison of Three Methods and a New Approach." *Journal of Studies on Alcohol*, 38, 554–562.

Lubalin, J., and J. Hornik. (1980). *Survey of the Normative Structure of Drinking in a Community: Final Report*. Bethesda: SysteMetrics, Inc.

Mäkelä, K. (1971). *Measuring the Consumption of Alcohol in the 1968–1969 Alcohol Consumption Study*. (Report no. 2). Helsinki: Social Research Institute of Alcohol Studies.

Mäkelä, K. (1975). "Consumption Level and Cultural Drinking Patterns as Determinants of Alcohol Problems." *Journal of Drug Issues*, 5, 344–357.

Mäkelä, K. (1978). Level of Consumption and Social Consequences of Drinking. In Y. Israel, F. Glaser, R. Popham, W. Schmidt, H. Kalant and R. Smart, eds., *Research Advances in Alcohol and Drug Problems*. Vol. 4. (pp. 303–348). New York: Plenum Press.

Mäkelä, K. (1981). *Scandinavian Drinking Survey: Construction of Composite Indicies of Drinking Attitudes and Personal Experiences Related to Drinking*. Oslo: National Institute for Alcohol Research.

Mäkelä, K., and J. Simpura (1985). "Experiences Related to Drinking as a Function of Annual Alcohol Intake by Sex and Age." *Drug and Alcohol Dependence*, 15, 389–404.

Mäkelä, K., R. Room, E. Single, P. Sulkunen, B. Walsh, with 13 others. (1981). *Alcohol, Society, and the State: 1. A Comparative Study of Alcohol Control.* Toronto: Addiction Research Foundation.

Mann, M. (1950). *Primer on Alcoholism.* New York and Toronto: Rinehart.

Mann, M. (1958). *New Primer on Alcoholism: How People Drink, How to Recognize Alcoholics, and What to do About Them.* New York: Holt Rinehart and Winston.

Mann, R., R. Smart, L. Anglin, and B. Rush. (1988). "Are Decreases in Liver Cirrhosis Rates a Result of Increased Treatment for Alcoholism?" *British Journal of Addiction, 83,* 683–688.

Marcus, A. (1962). *Some Remarks on "An Exploratory Study of Drinking in a Northern Ontario Community."* (Studies in Alcohol Education, Research Memo 7). Toronto: Alcoholism and Drug Addiction Research Foundation.

Martin, D. (1988). "A Review of the Popular Literature on Co-Dependence." *Contemporary Drug Problems, 15,* 383–398.

Maxwell, M. (1952). "Drinking Behavior in the State of Washington." *Quarterly Journal of Studies on Alcohol, 13,* 219–239.

Maxwell, M. (1958). "A Quantity-Frequency Analysis of Drinking Behavior in the State of Washington." *Northwest Science, 32,* 57–67.

McCready, W., A. Greeley, and G. Theisen. (1983). Ethnicity and Nationality in Alcoholism. In B. Kissin and H. Begleiter, eds., *The Biology of Alcoholism. 6. The Pathogenesis of Alcoholism: Psychosocial Factors.* (pp. 309–340). New York and London: Plenum.

McMillin, J. (1973). *Drinking Patterns in Sweden.* Ph.D. dissertation, Sociology, University of Southern Illinois (University Microfilms no. 74–6229).

Midanik, L. (1982). "The Validity of Self-Reported Alcohol Consumption and Alcohol Problems: A Literature Review." *British Journal of Addiction, 77,* 357–382.

Midanik, L. (1983). "Alcohol Problems and Depressive Symptoms in a National Survey." *Advances in Alcohol and Substance Abuse, 4,* 9–28.

Midanik, L. (1988). "Validity of Self-Reported Alcohol Use: A Literature Review Assessment." *British Journal of Addiction, 83,* 1019–1030.

Midanik, L. (1989). "Perspectives on the Validity of Self-Reported Alcohol Use." *British Journal of Addiction, 84,* 1419–1424.

Miller, N. (1984). Prohibitive Tendencies? The New Temperance Movement. *Boston Phoenix,* August 7, 1984, 1.

Milton, R., and R. Lee. (1967). "A Severity-of-Drinking Scale in Chronic Alcoholics." *The Medical Journal of Australia, 2,* 54th year, no. 16, 727–729.

Mohan, D., H. Sharma, K. Sundaram, and J. Neki. (1980). "Pattern of Alcohol Consumption of Rural Punjab Males." *Indian Journal of Medical Research, 72,* 702–711.

Moskowitz, M. (1983). New Attack on Drinking. *San Francisco Chronicle,* May 16, 1983, 52.

Mulford, H. (1964). "Drinking and Deviant Drinking, U.S.A., 1963." *Quarterly Journal of Studies on Alcohol, 25,* 634–650.

Mulford, H., and J. Fitzgerald. (1983). "Changes in Alcohol Sales and Drinking Problems in Iowa, 1961–1979." *Journal of Studies on Alcohol, 44,* 138–161.

Mulford, H., and D. Miller. (1960a). "Drinking in Iowa: II. The Extent of Drinking and Selected Sociocultural Categories." *Quarterly Journal of Studies on Alcohol*, *21*, 26–39.

Mulford H., and D. Miller. (1960b). "Drinking in Iowa: IV, Preoccupation with Alcohol and Definitions of Alcohol, Heavy Drinking and Trouble Due to Drinking." *Quarterly Journal of Studies on Alcohol*, *21*, 279–291.

Mulford, H., and D. E. Miller (1963). "The Prevalence and Extent of Drinking in Iowa, (1961): A Replication and Evaluation of Methods" *Quarterly Journal of Studies on Alcohol*, *24*:39–53.

Mulford, H., and D. Miller. (1964). "Drinking and Deviant Drinking, U.S.A., 1963." *Quarterly Journal of Studies on Alcohol*, *25*, 634–650.

Mulford, H., and R. W. Wilson. (1966). *Identifying Problem Drinkers in a Household Health Survey*. Washington: USGPO, Public Health Service Publication no. 1000, series 2, no. 16.

Murray, R., (1978). *Manitoba Health and Drinking Survey: The Social Epidemiology of Alcohol Abuse in Eastman Region*. Winnipeg: Manitoba Health and Drinking Survey.

Neff, J., and B. Husaini. (1982). "Life Events, Drinking Patterns and Depressive Symptomatology: The Stress-Buffering Role of Alcohol Consumption." *Journal of Studies on Alcohol*, *43*, 301–318.

Neff, J. A., and B. A. Husaini. (1984). Alcohol Use and Related Problems: Variation by Race and Urbanicity. Paper presented at the Annual Meeting of the American Public Health Association.

Neter, J., and J. Waksberg. (1965). *Response Errors in Collection of Expenditures Data by Household Interviews: An Experimental Study*. (Technical paper no. 11). Washington: U.S. Department of Commerce, Bureau of the Census.

Noble, E., ed. (1979). *Third Special Report to the U.S. Congress on Alcohol and Health: Technical Support Document*. (DHEW publ. no. (ADM) 79–832). Washington: USGPO.

Nusbaumer, M. R. (1981). "Religious Affiliation and Abstinence: a Fifteen Year Change." *Journal of Studies on Alcohol*, *42*, 127–131.

O'Farrell, T. J., and G. J. Conners. (1982). "Obtaining Drivers' License Records for Use in Evaluating Alcoholism Treatment." *Journal of Studies on Alcohol*, *43*, 1046–1052.

Park, P. (1983). Social-Class Factors in Alcoholism. In B. Kissin and H. Begleiter, eds., *The Biology of Alcoholism*, vol. 6: *The Pathogenesis of Alcoholism: Psychosocial Factors*. New York: Plenum.

Parker, D., C. Kaelber, T. Harford, and J. Brody. (1983). "Alcohol Problems among Employed Men and Women in Metropolitan Detroit." *Journal of Studies on Alcohol*, *44*, 1026–1039.

Pattison, E. M., M. B. Sobell, and L. C. Sobell. (1977). *Emerging Concepts of Alcohol Dependence*. New York: Springer, 1977.

Pearl, R. (1926). *Alcohol and Longevity*. New York: Alfred A. Knopf.

Péquignot, G., C. Charbert, H. Eydoux, and M. A. Courcoul. (1974). "Augmentation du Risque de Cirrhose en Function de la Ration d'Alcool." *Revue de l'alcoolisme*, *20*, 191–202.

Pernanen, K. (1974). Validity of Survey Data on Alcohol Use. In R.J. Gibbins et al., eds., *Research Advances in Alcohol and Drug Problems*. Vol. 1. (pp. 355–374). New York: Wiley.

Pittman, D. (1967). International Overview: Social and Cultural Factors in Drinking Patterns, Pathological and Nonpathological. In Pittman, D. ed. *Alcoholism*. (pp. 3–20). New York: Harper and Row.

Plaut, T. (1967). *Alcohol Problems: A Report to the Nation by the Cooperative Commission on the Study of Alcoholism*. New York: Oxford University Press.

Polich, J. M. (1980). Patterns of Remission in Alcoholism. In G. Edwards and M. Grant, eds., *Alcohol Treatment in Transition*. (pp. 95–112). London: Croom Helm.

Polich J. M. (1982). "The Validity of Self-Reports in Alcoholism Research." *Addictive Behaviors*, 7, 123–132.

Polich, J., and B. Orvis. (1979). *Alcohol Problems: Patterns and Prevalence in the U.S. Air Force*. Rand report no. 4-2308-AF. Santa Monica, CA: Rand Corp.

Polich, J., D. Armor, and H. Braiker. (1981). *The Course of Alcoholism: Four Years after Treatment*. Santa Monica: Rand Corp.

Popham, R. E., and W. Schmidt. (1978). "The Biomedical Definition of Safe Alcohol Consumption: A Crucial Issue for the Researcher and the Drinker." *British Journal of Addiction*, 73, 233–235.

Prentice, R. (1976). "Use of the Logistic Model In Retrospective Studies." *Biometrics*. 32, 599–606.

Quinn, R., and L. Shepard. (1974). *The 1972–1973 Quality of Employment Survey: Descriptive Statistics, with Comparison Data from the 1969–1970 Survey of Working Conditions*. Ann Arbor: Survey Research Center, University of Michigan.

Radloff, L. (1977). "The CES-D Scale: A Self-report Depression Scale for Research in the General Population." *Applied Psych. Measurement*, 1, 385–401.

Rappeport, M., P. Labaw, and J. Williams. (1975). *The Public Evaluates the NIAAA Public Education Campaign*. Princeton: Opinion Research Corp.

Reed, J. (1985). "Water, Water Everywhere: At Work and at Parties Americans Are Drinking Less and Enjoying It More." *Time*, May 20, 1985.

Riley, J., Jr., and C. Marden. (1947). "The Social Pattern of Alcoholic Drinking." *Quarterly Journal of Studies on Alcohol*, 8, 265–273.

Riley, J. W., C. F. Marden, and M. Lifshitz. (1948). "The Motivational Pattern of Drinking." *Quarterly Journal of Studies on Alcohol*, 9, 353–362.

Robins, L. N. (1966). *Deviant Children Grown Up: A Sociological and Psychiatric Study of Sociopathic Personality*. Baltimore: Williams and Wilkins.

Robins, L., W. Bates, and P. O'Neal. (1962). Adult Drinking Patterns of Former Problem Children. In D. G. Pittman and C. A. Snyder, eds., *Society, Culture, and Drinking Patterns*. (pp. 395–412). New York: John Wiley and Sons, Inc.

Robins, L., G. E. Murphy, and M. B. Breckenridge. (1968). "Drinking Behavior of Young Urban Negro Males." *Quarterly Journal of Studies on Alcohol*, 29, 657–684.

Robins, L., J. Helzer, J. Croughan, J. Williams, and R. Spitzer. (1981). *NIMH Diagnostic Interview Schedule III*. Rockville, MD: National Institute of Mental Health.

Rodin, M., D. Morton, and B. Becker. (1979a). *Lake View (Chicago) Survey on Community Dynamics and Drinking Behavior: Goals, Rationale, Procedures, and Statistics*. (Project no. 839, Technical Report no. 4). Chicago: University of Illinois School of Public Health, Project on Community Dynamics, Social Competence and Alcoholism in Illinois.

Rodin, M., D. Morton, and D. Shimkin. (1979b). *Social and Psychological Correlates of Drinking in the Lake View Community (Chicago)*. (Project no. 839). (Working Paper no. 6). Chicago: University of Illinois School of Public Health, Project on Community Dynamics, Social Competence and Alcoholism in Illinois.

Roizen, R. (1981). *The World Health Organization Study of Community Responses to Alcohol-Related Problems: A Review of Cross-Cultural Findings*. Geneva: World Health Organization.

Roizen, R., D. Cahalan, and P. Shanks. (1978). Spontaneous Remission among Untreated Problem Drinkers. In D. Kandell, ed., *Longitudinal Research in Drug Use: Empirical Findings and Methodological Issues*. (pp. 193–221). Washington, D.C.: Hemisphere Press-John Wiley.

Room, R. (1968). Amount of Drinking and Alcoholism. Presented at the 28th International Congress on Alcohol and Alcoholism, Washington, September (abstract In M. Keller and M. Majchrowicz, eds., *Proceedings of the 28th International Congress on Alcohol and Alcoholism, Vol. 1: Abstracts*, (pp. 97–98), Washington: Secretariat, 28th International Congress).

Room, R. (1970a). "Amount of Drinking Measured by Two Methods in a National U.S. Sample." *Drinking and Drug Practices Surveyor, 2*, 8–10.

Room, R. (1970b). "Asking about Amount of Drinking." *Drinking and Drug Practices Surveyor, 1*, 16.

Room, R. (1971a). Drinking in the Rural South: Some Comparisons in a National Sample. In J. Ewing and B. Rouse, eds., *Law and Drinking Behavior*. (pp. 79–108). Chapel Hill: Center for Alcohol Studies.

Room, R. (1971b). "Measures of Heavy Drinking: The Difference It Makes." *Drinking and Drug Practices Surveyor, 3*, 3–6.

Room, R. (1971c). "Survey versus Sales Data for the U.S." *Drinking and Drug Practices Surveyor, 3*, 15–16.

Room, R. (1972). "Drinking Patterns in Large U.S. Cities: A Comparison of San Francisco and National Samples." (Supplement no. 6, pp. 28–57). *Quarterly Journal of Studies on Alcohol*.

Room, R. (1974). "Interrelations of Alcohol Policies, Consumption and Problems in the U.S." *Drinking and Drug Practices Surveyor, 9*, 21–31.

Room, R. (1976). "Beverage Type and Drinking Problems in a National Sample of Men." *Drinking and Drug Practices Surveyor, 12*, 29–30.

Room, R. (1977). The Measurement and Distribution of Drinking Problems in General Populations. In G. Edwards, M. M. Gross, M. Keller, J. Moser, and R. Room, eds., *Alcohol-Related Disabilities*. (pp. 61–87). (Offset publication no. 32). Geneva: World Health Organization.

Room, R. (1980a). "New Curves in the Course: A Comment on Polich, Armor, and Braiker, 'The Course of Alcoholism'." *British Journal of Addiction, 75,* 351–360.

Room, R. (1980b). Treatment-Seeking Populations and Larger Realities. In G. Edwards and M. Grant eds., *Alcoholism Treatment in Transition.* (pp. 205–224). London: Croom Helm.

Room, R. (1983). Region and Urbanization as Factors in Drinking Practices and Problems. In B. Kissin and H. Begleiter, eds., *The Biology of Alcoholism, Vol. 6: The Pathogenesis of Alcoholism: Psychosocial Factors.* (pp. 555–604). New York: Plenum.

Room, R. (1984a). "Alcohol and Ethnography: A Case of Problem Deflation? With Comments and a Reply." *Current Anthropology, 25,* 161–191.

Room, R. (1984b). "A 'Reverence for Strong Drink': The Lost Generation and the Elevation of Alcohol in American Culture." *Journal of Studies on Alcohol, 45,* 540–546.

Room, R., and K. Beck. (1974). "Survey Data on Trends in U.S. Consumption." *Drinking and Drug Practices Surveyor, 9,* 3–7.

Rootman, I., and J. Moser. (1984). *Community Response to Alcohol-Related Problems: A World Health Organization Project Monograph.* (DHHS publication no. (ADM) 85–1371). Washington, DC: USGPO.

Rorabaugh, W. (1979). *The Alcoholic Republic: An American Tradition.* New York: Oxford University Press.

Rouse, B. A. (1970). "Comparison of Two Bases of Estimating Indices of Alcohol Consumption: Drinking Reported in the Past Week and Overall Estimate of Drinking in the Past Year." *Drinking and Drug Practices Surveyor, 2,* 6–7.

Rutledge, C., G. Carroll, and R. Perkins. (1974). *A Socio-Epidemiological Study of Alcoholism in East Baton Rouge Parish.* Baton Rouge, LA: School of Social Welfare, Louisiana State University

Sanchez, D. (1984). *NIAAA Quick Facts.* Rockville, MD: National Institute on Alcohol Abuse and Alcoholism.

Sandmaier, M. (1980). *The Invisible Alcoholics: Women and Alcohol Abuse in America.* New York: McGraw-Hill.

San Francisco Chronicle. (1982). "America's Boozing is Getting Worse." *San Francisco Chronicle,* July 15, 1982.

Sargent, M. (1970). "Methods of Measuring Drinking: Are Reported Habitual Drinking and Recent Occasion Drinking Comparable?, with an Exchange." *Drinking and Drug Practices Surveyor, 2,* 3–6.

Saunders, J., J. Walters, P. Davies, and A. Paton. (1981). "A Twenty-year Prospective Study of Cirrhosis." *British Medical Journal, 282,* pp. 263–266.

Schaef, A. W. (1986). *Co-Dependence: Misunderstood—Mistreated.* San Francisco: Harper and Row.

Schinke, S., and L. Gilchrist. (1983). Survey and Evaluation Methods: Smoking Prevention among Children and Adolescents. In J. Grabowski and C. S. Bell, eds., *Measurement in the Analysis and Treatment of Smoking Behavior.* (pp. 96–104). (NIDA Research monograph no. 48, DHHS publication no. (ADM) 83–1285). Washington: USGPO.

Schmidt, W., and J. de Lint. (1972). "Causes of Death of Alcoholics." *Quarterly Journal of Studies on Alcohol, 33,* 171–185.

Schmidt, W., and R. E. Popham. (1978). "The Single Distribution Theory of Alcohol Consumption: A Rejoinder to the Critique of Parker and Harman." *Journal of Studies on Alcohol, 39,* 400–419.

Schuckit, M. (1979). Alcoholism and Affective Disorder: Diagnostic Confusion. In D. Goodwin and C. Erickson, eds., *Alcoholism and Affective Disorders: Clinical Genetic, and Biochemical Studies.* (pp. 9–20). New York: Spectrum Publications Inc.

Simpura, J. (1986). Drinking Habits, Societal Change and Alcohol Policy: The Case of Finland, 1968–1984. Unpublished paper presented at the 32nd International Institute on the Prevention and Treatment of Alcoholism, Budapest, June 1986.

Simpura, J. (1987). Comparison of Indices of Alcohol Consumption in the Finnish 1984 Drinking Habits Survey Data. Presented at the annual meeting of the Alcohol Epidemiology Section, International Council on Alcohol and Addictions, Aix-en-Provence, June 1987.

Skog, O-J. (1980). "Liver Cirrhosis Epidemiology: Some Methodological Problems." *British Journal of Addiction, 75,* 227–243.

Skog, O-J. (1981). "Distribution of Self-Reported Alcohol Consumption: Comments on Gregson and Stacey." *Psychological Reports, 49,* 771–777.

Skog, O-J. (1982a). *The Distribution of Alcohol Consumption. Part I: A Critical Discussion of the Ledermann Model.* (SIFA mimeograph no. 64). Oslo: National Institute for Alcohol Research.

Skog, O-J. (1982b). *On the Risk Function of Liver Cirrhosis.* (Report from the National Institute for Alcohol Research, no. 61). Oslo: National Institute for Alcohol Research.

Skog, O-J. (1983). *The Distribution of Alcohol Consumption. Part II: A Review of the First Wave of Empirical Studies.* (SIFA-mimeograph no. 67). Oslo: National Institute for Alcohol Research.

Skog, O-J. (1984). "The Risk Function for Liver Cirrhosis from Lifetime Alcohol Consumption." *Journal of Studies on Alcohol, 45,* 199–208.

Skolnick, J. (1958). "Religious Affiliation and Drinking Behavior." *Quarterly Journal of Studies on Alcohol, 19,* 452–470.

Smart, R., and E. Adlaf. (1982). *Trends in Alcohol and Drug Use among Ontario Adults: Report of a Household Survey, 1982.* (Substudy no. 1234). Toronto: Addiction Research Foundation.

Smith, C., and R. Hanham. (1982). *Alcohol Abuse: Geographic Perspectives.* Washington, D.C.: Association of American Geographers.

Sobell, M., S. Maisto, L. Sobell, A. Cooper, T. Cooper and B. Sanders. (1980). Developing a Prototype for Evaluating Alcohol Treatment Effectiveness. In L. C. Sobell, M. B. Sobell and E. Ward, eds., *Evaluating Alcohol and Drug Abuse Treatment Effectiveness: Recent Advances.* (pp. 129–150). New York: Pergamon.

Social Research Group. (1974). Public Health and Drinking Practices Questionnaire. Unpublished Questionnaire (N4). Berkeley: Social Research Group.

Solomon, S., and T. Harford. (1984). "Drinking Norms versus Drinking Behavior." *Alcoholism: Clinical and Experimental Research, 8,* 460–466.

Straus, R., and S. Bacon. (1953). *Drinking in College.* New Haven: Yale University Press.

Streissguth, A., D. Martin, and V. Buffington. (1977). Identifying Heavy Drinkers: A Comparison of Eight Alcohol Scores Obtained on the Same Sample. In F. A. Seixas, ed., *Currents in Alcoholism,* vol. 2. (pp. 395–420). New York: Grune and Stratton.

Sulkunen, P. (1979). *Abstainers in Finland 1946–1976: A Study in Social and Cultural Transition.* Helsinki: State Alcohol Monopoly, Social Research Institute of Alcohol Studies.

Trocki, K. (1987). Situational Drinking Behavior and Situational Norms. Read at the Meetings of the Alcohol Epidemiology Section of the International Council on Alcohol and Addictions, Aix-en-Provence, France, June 1987.

Turner, T., E. Mezey, and A. Kimball. (1977a). "Measurement of Alcohol-Related Effects in Man: Chronic Effects in Relation to Levels of Alcohol Consumption, Part A." *John Hopkins Medical Journal, 141,* 235–248.

Turner, T., E. Mezey, and A. Kimball. (1977b). "Measurement of Alcohol-Related Effects in Man: Chronic Effects in Relation to Levels of Alcohol Consumption, Part B." *John Hopkins Medical Journal, 141,* pp. 273–286.

Tuyns, A., G. Péquignot, and J. Esteve. (1983). "Greater Risk of Ascitic Cirrhosis in Females in Relation to Alcohol Consumption." *International Journal of Epidemiology, 13,* pp. 53–57.

Vaillant, G. (1983). *The Natural History of Alcoholism: Causes, Patterns, and Paths to Recovery.* Cambridge: Harvard University Press.

Waksberg, J. (1973). The Effect of Stratification with Differential Sampling Rates on the Attributes of Subsets of the Population. *Proceedings of the Social Statistics Section, American Statistical Association.*

Wallack, L. (1978). *An Assessment of Drinking Patterns, Problems, Knowledge and Attitudes in Three Northern California Communities.* (Report C21). Berkeley: Alcohol Research Group.

Wallack, L., and D. Barrows. (1981). *Preventing Alcohol Problems in California: Evaluation of the Three Year "Winners" Program.* (Report C29). Berkeley: Alcohol Research Group.

Wallack, L., and D. Barrows. (1982–1983). "Evaluating Primary Prevention: The California 'Winners' Alcohol Program." *International Quarterly of Community Health Education, 3,* 307–335.

Warheit, G., S. Artey, and E. Swanson. (1976). "Patterns of Drug Use: An Epidemiological Overview." *Journal of Drug Issues, 6,* 223–237.

Wechsler, H., and M. McFadden. (1976). "Sex Differences in Adolescent Alcohol and Drug Use: A Disappearing Phenomenon." *Journal of Studies on Alcohol, 37,* 1291–1301.

Wechsler, H., H. Demone, and N. Gottleib. (1978). "Drinking Patterns of Greater Boston Adults: Subgroup Differences on the QFV Index." *Journal of Studies on Alcohol, 39,* 1158–1165.

Weisner, C. (1987a). *Paths to Treatment: A Study of Critical Events.* Dr.P.H. dissertation, School of Public Health, University of California, Berkeley.

Weisner, C. (1987b). The Social Ecology of Alcohol Treatment in the U.S. In M. Galanter, ed., *Recent Developments in Alcoholism*, vol. 5. (pp. 203–243). New York and London: Plenum.

Weisner, C., and R. Room. (1984). "Financing and Ideology in Alcohol Treatment." *Social Problems*, 32, pp. 167–188.

Weissman, M., and J. Myers. (1980). "Clinical Depression in Alcoholism." *American Journal of Psychiatry*, 137, 372–373.

Weissman, M. M., J. K. Myers, and P. S. Harding. (1980). "Prevalence and Psychiatric Heterogeneity of Alcoholism in a United States Urban Community." *Journal of Studies on Alcohol*, 41, 672–681.

Williams, G., S. Aitken, and H. Malin. (1985). "Reliability of Self-Reported Alcohol Consumption in a General Population Survey." *Journal of Studies on Alcohol*, 46, 223–227.

Williams, J. (1967). Waxing and Waning Drinkers. Presented at the Annual Meeting of the Society for the Study of Social Problems, San Francisco, August, 1967.

Wilsnack, R., S. Wilsnack, and A. Klassen. (1984). "Women's Drinking and Drinking Problems: Patterns from a 1981 National Survey." *American Journal of Public Health*, 74, 1231–1238.

Wilsnack, S., R. Wilsnack, and A. Klassen. (1984–1985). "Drinking and Drinking Problems among Women in a U.S. National Survey." *Alcohol Health and Research World*, 9, 3–13.

Wilsnack, S., R. Wilsnack, and A. Klassen. (1986). Epidemiological Research on Women's Drinking, 1978–1984. In National Institute on Alcohol Abuse and Alcoholism. *Women and Alcohol: Health Related Issues*. (NIAAA Research monograph no. 16). Washington: USGPO.

Windham, G. O., and M. J. Aldridge. (1965). *The Use of Beverage Alcohol by Adults in Two Mississippi Communities*. Preliminary report no. 6, Social Science Research Center. Mississippi State University.

Wiseman, J. (1976). Social Forces and the Politics of Research Approaches: Studying the Wives of Alcoholics. In V. Olsen, ed., *Women and Their Health: Research Implications for a New Era*. (pp. 22–27). (DHEW Publication no. (HRA) 77–3138). Washington, DC: USGPO.

Zobeck, T., G. Williams, and D. Bertolucci. (1986). "Trends in Alcohol-Related Fatal Traffic Accidents, United States, 1977–1984." *Alcohol Health and Research World*, 11, 60–63.

Contributors

RAUL CAETANO is a Senior Scientist at the Alcohol Research Group, Medical Research Institute of San Francisco. He holds an M.D. from Rio de Janeiro State University and Ph.D. in epidemiology from the University of California, Berkeley.

WALTER B. CLARK is a consultant to the Alcohol Research Group, Medical Research Institute of San Francisco, where he was formerly a Senior Scientist for many years. He holds an M.A. in sociology from Los Angeles State University.

BRIDGET F. GRANT is Chief of the Biometry Branch, Division of Biometry and Epidemiology, U. S. National Institute on Alcohol Abuse and Alcoholism. She holds a Ph.D. in experimental psychology and artificial intelligence from Rutgers University and a Ph.D. in epidemiology from Columbia University.

THOMAS C. HARFORD is the Director of the Division of Biometry and Epidemiology, U. S. National Institute on Alcohol Abuse and Alcoholism. He holds a Ph.D. in psychology from Boston University.

DEBORAH S. HASIN is an Assistant Professor of Clinical Public Health (Epidemiology), at Columbia University and a Research Scientist at the New York State Psychiatric Institute, New York, New York. She holds a Ph.D. in epidemiology from Columbia University.

DENISE HERD is an Assistant Professor in the Department of Social and Administrative Health Sciences, University of California at Berkeley. She holds a Ph.D. in anthropology from the University of California at San Francisco.

MICHAEL E. HILTON is now on the staff of the Prevention Branch of the National Institute on Alcohol Abuse and Alcoholism. His work on this book was as a Scientist at the Alcohol Research Group, Medical Research Institute of San Francisco. He holds a Ph.D. in sociology from Michigan State University.

ROBIN ROOM is a Senior Scientist at, and is Director of, the Alcohol Research Group, Medical Research Institute of San Francisco. He holds a Ph.D. in sociology from the University of California at Berkeley.

ROBERT L. SANTOS is now Director of Survey Operations for the Survey Research Center, Ann Arbor, Michigan. The article in this book reflects his sampling work at the Institute of Survey Research, Temple University, Philadelphia. He holds an M.A. in statistics from the University of Michigan.

Index

A

Abstainers. *See* Nondrinkers
Acculturation: alcohol-related
  problems and, 303-4; Hispanics
  and, 300, 303-7; Hispanic women
  and, 305-7; national alcohol survey
  (1984) and, 303, 305
Adult Children of Alcoholics
  (ACA), 153-54
Alanon. *See* Alcoholics Anonymous
Alcohol abuse. *See* Alcohol-related
  problems; Alcoholism
Alcohol and Longevity (Pearl), 40-42
Alcohol consumption rate: and
  alcohol-related problems, 213-16,
  222-32, 234-37; and average daily
  intake, 217, 219-20, 221-22,
  235-37; consumption response
  theory, 140; cyclical theory, 140-41,
  148, 151; demographics of, 39-40,
  73-75, 73-86, 194-96, 198-99,
  228-29, 250; and dependence,
  213-14; Finnish trends, 123; and
  gender, 128-30, 234-35; geographic
  variations in, 262-64, 271, 276-77,
  297-98; health aspects of, 40, 42,
  234-35, 249-50; measurement of, 3,
  33, 34-40; national alcohol survey
  (1984) and, 265-68; single-
  distribution theory, 105-6, 122-23;
  and social contexts, 253-54, 284-85;
  trends, 7-9, 122-23, 125-38, 139-41,
  150, 155-62; in United States,

9-10, 15-16, 23, 48, 151;
  "Volmax" measurement scale,
  108-9, 111-14, 119
Alcohol control policies: geographic
  variations in, 258, 271, 279
Alcohol dependence. *See*
  Alcoholism; Dependence
Alcohol Dependence Syndrome
  (ADS), 170-71
Alcoholics Anonymous, 6, 150,
  152-53, 166-67, 169, 174, 176, 177-78
Alcoholism: continuum concept of,
  165, 168, 170; and "craving,"
  166-67, 168-69; and dependence,
  53; disease theory of, 166-68,
  169-70; modified disease theory
  of, 171-72; nature and
  characteristics of, 6, 165, 166-67;
  psychiatric theory of, 170-71,
  213-14; survey research on, 27.
  See also Alcohol-related problems;
  Drunkenness
Alcohol-related problems, 3, 5-6, 8,
  42, 45-46; and acculturation,
  303-4; alcohol consumption rate
  and, 213-16, 222-32, 234-37;
  alcohol use and infrequency of,
  61, 65, 69-70; among Blacks, 93,
  99-100, 308-10; among Black
  women, 323; among Hispanics,
  93, 100, 293-94, 295-97, 298-99,
  301-2, 303, 306; among Hispanic
  women, 295-97, 301-2; characteristics of, 14; classification of, 165-66;

373